REFLECTIONS ON THE READINGS

Patrick J. Breen, O. Carm

Reflections on the Readings
for every day of the Church's year

the columba press

First published in 2011 by
the columba press
55A Spruce Avenue, Stillorgan Industrial Park,
Blackrock, Co Dublin

Cover by Bill Bolger
Origination by The Columba Press
Printed in Ireland by Gemini International Ltd, Dublin

ISBN 978 1 85607 732 3

Contents

Foreword

This collection was first begun in 2002 as an addition to the website of the Irish Province of the Order of Carmelites (www.carmelites.ie). Since then the reflections have been edited and produced in this volume. They are offered as a resource to provide some background information on the readings used and to provoke some thought on the texts.

Patrick J. Breen, O. Carm

THE SEASON OF ADVENT

SUNDAYS: YEAR A

First Sunday of Advent
Isaiah 2:1-5; Psalm 121; Romans 13:11-14; Matthew 24:27-44
Today we begin the Advent season in which we make our preparations for the Lord's birth into our lives at Christmas. The theme for today is very much of waiting but also of being ready for the moment which will arrive at a time we do not expect. The first reading from the Prophet Isaiah speaks of the mountain of the Temple of the Lord towering above all mountains and that in the Lord's time there will be peace and not war. In the second reading from his letter to the Romans, St Paul exhorts us to wake up and to live honest Christian lives because the Lord's time is at hand – we must show our faith in him by how we live and witness. In the gospel, Jesus is warning us to be prepared and ready because we do not know when the day of the Lord will arrive. It could be today, it could be next year, but, whenever, we must not be found wanting or caught off-guard – we must be alert and ready. We do this by reforming our lives every day and living according to the gospel precepts and commandments of God.

Second Sunday of Advent
Isaiah 11:1-10; Psalm 71; Romans 15:4-9; Matthew 3:1-12
Our readings today give us two key people and two important role models for us. The first is Isaiah who spoke of the Lord's arrival and who, in his way, prepared the way for the Lord's coming. The second is John the Baptist – the Lord's own cousin – who is spoken of by Isaiah and who prepared the way for the Lord in the Lord's own time. Isaiah tells us that a time will come when there will be peace and integrity, faithfulness and equity. The psalm reminds us that in the days of the Lord, 'justice shall flourish and peace till the moon fails.' In the gospel we are introduced to John the Baptist who is preaching repentance and who directly challenges the Pharisees and Sadducees who come to him for baptism. He has a stark warning for them and for us that

the Lord will sift through his people and separate the faithful from the unfaithful. He goes on to remind us that there will always be those who will be unfaithful. We are the successors to John and to his mission and by our baptismal promises we have taken on the duty to prepare the way in our own time for the Lord's imminent coming in power through the celebration of Christmas. Before we can be heralds of that great news we must first prepare a way for him to enter more deeply into our own hearts and we do that during these days of Advent. St Paul reminds us in the second reading that those who do not give up are helped in this work and so we too will be helped and strengthened if we continue to have faith in God and to work for the building of the kingdom.

Third Sunday of Advent – Gaudete Sunday
Isaiah 35:1-6, 10; Psalm 145; James 5:7-10; Matthew 11:2-11
The tone of our celebration for today is one of rejoicing at the fact that the coming of the Lord is very near. In the first reading from the Prophet Isaiah, the prophet is exalting the people to rejoice and to be glad for their God is coming to them. On that day 'the eyes of the blind shall be opened, the ears of the deaf unsealed, then the lame shall leap like a deer and the tongues of the dumb sing for joy.' The excerpt we have from St James' letter calls on the people to be patient and of joyful heart because the Lord is coming. He tells them that this should not just be for a time only but as a way of life for all time because in this way we will live the sort of lives which God asks of us and will encourage others to follow our example. We again have the Baptist in our gospel for today but this time he appears to be somewhat unsure about Christ. He sends his own disciples to find out if Jesus is the Christ. The reply which Jesus sends is based very much on the scriptures, particularly the Prophet Isaiah, and Jesus tells them to tell his cousin what they have seen – the blind being given sight, the lame walking again. Christ is the reason why we rejoice, he is the reason why we make an effort to amend our lives each year because it is he who is our Saviour and who will raise us with him to eternal life.

Fourth Sunday of Advent

Isaiah 7:10-14; Psalm 23; Romans 1:1-7; Matthew 1:18-24

In our first reading for today we read of an encounter between God and Ahaz, king of Judah. In the encounter, God tells Ahaz to ask for whatever he wants but Ahaz refuses to put the Lord to the test. As a result, the Lord tells him and the House of David that a maiden will give birth to a son who will be Emmanuel. In the gospel from St Matthew, we have another encounter, this time between Joseph and God's messenger. Joseph now knows that Mary is pregnant but the angel tells him to go through with the marriage for the child was conceived through the power of the Holy Spirit and his name will be Emmanuel. In the second reading from his letter to the Romans, St Paul tells his readers that he is writing to tell them about the Son of God who is a descendent of King David and who has the power of God. These three readings all refer to Jesus Christ whose birth as a human being we are about to celebrate. It is a reminder that there is now very little time to make our real preparations to worthily celebrate the season of Christmas.

SUNDAYS: YEAR B

First Sunday of Advent

Isaiah 63:16b-17; 64:1,3b-8; Psalm 79; 1 Corinthians 1:3-9; Mark 13:33-37

The readings today look forward to the Second Coming of Jesus, our Lord, asking that he reveal once again his mercy and his saving help. In the first reading from the prophet Isaiah, the prophet asks God to 'tear the heavens open' and come to the help of his people just as he came to help them when they were slaves in Egypt and in Babylon. The psalm asks God, the shepherd of Israel, to deliver the people he created: 'God of hosts, bring us back; let your face shine on us and we shall be saved.' The gospel warns us to be on our guard and to 'stay awake' if we are to be ready for the Second Coming of Christ at the end of time. Like somebody who leaves his servants to look after his house when he goes abroad, he can return when we least expect it. In the second reading, St Paul invites the community at Corinth to wait with patient endurance for the Lord's return.

Second Sunday of Advent

Isaiah 40:1-5,9-11; 64:1, 3b-8; Psalm 84; 2 Peter 3:8-14; Mark 1:1-8

The readings today focus on the role of John the Baptist in preparing a way for the Lord's coming through conversion. In the first reading, the Prophet Isaiah looks forward to the return of the exiled Israelites from Babylon by means of a road across the desert that the Lord would construct for that purpose. The psalm looks forward to the peace and justice that God will establish when his kingdom comes: 'Let us see, O Lord, your mercy and give us your saving help.' The gospel invites us to prepare for our celebration of the Lord's Incarnation by opening our hearts to the gospel message of conversion. In anticipation of Christ's Second Coming at the end of time, the second reading says that we should be found 'at peace' with God and with our neighbour when he comes.

Third Sunday of Advent – Gaudete Sunday

Isaiah 61:1-2a, 10-11; Psalm: Luke 1:46-50, 53-54; 1 Thessalonians 5:16-24; John 1:6-8, 19-28

The readings for this third Sunday of Advent anticipate the joy of the Second Coming of Jesus, our Lord – hence the name *Gaudete* – Rejoice. The first reading is the text Jesus quoted to announce his mission as the anointed Messiah, the one sent to bring good news to the poor and liberty to captives. The psalm, which is Mary's *Magnificat*, echoes the joy of the first reading, praising God for the wonderful things he has done for her and for all the people of Israel. The gospel describes John the Baptist as a witness of Jesus, a voice crying in the wilderness and calling people to conversion and baptism, but also recognising that he is not worthy to undo the sandal of the one who comes after him, the one who will baptise people with the Holy Spirit. The second reading invites us to see our Christian life, not just as a series of obligations towards God and neighbour, but as a joyful and prayerful way of life, recognising and thanking God for the many gifts of the Holy Spirit.

Fourth Sunday of Advent

2 Samuel 7:1-5, 8b-11, 16; Psalm 88; Romans 16:25-27; Luke 1:26-38

Rather than being dependant on David to build a dwelling place for God on earth, the first reading from the second Book of Samuel, presents God as ensuring that David's 'house' (that is, his dynastic line) will be continued. The psalm celebrates the abiding care and faithful love of God who honours the promise he made to ensure the survival of David's house and line: 'I will sing for ever of your love, O Lord.' The gospel describes the unexpected way in which the promise was fulfilled, through the birth of the 'Son of the Most High' from Mary who was betrothed to a man from the house of David, and hence, legally, herself of that house. Through her consent, 'I am the handmaid of the Lord: let what you have said be done to me,' God has come to live permanently in our human nature, building a house for himself in the womb of the Virgin Mary. The Ark for the Covenant, which David wished to build of wood, takes flesh in Mary who becomes the Ark which carries Christ. We too are called to be Arks to carry the good news of salvation wherever we go.

SUNDAYS: YEAR C

First Sunday of Advent

Jeremiah 33:14-16; Psalm 24; 1 Thessalonians 3:12-4:2; Luke 21:25-28, 34-36

In the first reading today from the Prophet Jeremiah we read that the Lord is about to fulfil the promise which he had made to the Houses of Israel and Judah. He is about to raise up the great successor to David which he had promised and whose kingdom shall last for ever. In the second reading from his first letter to the Thessalonians, St Paul urges us to grow in love as we await the coming of Christ. In the gospel, Jesus tells us to always stand ready for the moment when he returns. If we are ready and attentive to our Christian duties then we will have nothing to fear. Many people are waiting for the second coming of Christ at the end of time and often miss the rebirth of Christ at Christmas. Each Advent we await this rebirth of Jesus in our lives and we must prepare for that wondrous event by making love a greater part of the way in which we live.

Second Sunday of Advent
Baruch 5:1-9; Psalm 125; Philippians 1:4-6, 8-11; Luke 3:1-6
In our first reading from the Prophet Baruch we are told that the Lord will save his people and his city will become a place of beauty to which all will return triumphant. The psalm is a hymn of praise and thanksgiving for all that God has done for his people. In our second reading we see St Paul praising the Philippians for all that they have done in helping him to spread the word of God. He prays that God will bless them for their faithfulness. In our gospel passage from St Luke we read of the arrival of John the Baptist who came to prepare the way for Christ. All that he does fulfils the word of the prophet Isaiah who said that there would be a fore-runner to the Messiah. The readings point to the arrival of a greater age when peace will reign on the earth. That time begins each Christmas and our season of Advent is not just a time to prepare to live in that age but also a time to prepare ourselves to play our part in the building up of that kingdom.

Third Sunday of Advent – Gaudete Sunday
Zephaniah 3:14-18; Psalm: Isaiah 12:2-6; Philippians 4:4-7; Luke 3:10-18
The third Sunday of Advent is traditionally known as 'Gaudete Sunday' for the readings speak of rejoicing. In our first reading from the prophet Zephaniah the prophet tells the people that the Lord will forgive his people and he will redeem them from their enemies. The Lord is in the midst of his people and he will rejoice in them. The psalm is one of praise for God who is the strength of his people. In our second reading St Paul calls on us to be happy or to rejoice in the Lord for he is very near to his people. He calls on us to praise and thank God for all that he has done for us and continues to do for us. In the gospel today we see John the Baptist teaching the people and encouraging them to live what we call Christian lives – sharing with the poor and needy. Because of his teaching the people think that he is the Messiah but he tells them that he is not. John was the one who first brought the good news to the people and we too are called to do the same. We have received many blessings from the Lord and today is an opportunity to reflect on those and to give thanks and praise to God for them. Having done so we must

then go out and spread the Word of God to others in society so that they too may feel the presence of Christ this Christmas.

Fourth Sunday of Advent
Micah 5:1-4; Psalm 79; Hebrews 10:5-10; Luke 1:39-45
In our first reading we have a prediction about the birth of Christ which is to take place in Bethlehem – for a long time regarded as a low and insignificant village which couldn't produce anyone or anything of importance. Now it is to be the birthplace of the Lord's restoration. In the second reading from the letter to the Hebrews the author speaks about Christ's life and mission on earth. We are told that God did not want the sacrifices and holocausts which the Jews offered up to God in atonement for their sins. But to put an end to the sacrifices once and for all Christ was born in human form and became for us the ultimate sacrifice so that no sacrifice will ever again be necessary. All others are nothing by comparison to his sacrifice upon the cross. In our gospel for today we see Mary going to visit her cousin Elizabeth who is herself pregnant. Elizabeth rejoices at Mary's presence and tells us that even the child within her womb leapt for joy because he recognises in whose presence he now is. We too stand in the presence of God every time we come to church but do we rejoice as much as Elizabeth and her unborn son did all those years ago? If not, then now is the time to do something about it and to make a special place for Christ in our lives and in our families this Christmas.

THE WEEKDAYS OF ADVENT

Monday of the First Week of Advent
Isaiah 2:1-5; Psalm 121; Matthew 8:5-11

The readings throughout the Advent Season help us to prepare for the coming of Christ at Christmas by putting certain images and thoughts before us regarding the Son of God. We begin today with a text from the Prophet Isaiah which is one of the major prophetic writings of the Old Testament and which began to be written down in 744BC. In today's text we are told that people will stream to the Lord's Temple and that there will be a time of peace and prosperity between nations and peoples. The psalm takes up this theme and speaks of rejoicing when others say 'let us go to God's house.' In the gospel from St Matthew we have the cure of the centurion's servant. When Jesus said that he would go the centurion's house the man said that he didn't have to do that – all he had to do was to say the word and the servant would be cured. The man had tremendous faith in Jesus and in his word and it is this example of faith which we are to ponder on today. This is the faith that we are each called to have and to demonstrate if the birth of Christ at Christmas is to have any meaning in our lives and if we are to reach eternal life.

Tuesday of the First Week of Advent
Isaiah 11:1-10, 11-14; Psalm 71; Luke 10:21-24

The reading today from Isaiah speaks of an offspring of Jesse who will be king and who will rule with God's blessing. In his time there will be peace and prosperity for all and the kingdom will be sought after by the nations. On this king will rest the Spirit of the Lord who will bring him wisdom and insight, counsel and power, knowledge and fear of the Lord. The psalm continues this theme and says that 'In his days justice shall flourish.' In the gospel from St Luke we see that Jesus is filled with the Holy Spirit and proclaims that everything has been entrusted to him by the Father and that the only way to know the Father is through the Son. This means that the birth of Christ at Christmas is not a mere nicety or an excuse for a celebration – without getting to know Christ and accepting him into our hearts we cannot really know the Father. If we are to enter eternal life then we need to strengthen our relationship with both which we do in these days of Advent.

Wednesday of the First Week of Advent
Isaiah 25:6-10; Psalm 22; Matthew 15:29-37
In our first reading from the Prophet Isaiah we see the Lord inviting us to a banquet on his holy mountain. At that banquet the Lord will bring peace to our lives, he will remove all mourning and all embarrassment from our lives. Most importantly, he will destroy death itself. In the gospel from St Matthew we see that many people have come to Jesus bringing their sick who he cures. In the second part of the text we see him feeding this multitude of people from very meagre resources. In both readings the Lord feeds his people and changes their lives, giving them hope for the future.

Thursday of the First Week of Advent
Isaiah 26:1-6; Psalm 117; Matthew 7:21, 24-27
In the text from the Prophet Isaiah today we read that the Lord has set up a strong city for his people. Those who lived in the high citadels have been knocked from their thrones so that even the poor trample on them. The psalm reminds us that 'It is better to take refuge in the Lord than to trust in men [or] princes.' In the gospel passage we see Jesus teaching the people and telling them that it is very easy for people to call out his name and seek his help but this does not win entry to heaven. We must have faith in Christ but we must put that faith into practice and carry out the will of God if we are to enter heaven. While faith may be a personal thing to each one of us it is something which must be lived out in a communal way in that what we believe must be seen by others in the way in which we live. If we haven't been living out our faith then we need to look at that carefully and make a change if we are to worthily receive the gift of Christ in our lives in a few weeks' time.

Friday of the First Week of Advent

Isaiah 29:17-24; Psalm 26; Matthew 9:27-31

Our reading from Isaiah continues to speak of how things will be different in the day of the Lord when the Messiah shall come among the people. Those who are lowly will be raised up, those who plot evil against the good will be silenced, shame will be removed. The psalm asks the Lord that we live in his house for ever. In the gospel we see Jesus restoring sight to two blind men but only after they had affirmed that they had faith in him and his ability to cure them. This is the sort of thing which the first reading spoke of and so we can see that Jesus is the one to whom the first reading refers. It is now time for us to affirm our faith in Christ as we move towards the celebration of his birth.

Saturday of the First Week of Advent

Isaiah 30:19-21, 23-26; Psalm 146; Matthew 9:35-38, 10:1, 5-8

Our first reading speaks of the people being punished and how miserable life will be. But it also speaks of the Lord healing his people and how he will be gracious to them when he hears them cry out to him. In our gospel passage we see that Jesus has been travelling throughout the countryside and teaching people in various towns and villages. He feels sorry for them because they want the message he has but he has not enough time to get around to them all. So he sends out the Twelve to preach in his name and to heal the sick. There is a reminder here that we too should preach the good news wherever we go and we can do this very effectively by the way in which we live our lives. A good life demonstrating the gospel values can speak more than a good sermon, for actions speak louder than words. The harvest today is still vast and we each have a role to play in the building up of the kingdom so that the celebration of Christmas may have greater meaning for all of us.

Monday of the Second Week of Advent

Isaiah 35:1-10; Psalm 84; Luke 5:17-26

We again begin this week with a text from Isaiah and today we read that the Lord himself is coming to his people and when he does the lame shall walk, the blind shall see and the deaf shall hear. Upon his arrival the barren lands shall become prosperous and dry lands shall be watered. The psalm continues this theme of the Lord coming to save his people. The gospel text from St Luke recounts the cure of a lame man whose stretcher had to be let in through the roof because of the crowds. Jesus tells the man that his sins are forgiven and this does not sit well with the Pharisees who had come to hear him, for they believed that only God himself could forgive. The text can be seen to fulfil the first reading in that this is God himself among the people and therefore Jesus does have the authority to forgive. This is important for us at this time as we need to look at our own lives and not just ask whether or not we believe Jesus to be the Son of God, but to also acknowledge our failings – openly and honestly – and ask the Lord for forgiveness as we approach the celebration of his birth.

Tuesday of the Second Week of Advent

Isaiah 40:1-11; Psalm 95; Matthew 18:12-14

In our first reading from the Prophet Isaiah we read of how God will come to console his people and to tell his people that their sin has been atoned for. The concluding part of the text tells us that God is like a shepherd who will feed his flock and gather his lambs in his arms. The psalm continues this theme and also praises God. In our very short gospel text Jesus uses a parable about a shepherd who goes in search of one stray sheep and then rejoices when he gets it back. Jesus concludes by saying that God rejoices when someone who has strayed from the right path returns to the true path. This again is a reminder to us to look closely at our own lives and to make amends for anything that it is not in keeping with the values of the gospel. Now is the time to repent of our sins while knowing that God is our consolation and that he rejoices at our return.

Wednesday of the Second Week of Advent

Isaiah 40:25-31; Psalm 102; Matthew 11:28-30

Our first reading today reminds us of the power of God and that there is no one else like him in creation for he is the Creator of all – he alone can bring us consolation and peace. Our very short gospel passage sees Jesus calling the people to himself, particularly those who are burdened and weary. The Lord tells us that he has a yoke to be carried but that his yoke is easy and light. The readings remind us again that we need to look at our lives and at our faith and acknowledge that God is the Lord of all and that Jesus is his Son and our Saviour.

Thursday of the Second Week of Advent

Isaiah 41:13-20; Psalm 144; Matthew 11:11-15

In our first reading from the Prophet Isaiah we again have the theme of the Lord coming to his people to console them and so change their lives for ever. The psalm praises God for his kindness and compassion. In our gospel passage Jesus introduces the figure of John the Baptist and tells us that all the prophecies were pointing towards him. He also tells us that a greater than John the Baptist has never been seen but at the same time even the least person is as great as John. Like John, we all have a role to play in the building up of the kingdom and in the spreading of the good news. However, we might not all do it in the same way as John but it is important that we do make a serious effort knowing that God values each of us as much as he valued John.

Friday of the Second Week of Advent
Isaiah 48:17-19; Psalm 1; Matthew 11:16-19
In our last text from Isaiah for a while we read how the Lord laments the fact that the people were not open to keeping his commandments for if they had been their happiness would be so much greater. The psalm reminds us that those who do follow the Lord and keep his commandments and live as he asks 'will have the light of life'. Our gospel text for today is a continuation of yesterday's in which Jesus is talking about his cousin, John the Baptist. He reminds the people that when John came living a good life they called him a mad man and that when he, Jesus, arrived living the life they wanted John to live they called him a drunkard and a glutton. There is a reminder here that we cannot create God to be who we want him to be. The readings remind us that if we reject God and his Son as they are, then we will never be truly happy. We are challenged today to look at our image of God and see if it is an image we have made ourselves and use to justify how we live, or do we believe in God as he really is and so live our lives according the gospel.

Saturday of the Second Week of Advent
Sirach 48:1-4, 9-11; Psalm 79; Matthew 17:10-13
Our first reading today comes from the Book of Ecclesiasticus or Sirach and reminds us of the Prophet Elijah and of all that he did. It tells us that he will come again and it reminds us of the gospel passage on Thursday in which Jesus implied that John the Baptist was Elijah returning. In the gospel text we see Jesus speaking with his disciples and they ask him why Elijah has to come back. He tells them that this has to happen to make sure that all is as it should be. He then says that Elijah has indeed come back and they understand this to be John the Baptist. This takes place after John has been beheaded. It is also a reminder that we too have to make sure all is ready for the celebration of the Birth of Christ. The most important preparations concern the faith and not expensive presents and glittering wrapping paper. If we fail to prepare properly for Christmas then we will be missing out on the most important gift of all – the presence of Christ in our hearts.

Monday of the Third Week of Advent
Numbers 24:2-7, 15-17; Psalm 24; Matthew 21:23-27
Our first reading today comes from the Old Testament Book of Numbers and recounts a poem by Balaam, son of Beor. In the poem Balaam recounts what the Lord tells him and he declares that one from the tribe of Jacob shall take the leadership and he will be a great king. In the gospel we see Jesus being challenged by the chief priests and the elders of the Temple. They want to know where he gets his authority from. We know that Jesus is a descendent of Jacob and so he is the great king spoken of in the first reading. However, he is also the Son of God and is himself God and there is no greater authority than this. The challenge for us today is to ask ourselves whether or not we really see him this way, for this is one of the cornerstones of our faith.

Tuesday of the Third Week of Advent
Zephaniah 3:1-2, 9-13; Psalm 33; Matthew 21:28-32
In our first reading today from the Prophet Zephaniah, who was writing about 620BC, we read that trouble 'is coming to the rebellious, the defiled, the tyrannical city!' The Lord says that he will change peoples' ways and that truth will be spoken and shame will be removed. This very much echoes themes we have heard over the past two weeks from Isaiah. In the gospel we see Jesus telling the Pharisees that the very people they regard as sinners – tax collectors and prostitutes – are living better lives than the Pharisees are because they believed in the words of John the Baptist and took them to heart. The Pharisees were often seen as men who taught people one thing but did something else themselves. The readings ask us to look at our lives and to see how we are living them. Specifically we need to ask ourselves if we are like the Pharisees – happy to call ourselves Christian but not really living Christian lives in keeping with the gospel. In the few days that are left before Christmas we need to answer this question honestly and make a change to our lives.

Wednesday of the Third Week of Advent

Isaiah 45:6-8; Psalm 84; Luke 7:19-23

Today we return to the book of the Prophet Isaiah and today's text reminds us that it is God who created everything and that he has no equal. It also reminds us that what comes from the mouth of the Lord is truth. In our gospel from St Luke we see two of John the Baptist's disciples coming to Jesus to ask if he is the one who is to come. Rather than answer 'yes' or 'no' Jesus simply tells them to report what they have seen – Jesus curing the sick, restoring sight, casting out spirits, the dead raised to life and the good news proclaimed. He finishes by saying that 'happy is the man that does not lose faith in me.' That last line is a challenge for us today and is something we need to think about in the coming days as we move towards Christmas. Do we really believe that Christ is the Son of God, our Saviour? If we really do then we will be truly happy, but if not then we need to look closely at our faith and see what needs to be changed in order to achieve true happiness this Christmas.

Thursday of the Third Week of Advent

Isaiah 54:1-10; Psalm 29; Luke 7:24-30

Our first reading from Isaiah tells us that the Lord will take pity on us and our lives will be so much better as a result. The Lord tells us that 'my love for you will never leave you and my covenant of peace with you will never be shaken.' In the gospel Jesus is speaking to the people about John the Baptist and the baptism which he brought. He tells them that because the Pharisees refused to be baptised by John they have thwarted God's plan for them. God's plan for us is that we accept the love and peace he promised us in the first reading which comes to us by listening to the words of Christ and believing in him as our Saviour. This is what the Pharisees were also asked to do but they refused and so lost what God had in store for them. As we approach the Season of Christmas we need to look honestly at our lives and ask ourselves whether or not we have fully accepted Christ as our Saviour.

Friday of the Third Week of Advent
Isaiah 56:1-3, 6-8; Psalm 66; John 5:33-36
Our first reading today from the Prophet Isaiah speaks of the
Lord gathering his people into his house. We are all invited to
this house but, in order to enter, we must 'Have a care for justice, act with integrity' and observe the Sabbath. The Lord also
says that 'foreigners' who believe will also be welcomed. In our
gospel text from St John we see Jesus telling the people that he
does not rely on the testimony of John the Baptist or anyone else
because what he speaks comes directly from God and is truth.
However, John came to help the people to understand and to believe. It is for us to decide whether or not we are going to believe
in Christ and his message, knowing the great invite to and
promise of eternal life which awaits those who do believe and
who do live a life in keeping with the gospel values.

DECEMBER 17–24

17 December
Genesis 49:2, 9-10; Psalm 71; Matthew 1:1-17
The readings for these final days leading up to Christmas all set
the scene for the birth of Christ. Today we read from the Book of
Genesis – the first book of the Bible – and in it we see Jacob blessing his twelve sons prior to his death. Our passage comes from
the blessing of his son Judah who will also be blessed by his own
brothers. Jacob also says that the sceptre shall not pass from
Judah until the one comes to whom it rightfully belongs. Our
gospel text comes from St Matthew and presents the genealogy
of Jesus Christ from Abraham. Judah was the great-grandson of
Abraham and is one of the fore-fathers of Jesus. Therefore, Jesus
is the one to whom the sceptre rightfully belongs. This helps to
make sense of the readings of the past three weeks which spoke
of a mighty king coming to rule the people and bring them
peace. This person is Jesus Christ.

18 December
Jeremiah 23:5-8; Psalm 71; Matthew 1:18-24

Today we turn to the Book of the Prophet Jeremiah which was put together in 605BC and in our text we have a similar theme to yesterday's text from Genesis. Today we are told that a descendent of King David will reign as true king. Having read the genealogy of Jesus yesterday we know that Jesus is a descendent of King David. Our gospel text tells us of how Joseph and Mary came to be together and the dilemma Joseph had when he discovered that Mary was already pregnant. We have in the text the annunciation to Joseph in which he is told that this child is no ordinary child but one who will save people from their sins. Being a man of faith, Joseph heeds the dream and takes Mary as his wife. Joseph's 'yes' to God is one we are called to have in our lives.

19 December
Judges 13:2-7, 24-25; Psalm 70; Luke 1:5-25

Our first reading today from the Book of Judges recounts the annunciation to the wife of Manoah of the tribe of Dan in which she is told that she would bear a son. This child was Samson who was a great champion against the Philistines. In the gospel we read of the annunciation to Zechariah, the priest, by the angel Gabriel. The angel tells him that Elizabeth, his wife and cousin of Mary, will bear a son despite her years. The angel tells Zechariah that he is to name the child John and that he will be great in the sight of the Lord, bringing many people back to the Lord. Zechariah doubts what the angel says and looses the power of his speech as a result.

20 December
Isaiah 7:10-14; Psalm 23; Luke 1:26-38

In the first reading from the Prophet Isaiah we see King Ahaz refusing to put the Lord to the test. The Lord then gives the people a sign and the sign is that of a maiden with child. This child will be special and will be called 'Immanuel.' Over the past few days we have read of various annunciations to people by the Lord's angel and all were about the birth of a child. Today we have the most important of those annunciations and this is to Mary. She is the maiden spoken of in the first reading and her child is to be great and is to be named 'Jesus'. Of importance in this text is the fact that Mary, despite being undoubtedly surprised by the visit, readily says 'Yes' to the angel's word. This attitude of Mary, like Joseph's own response to his annunciation, is the attitude we are all called to have as we approach the great season of Christmas – an attitude of openness and receptiveness to the will of God in our lives.

21 December
Songs 2:8-14 or Zephaniah 3:14-18; Psalm 32; Luke 1:39-45

Our first reading today comes from the Song of Songs which has often been seen as an allegory of the story of God and his people. Seeing it in this way the groom represents God and in our passage we see him inviting his beloved to come to him and to live with him in happiness. In the alternative reading from the Prophet Zephaniah the people are told to rejoice for the Lord is in their midst and that he has driven away their enemies and renewed them. Looking to the gospel text we see Elizabeth and her unborn son rejoicing when Mary and her unborn child come into their presence. In our gospel text we see Mary travelling to the hill country of Judah to be with her cousin, Elizabeth, and to rejoice in Elizabeth's pregnancy. As soon as Elizabeth hears Mary's voice the child in her womb leaps for joy – John has recognised who the child Mary is carrying is. At the same time Elizabeth acknowledges that Mary carries the Lord and that therefore she is most blessed.

22 December

1Samuel 1:24-28; Psalm: 1Samuel 2:1, 4-8; Luke 1:46-56

Today's first reading comes from the first Book of Samuel and our text recounts the birth of Samuel himself. His mother was barren and had pleaded with the Lord to give her a child. This the Lord did and she brings the child to the temple at Shiloh to dedicate him to the Lord in keeping with the promise she had made. In our gospel we continue yesterday's meeting between Mary and Elizabeth. We have the *Magnificat* – Mary's hymn of praise as written by Luke for the wondrous thing the Lord has done for her. We are told that Mary stayed for three months with Elizabeth and then returned home.

23 December

Malachi 3:1-4, 23-24; Psalm 24; Luke 1:57-66

In our first reading from the Prophet Malachi we read that the Lord will send a messenger to prepare things before his arrival. This messenger will be Elijah who appeared in our texts in the second week of Advent and in those texts there was the implication that John the Baptist was the new Elijah. In our gospel text we have the birth of John the Baptist and how his father's speech was restored when he said that the child was to be named John. We are told in the concluding sentence that 'the hand of the Lord was with' John. The connection between the first reading and the gospel text is quite clear.

24 December (Morning Mass)

2 Samuel 7:1-5, 8-12, 14, 16; Psalm 88; Luke 1:67-79

Our first reading for today from the second book of Samuel tells of a message for King David given to Nathan by the Lord. In the message the Lord says that David's house will be a great house which will be established for ever. This house will be one to which all peoples will come. Our gospel text comes from the birth of John the Baptist and today we see his father – Zechariah the priest – proclaim a hymn of praise for God – the *Benedictus*. In this hymn, Zechariah blesses God and says that he has come to the help of his people by raising up one from the house of David. He says that his own son, John, 'shall be called Prophet of the Most High and will go ahead of the Lord to prepare the way before him.' The season of Christmas is now upon us and the scene has been fully set for the celebration of Christ's birth. All the signs of the past few weeks, and particularly of the past eight days, have pointed to this moment and it is now time for us to rejoice in the birth of our salvation. At the same time we must not let this opportunity pass – the preparations we have made over the past few weeks must not be allowed to lapse but our 'new lives' must continue into the season of Christmas and beyond as people of renewed and invigorated faith.

THE SEASON OF CHRISTMAS

December 24 Christmas Eve – Vigil Mass
Isaiah 62:1-5; Psalm 88; Acts 13:16-17, 22-25; Matthew 1:1-25
Our first reading this evening from the prophet Isaiah speaks of the Lord coming to his people. There is one reason for this – 'the Lord takes delight in you.' In the second reading from the Acts of the Apostles we see St Paul witnessing to Christ. He reminds the people that Jesus is of David's line – the successor who had been promised by God. Jesus' immediate predecessor was John the Baptist and Paul quotes from John: 'I am not fit to undo his sandal.' The first part of our gospel from St Matthew gives the genealogy of Jesus going back to Abraham. The second part of the passage tells us how Jesus came to be born but the story centres on Joseph rather than the actual birth. Joseph was aghast to find out that his young bride was pregnant but at the word of God he accepted what was happening and looked after Mary and the Child. Joseph is our role model because, like him, we too have doubts, but, also like him, we are called on to believe in the word of God and to truly accept Jesus as our Lord and to carry out his will.

Midnight Mass
Isaiah 9:1-7; Psalm 95; Titus 2:11-14; Luke 2:1-14
Our first reading from Isaiah speaks of the Son that is given to us. This Son will destroy war and oppression. He will assume all authority and the peace he brings will have no end. In the second reading St Paul tells us that the grace of God has been revealed – it has been revealed in Christ. But he also reminds us that we are waiting for the second coming of Christ and until then we should have no ambition other than to do good. Our gospel passage from St Luke tells of the lowly birth of Christ at Bethlehem. The shepherds were the first to hear the glad tidings and we too are called on to hear these same glad tidings and to believe in our Saviour and to worship him.

December 25 Christmas Day – Dawn Mass
Isaiah 62:11-12; Psalm 96; Titus 3:4-7; Luke 2:15-20
Isaiah tells us in the first reading this morning that our Saviour comes – he has been born for us. St Paul reminds us in his letter to St Titus that the Saviour came to us for no other reason than the fact that he had compassion for us. Despite all we had done and continue to do the Lord has compassion for us and still wants to save us. In the gospel passage from St Luke we see the shepherds coming to worship their new-born King and Saviour. They were the first to hear the great news and they readily came and worshipped. We too are called on this day to worship our Saviour who has been born anew for us.

Mass during the Day
Isaiah 52:7-10; Psalm 97; Hebrews 1:1-6; John 1:1-18
Today we read in Isaiah how the Lord has come to redeem his people and how 'all the ends of the earth shall see the salvation of our God.' The author of the Letter to the Hebrews tells us in the second reading that God had spoken to his people in past times through various prophets and in various other ways. But now he has spoken to us through his own Son, a Son who has destroyed the power of sin and death. In the gospel, we read the opening passage of St John's gospel in which he speaks of Christ as being the Word of God, a Word which has been with God since the beginning, a Word which was God. He reminds us that this Word was in the world from the very beginning but the world did not recognise it. Those who did recognise it and accept it were saved. We too will be saved if we truly accept that the Son who is born to us today is the Son of God and has the power to save.

December 26-28: *See Readings for Feastdays and Memorials*

December 29: Fifth Day in the Octave of Christmas
1 John 2:3-11; Psalm 95; Luke 2:22-35
In our first reading today St John reminds us of the commandment to love one another, a love which must be as self-sacrificing as the love of Christ for us. By living out this commandment we will come to perfection in God and we will truly be living Christian lives. Failure to live by love removes us from the light

of Christ so that we become the people who walk in darkness. In our gospel passage we read of the presentation of the Child Jesus in the Temple in accordance with the Law. While there, the Holy Family are met by Simeon who blesses them and thanks God for letting him see the Messiah before he dies, which he can now do in peace. He also warns them – especially Mary – that though this child is the Son of God there will also be suffering associated with him.

December 30: Sixth Day in the Octave of Christmas
1 John 2:12-17; Psalm 95; Luke 2:36-40

In our first reading from St John we are again reminded to keep faithful to God and to live according to his will by avoiding the obstacles which the world places before us. The spirit of good-will which marks this joyful season must permeate our lives not just for these few weeks each year but every day of our lives. It is a challenge to live this way but a challenge which we can live up to because we have the love of God to support us. Our gospel is the end section of the Presentation text and today we see Anna greeting the Child and telling all present that he is the Saviour of Jerusalem. Having fulfilled the Law, the Holy Family then return to Nazareth.

December 31: Seventh Day in the Octave of Christmas
1 John 2:18-21; Psalm 95; John 1:1-18

In the reading from the first letter of St John we are again re-minded that we are all children of God and that we have already received the truth and the knowledge of God. John was writing to those who live in modern day Turkey and rebuking them for having abandoned the Christian way, which he sees as a sign of the coming of the antichrist. For John, those who are true believ-ers would never abandon the faith and the Christian calling so easily. Our gospel text today is the prologue to St John's gospel in which the evangelist tells us that Christ is the Word of God and that he has existed since the beginning. He also tells us that those who accept Christ as their Saviour and Lord will become children of God. As believers and children of God we have a duty and responsibility to live Christian lives and to proclaim Christ as our Saviour and Lord, and especially having just cele-brated his birth.

January 1: Solemnity of Mary, Mother of God

Numbers 6:22-27; Psalm 66; Galatians 4:4-7; Luke 2:16-21

In our first reading today from the Book of Numbers we see God telling Moses how to bless the people in his name: 'May the Lord bless you and keep you ...' In our reading from Galatians we are reminded that Christ was born of a woman and therefore he was as human as we are. However, in so doing he has enabled each of us to become children of God just as he is the Son of God. In the gospel passage we see the Holy Family still in the stable or cave when the shepherds come, having been sent by the angels. The second part of the text recalls how the child was named Jesus in accordance with the instruction of Gabriel at the annunciation.

January 2

1 John 2:22-28; Psalm 97; John 1:19-28

St John exhorts us to remain faithful to God in our first reading and to be faithful to the teaching which we have received from Christ and to be wary of those false teachers who deny that Jesus is the Messiah. If we remain steadfast then we will receive the promise which God made to us – that is eternal life. We can be steadfast because we have been anointed with the Holy Spirit who will protect us whenever we ask for that strength and protection. In our gospel we read about John the Baptist who was sent to prepare the way for Jesus. We are called on to be modern day successors of John and to proclaim the kingdom by what we do and say and think. John told his questioners that the Messiah stood among them though they did not know it – and that is still true today – Jesus walks among us though we, sadly, do not always recognise him.

January 3

1 John 2:29-3:6; Psalm 97; John 1:29-34

In our first reading today we are reminded that those who truly know God do not sin because they live according to his will and are his children. The title 'Son of God' was reserved for those in Old Testament times who lived uprightly in the sight of God. St John is challenging us to live up to the fact that we are the Sons and Daughters of God. In our gospel text we see John the Baptist witnessing to Jesus and telling his listeners that Jesus is truly the Son of God who is filled with the Spirit of God. The two readings call on us to reaffirm our allegiance to God and to witness to him at all times.

January 4

1 John 3:7-10; Psalm 97; John 1:35-42

In our first reading today, St John tells us that a sinful way of life is not in keeping with God's love for us. We are the children of God and so cannot sin if the seed of truth and the Spirit of God are within us. In today's gospel we read of the calling of the first apostle – St Andrew – who went and called his brother, St Peter, proclaiming that he had found the Messiah. We have heard about Jesus all our lives but how long is it since we proclaimed him as the Messiah?

January 5

1 John 3:11-21; Psalm 99; John 1:43-51

St John continues to exhort us to live according to the will of God and to love one another by showing us what love is not– the slaying of Abel by his brother Cain. For John, showing hatred to another person is to imitate Cain. For him, our love should not be mere lip-service, but should be seen in all our actions. In the gospel passage for today we see Philip and Nathanael witnessing to Jesus as he calls them to be his disciples. We too are called on to witness to Christ and to the kingdom through loving others at all times no matter what they may do to us, and to bring the love and peace which God bestowed on us at Christmas to the world.

The Epiphany of the Lord
Isaiah 60:1-6; Psalm 71; Ephesians 3:2-3a, 5-6; Matthew 2:1-12
The feast of the Epiphany celebrates the first formal presentation of the Christ-child to the world, represented by the three
wise men from the east. The first reading from the Prophet
Isaiah speaks of the glory of the Lord now becoming visible and
of the great joy that this brings to the earth. The psalm continues
this theme and tells of how all the people shall worship and give
glory and praise to God. In the second reading from his letter to
the Ephesians, St Paul tells his readers that the message of God
through Christ is meant for all people – not just the Jewish people but all peoples. The gospel text from St Matthew recalls how
the three wise men came to find the child and the homage they
pay to him. The three wise men in particular represent all
peoples – Jew and Gentile alike – and on our behalf they pay
homage to our infant king while also giving him gifts from us.
We cannot give him presents as the wise men did for he is no
longer physically present but we can give him the gift of believing in him and of proclaiming the gospel. As the Christmas carol
says – 'what I have I give him, give my all.'

*Where Epiphany is celebrated on the 6th then the readings for the fol-
lowing days go by the date (Ireland).*
*Where Epiphany is celebrated on the Sunday not the 6th then the read-
ings follow the day of the week (UK and USA).*

January 6: *(where Epiphany is on 7 or 8)*
1 John 5:3-15; Psalm 147; Mark 1:6-11
St John, in the first reading, reminds us that those who believe in
Christ and live in Christ will have eternal life while those who
reject him or are indifferent to him will not have eternal life.
John reminds us that Christ was baptised in water and shed his
blood so that we might have eternal life. In our gospel passage
today we read of the baptism of Jesus by John the Baptist after
John had been speaking of Jesus and how he would baptise with
the Spirit while John baptised with water. Both readings speak
of God himself witnessing to Jesus – 'You are my Son, the
Beloved; my favour rests on you' – and there is no greater testimony to the person of Christ than this. Those same words could

also be said of those who truly live according to the Law of God and the gospel values, while witnessing to Jesus.

January 7: *(where Epiphany is on 7 or 8)*
1 John 5:14-21; Psalm 149; John 2:1-12
In our first reading St John tells us that if we ask God for anything that he will hear us, especially if we are striving to live the Christian life. He encourages us to pray for others that their faith may be strengthened. However, he also reminds us to keep faithful and to avoid sin because we are children of God in Christ. In the gospel, we read of the miracle at the wedding feast at Cana. We also note that Jesus worked this miracle at the request of his mother. Therefore we have an advocate before Christ and the Father in the person of Mary who is both Mother of Christ and Mother of God.

January 7: *(or Monday after Epiphany)*
1 John 3:22-4:6; Psalm 2; Matthew 4:12-17, 23-25
St John reminds us in the first reading that those who keep the commandments, believe in Christ and love one another will have God in them. He also warns the people of Asia Minor about false prophets who were about at the time diluting the message given by Christ. One of the marks of a true prophet or believer in Christ was that the preacher fully accepted the Incarnation. We are reminded that the language of belief is often alien in our world today and so we must persevere all the more and not believe the false prophets who come speaking the language that people want to hear. In the gospel from St Matthew we read of the beginning of Jesus' public ministry or his first appearance in public following the arrest of John the Baptist. Jesus' fame and reputation quickly spread as he goes about preaching and curing.

January 8: *(or Tuesday after Epiphany)*
1 John 4:7-10; Psalm 71; Mark 6:34-44
In the first reading today St John reminds us of the great love of God which is far beyond our love. Not alone does he tell us that God loves us but he tells us that God *is* love and that this love was clearly seen in the death of Christ for us. In the gospel text

from St Mark we read of the miracle of the loaves and fish. It shows Christ's concern for those who followed him and had spent all day listening to him. However, for Mark, it also shows that Christ is a great prophet and that he is the Chosen One of God. The readings call on us to love God and to devote ourselves as much to his Word as did the people who had listened to Jesus all day.

January 9: *(or Wednesday after Epiphany)*
1 John 4:11-18; Psalm 71; Mark 6:45-52
In today's continuation of the letter from St John we are told that as God has loved us greatly therefore we too should love much. Those who truly love others have God living in them and those who live by the law of love will never fear anything because love brings perfection to them. In the gospel from St Mark we see Jesus leaving the crowds and the disciples to go into the hills to pray by himself. When he returns to the disciples he walks across the water to them. This is further proof of how great he is though the disciples still do not understand. Like the first reading, he reminds them not to be afraid for he is with them. We are challenged today to love much and to believe without fear in Jesus as the Saviour of the world.

January 10: *(or Thursday after Epiphany)*
1 John 4:19-5:4; Psalm 71; Luke 4:14-22
We continue reading today from St John's passage on love. He again tells us to love much and he reminds us that if we do not love the one we see then we cannot love the One who is always present though unseen. He tells us that we must love our brother but in this John is not simply referring to our blood relations but to all peoples because we are all brothers and sisters in Christ. There is a strong reminder of the connection between love and faith. In today's gospel text from St Luke we see Jesus reading in the synagogue. He reads from the Prophet Isaiah and tells the people that he is the fulfilment of the passage. We too are called on to 'bring the good news to the poor, to proclaim liberty to captives ...' It is a further manifestation that the One whose birthday we celebrated at Christmas is truly the Son of God and the promised Messiah.

January 11: *(or Friday after Epiphany)*
1 John 5:5-13; Psalm 147; Luke 5:12-16
St John tells us in the first reading that only the one who believes
in Christ can overcome the world and have eternal life. God
himself has said this and there is no greater witness than this.
John also talks of Jesus' baptism by water and the shedding of
his blood for us. In the gospel reading from St Luke we again
read of the great power which Jesus had. In the text we see him
cure a man of his leprosy and what is significant is that he tells
the man that he wants to cure him. Jesus wants to save each one
of us but we too must want that just as the leper wanted to be
cured. While Jesus wants to save he will not force his ways on
anyone and so we must show our desire to be saved by living
out his commandments and loving one another.

January 12: *(or Saturday after Epiphany)*
1 John 5:14-21; Psalm 149; John 3:22-30
In our text today from St John's first letter we are told to pray to
God for what we need, safe in the knowledge that he will hear
and will answer us. He also tells us that we belong to God and
not to this earth but that we must be wary of the false gods who
will keep us tied to the things of this earth and not to our true
God in heaven. One of the main themes of the letter we now
conclude comes through: sin should have no place in the life of a
Christian. In the gospel we read of John the Baptist's continuing
testimony to Jesus. He tells his listeners that Jesus must grow
greater as he, John, must decrease in popularity. This is because
his job of preparing the way for Jesus has finished.

The Second Sunday after Christmas
Sirach 24:1-2, 8-12; Psalm 147; Ephesians 1:3-6, 15-18; John 1:1-18
The first reading and the gospel today are linked together because they both speak about the Wisdom of God coming to dwell
among his chosen people. Jesus is that Wisdom and he lived on
this earth as a human being, as one of his own creation and one
of his own people. St Paul tells us in the second reading that in
this way we are all sons of God because, through the Incarnation,
Christ restored us to glory and we are all saved through him if
we earnestly seek that salvation and the inheritance he promised

us. Paul is asking us to think about this great mystery and to re-alise the hope which is now before each one of us.

Feast of the Holy Family: Year A
Ecclesiasticus 3:2-6, 12-14; Psalm 127; Colossians 3:12-21; Matthew 2:13-15, 19-23
In our first reading today we are told to honour and look after our parents without conditions. The author tells us that in so doing we also respect, honour and obey the Father of us all. In our second reading St Paul tells us how we should live in fami-lies with the underlying rule being that of love and respect. Everything we do in our families should be done with the wis-dom which comes from God. In the gospel text from St Matthew, we read of the angel appearing to Joseph and telling him to take the Child and Mary into Egypt until it was safe to return. It would have solved a number of problems for Joseph if the child were to die and yet he carried out the angel's instruction, showing himself to be a true father and guardian to Jesus. Today we are called on to honestly evaluate our relationship with our family and to do what we can to live the ideal found in today's readings.

Feast of the Holy Family: Year B
Genesis 15:1-6, 21:1-3; Psalm 104; Hebrews 11:8, 11-12, 17-19; Luke 2:22-40
Our first reading from the Book of Genesis sees the Lord telling Abram that he will be the father of a multitude of believers. Abram is taken aback because he has no child by his wife so, to fulfil his promise, the Lord completes Abraham's family through Sarah's giving birth to Isaac. In the second reading St Paul reminds us of the great faith that Abraham had even to the point of sacrificing his only son which would have rendered God's promise null and void. In the gospel, we see Jesus being brought to the Temple by Mary and Joseph to fulfil the Law. There they are met by Simeon and Anna who praise God for having seen the Saviour. We are called on to have faith like Abraham and Sarah, Simeon and Anna, and to believe in God and his Word even when we do not fully understand what it is that we are believing. If we do have faith then the promises of salvation which have been made to us will be fulfilled for us.

Feast of the Holy Family: Year C

1 Samuel 1:20-22, 24-28; Psalm 83; 1John 3:1-2, 21-24; Luke 2:41-52
In our reading from the first book of Samuel we read of the birth of Samuel. Hannah had prayed to the Lord for a child and promised that the child would be dedicated to God forever. The child is born and Hannah gives praise and thanks to God for the gift of new life and, when the child is a year old, she brings him to the Temple to dedicate him to God as she had promised. The child grew and became one of the greatest judges in the history of Israel. In the second reading St John asks us to think about the love which God has lavished upon us, in particular by letting us be known as his sons and daughters. All we have to do in return is to live by the gospel precepts. In our gospel passage from St Luke we have the story of the finding of the child Jesus in the Temple by his very worried parents. When questioned he tells them that he was carrying out his Father's will. Though his true Father was in heaven he still lived under the authority of both Mary and Joseph and grew strong in the sight of his peers. This is the ideal to which all families are called – an ideal based on love and respect.

Baptism of the Lord: Year A

Isaiah 24:1-4, 6-7; Psalm 28; Acts 10:34-38; Matthew 3:3-17
In our first reading from Isaiah we see the Lord speaking about his servant. This servant enjoys the favour of the Lord and has been sent to be the 'covenant of the people and the light of the nations.' Our gospel passage recounts Christ's baptism by John as told by St Matthew. In it, the Father witnesses to his own Son and says that he is the Chosen One in fulfilment of the text from Isaiah. In the second reading from the Acts of the Apostles we see St Peter preaching and he tells us that Christ was filled with the Holy Spirit, that he cured those who came to him, and that he is the Lord of all people. He also tells us that God has no favourites – each one who does the will of the Father will receive the inheritance promised if they believe in Christ.

Baptism of the Lord: Year B

Isaiah 55:1-11; Psalm: Isaiah 12:2-6; 1 John 5:1-9; Mark 1:7-11

In our first reading from the Prophet Isaiah we see the people being called by God to return to him and to abandon their wicked ways. The symbol of water is very evident in this reading as it is in all of the readings today. In the second reading from St John's first letter we are told that we should love those with whom we come into contact because if we do not love them then we cannot possibly love God whom we cannot see. Our gospel passage recounts Christ's baptism by John as told by St Mark. In it, the Father witnesses to his own Son and says that he is the Chosen One in fulfilment of the text from Isaiah.

Baptism of the Lord: Year C

Isaiah 40:1-5, 9-11; Psalm 103; Titus 2:11-14, 3:4-7; Luke 3:15-16, 21-22

Our first reading today from the Prophet Isaiah is a call to the people to rise up and be consoled for their liberation is now at hand. The Lord has now come to them and he will gather them together as a shepherd gathers his sheep. It is an appropriate text for the celebration of the Lord's baptism because with his baptism Jesus began his public ministry – at his baptism he was revealed to the people and God signalled his approval of him. At the Epiphany we celebrated the revelation of our salvation to the Magi but now we celebrate his revelation to all the people and the preaching of the Good News. Our gospel passage recounts Christ's baptism by John in the Jordan as told by St Luke. In it, the Father witnesses to his own Son and says that he is the Chosen One in fulfilment of the text from Isaiah. In the second reading St Paul tells us that Christ became a sacrifice for us simply because he had compassion for us – we had done nothing to merit it. Now, however, we must live good and religious lives in this present world while we wait for the blessings of the world to come. At our own baptism we became God's chosen ones in a special way and by living out Paul's instructions in the second reading we will help to bring Christ's glory to the whole world.

THE SEASON OF LENT

SUNDAYS: YEAR A

The First Sunday of Lent
Genesis 2:7-9, 3:1-7; Psalm 50; Romans 5:12-19; Matthew 4:1-11
The first reading from Genesis reminds us of the creation of the world and of the first humans – Adam and Eve. Having reminded us of the beauty of Creation and of all the good that was in it, it then recalls the great sin of Adam and Eve as they gave in to temptation. The psalm asks for forgiveness from God for our sins. St Paul tells the Romans that sin came through one man (Adam) but that all people have been redeemed through another man – Christ. As man brought separation from God so the unity has been restored by Man because whatever sins were committed God's freely given grace is always greater. In the gospel we see Jesus – truly man like us – being tempted by the devil while fasting in the wilderness. He resists these temptations because of his adherence to the word of God and because of his faith in God. We are called on in the readings to be faithful to God, to trust him at all times, and to call on Christ who knows what it is to be tempted.

The Second Sunday of Lent
Genesis 12:1-4; Psalm 32; 2 Timothy 1:8-10; Matthew 17:1-9
Our first reading for today is from the Book of Genesis and recounts the call of Abram and the promise made to him by God – the promise to make of him a great nation if he answers the call of the Lord. St Paul reminds us in the second reading that God has saved us and has given us his grace, a grace which had been granted before the beginning of time but which has only appeared with the Incarnation. He also reminds us that there will be hardships to bear because we are Christians but that the reward is immortality. The text from St Matthew is that of the Transfiguration of the Lord before the three disciples. The glory of the Lord is already being revealed to his disciples though they are not allowed to reveal this until after his resurrection. The disciples are encouraged and strengthened for what is to follow by what they have just seen. We are called to believe like them and to have faith and confidence in God as Abram had. This time of penance and transformation is about

making ourselves ready for that great day when our true glory will be revealed as was Christ's glory on the mountain top – a glory which is ours if we but strengthen our faith and remove sin from our lives.

The Third Sunday of Lent
Exodus 17:3-7; Psalm 94; Romans 5:1-2, 5-8; John 4:5-42
Our reading from Exodus shows the Jewish people in their wanderings in the wilderness having fled from Egypt. However, they are now complaining and Moses has to intercede for them before God. St Paul reminds us in the second reading that we have all received God's love and grace through the life, death and resurrection of Christ. That love and grace is not a lie but is very real: Christ did not wait until humankind stopped sinning to die but did so while humankind was still sinning. The story of the Woman at the Well is found in today's gospel passage. Christ speaks to her of the 'living water' which is himself. She believes and brings many others to the well and they in turn also believe in Christ and his message. It also shows how important it was for Christ to bring his message to all peoples because, in his day, the Samaritans were not considered 'proper Jews' because they did not worship in the Temple in Jerusalem. Christ knew her life story and wanted her to be whole again. He spoke with her and showed her the way to true life through acknowledging her past and letting her see his love and concern for her. Her experience of the Messiah brought many others to experience the Messiah also. We have a duty to follow the example of the Samaritan woman by actively seeking after the living water and to bring that refreshment to others.

The Fourth Sunday of Lent – Laetare Sunday
1 Samuel 16:6-7, 10-13; Psalm 22; Ephesians 5:8-14; John 9:1-41
In the text for our first reading today from the book of the Prophet Samuel we see Samuel out looking for a successor to Saul – Israel's king. He goes to Jesse of Bethlehem who presents each of his sons except the youngest who is out minding the herd. However, the Lord chooses none of those presented but instead singles out the youngest boy – David – for service as the anointed King of Israel. St Paul reminds us in the second reading from his letter to the Ephesians, that, as Christians, we are children of the light (that is, of Christ) and that we are to live by that

light in all things. Only by right living can we really be children
of the light and know what path the Lord is marking out for us
in this life. In our gospel text for today we see Jesus on a Sabbath
day giving sight to a man born blind. The miracle itself receives
little print but the reaction of the Pharisees and officials receives
a lot of print as John records for us that reaction. The Pharisees
maintained that the man had been born blind because of sins
committed either by his parents or by himself, though Jesus tells
us that this was not the case. They question the man and his parents and the man answers back quite strongly and so receives a
rough time from the Pharisees. This incident began to drive a
wedge among some of the Pharisees and between the Pharisees
and the followers of Christ. The first reading and gospel remind
us that how we perceive the world is not always how God per-
ceives it and that often times God chooses those whom the
world rejects (such as the boy David) to lead his people.

The Fifth Sunday of Lent
Ezekiel 37:12-14; Psalm 129; Romans 8:8-11; John 11:1-45
The first reading from the Prophet Ezekiel recounts the Lord
telling his people that he will give them his spirit and they will
live. St Paul in our second reading, which comes from his letter
to the Romans, continues this theme and says that the spirit of
God has been given to the people and that it is life-giving for
them. This is because their only interest is in spiritual things and
not things of an unspiritual nature. In the gospel, we have the
story of the raising of Lazarus from the dead. This reminds us of
the death of Jesus and of his resurrection but also provokes us to
think about our own death in baptism and resurrection at the
end of time. While Lazarus returned to life we know that he
died again but that final death was so that he could live in life
eternal.

Palm (Passion) Sunday
Isaiah 50:4-7; Psalm 21; Philippians 2:6-11; Matthew 26:14-27:66
The readings today all point to the person of Christ. Isaiah
speaks of Christ as one who came to preach but who was beaten
and insulted. St Paul in the second reading speaks of the divinity
of Christ and what he gave up in order to become one of us. The
gospel from St Matthew recounts the passion and death of
Christ for us. While Palm Sunday recalls the triumphant entry

of Christ into Jerusalem it is also the beginning of the end of his earthly life and gives us a contrast which helps us to focus on what is to happen later this week. Seeing the Christ suffer for us, it also helps us to carry our sufferings for him. Between today's reading of the Passion and that on Friday we have a final opportunity to reflect on the history-changing events which are about to happen and of their significance for each and every one of us.

SUNDAYS: YEAR B

The First Sunday of Lent
Genesis 9:8-15; Psalm 24; 1 Peter 3:18-22; Mark 1:12-15
As we begin our Lenten preparation for the celebration of Easter we are reminded of the reason behind this time. In the first reading we see God talking with Noah and making a new covenant with him, and not just with him but with all of creation right down to our own time. The rainbow in the sky is a reminder of that covenant. In the second reading St Peter reminds us that the waters of baptism save far more than were saved by the ark in Noah's time. We read very briefly in St Mark's gospel of Jesus' temptations in the wilderness and how he did not succumb to Satan's promises. After this episode Jesus begins preaching repentance for the sake of the kingdom. We know that what awaits us is a much greater promise than awaited Noah and so we should use this time well by examining our own life and making sure that it is in keeping with the covenant.

The Second Sunday of Lent
Genesis 22:1-2, 9-13, 15-18; Psalm 115; Romans 8:31-34; Mark 9:2-10
Today we read of Abraham's sacrifice of his only son, Isaac. He did so out of love for God and out of a desire to do the will of God even if that appeared to negate the earlier promise of being a father to a great multitude. In the second reading from the letter to the Romans, we are reminded that God gave up his only Son for our sake so that we might have eternal life once again, and that this Son now sits at God's right hand to plead for us. In the gospel, we read St Mark's account of the Transfiguration of the Lord. For a moment Christ was seen in dazzling white robes and it is a foretaste of what we too can be – pure as Christ. Our readings put before us the need for this penitential season as we move towards the great festival of Easter. We will become pure as Christ and enter heaven through our own purification which

we must carry out as willingly as Abraham was willing to sacrifice his own son.

The Third Sunday of Lent
Exodus 20:1-17; Psalm 18; 1 Corinthians 1:22-25; John 2:13-25
In our first reading today we are presented with the ten commandments – the most basic law for moral living. The psalm
tells us that 'the law of the Lord is perfect, it revives the soul.' In
the second reading St Paul tells us that while others may scoff at
the notion of a crucified Christ, we as Christians know that
Christ is the wisdom of God and that, following his law, we too
will enter into the Father's glory. In the gospel, we see Jesus
driving the money changers out of the Temple and predicting
his own death and resurrection – the very folly that Paul spoke
of. Yet we know that through Christ's death and resurrection we
are given the supreme example of love – the love of God for us
who died that we might have life. In the light of this we are challenged to really look at our lives in the light of the ten commandments – which are very short indeed – and to live by them in
order to win the glory promised us.

The Fourth Sunday of Lent – Laetare Sunday
Chronicles 36:14-16, 19-23; Psalm 136; Ephesians 2:4-10; John 3:14-21
In our first reading from the Book of Chronicles we read how
the people had defiled the Temple of the Lord and for this they
were punished with deportation. However, the Lord is full of
mercy and compassion and so he moved the heart of the king to
allow his people to return home and start the Temple afresh in
Jerusalem. In the second reading from St Paul we are reminded
that we are dead because of our sins but through the grace of
God we are raised to life again. In our gospel, we see Jesus
speaking with Nicodemus and he tells him that the Son of God
must be raised up as a sign for all the people – a sign which, if
they believe, will bring them to everlasting life. But part of this
believing is that we live as people of the light and allow others
to clearly see that we are believers and that we play our part in
the spread of the gospel. Lent is about purifying ourselves of sin
but also about strengthening our resolve to be heralds of the
gospel of Christ.

The Fifth Sunday of Lent

Jeremiah 31:31-34; Psalm 50; Hebrews 5:7-9; John 12:20-30

In our first reading from the Prophet Jeremiah we see God telling his people that he will make a new and everlasting covenant with them which will be unlike any of the previous covenants. With this covenant he will wipe away their sins and not call them to mind. St Paul tells us in the second reading that Christ obeyed the Father and suffered for us and in that suffering he became the source of eternal salvation for all people. We as Christians know that Christ is the everlasting covenant spoken of in the first reading and so we must believe in him with our whole hearts. If we believe in him then we will give up our selfish ways and live only for him so that we may yield the rich harvest which Jesus speaks of in the gospel. He died so that we might all be drawn to him and we will only be drawn to him if we spend time in prayer and living the life to which we are called. When we suffer, we do not do so alone because Christ is with us and so our suffering is not for nothing.

Palm (Passion) Sunday

Isaiah 50:4-7; Psalm 21; Philippians 2:6-11; Mark 14:1-15:47

The readings today all point to the person of Christ. Isaiah speaks of Christ as one who came to preach but who was beaten and insulted. St Paul speaks of the divinity of Christ and what he gave up in order to become one of us. The gospel from St Mark recounts the Passion and death of Christ for us. While Palm Sunday recalls the triumphant entry of Christ into Jerusalem it is also the beginning of the end of his earthly life and gives us a contrast which helps us to focus on what is to happen later this week. It begins the week on a sad note and sets a very sombre tone for the days to come. Mark's text very much highlights the fact that while Christ arrived in triumph he ended the week in abject abandonment – abandoned by those who turned out to welcome him to the city, abandoned by his closest friends. However, there is also a note of victory because we have the benefit of knowing the full story – that story being that Christ triumphed over death and won for us our salvation.

SUNDAYS: YEAR C

The First Sunday of Lent
Deuteronomy 26:4-10; Psalm 90; Romans 10:8-13; Luke 4:1-13
In our first reading from the book of Deuteronomy we see
Moses instructing the people. He tells them that they must bring
their first fruits to the Lord and to declare their faith in him. This
will be their way of thanking God for all that they have received
from him. In our second reading, St Paul also speaks about
creeds and tells us that the creed of the Christian is that Christ
rose from the dead and redeemed us regardless of race or
colour. In our gospel reading from St Luke we read of the temptation of Christ in the wilderness during his fasting and prayers
of forty days. Despite all that Satan offered him he remained
faithful to his Father and to his mission. Our Lenten season is
about facing up to the times when we have given in to temptation and resolving to say 'no' to them in the future. It is also
about preparing to celebrate the events which are central to our
faith and which bring us salvation.

The Second Sunday of Lent
Genesis 15:5-12, 17-18; Psalm 26; Philippians 3:17-4:1; Luke 9:28-36
In our first reading today we see Abram putting his trust in God
yet again. He has already left his homeland to go to a place
which the Lord pointed out even though he did not know what
lay in the future for him. Again he puts his trust in the Lord and
this time the Lord promises to give his descendants the land he
is now living in despite the fact that he has no children and Sara
is barren. As we know, God did fulfil his promise and gave
Abram a son and made him the father of a multitude. In the
gospel text we have St Luke's account of the Transfiguration of
Christ. Jesus and some of his closest friends had climbed the
mountain, where he was transfigured in their sight and appeared in radiant glory and stood between Moses and Elijah –
the two key figures for the Jews from the Old Testament. The
apostles got a glimpse of Christ's true glory on the mountain
and it was only after the resurrection that they truly understood
what they saw. The Transfiguration also has an important implication for each of us and this is brought out by St Paul in the
second reading in which he tells us that Christ will transform
our mortal bodies and make us like his own in glory. The

Transfiguration didn't just give the apostles a glimpse of their glorified Lord – they also got a glimpse of what they too would be like when they joined him in eternity. That glory awaits those of us who have been faithful to God in this life, and this season of Lent is about making us aware of what we need to do in order to attain that perfection and ultimately the glory which awaits us.

The Third Sunday of Lent
Exodus 3:1-8, 13-15; Psalm 102; 1 Corinthians 10:1-6, 10-12; Luke 13:1-9
In our first reading we see the Lord appointing Moses to go and bring his message to his people in Egypt who have been held in slavery by a people with whom they once had equality. What is important for us to note in the account is not the fact that the bush was unharmed or that Moses was tending a flock, but that the Lord has seen the plight of his people and has resolved to free them from that plight. Today many people are oppressed by their own false gods and habits but the Lord still wants them to be freed and so we have this season of Lent to help us identify our false gods and to accept God's help in freeing ourselves from the things which oppress us. St Paul reminds us of this in the second reading. In the gospel we see Jesus calling the people to repentance. If the people repent then they will have life but if not they will perish. The choice placed before us today is quite clear: if we accept the Lord's love and compassion and turn away from our false gods which lead us into sin then we will be saved and receive eternal life, but if not then, while we may live this life according to our own rules, we will not enter the kingdom in the next life.

The Fourth Sunday of Lent – Laetare Sunday
Joshua 5:9-12; Psalm 33; 2 Corinthians 5:17-21; Luke 15:1-3, 11-32
In our first reading we see that the Israelites have arrived in the Promised Land and so cease to feed on manna. The Lord has fulfilled his promise to his Chosen People and removed the shame of slavery from them. In our gospel for today we have the story of the Prodigal Son, a story which reminds us of the great love of the Father for his people even when they stray from his love. He is always ready to accept back into his family those who repent of their wrong-doing and acknowledge his love and their dependence on that love. This is re-enforced in the second reading

in which St Paul tells us that it was through Christ that God's forgiveness and reconciliation were given to us. Not alone have we been reconciled with God through Christ but we are now ambassadors of that reconciliation – we have a duty and responsibility as baptised Christians to bring that reconciliation to those whom we meet, beginning at home and then going out into the workplace. This season of Lent is about reminding ourselves of how much God loves us and wants to keep us part of his family but also a reminder that it is for us to make the choice – God will not force his love on any of us.

The Fifth Sunday of Lent
Isaiah 43:16-21; Psalm 125; Philippians 3:8-14; John 8:1-11
Our first reading today from the prophet Isaiah tells us that our past deeds are not called to mind by God or held against us. He has redeemed us and now all we have to do is to accept that redemption. The psalm reminds us that the Lord has delivered his people from their bondage and redeemed them. In our gospel we see Jesus confronted with the woman who has been caught in adultery and who the elders were about to stone in accordance with the Law. But Christ turns the situation around and confronts the elders making them face their own sinfulness. The woman is sorry for what she did and so Christ forgives her and wipes out her guilt – it will never again be called to mind. The Lord does not condemn and is simply waiting for us to turn to him for forgiveness. St Paul tells us that adherence to the Law is not enough for us to achieve perfection, which is what the elders were doing in the gospel. Fulfilling the Law is important because it helps us along the path to freedom but it is useless if it is not backed up and grounded in a deep-rooted faith in God. Without faith adherence to the Law is nothing but a hollow gesture and will not bring us freedom.

Palm (Passion) Sunday
Isaiah 50:4-7; Psalm 21; Philippians 2:6-11; Luke 22:14-23:56
The readings today all point to the person of Christ. Isaiah speaks of Christ as one who came to preach but who was beaten and insulted. St Paul speaks of the divinity of Christ and what he gave up in order to become one of us. The gospel from St Luke recounts the Passion and death of Christ for each one of us. While Palm Sunday recalls the triumphant entry of Christ into

Jerusalem it is also the beginning of the end of his earthly life and gives us a contrast which helps us to focus on what is to happen later this week. It begins the week on a sad note and sets a very sombre tone for the days to come. However, there is also a note of victory because we have the benefit of knowing the full story – that story being that Christ triumphed over death and won us our salvation.

THE WEEKDAYS OF LENT

Ash Wednesday
Joel 2:12-18; Psalm 50; 2 Corinthians 5:20-6:2; Matthew 6:1-6, 16-18
Today we enter Lent – the great penitential season of the Church's year – in preparation for the death and resurrection of Christ for the salvation of each of us. The readings today speak about repentance, about fasting, about preparation. We are called to prepare for the glory of the resurrection and our salvation by prayer, fasting and almsgiving. In the gospel, we are told that what we do is to be done quietly and without drawing attention to ourselves for that means nothing in the sight of God. Throughout Lent, many people give up various things, such as chocolate or sugar, etc, but what we are asked to give up in the readings has far greater impact not just on ourselves but on others, for we are asked to give up sin and hypocrisy.

Thursday after Ash Wednesday
Deuteronomy 30:15-20; Psalm 1; Luke 9:22-25
In today's Old Testament reading Moses sets before the people a choice – life or death. To gain long life they must live according to the commandments of God. To gain death they need only ignore God. The psalm speaks of the happiness of those who do turn to God. Similar to the first reading, Jesus too gives us a choice – life or death. If we opt to follow him in all that we do and say then we will gain an eternal reward, though this may mean loosing our physical life here on earth but it will certainly mean entering into life with Christ. The purpose of the readings each day is to make us think about our lives and where they are going. The readings today encourage us to reflect, at this early part of Lent, on what we have to change over the next few weeks in order to make us more worthy of the great sacrifice made for us by Christ.

Friday after Ash Wednesday
Isaiah 58:1-9; Psalm 50; Matthew 9:14-15

Through the Prophet Isaiah the Lord tells us the sort of fast that is false – one which is trumpeted before others while putting on a false impression of being miserable. Instead, God wants a quiet, private fast. He also wants all oppression to cease and for all people to show charity to their neighbours. Isaiah spells out practical works of mercy that do please God. We might imitate these ourselves in a variety of ways throughout this penitential season. In the gospel, the Pharisees are admonishing Jesus for his disciples' lack of fasting but he tells them that because he (the bridegroom) is with them, they will not fast. When he is gone, then the time will be right for fasting.

Saturday after Ash Wednesday
Isaiah 58:9-14; Psalm 85; Luke 5:27-32

The Lord continues to tell his people how they should live if they are to enjoy his favour. They must do all that he has commanded them and must bring about an end to tyranny and oppression. It reminds us of the blessings and rewards that lie in store for us if we practise kindness and compassion towards others. Our gospel text reminds us that the Word of God is not just for those who believe and live their lives in accordance with his wishes for they are not in need of conversion. His Word is for all people and particularly for those who are not living a life worthy of him – and he is the judge of what is worthy of him.

Monday of the First Week of Lent
Leviticus 19:1-2, 11-18; Psalm 18; Matthew 25:31-46

The readings today show us how to make our lives more holy during Lent by treating other people the way we should treat them. The Lord speaks to Moses in the reading from Leviticus and through him gives the people instructions for living properly in his sight, particularly how to act towards members of our family, friends and neighbours. The psalm sings the praises of God's law and reminds us that this law gives wisdom and refreshes the soul. In the gospel, Jesus gives a further instruction for proper living: we must reach out to others and help them in any way we can because God dwells in them just as much as he does in us. At the start of this first full week of Lent we are reminded that good works – as well as faith in God – are necessary in life.

Tuesday of the First Week of Lent
Isaiah 55:10-11; Psalm 33; Matthew 6:7-15
In the reading from Isaiah, God says that his word goes out and achieves what it was sent to do. This reminds us that God's will is perfectly carried out in heaven and that we pray for this to happen here on earth. In the gospel, Jesus gives us the most perfect prayer – the Our Father. It is perfect because it is past, present and future. It is perfect because it gives praise to God for what we have received; it asks for what we need to continue living; it seeks forgiveness for the wrongs we have done; it asks for the strength to forgive; and it asks for protection. The whole gospel is summed up in this one prayer and as we pray it the word of God is fulfilled.

Wednesday of the First Week of Lent
Jonah 3:1-10; Psalm 50; Luke 11:29-32
Todays readings remind us of the importance of penance and of its reward. In the first reading we see Jonah has been sent to Nineveh to warn the people of God's wrath at their wrong-doing and of God's intention to punish them. When they hear the warning they repent and when they repent the punishment they were to receive is set aside, and their friendship with God is restored. The psalm takes up this theme of repentance and the plea for forgiveness. Jesus, in the gospel, is giving the same warning to the people of his day as Jonah gave to the Ninevites. The message is given to us in our day also. We must turn away from sin and return to the ways of the Lord if we are to be saved.

Thursday of the First Week of Lent
Esther 14:1, 3-5, 12-14 (Vulgate); Psalm 137; Matthew 7:7-12
Today's readings remind us of just how important a life of prayer is and that we should cultivate this during the Lenten season. In the first reading we see Queen Esther – a Jew – whose husband, King Ahasuerus, had just been tricked into destroying the Jews. In our passage today from Esther, we see that she has just received word of this and pleads to the Lord to be with her in this time of great peril as she attempts to save her people, and in which she is ultimately successful. In the gospel passage, Jesus speaks of the importance of prayer and the fact that no prayer goes unanswered. While we may not always be happy with the answer we receive, we do still receive

an answer to our prayer, an answer which God deems to be best for us in our situation.

Friday of the First Week of Lent
Ezekiel 18:21-28; Psalm 129; Matthew 5:20-26
The readings today remind us of the importance of interior conversion. In the reading from the Prophet Ezekiel we are told that God does not rejoice in the death of a wicked man but rejoices to see that person converted. More distasteful in his sight is a righteous man turning to wicked ways than a wicked man living wickedly. In the gospel, we are told that our virtue must be more than the mere lip-service of the Pharisees – we must live and act from a deeply held conviction and faith and not just go through external emotions. God sees the inmost heart and judges accordingly. Jesus also reminds us to be reconciled with our family for any wrong we have done to them or they have done to us. Where we fall short on this we must take concrete steps towards conversion.

Saturday of the First Week of Lent
Deuteronomy 26:16-19; Psalm 118; Matthew 5:43-48
In the reading from the Old Testament Book of Deuteronomy, we see that God has promised life to his people but only if they keep the commandments – those simple instructions and rules for living which make life so easy and happy. The psalm tells us that those who do keep the commandments and the law of God will live in happiness. Jesus reminds us in the gospel that we must love all people – good and bad alike. For him, this is a simple extension of the commandments and something we should have no problem doing if we are truly living out the commandments. We must always act perfectly in the same way that God is perfect and we are seeking to become one with him.

Monday of the Second Week of Lent
Daniel 9:4-10; Psalm 78; Luke 6:36-38
In our first reading we see Daniel speaking to the Lord and contrasting the goodness of God with the wickedness of the people. The reading reminds us that while we may sin and rebel against God, he never fails to forgive us when we seek forgiveness. The message is that as we are forgiven so we must forgive those who we perceive to have wronged us. The psalm continues this

theme and asks God not to treat the people according to their sins. In the gospel reading from St Luke, Jesus tells us to forgive others and we too will be forgiven; if we give to others we too will receive. When we judge others we should be careful that the yardstick we use on them is the same which we apply to ourselves. There is often a difference between judging and justice and we must err on the side of the latter.

Tuesday of the Second Week of Lent
Isaiah 1:10, 16-20; Psalm 49; Matthew 23:1-12
In the Prophet Isaiah we are called to turn back to God but we must do more than just repent of what sins we have already committed. We must resolve to do good from now on and to commit no wrong. We must put into practice the words which we ourselves speak. Christ takes up this theme in the gospel text and tells us that we must practise what we preach. If we have authority over others then we should not ask them to do what we ourselves would not do but should help others to carry their burdens rather than piling more burdens on them. There is no point in doing good acts if we do not believe in the reason for them or if we are simply doing it for the praise of others. We must be a humble people before others and before our God.

Wednesday of the Second Week of Lent
Jeremiah 18:18-20; Psalm 30; Matthew 20:17-28
In our first reading we read that the people have turned against Jeremiah and he prays to God for his safety. The plotting against Jeremiah reminds us of the plotting that will take place against Christ as we near Holy Week and, ultimately, the outcome of that plotting. The psalm continues this prayer for help, reminding us that in God alone is our safety and our salvation. In the gospel passage from St Matthew we have the first prediction by Christ of his coming death. Zebedee's wife asks that her two sons be closest to him in heaven but he tells them that they will have to suffer first and they reply that they are happy to do so. Turning to the others he tells them that places at table are insignificant because he came to serve rather than to be served. We too must serve if we are to be fit for heaven.

Thursday of the Second Week of Lent

Jeremiah 17:5-10; Psalm 1; Luke 16:19-31

Both the first reading and the psalm today tell us that man must put his trust in God alone for only God is our saviour and salvation. In the gospel, Christ tells the story of the poor man, Lazarus, and the rich man outside whose house Lazarus used to sit. The rich man is not condemned because of his wealth but because of what his wealth had made him, that is, indifferent to the plight and true dignity of others. We are all given choices in life and the readings today implore us to make the right one: that is to live by the law of God and to believe in him alone while treating others as he wants us to, seeing Christ in each person.

Friday of the Second Week of Lent

Genesis 37:3-4, 12-13, 17-28; Psalm 104; Matthew 21:33-43, 45-46

Today's passage from the Book of Genesis recounts the story of Joseph being sold into slavery by his brothers. There is an echo in the story of Joseph – whose brothers rejected him, plotted against him and tried to kill him – of the story of Jesus who was also rejected, plotted against and eventually put to death. In the gospel, Jesus uses a parable to speak of himself to the people. He tells the story of a vineyard owner whose workers have rebelled and killed his messengers. In the end he sends his son and they kill him too. The kingdom was being offered to the Jews first but they would not produce the harvest so it was offered to the gentiles who accepted the task and have produced a harvest. We are now heirs of those gentiles and are reminded of who our vineyard owner is. The story is also one of missed opportunities, a betrayal of trust, and ingratitude in the face of the vineyard-owner's overwhelming generosity. It is a reminder to us to examine our lives and to ensure that we are not like the bad tenants, and, if perchance we are, to take this opportunity to make up for the opportunities which have already passed us by.

Saturday of the Second Week of Lent

Micah 7:14-15, 18-20; Psalm 102; Luke 15:1-3, 11-32

The reading from Micah asks God to lead us in the right path and to remember his covenants. There is a reminder that God does not remember our sins for ever but that he forgives us and casts our sins away. The gospel recounts the well-known parable of the Prodigal Son. The father in the story represents God and each of us is represented by the younger son because we all turn from God and try to hide from him at some time or other. As the younger son was welcomed back with open arms, so too will God welcome us back. We must also be careful not to be like the eldest son, who failed to forgive and so distanced himself from his loving father which made his sin all the more grievous. The readings challenge us to look at how we have lived and to return to the Lord seeking forgiveness for whatever we have done that is not in keeping with his will. Whether we return to him sooner or later, he will always be there waiting with open arms for us to return .

Alternative Readings for the Third Week of Lent
These readings may be used any day this week, especially in Years B and C, when the Gospel of the Samaritan Woman is not read on the Third Sunday of Lent.
Exodus 17:1-7; Psalm 94; John 4:5-42
In our first reading from the Book of Exodus we see that the people are now free of slavery in Egypt and have begun the journey back to the land of their forebears. However, they begin to complain to Moses and forget the reasons why they have been freed and the promises made to them by the Lord. The spark this time is about water and the lack of fresh water for the people. Moses asks God for help and the people receive water. The theme of water is also found in our gospel text where we see Jesus taking a break from his travels beside a well. His companions go in search of food and while alone a Samaritan woman comes to the well. Despite the norms of the time Jesus speaks to her and asks her for water. Through the conversation which follows the woman becomes a believer and she brings many of the townspeople to Jesus and they too believe. Jesus saw the woman's thirst for true water and for life and this was granted to her because she listened and had faith. We too are challenged to listen to the word of God, to place our trust in him and to have faith in him.

Monday of the Third Week of Lent
2 Kings 5:1-15; Psalm 41; Luke 4:24-30
In the text from the second book of the Kings we see one of the King of Aram's commanders – Naaman – being cured of leprosy by the Prophet Elisha. At this the commander declares that only

in Israel is there a true God. In the gospel passage, Jesus refers to the text from Kings and Naaman the leper and tells his listeners that he, like Elijah and Elisha, was not sent only to the Jews but to all peoples. The story of Naaman also reminds us of Easter baptism: there is a link between Naaman's cleansing in the Jordan and the baptism of Christ in the same waters. We have a duty not to keep the gospel message to ourselves but to bring it to others. Christ brought his message to his people first but they failed to see in his simplicity and ordinariness, the true power and presence of God. They sought something spectacular but did not see it. If we are looking for something spectacular then we too will be disappointed for the message of Christ is profound while still being simple.

Tuesday of the Third Week of Lent
Daniel 3:25, 34-43; Psalm 24; Matthew 18:21-35
In the Book of the Prophet Daniel there is recounted the story of three young men – Hananiah, Mishael and Azariah – who refused to abandon their religion for King Nebuchadnezzar. The king had them bound and thrown into a fiery furnace but the angel of God joined them there and they walked through the furnace unharmed. Our passage today from Daniel sees Azariah speaking to God from within the furnace and asking God to look kindly on them and on their people and to forgive the sins of the people which have brought them such torment. The psalm continues this theme. In the gospel, Jesus tells his disciples that prayer on its own is not enough – we must also forgive our neighbours whenever they wrong us. And that forgiveness must come from the heart and not just from the lips. If we do not forgive others how then can we stand before God and expect him to forgive us when we withhold forgiveness?

Wednesday of the Third Week of Lent
Deuteronomy 4:1, 5-9; Psalm 147; Matthew 5:17-19
In the first reading, Moses has given the people their laws and tells them to be careful to observe them because they come from God. It is a reminder of the importance of the command of God in our daily lives. Christ, in the gospel, tells us that he came to complete the laws given to us by Moses and that they are to be obeyed. While some use Jesus as an excuse to be a rebel we see him today upholding the tradition and Law of the

Jewish people, but what is important is that Jesus wants us to live the spirit of the law and not just the mere letter of the law, and while this at times is harder to do it is infinitely more rewarding and more pleasing to God. The ten commandments may have been given many centuries ago but they are not outdated and are still to be obeyed by all.

Thursday of the Third Week of Lent
Jeremiah 7:23-28; Psalm 94; Luke 11:14-23
In today's reading from the Prophet Jeremiah, God tells us what commands he had given the people. The people, however, have abandoned the Lord and his commands. It is a reminder to us not to harden our hearts to God but to always be receptive to his ways no matter where they lead us or what they may ask of us. In the gospel some of the people are afraid of Jesus and believe that he can cast out devils because he is one himself. He tells them that this is not the case because the kingdom would soon die if that were so. He goes on to tell them that if they are not for him then they are against him. We know that being for Jesus is not just something we say but is a complete way of life and one which we cannot shy away from, because when we refuse to make the commitment to live this way of life then, at that moment, we put up a barrier to closer union with God.

Friday of the Third Week of Lent
Hosea 14:2-10; Psalm 80; Mark 12:28-34
In the first reading from Hosea, the Lord is calling his people back to him and reminding them that when they seek help that it is he who gives it. God assures them that he loves them freely and that he will shower his blessings on them despite their transgressions. The psalm continues this theme of God calling his people. In the gospel, Jesus gives the supreme commandment of love – love of God followed by love of neighbour. He quotes from the Old Testament, or the Jewish scriptures, from the Book of Deuteronomy, which reminds his listeners of the covenants made with God and of their failure to live by it even in the simplest of things. If we live by the command of love then we will have no problem in keeping all the commandments.

Saturday of the Third Week of Lent
Hosea 5:15-6:6; Psalm 50; Luke 18:9-14

We read in the prophet Hosea that what God wants from us is true love – not sacrifices and fleeting emotions when we are in difficulty. We must always love him and seek to do his will with sincerity. We must never be superficial people when it comes to God. The psalm echoes this. In the gospel, Jesus tells the story of two men in the Temple – one who went to the front and told God how good he was, believing that his goodness and righteousness was of his own creation; the other who stayed at the back and asked God for mercy acknowledging that he was a sinner. We are called to be like the second man – to be honest before God and to acknowledge that we do wrong. We are also reminded that all goodness comes from God and not from ourselves and this is what the tax collector realised and which made him righteous before God – God has no time for insincerity. The lesson put before us today is that true love for God is genuine and humble.

Alternative Readings for the Fourth Week of Lent
These readings may be used any day this week, especially in Years B and C, when the Gospel of the man born blind is not read on the Fourth Sunday of Lent.
Micah 7:7-9; Psalm 26; John 9:1-41

In our first reading from the Prophet Micah we see someone who is declaring their trust and their faith in God. Even though there may be difficult moments in their life they still trust in God knowing that he will come to their rescue and that he will take them from darkness into light. We have a similar theme in the gospel where we read of a man who is given the gift of sight by Jesus on a Sabbath day. The man had been born blind and it was the belief of the time that this was because the man, or his parents, had sinned. In the full text we read of the unwanted and negative attention which the man and his parents received following the miracle. Despite this, and the very poor way he was treated by the authorities, the man believed in Jesus and stands up to the authorities. We have believed in Jesus to some extent or other from our earliest days but are we brave enough to stand up for what we believe against those who do not want to believe despite the proof of the presence of God?

Monday of the Fourth Week of Lent
Isaiah 65:17-21; Psalm 29; John 4:43-54
God tells us through the Prophet Isaiah that he will establish his kingdom on earth and it will be one of happiness because he will be with us. In the text we have, God tells us that those blessings will mean that the sound of weeping will no longer be heard and that infants would no longer die after a few days. In the text from St John's gospel we see Jesus fulfilling the text from Isaiah as he cures the son of a court official which also removes the mourning veil from over the official's house. The official had wanted Jesus to come to the house and cure the boy but Jesus would not go, preferring instead to tell the man his son was saved. The man believed and went on his way. We are asked to have faith in Christ as this official did and to live according to his ways. If we do so, then we will inherit the kingdom God spoke of in the first reading. Christ's message is not just for the Jews or the poor, but for all people be they rich or poor, powerful or powerless.

Tuesday of the Fourth Week of Lent
Ezekiel 47:1-9, 12; Psalm 45; John 5:1-3, 5-16
In the first reading from the Prophet Ezekiel we read of a stream of water coming from the Temple which gives life to everything it comes into contact with. This reading reminds us of the new life that the waters of baptism bring to our souls. In the gospel, Jesus is at the Sheep Pool in Jerusalem which was believed to have curative powers. Jesus cures a man by simply telling him to get up and walk. The authorities are annoyed because he did this on a Sabbath. They failed to see that what was at work was the power of God, something which does not rest even on a Sabbath. Jesus is the Temple of the first reading, and the stream of water is the water of baptism. We are represented by the trees and fish and other things that are nourished by the water.

Wednesday of the Fourth Week of Lent
Isaiah 49:8-15; Psalm 144; John 5:17-30
The text from the Prophet Isaiah for today comes from the second song of the servant of God and in it the servant is told that he is the covenant of the people who has been appointed to bring the people back to God and to rescue them from wherever they have been scattered. We are reminded that the love of God

is far more tender than a mother's love for her child. In the gospel passage, we see that Jesus is the covenant of the people – the one who was sent to redeem the people. He also makes it quite clear that he and the Father are one and they both act in the same way: as Jesus is merciful to those who come to him, so too is the Father. As Jesus was tender and compassionate, so too is our Father.

Thursday of the Fourth Week of Lent
Exodus 32:7-14; Psalm 105; John 5:31-47
The people, in the reading from the book of Exodus, have turned against God and God is about to punish them. Moses, however, pleads on their behalf and reminds God of the covenant he made with Abraham, Isaac and Jacob. The psalm tells of the sins of the people and for which God was about to deal harshly with them. Jesus is speaking to the Jews in the gospel text and telling them that if they truly believed in Moses then they would believe in him too. The authorities had become too set in their ways to realise in whose presence they stood. They had shut their eyes and ears to the truth. We are challenged today to really look at our own lives and ask ourselves if we have shut ourselves off from the real Jesus. If we have shut ourselves off from him then we need to resolve to do something about it today, rather than waiting until tomorrow.

Friday of the Fourth Week of Lent
Wisdom 2:1, 12-22; Psalm 33; John 7:1-2, 10, 25-30
The reading from the Book of Wisdom is prophetic in that it speaks of the death of the virtuous man – which we can understand as being the death of Jesus. Everything that is said in it speaks of Jesus and how the people did not wish to follow him because his way was different and challenging and he pointed out their sins and transgressions. The gospel continues this story and we see that some of the people have decided to be rid of Jesus. Jesus tells us that he came not for himself but for God and for his people. He came not just to tell us about God but to show us God. We too should make every effort to get to know God personally and not just talk about him.

Saturday of the Fourth Week of Lent

Jeremiah 11:18-20; Psalm 7; John 7:40-53

The Prophet Jeremiah in our first reading speaks of the innocent man being led to the slaughter house like a lamb. Yet the just man continues to trust in God and in his help, just as Jesus did as he faced his own death. In the gospel, we are coming nearer to the arrest and Passion of Christ. The authorities have now decided to be rid of Jesus and are seeking the moment to seize him. One of the Pharisees – Nicodemus – speaks up and says that Christ deserves a trial under the Law. The Pharisees regard themselves as the only ones who know the Law and want to act as they see fit and tell the people what to do and believe. The question before us today is whether we are open to the message of Christ, which should change our lives every day, or will we be like the authorities who wanted to protect their comfortable existence and so continue in our imperfect ways.

Alternative Readings for the Fifth Week of Lent

These readings may be used any day this week, especially in Years B and C, when the Gospel of the raising of Lazarus is not read on the Fifth Sunday of Lent.

2 Kings 4:18-21, 32-37; Psalm 16; John 11:1-45

In our first reading from the Second Book of the Kings we see the Prophet Elisha coming to the home of the Shunammitess with whom he often stayed. As a reward for her hospitality the woman gave birth to a son at the intercession of the prophet. In today's text we read how the boy dies in his mother's arms and she lays him on the prophet's bed. Elisha spends time alone with the body and in prayer to God and eventually the boy is restored to life. This same theme is found in the gospel text where we read of the death of Lazarus, a friend of Jesus. Jesus travels to Bethany to be with Martha and Mary and despite the threat to their own lives for being with him, the Apostles travel with him. While there we see Jesus grieve for his friend but it also becomes a moment of instruction as Jesus proclaims that he is the resurrection and the life and that whoever believes in him will never die. This reading gains its importance as we move towards the death and resurrection of Jesus next week and it also reminds us of what lies in store for each of us – resurrection to life eternal.

Monday of the Fifth Week of Lent
Daniel 13:1-9, 15-17, 19-30, 33-62; Psalm 22; John 8:1-11
Our readings today remind us that God himself defends those
who are innocent, particularly when they cannot defend themselves. In the reading from Daniel we see that two judges have
become infatuated with Susanna and have lied to save themselves, condemning her to death for something she did not do.
She is only saved by asking God for help. He heard her cry and
sent the boy Daniel to save her. In the gospel we see another
woman about to be stoned for committing adultery. She is saved
by Jesus who forgives her of her sins and tells her to sin no more.
In both cases, those who had themselves sinned were quick to
condemn others while covering up their own wrong doings. We
often find ourselves in the situation of the women in today's
texts – we find ourselves in need of Jesus' healing and compassion. During this time of preparation we are called on to acknowledge our own sins and to ask forgiveness for them, while
resolving to do better in the future.

Tuesday of the Fifth Week of Lent
Numbers 21:4-9; Psalm 101; John 8:21-30
Today's reading from the Book of Numbers shows the Israelites
turning against God even though he had just won their release
from slavery in Egypt. In this episode the Jews turned against
God in the wilderness and began worshipping false gods.
Moses fashions a bronze serpent which saves those who look at
it. In the gospel, Jesus is speaking about himself and telling the
people that only when they have killed him will they realise that
he is the Son of God because only then will they see his glory.
Like the bronze serpent on the pole, Christ on the cross will
bring us new life. We are called to believe in Jesus though we
have not seen him with our own eyes. The Jews in Egypt saw
God's power when he led them to freedom, yet they turned
against him. We must not turn against him, but must put our
total trust in him, serving his gospel throughout our lives.

Wednesday of the Fifth Week of Lent
Daniel 3:14-20, 24-25, 28; Psalm: Daniel 3:52-56; John 8:31-42
In the Book of the Prophet Daniel there is recounted the story of
three young men – Hananiah, Mishael and Azariah – who refused to abandon their religion for King Nebuchadnezzar, part
of which we read two weeks ago. The king had them bound and

thrown into a fiery furnace but the angel of God joined them
there and they walked through the furnace unharmed. At the
end of the reading, the king too praises the true God. The reading reminds us that when we are truly free in heart, nothing can
trouble us or separate us from the love of God. The psalm continues this theme. In the gospel, Jesus tells his listeners that they
will only be free if they listen to his word and live by it, because
only then will they be free from the slavery to sin and so be his
true disciples. God's word is available to us but it is up to us to
accept it and to let it take root in our lives.

Thursday of the Fifth Week of Lent
Genesis 17:3-9; Psalm 104; John 8:51-59
In the reading from Genesis we see God making his covenant
with Abraham and his descendents. This covenant was fulfilled
in the person and life of Jesus. In the gospel, Jesus is speaking of
Abraham and telling his listeners that Abraham longed to see
Christ's day. He reveals himself to his listeners with the words 'I
Am,' which is the name God used for himself when he spoke
with Moses. Jesus is telling them that the God of Moses,
Abraham, and Isaac is the same person who is now speaking to
them. He goes on to tell us that even though we may suffer and
die in this world, suffering and death have no power over us if
we believe in him alone. That which was promised to Abraham
has come to pass in the person of Jesus and it is a saving
covenant for us who believe it.

Friday of the Fifth Week of Lent
Jeremiah 20:10-13; Psalm 17; John 10:31-42
The Prophet Jeremiah is being persecuted by the people but he
still places his trust in God and still praises him. It is a reminder
of Jesus who is soon to be arrested and who will also pray to the
Father for guidance and strength while never abandoning faith
in the Father. The psalm is a prayer of confidence in God by one
who is being persecuted. Our gospel reading shows Jesus being
persecuted by some of the Jews. He, like Jeremiah, is under
God's protection and so is saved from them until the hour of his
glory. We too will be saved and supported if we praise God all
our days and turn to him in confidence. But we must not forget
him when things are going well for us.

Saturday of the Fifth Week of Lent
Ezekiel 37:21-28; Psalm: Jeremiah 31:10-13; John 11:45-56
In our first reading we see the Prophet Ezekiel looking forward
to a day when the Lord will unite the people under a new leader
as a redeemed nation. In the gospel, we see the Pharisees taking
the decision to kill Jesus. They did so in order to save their people because they feared that Jesus' talk of a supreme power and
authority would cause a revolt which the Romans would crush
as ruthlessly as the previous ones. While their motives may
have been honourable, it was they who were misguided because
they had closed their minds to the word of God and believed the
Messiah to be a political and military leader. The words of
Caiaphas also suggest that the death of Jesus might unite the
people – an echo of the first reading. They never thought that
the Messiah would free them in spirit which is a far greater
thing. If we truly open our hearts to God then the unity which
the gospel speaks of will take place as the kingdom takes shape
in our world.

HOLY WEEK

Monday of Holy Week
Isaiah 42:1-7; Psalm 26; John 12:1-11
Our first reading from Isaiah points to the person of Christ who
is the fulfilment of the covenants made so long ago. We could in
a way see the reading as God dedicating his Son for the work he
is about to accomplish. The psalm speaks of the Lord as our light
and our help. The gospel passage is leading up to the Passion at
the end of this week. Today we see a woman named Mary
anointing the feet of Jesus and he tells those with him that she
will need this ointment again for his burial. While Judas was indignant at the ointment being used in this way, Jesus sided with
Mary because the intention in her heart was pure and well
placed. The reading also prepares us for the betrayal by Judas
later this week. Meanwhile, the chief priests continue to plot his
death.

Tuesday of Holy Week
Isaiah 49:1-6; Psalm 70; John 13:21-33, 36-38
The Prophet Isaiah today speaks beautifully of the servant of
God, one who will be the light of the nations. Each of us is called
to witness for God before men and women so that this passage

may be said of each of us. We could in a way see the reading as
Jesus speaking about his destiny as redeemer of the world. The
psalm is the prayer of a man persecuted by his enemies and
who seeks the help of God. In the gospel we have the scene at
the Last Supper. We are confronted with the fact that Judas is
about to hand Jesus over to his accusers while St Peter will fail
to stand up for Christ despite his vow. We too can fail God
when the crunch comes but if we believe in his power and pray
to him as the psalmist does in today's psalm, then he will stand
by us and we will be the light of the nations.

Wednesday (Spy Wednesday) of Holy Week
Isaiah 50:4-9; Psalm 68; Matthew 26:14-25
The reading from Isaiah takes up the theme found in yesterday's first reading – that of answering God's call and witnessing
for him before our fellow men and women, which may at times
bring suffering and persecution. The psalm is of a man in great
distress who calls on God for help against his enemies. The
gospel reading sees Judas accepting thirty silver pieces for
handing Jesus over to the Jewish authorities – hence the name
'Spy Wednesday.' We all have the ability to be like Judas at
times and to deny Christ for the sake of our other gods. Judas
realised too late that what he was doing would not work and in
his sorrow he repented in the only way he knew how. How
often do we truly feel sorry for having betrayed the Lord for the
ways of this world and if we did feel sorry, when did we last
truly do penance for it? We are called to rely on God's help and
believe in the reprieve Christ gained for us so that we will become the witnesses Isaiah speaks of.

THE EASTER TRIDUUM

Holy Thursday – Chrism Mass
Isaiah 61:1-3, 6a, 8b-9; Psalm 88; Apocalypse 1:5-8; Luke 4:16-21
This celebration takes place in the Cathedral in every diocese
on the morning of Holy Thursday and is presided over by the
bishop as head of the diocese. During this Mass the sacred oils
(the Oil of the Sick and the Oil of Catechumens) are blessed
and the Oil of Chrism consecrated. They are then distributed
to the churches throughout the diocese for use in the coming
year. Also at this Mass, the bishop is joined by clergy from

throughout the diocese which represents the unity of the diocese and of the universal Church. The clergy renew their commitment to priestly service before the bishop and the people.

The first reading for this celebration from the Prophet Isaiah speaks very much of the presbyteral order – of those ordained to sacred ministry and who will carry on the work of God following the example of Christ. The second reading from St John's vision in the Apocalypse speaks of what Christ has done for us by washing away our sins with his blood. It also says that those who pierced him will now see his glory. The gospel text from St Luke echoes the first reading and in it we see Jesus preaching in the synagogue in his home town of Nazareth. Through baptism we all have a common priesthood – that of spreading the gospel of Christ across the world, beginning in our own small corner of that world. While this morning is a celebration of the ordained ministers gathered with their bishop, it is also a celebration of the commitment we each have to work for the building of the kingdom of God.

Evening Mass of the Lord's Supper
Exodus 12:1-8, 11-14; Psalm 115; 1 Corinthians 11:23-26; John 13:1-15
The Lord's Supper is celebrated in the evening time – just as the Passover meal was celebrated in the evening to recall the first Passover in which the Jews left Egypt. As the blood of the lamb saved the Jews, so the blood of Christ brings salvation to the whole world. The first reading from the Book of Exodus recounts the instructions given to the people regarding the Passover meal. The letter of St Paul tells of the institution of the Eucharist when Christ gave his disciples bread and wine as his very own body and blood. The gospel shows us the scene in the upper room and in it we see Jesus washing the feet of those who were with him. In this way he showed that they were to be servants of all. After the gospel is read, the washing of feet takes place as a reminder to us today of the instruction Christ gave us. At the end of the eucharistic celebration the Blessed Sacrament is removed from the tabernacle to the Altar of Repose and the altars stripped and crucifixes covered. This gives us a stark reminder that the Lord has been taken from us.

Good Friday – Celebration of the Lord's Passion

Isaiah 52:13-53:12; Psalm 30; Hebrews 4:14-16, 5:7-9; John 18:1-19:42

This celebration should take place in the mid-afternoon as this corresponds to the time when Jesus went to Calvary to be crucified. The Prophet Isaiah speaks of the suffering servant, of the one who died for our sake. It gives an account of the terrible suffering he underwent and the fact that it was our sins which caused that suffering. The passage from the Letter to the Hebrews speaks of Christ as the one who lived a human life like us and, because he trusted in God and interceded for us, brought about our salvation. The gospel of St John recalls the Passion and death of Christ. The celebration begins with a silent procession to the sanctuary – the silence reminding us of the importance of what is happening. The Liturgy of the Word is followed by the Intercessions and then the Veneration of the Cross. The Veneration begins with the presentation of the Cross to the people before each person present goes forward and kisses the cross – the sign of their salvation. The Cross is then placed in a prominent position before the people as a reminder to them of what their sins have bought. The Celebration concludes with the Holy Communion.

Holy Saturday – The Easter Vigil

The Triduum reaches its climax on this night with the celebration of the Easter Vigil. The vigil begins with the Service of Light in which the Easter Fire is lit and the new Paschal Candle blessed. From this each of the faithful lights a candle and carries it in procession into the church. When the procession reaches the sanctuary the great Easter Proclamation (*Exsultet*) is sung. This great hymn reminds us of what Christ and God have done for us. The Liturgy of the Word follows and the readings trace the history of salvation from the story of Creation to the Resurrection of Christ on this night. Where possible, the sacrament of Baptism now takes place. If there is no one to be baptised then Easter water is blessed and the faithful renew their baptismal promises before being sprinkled with the Easter water. The Liturgy of the Eucharist is now celebrated for the first time since Holy Thursday and for this the altar is again covered with a cloth and burning candles are placed on or near it. The whole feeling of the Vigil is one of great joy and celebration for our salvation has been won for us and Christ has been glorified by his Father.

THE SEASON OF EASTER

SUNDAYS:YEAR A

Easter Sunday

Acts 10:34, 37-43; Psalm 117; Colossians 3:1-4 (or 1 Corinthians 5:6-8); John 20:1-9

In the reading from the Acts of the Apostles, St Peter is proclaiming the Risen Lord and saying that not only has Christ risen but he has also appeared to his followers, and Peter himself has witnessed this. The psalm is a hymn of praise for this day – the day of the resurrection of the Lord. St Paul in his letter to the Colossians speaks of us becoming new people, living as Christ commanded, and looking to heaven and to God for that is where our future lies. The gospel tells of the finding of the empty tomb and the realisation that scripture had pointed to this moment – the resurrection of Christ.

Second Sunday of Easter – Divine Mercy Sunday

Acts 2:42-47; Psalm 117; 1 Peter 1:3-9; John 20:19-31

Today's reading from the Acts of the Apostles gives us a glimpse of how the early Christian communities lived – everything was held in common for the good of all. It shows us that the message of Christ can be put into practice for the good of everyone in the community. This Sunday has also been designated 'Divine Mercy Sunday,' a special day when we give thanks to God for all that we have received from him. This is brought out in the psalm which is a hymn of praise and thanks to God. The second reading from St Peter continues this theme, the central point of which reminds us that in his great mercy God has given us a new birth as his sons and daughters through the death and resurrection of Christ. The gospel for today sees Jesus appearing to his disciples and then coming back a second time when Thomas was present. In his doubt, Thomas represents each of us, he represents all those who have not physically seen the Lord. His great acclamation – 'My Lord and my God' – is the confirmation which we all need that what we have been told did in fact take place. Jesus Christ is truly risen from the dead – he is our Lord and God.

Third Sunday of Easter
Acts 2:14, 22-33; Psalm 15; 1 Peter 1:17-21; Luke 24:13-35
In the first reading from the Acts, St Peter is addressing the gathering and boldly speaking to them of the Risen Lord. He is telling them that it is impossible for Christ to be held in Hades because he now has power over life and death. In the second reading, Peter is telling the people to remain faithful to Christ and to be on their guard whether they be at home or abroad. He reminds them of the tremendous ransom that was paid on their behalf, a ransom which cannot be equated with anything they or the world could ever possess. The gospel passage from St Luke recounts the story of the two disciples on the road to Emmaus. In the story, Christ meets two men but we are only given one name which suggests that Luke sees the second man as representing all the followers of Christ who have doubts. Christ appears to them and asks how they are and gradually he opens their eyes to him. So too he opens our eyes in many and different ways.

Fourth Sunday of Easter
Acts 2:14, 36-41; Psalm 22; 1 Peter 2:20-25; John 10:1-10
In our first reading today from the Acts of the Apostles, St Peter is teaching the people about Christ, and they are so moved by what he says that they ask for baptism – 3,000 of them. The psalm, the text from Peter's first letter and the gospel passage from St John, use the image of the shepherd. Christ is the good shepherd who looks after his flock and keeps them all in view. Like a shepherd, he protects his people from evil and keeps them safe in his care. This protection is given to all those who believe in him, listen to his word and put that word into action in their lives. Today is also designated Vocations Sunday – a day when we pray in a special way for vocations. We must remember, though, that the word 'vocation' is more than just a call to serve the Lord in the ministerial priesthood or religious life. By our very baptism we are all called to serve the Lord in whatever way we can. While we pray for vocations to the priesthood and religious life, we also pray that we may all have the strength to live out our Christian vocation in the married or celibate state, as parents and teachers, and simply as Christians.

Fifth Sunday of Easter
Acts 6:1-7; Psalm 32; 1 Peter 2:4-9; John 14:1-12
In the first reading we see the Twelve calling a meeting. This was in response to a complaint that some of the people in the early Christian community were being overlooked when it came to charity. At the meeting, the Twelve prayed and appointed seven men – the first to fulfil the role of deacons – to help minister to the people. In a very short space of time the Church has begun to evolve to meet the growing pastoral needs of the flock. The second reading exhorts us to place our trust in Christ because he is the cornerstone of everything we have and do and are. In this passage, St Peter also tells us that we are 'a chosen race, a royal priesthood, a consecrated nation, a people set apart' and so we must live in this way. In the gospel from St John we see Jesus teaching his disciples and telling them that he is the way to the Father and to eternal life but that we must put our trust and belief in him if we are to succeed along this way.

Sixth Sunday of Easter
Acts 8:5-8, 14-17; Psalm 65; 1 Peter 3:15-18; John 14:15-21
The first reading from the Acts of the Apostles again tells us of the spread of the Church and the message of Christ. The people of the Samaritan town have little difficulty in believing all that they have been told about Christ. The second reading calls on us to treasure Christ in our hearts and to have an answer ready for those who do not understand why we believe in him, even if this may bring trouble our way. In the gospel, Jesus is promising his listeners the gift of the Holy Spirit to help and strengthen them. Those who love him love the Father and so will be able to keep the commandments and gain eternal life.

Seventh Sunday of Easter
Acts 1:12-14; Psalm 26; 1 Peter 4:13-16; John 17:1-11
After the Ascension, the disciples return to Jerusalem and gather to pray. The second reading tells us that if we suffer for doing the work of Christ then we are truly blessed. The gospel shows us Jesus praying to the Father and in it he lets us see what we need to do to gain eternal life – we must believe in him and his message and live that in our lives.

Ascension of the Lord

Acts 1:1-11; Psalm 46; Ephesians 1:17-23; Matthew 28:16-20

The first reading from the Acts of the Apostles tells us of the ascension of Jesus when he was taken up into heaven in the sight of his followers. Those who were with him continued to look into heaven because they had not realised what had actually taken place. They had to be told by two strangers that the Lord had returned to heaven. The reading from Ephesians tells us that Christ, now he has ascended into heaven is seated at the right hand of God and that everything is now subject to him. The reading is in the form of a prayer that the Holy Spirit will come to guide the people so that they can see the glory of God and his plan for his people. The gospel text sees Jesus meeting the disciples and giving them the great command to go out and to preach the good news to all nations and peoples. This is what we too are called to do in our day and to help make the kingdom truly visible here on earth, knowing that the Lord and Holy Spirit are always with us.

Pentecost Sunday

Acts 2:1-11; Psalm 103; 1 Corinthians 12:3-7, 13-12; John 20:19-23

Our first reading today from the Acts of the Apostles tells us of the descent of the Holy Spirit upon the followers of Christ and of the effect it had on them. The Apostles were in one room together when the Holy Spirit came down upon them and they were able to speak in different languages. They went out into the streets and began to teach about Jesus and all those who were in the city were able to understand what was being said. This is the birth of the Church. The second reading tells us that there are many gifts given by this Holy Spirit but that we are all one in this Spirit and therefore we all make up one body – the body of Christ which is his Church. The gospel sees Jesus meeting with his followers and telling them that they must continue his work now that they have received the Holy Spirit. As heirs of the Apostles we too have received the Holy Spirit, most notably at Baptism and Confirmation, and it is up to us to respond to the promptings of the Holy Spirit in our lives and to give praise and glory to God by the lives we lead. We should also follow the example of the Apostles on Pentecost Day and spread the good news about the kingdom of God.

SUNDAYS: YEAR B

Easter Sunday
Acts 10:34, 37-43; Psalm 117; Colossians 3:1-4; John 20:1-9
In the reading from the Acts of the Apostles, St Peter is proclaiming the Risen Lord and saying that not only has Christ risen but he has also appeared to his followers, and that he himself has witnessed this. The psalm is a hymn of praise for this great day – the day of the resurrection of the Lord. St Paul in his letter speaks of us becoming new people, living as Christ commanded, and looking to heaven and to God for that is where our future lies. The gospel tells of the finding of the empty tomb and the realisation that scripture had pointed to this moment – the resurrection of Christ. If we too follow the path Christ has marked out for us, then we too will inherit eternal life.

Second Sunday of Easter – Divine Mercy Sunday
Acts 4:32-35; Psalm 117; 1 John 5:1-6; John 20:19-31
In our first reading today we read of the ideal way of living the Christian message – everyone united together in faith, looking out for one another and sharing their possessions for the good of all. Our psalm is a hymn of praise to God. St John tells us in the second reading that those who truly believe in Christ are the sons and daughters of God and will overcome the world. We do this by loving God and our neighbour and by keeping the commandments which, John tells us, are not difficult to keep if we put our mind to it. Our gospel text recounts the first visit of Jesus to his disciples eight days after the resurrection. They are amazed but they were also filled with joy and he sends them out to preach the good news to all peoples. Important for us in this text is the fact that St Thomas was not there and because he did not see Jesus he refuses to believe. He is there the next time Jesus returns and is told to put his finger in the wounds showing that Jesus knew what Thomas had said. We all doubt from time to time, as did Thomas, but Thomas represents each of us and received the proof on our behalf. Therefore, with him we are called on to say 'My Lord, and my God.' Another way of looking at this text is that perhaps Thomas refused to believe because of who it was he was listening to. Perhaps we too fail to

accept something as true because of how we view those who are telling us. No matter who spreads the faith, the faith has Christ and the Holy Spirit behind it to confirm it and so we need to listen and to believe.

Third Sunday of Easter
Acts 3:13-15, 17-19; Psalm 4; 1 John 2:1-5; Luke 24:35-48
In our first reading we see St Peter still teaching the people about Christ and telling them that they had betrayed the Prince of Life for a murderer. However, despite the gravity of the charge he lays against them he goes on to tell them that they will be saved if they repent of their sins and return to God. In the second reading St John tells us that all our sins are taken away by Christ who is our advocate before the Father, so we should never despair when we do wrong but should turn to God in confidence knowing that his love is far greater than ours. In our gospel, we have St Luke's account of the appearance of Jesus to the disciples. He greets them and then shows them his wounds and invites them to touch him so that they can see that it really is him. They heard others tell about seeing him and yet they still doubted the veracity of the resurrection. But now he teaches them again and they come to see that all that is happening has been foretold in scripture. We too are called on to have true faith in the risen Lord because he is still merciful and will intercede for us before the Father no matter how often we fall. The Lord reminds us that repentance is to be preached to the whole world and that we are to do the preaching.

Fourth Sunday of Easter
Acts 4:8-12; Psalm 117; 1 John 3:1-2; John 10:11-18
In our first reading we see St Peter talking to the elders a short while after he had cured a cripple, which the elders were not pleased with because he had done so in the name of the Risen Lord. They had hoped that in killing Jesus they would kill off his support as well and yet here was Peter and his companions preaching and healing in Christ's name. Peter reminds them of what they did and tells them that Christ is the keystone, the only name by which we can be saved. St John tells us in the second reading that, as followers of Christ and children of God, we are

outcasts from the world which does not want to know us. But because of the Father's great love, those who believe in him and live by his commandments will live in glory with God. In the gospel, we have the 'Good Shepherd' passage from St John in which Jesus tells us that he is the good shepherd who willingly gives his life for his sheep. Those who believe in him listen to his voice and do as he commands and will be gathered together into the one true fold. The challenge for us is to live as outcasts from the world and to shun the ways of this world for the glory which has been promised us through the death and resurrection of Christ.

Fifth Sunday of Easter
Acts 9:26-31; Psalm 21; 1 John 3:18-24; John 15:1-8
Our first reading sees Saul after his conversion on the road to Damascus. The disciples still feared him but Barnabas speaks on his behalf and they accept him. However, his time with them is short lived because he has to flee from those who wanted to kill him because of his positive preaching about the Risen Christ. In the second reading, St John reduces the commandments to two basic instructions: belief in Christ and love of neighbour. This is nothing new, for Christ had said this himself but John is reminding us to keep these two commandments knowing that if we do then God will live in each of us. In the gospel, Christ tells us that he is the true vine and we are the branches. Those of us who believe in Christ will be looked after but those who ignore him will wither and be gathered up for burning as rubbish. Only if we believe in him can we achieve eternal happiness and bear much fruit and thereby give glory to God.

Sixth Sunday of Easter
Acts 10:25-26, 34-35, 44-48; Psalm 97; 1 John 4:7-10; John 15:9-17
In our first reading St Peter is teaching a group of pagans who receive the gift of the Holy Spirit as he speaks to them. Some of his Jewish followers are amazed that pagans should receive the gift that they believed only true followers could receive, but Peter reminds them that God's message is for all people regardless of their nationality or race or skin colour. St John speaks to us in the second reading about the love of God and tells us that

God is love and that he revealed his love by sending his Son into the world for us. This theme of love is continued in the gospel where Christ tells us to remain in his love and we do this by keeping the commandments and loving God above all else. If we live in love we will reach out to others no matter where they come from and we will work to build up the kingdom of God in peace, harmony and love. In the text, Christ also tells us that he is commissioning each of us to go out and spread this love where ever we may find ourselves. He has called us and he is waiting for our reply and our full commitment.

Seventh Sunday of Easter
Acts 1:15-17, 20-26; Psalm 102; 1 John 4:11-16; John 17:11-19
In today's first reading we see St Peter speaking with his companions about the vacancy left in their number by the death of Judas. They pray for a time for guidance and then chose Matthias who became one of the Twelve. Our second reading continues the theme of love which we found in the second reading last week. Those who live in love will have God living within them. Our gospel text today is a reminder that belief in the Lord is not without its trials. In the text we see Christ praying to his Father that those who believe in him may be protected and strengthened against a world that does not want to know them. That text is still valid even today for the world does not really want to know the Christian way of life as it is too much of a challenge to the *laisser-faire* ways of modern life. We are reminded as we move towards the end of the Season of Easter of the necessity to pray to God and to believe in him no matter what others may think or say about us.

Ascension of the Lord
Acts 1:1-11; Psalm 46; Ephesians 4:1-13; Mark 16:15-20
Our first reading today recounts the ascension of Jesus into heaven. It was now forty days after his resurrection and he had appeared to the apostles on numerous occasions but now they see him face to face for the last time. As they are speaking he is taken up into heaven. St Paul in the second reading implores us to live a life which is worthy of our vocation. We all have the common vocation of being God's sons and daughters and living

as Christians but the vocation manifests itself in different ways according to the skills each of us has. In the gospel we read St Mark's account of the ascension and before he leaves them we see Jesus sending his disciples out into the world to preach in his name. As the successors to the disciples, we too are commissioned to go out and to preach the word of God to all peoples and to let them see and feel his compassion and his love.

Pentecost Sunday
Acts 2:1-11; Psalm 103; Galatians 5:16-25; John 15:26-27, 16:12-15
In our first reading we read of the descent of the Holy Spirit on the Apostles and how they immediately went out and began preaching to people about the Risen Lord. Not only did they preach but they were able to do so in many languages so that everyone who heard them that day could understand what they were saying, such was the power of the Holy Spirit at work in them. St Paul urges his readers in the second reading to live by the Holy Spirit because if we don't then we cannot inherit the kingdom which has been promised to us. The Spirit is life and so we must allow ourselves to be directed by the Spirit. In the gospel, Jesus tells the disciples that he will send them the Holy Spirit and he tells them that the Spirit will help them to come to the complete truth. They will then be his witnesses before the whole world and what they proclaim will be Christ's message.

SUNDAYS: YEAR C

Easter Sunday
Acts 10:34, 37-43; Psalm 117; Colossians 3:1-4; John 20:1-9
In the reading from the Acts of the Apostles, St Peter is proclaiming the Risen Lord and saying that not only has Christ risen but he has also appeared to his followers, and that he himself has witnessed this. The psalm is a hymn of praise for this great day – the day of the resurrection of the Lord. St Paul in his letter to the Colossians speaks of us becoming new people, living as Christ commanded, and looking to heaven and to God for that is where our future lies. The gospel tells of the finding of the empty tomb and the realisation that scripture had pointed to this moment – the resurrection of Christ. If we too follow the path Christ has marked out for us then we too will inherit eternal life.

Second Sunday of Easter – Divine Mercy Sunday
Acts 5:12-16; Psalm 117; Revelation 1:9-13, 17-19; John 20:19-31
In our first reading today we see that the apostles have continued to preach about Christ and his resurrection. This teaching has had a great effect and many people have now come not just to listen to their teaching but to seek cures for their illnesses. All that the apostles do is done in the name of Jesus and it is Christ who grants healing through their actions and words. The psalm reminds us that the love of the Lord has no end. Our second reading comes from the opening chapter of St John's Revelation in which John tells us that he has been imprisoned for having preached the word of God. During this imprisonment he had a vision from God in which he is visited by Christ who tells him that he has not died but lives for ever. In our gospel we see Jesus appearing to the disciples where they have locked themselves away for fear of the Jews. He gives them his Spirit and sends them out to preach in his name. Of particular importance to us is the absence of St Thomas. When the others told him that Jesus had appeared he refused to believe and only believed when Jesus appeared eight days later. Thomas represents all of us who find the idea of resurrection difficult to grasp and the reading also reminds us that the first apostles were also slow to come to

full belief. He also represents us when he makes his great declaration of faith – 'My Lord and my God!' This is the declaration which we too must make if we are to inherit eternal life through the Lord's resurrection.

Third Sunday of Easter
Acts 5:27-32, 40-41; Psalm 29; Revelation 5:11-14; John 21:1-19
In our first reading we see St Peter and the apostles being reprimanded by the authorities for preaching in Christ's name. But far from being cowed by them they are happy to have suffered for the sake of their Lord and continue to speak about him. Our second reading comes again from St John's vision and in today's extract we see all living things giving praise and glory to the lamb of sacrifice. This is not the lamb that was offered up regularly in the Temple or even the lamb that secured freedom for the Jews in Egypt. It is Christ, the true Lamb who was sacrificed for all people and through whom all people are redeemed. In our gospel text we read of another meeting between the disciples and the Risen Lord, this time while they are fishing. When they come ashore the Lord is there with breakfast ready and, when the meal is over, he asks Peter three times if he loves him. Peter replies that he does and becomes upset that the Lord asked him the same question three times – no doubt his triple denial of Jesus on Holy Thursday still worries him. But in response Jesus instructs Peter to look after and feed his sheep – he is to be a spiritual guide and leader for the faithful. The passage ends with Jesus giving an indication to Peter that Peter's life will not go as smoothly as he might like. Unlike Holy Thursday however, Peter will not turn his back on the Lord this time but will, ultimately, give his life for his Lord.

Fourth Sunday of Easter
Acts 13:14, 43-52; Psalm 99; Revelation 7:9, 14-17; John 10:27-30
In today's first reading we see Sts Paul and Barnabas teaching the people about God after they themselves had faithfully attended the synagogue. Some of the Jews, however, are not happy with their presence and their teaching and so they have them driven from the synagogue. No longer welcome, the two apostles turn to the pagans and proclaim the good news to them

and the pagans happily receive the word and become believers. In the second reading we read that the Lamb of Sacrifice, who is Christ, will shepherd his people and he will lead them to living water. Those who have been redeemed by him now sing his praises in his presence in the kingdom. This theme of shepherding is found in the gospel in which Christ tells his followers that those who listen to him and follow his word will receive eternal life from him. No one else can give us eternal life no matter what they say and only those who believe in Christ as their Lord and God can receive this most precious of gifts. This gift is ours if we have the courage to teach like Paul and Barnabas in the first reading, even if that means making ourselves outcasts in the eyes of the world.

Fifth Sunday of Easter
Acts 14:21-27; Psalm 144; Revelation 21:1-5; John 13:31-35
In the first reading we see Sts Paul and Barnabas going back to some of the places where they had earlier visited and brought the word of God. As they travel they encourage the people to remain faithful to the message they had given them. The news of the faith of other groups encouraged the faithful and they in turn remained faithful. In the second reading from St John's vision we are told about the New Jerusalem. It will be a place of peace and happiness for all eternity, will be created by God and he himself will live there. This is the new kingdom towards which we are all striving and about which Christ taught us. In our gospel text we go back to the scene on Holy Thursday night just as Judas leaves the upper room. Christ declares that the time for his glorification has now come and before he departs he gives the disciples a new commandment and tells them that they must love one another in imitation of his love for them. If we are to be the Lord's disciples and if we are to be worthy of heaven, the New Jerusalem, then we too must love one another. If we live a life of love then others will see that we really are Christians and, through our example, their own faith may be renewed and strengthened as in the first reading.

Sixth Sunday of Easter

Acts 15:1-2, 22-29; Psalm 66; Revelation 21:10-14, 22-23; John 14:23-29
We read in the first reading from the Acts of the Apostles that some people have been preaching in Christ's name but they have been adding certain practices to Christ's teaching and insisting that the people comply. Sts Paul and Barnabas and the community are not happy with this and so send Paul, Barnabas and others to speak with the apostles in Jerusalem about this matter. They do not want the basics of the faith lost or muddied by unnecessary laws. The apostles in Jerusalem write a letter to the faithful explaining their decision which they entrust to Paul and his companions. Again today, our second reading speaks of the New Jerusalem which God has created. The new city will not have any temples because God himself will live in the midst of the city. There will also be no need for sun or moon because 'the radiant glory of God and the Lamb' will be its light. In our gospel text we see Jesus preparing the disciples for his departure but comforting them with the knowledge that when he has gone he will send the Holy Spirit who will be their guide and their strength. This same Holy Spirit was given to each one of us and is always with us to guide and strengthen us if we but ask for his help. The Spirit will bring us to the new Jerusalem where we will live in God's presence for ever.

Seventh Sunday of Easter

Acts 7:55-60; Psalm 96; Revelation 22:12-14, 16-17, 20; John 17:20-26
In our first reading today we read of the martyrdom of St Stephen – the first to be martyred for the faith. Stephen could have softened his teaching and remained alive but instead he opted for eternal life and preached about the Risen Lord. At his martyrdom he echoed Christ's words on the cross and forgave those who killed him while commending his spirit to God. Looking on was Saul who would later become one of the greatest apostles. In today's reading from St John's vision, we hear Jesus telling John through the angel that he will soon be back with his people to bring to the faithful their reward. He also reminds John that he is of David's line and that he has always existed. In our gospel reading we see Jesus praying to the Father and asking that his followers may be united and that those who hear the

word from them may be united with them. In this way those who see them will realise that they are Christians and so may come to eternal life themselves. We are called to be one with the Church and the message of God and to have the faith and courage of Stephen who willingly gave his life for the sake of the kingdom.

Ascension of the Lord
Acts 1:1-11; Psalm 46; Hebrews 9:24-28, 10:19-23; Luke 24:46-53
Our first reading today recounts the ascension of Jesus into heaven. It was now forty days after his resurrection and he had appeared to his disciples on numerous occasions but now they see him face to face for the last time. As they are speaking he is taken up into heaven. In the second reading the Hebrews are reminded that when Christ ascended he went straight to heaven and not to anything human. He went to heaven to be in the presence of God where he would intercede on behalf of his followers. The author also tells them that because Christ had sacrificed himself there would be no need for any other sacrifice for sin and wrong-doing – Christ's sacrifice wipes away all sin and is eternal. Our gospel reading gives St Luke's second account of the ascension in which Christ promises the disciples the Holy Spirit who will lead and strengthen them. As soon as he has blessed them he is taken from them for ever. It is our Christian hope that as Christ has ascended into heaven, we too will follow him and will join him in the kingdom. But we can only do this if we remain faithful to his teaching handed on through the apostles while being open to the promptings of the Holy Spirit in our lives.

Pentecost Sunday
Acts 2:1-11; Psalm 103; Romans 8:8-17; John 14:15-16, 23-26
In our first reading we read of the descent of the Holy Spirit on the Apostles and how they immediately went out and began preaching to the people about the Risen Lord. Not only did they preach but they were able to do so in many languages so that everyone who heard them that day could understand what they were saying, such was the power of the Holy Spirit at work in them. Our psalm is a hymn requesting the Father to send the Holy Spirit among us and, through him, to renew the face of the

earth. In the second reading, the Romans are told that if they have the Spirit within them then what they do will be directed towards God at all times – the things of this earth will be of no great interest or lasting value to them. In the gospel reading from St John, we see Jesus telling his disciples that he will send them the Spirit – whom he calls the Advocate – to be with them to strengthen and to guide them. This is the Spirit who is sent in the first reading. As heirs of the Apostles we too have received the Holy Spirit, most notably at Baptism and Confirmation, and it is up to us to respond to the promptings of the Holy Spirit in our lives and to give praise and glory to God by the lives we lead.

THE WEEKDAYS OF EASTER

Monday of Easter Week
Acts 2:14, 22-33; Psalm 15; Matthew 28:8-15

Today's readings testify to the resurrection of Christ. St Peter, along with his fellow disciples, is speaking to a crowd and speaking to them of Christ and is part of the first ever Christian sermon. The basis for his preaching and that of the apostles is clearly their own personal encounter with the Risen Lord. Like the sermons recorded in the Acts of the Apostles they are personal testaments to the death and resurrection of Christ. In the gospel, Jesus appears to the women and tells them to go and get the disciples and to tell them to go to Galilee where he will meet them. Galilee represented normality and everyday life for the disciples and it reminds us that we too will find Christ in the normality of our lives.

Tuesday of Easter Week
Acts 2:36-41; Psalm 32; John 20:11-18

Today's reading from the Acts of the Apostles is a continuation of yesterday's reading and in it we see St Peter still teaching the people. So moved are the people by his personal testimony that they believe in his message and in Christ as their Risen Lord and Saviour. Peter begins by telling the people how they had put to death the promised Messiah. That day, we are told, about 3,000 people converted to Christianity. Today's gospel text is a further telling of the resurrection, this time from St John. Here we see Christ talking to Mary Magdalene and telling her to tell the disciples that he has risen and is preparing to ascend to the Father, who is also our Father.

Wednesday of Easter Week
Acts 3:1-10; Psalm 104; Luke 24:13-35
St Peter and his fellow disciples have been strengthened by the resurrection of Christ and are now going about preaching his message and curing the people in his name. Today we see them run into conflict with the Jewish authorities for doing the very things that the authorities had crucified Jesus for. The disciples are aware of this and yet they continue unafraid. The gospel text is the familiar story of Christ's appearance to two of his followers on the road to Emmaus. They only recognise him at the breaking of bread because they had not believed all that he had told them while he was still alive. The breaking of the bread is also a reminder to them of the importance Christ placed on his institution of the Eucharist and of the necessity of doing this in his memory. When they did realise that it was the Lord, their hearts burned with joy. When did our hearts last burn with joy in the presence of Christ in the Blessed Eucharist? We are called on to have faith like Peter and the disciples and to openly proclaim our faith in Christ.

Thursday of Easter Week
Acts 3:11-26; Psalm 8; Luke 24:35-48
In the Acts of the Apostles we again see St Peter and the disciples proclaiming the message of Christ and his resurrection. Peter also insists that it was trust in the name of Jesus that cured the lame man in our text. The 'you' of the last paragraph is addressed very strongly to today's listeners. Today's gospel passage tells of the first encounter the disciples as a group have with the Risen Jesus. He comes to visit them and they are afraid but, having touched him, they believe. He opens their minds so that they understand clearly that his life is a fulfilment of all that sacred scripture had said about the Messiah.

Friday of Easter Week

Acts 4:1-12; Psalm 117; John 21:1-14

In our reading from the Acts of the Apostles for today, St Peter addresses the elders who have arrested himself and St John. He tells them that there is only one name in all the world that can save us and that is the name of Christ. It is strengthening to see Peter – a former fisherman from Galilee – taking on the most powerful of the Jewish authorities and boldly proclaiming the very things that they forbade Jesus from proclaiming and ultimately put him to death for. Today's gospel text from John tells of another meeting with Jesus and the disciples after the resurrection. The meeting we read of today took place by the Sea of Tiberias. When the disciples come ashore they find that Jesus has prepared breakfast for them and as they gather he gives bread to them – reminding them of what he did in the upper room on Holy Thursday night and of his instruction to repeat that sacred action.

Saturday of Easter Week

Acts 4:13-21; Psalm 117; Mark 16:9-15

Today's first reading continues with the trial of St Peter and St John before the elders of the people. They are warned not to preach about Christ again but they reply by saying that they cannot promise this – so strong is their belief in Christ now. We also see that the authorities are once again afraid of public opinion which is in favour of the apostles and their message. The text from St Mark's gospel tells us of the meeting of Christ with his disciples. They have not accepted the word of those who said they had seen the risen Lord and he rebukes them for their lack of faith. The gospel ends with the great mandate to 'Go out to the whole world; proclaim the good news.' The commitment of Peter and John in the first reading shows that they have taken this mandate to heart and are actively carrying it out. This mandate is also given to each of us to carry on, no matter where we find ourselves in life.

Monday of the Second Week of Easter

Acts 4:23-31; Psalm 2; John 3:1-8

Today's reading from the Acts of the Apostles takes up where we left it on Saturday. Saints Peter and John have been released and now they continue to boldly preach the good news in spite of the warning of the elders. We also learn that the early Christian community – rather than being depressed at the troubles and persecutions that lay ahead – fearlessly pray to God for protection. In the gospel passage, Jesus is speaking with Nicodemus and is telling him that it is essential for a person to be baptised and to live out that faith in order to be saved. This means that we must study, understand and live out our faith and develop our own spiritual lives. We, as baptised people, have an obligation to proclaim the Risen Lord as did Peter and John.

Tuesday of the Second Week of Easter
Acts 4:32-37; Psalm 91; John 3:7-15
In the first reading for today we get a glimpse of the early Christian Church at work and we are told that the disciples continued to proclaim Christ while those who believed looked after each other and saw to it that none of the community was ever in need. This strong community life enables them to live fearlessly and to give strong witness to the Risen Lord. One person in particular is mentioned for his Christian values – Barnabas. Jesus' conversation with Nicodemus is continued in today's text from St John's gospel and again Jesus tells us that faith in him is essential for salvation – faith and belief like that of Barnabas.

Wednesday of the Second Week of Easter
Acts 5:17-26; Psalm 33; John 3:16-21
We read today that St Peter and the apostles are again imprisoned for speaking about Christ. This time, they are miraculously set free and go immediately to the Temple where they again preach openly about Jesus. The text for today ends with Peter giving witness in the Jewish supreme court to the resurrection of the Christ. In the gospel, Jesus is telling Nicodemus that he was sent into the world because of the Father's great love for his creation and that salvation awaits those who believe in him. We are called on to have belief in the Lord just as Peter and the apostles had, but also to let that faith be seen by those with whom we come into contact.

Thursday of the Second Week of Easter
Acts 5:27-33; Psalm 33; John 3:31-36

Our first reading today from St Luke's Acts of the Apostles continues St Peter's trial before the Jewish supreme court and he speaks so strongly about Christ that they wish to kill him but are unable to do so. In the gospel, John the Baptist is speaking to his own followers in the passage from St John and he is telling them that belief in Christ leads to eternal life. No one else can bring us to the kingdom or offer us what Christ has offered to each of us through his blood on the cross.

Friday of the Second Week of Easter
Acts 5:34-42; Psalm 26; John 6:1-15

We read of the conclusion of the trial of St Peter and his companions before the Jewish supreme court. Peter and the others have been helped by Gamaliel – a rabbi and former teacher of St Paul – who says that if they are frauds then their preaching will come to nothing. The other elders listen to him and instruct Peter and company to be flogged, having been warned not to preach again. However, it has no effect as the Apostles are happy to suffer humiliation for the sake of Christ and it encourages them to preach all the more earnestly. The gospel text from St John sees a miracle of the loaves and fish taking place. It is often regarded as John's equivalent of the Institution Narratives in the synoptic gospels. Christ gives bread to the people and then fish – both of which are symbolic of himself. This giving of loaves and fish was also repeated in one of the appearances of the Risen Lord to the apostles after they had been fishing all night. If we acknowledge our own poverty and our dependence on God then he will fill us with his riches.

Saturday of the Second Week of Easter
Acts 6:1-7; Psalm 32; John 6:16-21

In the Acts of the Apostles today we see that the number of believers has grown and with it a conflict between two different groups of Jewish-Christians – the Hellenists and the Hebrews. To help settle the dispute and to make sure that there are enough ministers for the minor matters to allow the disciples to look after their role, they institute the diaconate. They spend time in prayer and then choose seven men on whom they lay their hands to invoke the Holy Spirit – a gesture which is central to the Ordination Rites of the Church today. In the gospel, Jesus walks on water to the disciples out on the lake demonstrating that he is Lord of creation and can overcome the natural world and its rules as he wishes.

Monday of the Third Week of Easter
Acts 6:8-15; Psalm 118; John 6:22-29
Today's first reading sees the arrest of St Stephen for proclaiming the message of Christ and the gospel. Stephen is undaunted because all that he says is being guided by the Holy Spirit and Stephen is content – so much so that 'his face appeared to them like the face of an angel'. In the gospel, we have the continuation of the sixth chapter of St John and in it we see the people following Jesus because they want more of the bread that he had given them. He tells them that the bread they must work and long for is the bread of eternal life and that they must believe in him. We are called to believe in Christ even to the point of suffering for him like Stephen did.

Tuesday of the Third Week of Easter
Acts 7:51-8:1; Psalm 30; John 6:30-35
The reading from the Acts of the Apostles tells of the trial of St Stephen and of how he tells those who are persecuting him that they have killed the long-awaited Messiah. However, Stephen finds comfort in the knowledge that the Messiah is waiting to receive him in to eternal life and so Stephen becomes the first martyr for Christ. As he dies, Stephen asks God to forgive those who have persecuted him. The words of the psalm could easily have come from Stephen's lips as he was being martyred. The people in the gospel ask Christ for bread and remind him of the manna in the desert. He tells them that the only true bread is the bread of life – which is himself. We are called to put our total trust in Christ and in the Father as Stephen did.

Wednesday of the Third Week of Easter

Acts 8:1-8; Psalm 65; John 6:35-40

Our reading today from the Acts of the Apostles shows that the persecution of the early Church did not end with the death of the first martyr, Stephen. It increased and we are now introduced to one of the greatest of those persecutors – Saul of Tarsus. Many now leave the area but as they travel they spread the gospel wherever they go. In the gospel text for today, Jesus speaks of himself as the bread of life and that those who believe in him shall have eternal life. Again, the readings this week remind us of what took place during the Triduum and of what has been won for us: salvation and eternal life. We are reminded to believe in Christ and in him alone.

Thursday of the Third Week of Easter

Acts 8:26-40; Psalm 65; John 6:44-51

The Acts of the Apostles today tells of St Philip and his work of preaching and baptising in the name of Christ as he travelled. On one of his journeys he meets an Ethiopian official who is having difficulty understanding some of the texts from the Prophet Isaiah. Philip travels with the official and begins to tell him about Christ as the suffering servant the official has been reading about. The official then asks for baptism. The psalm could have been used by Philip as he travelled and preached. Today's gospel continues the theme of yesterday's text – Christ is the bread of life and we are all called to believe in him in order to have eternal life.

Friday of the Third Week of Easter

Acts 9:1-20; Psalm 116; John 6:52-59

Today we read of the conversion of Saul on the road to Damascus, an event of major significance for the early Church. The event had such a profound effect on Saul that he became a firm believer in Christ and became a fearless preacher of the good news. The gospel is from the sixth chapter of St John's gospel in which Jesus is clarifying all that he has said so far about being the bread of life which brings eternal life to the believers who receive him into their hearts. With the image of the conversion of St Paul before us today we are challenged to look closely at our lives and to accept Christ as our Saviour and so spread the good news of the kingdom wherever we may go.

Saturday of the Third Week of Easter
Acts 9:31-42; Psalm 115; John 6:60-69

As we continue reading from the Acts of the Apostles we see that with the conversion of Saul (who now goes by his Roman name of 'Paul' rather than the Jewish 'Saul') the Christians are now free to preach and to proclaim the Risen Christ. St Peter continues his travels and in the name of Christ he cures people and restores the dead to life. In our gospel text for today we come to the end of our reading of St John's sixth chapter and we see that many who have been listening to Christ are unable to believe or to accept what he has been saying about being the bread of life. When he asks the apostles what they think, Peter replies that there is nobody else to go to for he is the one who has the message of eternal life. This is the faith that we are called to profess.

Monday of the Fourth Week of Easter (Year B &C)
Acts 11:1-18; Psalm 41; John 10:1-10

In the reading from the Acts of the Apostles, St Peter is being criticised for associating with uncircumcised people. He tells those who are criticising him that what he did was instructed by God. Clearly, the message of God is meant for all people to hear and to believe regardless of their current beliefs. In the gospel text Jesus speaks to the people and likens himself to a shepherd: when the sheep hear the voice of the shepherd they follow him, they do not follow those they do not recognise. It is also impor-tant to note that the good shepherd leads the sheep – he does not drive them but leads them and they follow. We are also told that there is only one way to enter heaven and that is through belief in Christ as the Son of God. Therefore Christ is our shepherd and we are called on to listen to his voice alone and to trust in that.

Monday of the Fourth Week of Easter (Alternative gospel for Year A)
Acts 11:1-18; Psalm 41; John 10:11-18

In the reading from the Acts of the Apostles, St Peter is being criticised for associating with uncircumcised people. He tells those who are criticising him that what he did was instructed by God. Clearly, the message of God is meant for all people to hear and to believe regardless of their current beliefs. In the gospel text – a continuation of that for the Fourth Sunday of Easter – Jesus speaks to the people and likens himself to a shepherd, but a shepherd who lays down his life for his sheep. Christ tells us that many shepherds run away at the first sign of trouble but that the Good Shepherd, the true shepherd who has concern for his flock, freely lays down his life to save those entrusted to him. There is also the suggestion that others outside the Church will also be saved by Christ.

Tuesday of the Fourth Week of Easter
Acts 11:19-26; Psalm 86; John 10:22-30
Our continuous reading from the Acts of the Apostles gives us a constant reminder of the sort of life we are called to – one which proclaims Christ and his gospel in word and deed. Today's reading notes that the name 'Christian' is used for the first time. It also notes that the good news is deliberately preached to the Gentiles for the first time thanks to the teaching of St Philip in Samaria and St Peter's contact with Cornelius, a Roman centurion. In the gospel, the theme of sheep and shepherd is used again today. Despite all that Christ has said to this point, many of those who have heard him have failed to understand what he has been saying. They have failed because they are not the sheep of his flock but follow another shepherd.

Wednesday of the Fourth Week of Easter
Acts 12:24-13:5; Psalm 66; John 12:44-50
Saints Paul and Barnabas have just completed their work in Antioch (one of the largest cities in the world at the time) in today's first reading. However, they are again called by the Holy Spirit and so resume their travels in the name of Christ once more, this time travelling to the Gentiles in Cyprus and southern Turkey. In the gospel, Christ proclaims that he is the light of the world who has been sent by the Father to bring all those who believe in him to eternal life, and that to believe in Christ is to believe in the Father.

Thursday of the Fourth Week of Easter
Acts 13:13-25; Psalm 88; John 13:16-20

In our first reading today St Paul begins teaching about Christ in
a synagogue, something which would not have gone down too
well with his former colleagues in the Pharisees. In the sermon,
Paul traces salvation history from the Old Testament up to John
the Baptist. Our gospel passage today sees Christ and the disciples at the Last Supper where Christ has just washed their feet.
He tells them that they must accept those who will be sent by
him and they are not to turn them away. We too must listen to
those who have been sent by God and accept what they say as
the message of God. First and foremost they are to serve God
through their love for and service of others following his example.

Friday of the Fourth Week of Easter
Acts 13:26-33; Psalm 2; John 14:1-6

St Paul, in our first reading, continues teaching the people in the
synagogue in Pisidia and tells them that when the Jews in
Jerusalem had Jesus put to death, they did no more than fulfil
sacred scripture. In the gospel, Jesus tells us – in response to a
pessimistic remark from St Thomas – that he is the way, the
truth and the life and that if we believe in him, we too will have
life. Christ is the only way to the Father – as we heard earlier this
week – there is no other and any other which appears to suit us
better and be more in line with our own views will not bring us
to eternal life. Christ is the embodiment of the truth he speaks
about and he is the one who gives life to our Eucharistic celebration.

Saturday of the Fourth Week of Easter
Acts 13:44-52; Psalm 97; John 14:7-14

In our passage from the Acts of the Apostles we read that many
more people are now coming to the synagogue to hear Saints
Paul and Barnabas and the message they bring. The Jews are
not happy at this but the people are because not all of them are
Jews and yet the message is being preached freely to everyone
regardless of their current beliefs. In the gospel, Jesus continues
to teach his disciples that he and the Father are one and that in

believing in him they are believing in the Father. St Philip is slow to believe or to understand that God the Father and God the Son are one and the same person though he has heard this many times from Christ's own mouth. We have heard these words all our lives and must ask ourselves whether we believe them or whether we're a little hesitant. True faith is when we accept such mysteries without waiting for proof.

Monday of the Fifth Week of Easter
Acts 14:5-18; Psalm 113; John 14:21-26
In our first reading from the Acts of the Apostles we see that Saints Paul and Barnabas are forced to flee because the authorities wish to kill them for preaching about Christ. They travel to Laconia – in modern day southern Turkey – and are very well received there. According to legend, the gods Zeus and Hermes visited here and were rejected by the people who were in turn destroyed by the two gods. Having witnessed what Paul and Barnabas can do, the people fear that if they don't treat these 'gods' well that they will be destroyed like the old tale. In the gospel text, Jesus tells his disciples that after he has gone they will be given the Holy Spirit who will teach them everything and remind them of all he had said. This Spirit is the one who caused Paul and Barnabas to work as they did. That same Spirit has been given to us and will work in us only if we allow him to and, in so doing, bring glory to God.

Tuesday of the Fifth Week of Easter
Acts 14:19-28; Psalm 144; John 14:27-31
In our first reading today we see that Saints Paul and Barnabas are still suffering for their preaching but they continue to preach and to give strength to the Christian communities which they visit. Paul also reminds the faithful that believing in Christ will cause hardship as he himself can testify but the reward is worth the suffering. In the gospel, Jesus gives his peace to the disciples before he leaves them. It is a peace which is not of human origins and therefore is greater and more liberating. It is a peace which this world badly needs but does not want to try. It is for us as Christians to convince the world that this is the only way to true happiness and fulfilment.

Wednesday of the Fifth Week of Easter

Acts 15:1-6; Psalm 121; John 15:1-8

In today's first reading we see that Saints Paul and Barnabas are now back in Antioch following their first missionary journey to the Gentiles. We see them in a debate with other Christian preachers and Pharisees about circumcision and are being sent to Jerusalem to speak with the Apostles on the matter. In the gospel, Christ says that he is the true vine and that we are its branches. If we believe in him then we will bear much fruit, but if we do not believe, then we are good for nothing and will be pruned away. If we believe in him he will grant all our prayers especially if that prayer is a prayer for an increase in our own faith so that we can do his will.

Thursday of the Fifth Week of Easter

Acts 15:7-21; Psalm 95; John 15:9-11

Today's first reading marks a key moment in the early Christian Church. The first Council of the Church is held in Jerusalem at which the practice of preaching to the Gentiles without them having to undergo circumcision is approved. It is a turning point also because the new Church has now broken away from the Jewish faith and laws and begins making its own laws and traditions. It is also the last time that St Peter and the Apostles are mentioned as St Luke now concentrates on the growth of the Church among the Gentiles which is the particular ministry of St Paul. In today's gospel text, Christ tells his listeners that they are to love one another in the same way that he has loved them. To love like Christ is to make our decisions in a Christ-like manner and so overcome the hurt that others may have inflicted upon us. To love like Christ is not always easy, but when we realise that Christ is present in each one of us, then we also realise that what we do to another person we do to Christ.

Friday of the Fifth Week of Easter

Acts 15:22-31; Psalm 56; John 15:12-17

The Council in Jerusalem now sends Saints Paul and Barnabas back to Antioch with chosen helpers to strengthen the people and to inform them of their decision which was guided by the Holy Spirit. The letter which Paul and his companions carry to the new communities to explain the decision of the Council of Jerusalem is a prototype of the official documents and encyclicals which have been issued by popes ever since. Continuing yesterday's theme of love, today's gospel passage sees Christ giving his followers the commandment to love more forcefully than in yesterday's text. In the Old Testament, Moses and the prophets were known as 'servants of God' but Jesus calls us his friends which implies a far more personal relationship which is available to each and every one of us. Christ was willing to give his life for his friends so we should be willing to give our lives for Christ – our brother and our friend.

Saturday of the Fifth Week of Easter
Acts 16:1-10; Psalm 99; John 15:18-21
Today's reading from the Acts of the Apostles sees St Paul setting out on his second missionary journey to the Gentiles which will take him as far as Corinth in Greece. He has a vision from God who tells him to spend time bringing the faith to what is modern day Greece. He is joined by St Timothy and also, scholars believe, by St Luke the Evangelist and author of the book. This is suggested by the use of the word 'we' in the last paragraph which tells us that Luke was a witness to part, at least, of what he records in the Acts. In the gospel, Christ tells his listeners that they will be persecuted for the sake of his name just as he too was persecuted. We all suffer in some way – from broken relationships, bad health, financial difficulties. But how much, if any, of our sufferings are a result of our being Christian? The world rejected Christ 2,000 years ago and, in truth, it hasn't improved much since but continues to reject that which shows up its own weaknesses and shortcomings. As Christians we should be willing to be rejected by the world but that will only happen if we are brave enough to be real Christians. Paul was persecuted for Christ but it did not stop him carrying out his work for the Lord, and look at the legacy which he left. What sort of a legacy could we collectively leave were we to openly follow the path of Christ?

Monday of the Sixth Week of Easter
Acts 16:11-15; Psalm 149; John 15:26-16:4
In the reading from the Acts of the Apostles we see St Paul on

his second mission to the Gentiles to preach the gospel of Christ, this time in the area of Macedonia. He begins preaching in Philippi and is well received by the people. His preaching is so powerful and full of the Spirit that people readily accept Jesus as their Saviour. In the gospel, Jesus is assuring his followers that he will leave them a strong witness to assist them after he has gone from them. The witness is the Holy Spirit. Christ is fully aware of the trials and persecutions which are to befall his followers but he is equally aware that with the aid of the Holy Spirit they will be able to endure and so be victorious. We too will be strengthened if we allow the Spirit to work in us.

Tuesday of the Sixth Week of Easter
Acts 16:22-34; Psalm 137; John 16:5-11
Today's first reading tells us of the imprisonment of St Paul and his companion Silas. They had freed a girl of an evil spirit which now meant that she was useless to her masters. These same masters had Paul and Silas imprisoned because of their lost earnings now that she was freed from possession. However, this is turned into an occasion of teaching and conversion when they are freed from their chains and the gaoler sees this. As a result, the gaoler is converted to the faith. In the gospel, Jesus tells his followers that if he were to remain with them they would not receive the Holy Spirit. By his going all is accomplished and the reign of the Spirit in the hearts of all humankind can begin. The Spirit is always with us but unless we undergo personal conversion – like the gaoler in the first reading – the Spirit's presence will be lost to us.

Wednesday of the Sixth Week of Easter
Acts 17:15, 22-18:1; Psalm 148; John 16:12-15
In the first reading St Paul is now in Athens, the artistic and spiritual centre of Greece in Paul's day. Paul's first impression of the city is not a good one and he resolves to bring about change in the hearts of the people. He preaches at the Areopagus and uses the philosophy of the ancient Greeks in his arguments. Some laugh at his teaching while others believe and follow him. Jesus, in the gospel text, continues to talk to the disciples about the Holy Spirit. With the Holy Spirit we too will be led to the

complete truth but only if we truly believe and are open to that truth and are willing to listen to the Spirit in our midst. If not, we will be no better than those who laughed at Paul in Athens.

Thursday of the Sixth Week of Easter
Acts 18:1-8; Psalm 97; John 16:16-20
Today we see St Paul in southern Greece, in the city of Corinth, a city well known for its sexual immorality. Paul goes several times to the synagogue to persuade the people about Jesus but when they refuse to listen to him he goes instead to the Gentiles. Again his Spirit-filled teaching wins over many new believers. The gospel passage from St John sees Jesus preparing the disciples for his ascension which quickly approaches. While they will be sorry to loose his physical presence they will rejoice in his glory and in the spread of the gospel. So too, we should rejoice in the gospel and its message to all peoples.

Friday of the Sixth Week of Easter
Acts 18:9-18; Psalm 46; John 16:20-23
Today's reading from the Acts sees St Paul being assured by Christ himself in a vision, that those in Corinth who speak against him will never be able to silence or hurt Paul. With this knowledge Paul preaches all the more earnestly. A group of Jews even bring him before the civil courts because of his preaching but Paul is allowed to go as the proconsul refuses to get involved in religious matters. Paul now heads for Antioch. Again in the gospel, Christ is assuring his followers that their sorrow at his departure will only be temporary and that soon after they will rejoice as the kingdom of God spreads across the earth. We have a duty to help spread that kingdom as did the first followers of Christ.

Saturday of the Sixth Week of Easter
Acts 18:23-28; Psalm 26; John 16:23-28
In the first reading from the Acts we see St Paul visiting the Christian community in Antioch. From here he sets off on his third missionary journey, this time to Galatia in modern-day Turkey. We are also introduced to Apollos, an Alexandrian Jew, who openly teaches about Christ and helps the believers. In the

gospel, Christ is again reassuring the disciples as he prepares to leave them. He tells them that we should pray earnestly to God with full confidence while making all our prayers in the Lord's own name.

Monday of the Seventh Week of Easter
Acts 19:1-8; Psalm 67; John 16:29-33
In our first reading from the Acts of the Apostles today we see St Paul on his third missionary journey in what is present-day Turkey. Paul arrives in the port town of Ephesus, where he will remain for almost three years – the longest he stayed anywhere. Today we learn from him that baptism in to the Christian faith does not complete our lives. Only the gift of the Holy Spirit can do this. In the gospel, Christ tells the disciples that they are about to leave him and be scattered. They will do so in order to spread the gospel throughout the world. He also tells them that this will not be an easy task. We, as heirs of the first disciples, have a duty to help spread the gospel and we should have no fear in this for Christ, as he says in the text, has already conquered the world.

Tuesday of the Seventh Week of Easter
Acts 20:17-27; Psalm 67; John 17:1-11
Today's reading from the Acts sees St Paul bringing his time with the Ephesians to a close after almost three years. He is leaving to go to Jerusalem though he does not know what lies in store for him there. The parting is sad and emotional. In our gospel today, Christ is praying to the Father and making an account of his doings on earth. His work has finished but those who are left behind must now continue the spread of that work.

Wednesday of the Seventh Week of Easter
Acts 20:28-38; Psalm 67; John 17:11-19
Today's first reading continues St Paul's emotional farewell to the Ephesians. He warns them that they will face trials of faith after he has gone but he commends them to God's protection. The reading also reveals the affection the Ephesians had for Paul. Jesus is praying to the Father in the gospel and asking that his followers be kept faithful and unified in their work

and belief. He then calls them together so that they may dedicate themselves to the work he is leaving them.

Thursday of the Seventh Week of Easter
Acts 22:30, 23:6-11; Psalm 15; John 17:20-26
Today's reading from the Acts sees St Paul on trial in Jerusalem where many of the Jewish community are not happy that he has abandoned aspects of the Law of Moses. Paul has been arrested – partly for his own safety – and he now stands trial before the Sanhedrin (the religious supreme court of the Jews). From this too he has to be rescued by the tribune who fears for Paul's safety. In a vision at the end of the text, the Lord tells Paul that he is now to go to Rome. In the gospel, Jesus prays to the Father and asks that all believers may be unified. He also prays for strength for his followers who carry his Gospel to all peoples. We too are called on to witness to Christ wherever he may send us knowing that he is always with us to guide and protect us.

Friday of the Seventh Week of Easter
Acts 25:13-21; Psalm 102; John 21:15-19
In our first reading from the Acts of the Apostles we see that following his unfinished trial before the Sanhedrin a group of Jews conspire against St Paul. He is now in Caesarea but knows that he won't get a fair trial in Jerusalem and so asks that, as a Roman citizen, he be tried in Rome itself. In this Paul is complying with Christ's vision for him to go and preach the Gospel in Rome from the end of yesterday's reading. Today's gospel text is a well-known one in which Christ asks St Peter if he loves him. He also gives Peter a hint as to how Peter is to die. Peter, having denied Christ three times, now affirms three times that he does indeed love him. While it is easy for us to say we love Christ, would it be easy for others to see it by how we live our lives?

Saturday of the Seventh Week of Easter
Acts 28:16-20, 30-31; Psalm 10; John 21:20-25
St Paul has now arrived in Rome in our first reading, and quickly sets about teaching about Christ while still under house arrest. This is the conclusion of the Acts of the Apostles and St Luke ends it here to show that the fledgling church has now spread

well beyond Jerusalem and has now reached Rome – the centre
and capital of the world as they knew it. In today's reading from
St John's gospel we have the closing verses of that gospel. The
author tells us that though a lot has been written about Christ
there is so much more that could be written. What we have is all
that we need for our faith – if we are willing to accept it.

ORDINARY TIME

SUNDAYS: YEAR A

In Year A the gospel is taken from St Matthew's gospel which appears to have been written to strengthen the faith of the community to which he belonged and possibly as a text for use in liturgies. The emphasis is on the kingdom of God and also on Jesus as the Christ, though both need to be seen together. There is also an emphasis on the Law but with the stress being on Jesus' teaching on the law of love rather than strict observance of the Mosaic Law. It is dated to between 80 and 90AD which would suggest that it was not written by the Apostle Matthew but from within his community. The Old Testament texts are chosen in respect of the texts from this gospel.

The second reading texts for this year all come from St Paul:
Week 1: The Lord's Baptism.
Weeks 2-8: 1Corinthians was written about the year 54AD by Paul. It was probably written following reports Paul had received from some of his friends who had passed through or come from Corinth.
Weeks 9-24: The Letter to the Romans in late 57 or early 58AD by Paul ahead of his visit to Rome. The Church in Rome was not founded by Paul and he had not been there at this time and so it contains many important teachings for the early Church but does not contain all of Paul's held beliefs.
Weeks 25-28: The Letter to the Philippians appears to be a collection of texts and so its authorship stretches from 54-58AD. The initial part sees Paul giving thanks for a gift he received while he was in prison. The second part is in response to reports Paul had heard that there were now difficulties in Philippi between Christians and non-Christians and for which Paul urges greater unity within the Christian community. The final section is a warning against itinerant Christian preachers as some of those who were travelling around did not always preach the true faith but had their own 'slant' on things.
Weeks 29-34: 1 Thessalonians is the oldest text in the New Testament and gives us a clear insight into the importance of the death and resurrection of Christ to the early Church. It was written in 50AD shortly after Paul had left Thessalonica following reports he had received from Timothy.

First Sunday in Ordinary Time – The Baptism of the Lord

Isaiah 24: 1-4, 6-7; Psalm 28; Acts 10:34-38; Matthew 3:3-17

In our first reading from Isaiah we see the Lord speaking about his servant. This servant enjoys the favour of the Lord and has been sent to be the 'covenant of the people and the light of the nations'. Our gospel passage recounts Christ's baptism by John as told by St Matthew. In it, the Father witnesses to his own Son and says that he is the Chosen One in fulfilment of the text from Isaiah.

The second reading from the Acts of the Apostles sees St Peter addressing Cornelius and his household and teaching them about Jesus Christ. In the text he speaks about the baptism of Christ by John and about the Father anointing Christ for the work which he then began. We too were baptised and anointed and so we have a duty to spread the gospel as Jesus did following his baptism in the Jordan.

Second Sunday in Ordinary Time

Isaiah 49:3, 5-6; Psalm 39; 1 Corinthians 1:1-3; John 1:29-34

Today's gospel from St John sees John the Baptist giving Jesus the title, 'Lamb of God.' The lamb was traditionally sacrificed in the Temple to atone for sins, to intercede, and to give thanks on behalf of the people. Jesus is the ultimate lamb, the ultimate sacrifice. We are also reminded that at the Passion, Jesus died at the same time that the lambs were being sacrificed in the Temple for the Passover ceremonies. The first reading from the Old Testament prophet Isaiah talks about the Lord's servant being the one to bring salvation to the whole world. This links in with the gospel where John says that Christ is that servant.

Our second reading for the next seven weeks comes from St Paul's letter to the Christian community in Corinth. In today's passage Paul tells us that the Lord is for all peoples – he came to save all nations, not just the Jewish people. We are challenged today to say, with conviction, the words spoken by John the Baptist, 'Yes, I have seen and I am the witness that he is the Chosen One of God.'

Third Sunday in Ordinary Time

Isaiah 8:23-9:3; Psalm 26; 1 Corinthians 1:10-13, 17; Matthew 4:12-23.
Today we begin the cycle of readings from St Matthew's gospel
which will continue throughout the Sundays of Ordinary Time
for this year. In today's passage we see Jesus settling in
Capernaum and calling his first disciples. By settling in
Capernaum he is fulfilling the words in our reading from Isaiah
which say that this area is where the glory of the Lord will come
from, an area which had been humbled in the past. Isaiah also
speaks about the people being freed from a great darkness and
their yoke being lifted from their shoulders. He speaks of joy
and gladness and rejoicing and of how a great light has shone on
the land that was shrouded in darkness. This is what Christ
came to bring to the people of God who believe in him – liberation from that which oppresses them. In our day too he brings
liberation from all that oppresses us and keeps us separated
from the love of God which knows no bounds.
St Paul reminds us in the second reading taken from his first letter to the Corinthians that we can only be for one person and
that person must be Jesus Christ. There may be many great ora-
tors to show us the way but it is not them that we are to follow
but the Christ about whom they preach.

Fourth Sunday in Ordinary Time

*Zephaniah 2:3, 3:12-13; Psalm 145; 1 Corinthians 1:26-31; Matthew
5:1-12*
The first reading from Zephaniah speaks to us about acting with
humility and being honest before the Lord. Those who live by
humility and seek the Lord will find shelter in the Lord and un-
interrupted rest. In our gospel passage from St Matthew, we
have the Beatitudes from the Sermon on the Mount. As well as
being a well known passage it is a radical way of living, something that could bring great good to our world but only if people
choose to live it. Matthew tells us that the sermon took place on
top of a mountain reminding us of Moses, and the fact that Jesus
was seated which emphasises his authority. The connection between this and the first reading is the theme of humility.
St Paul tells us in the second reading from his first letter to
the Corinthians that God often chooses what we regard as

something foolish or lowly and turns it into something great, such as humility or what many regard as weakness or foolishness. Paul tells us that what the world regards as foolish and weak is actually turned into something powerful and transforming by the Lord.

Fifth Sunday in Ordinary Time
Isaiah 58:7-10; Psalm 111; 1 Corinthians 2:1-5; Matthew 5:13-16
In this Sunday's first reading the Prophet Isaiah gives us a few simple instructions on how to live our lives, particularly where the poor are concerned. He talks about light shining out for others to brighten their lives. Continuing the theme of light, Jesus tells his disciples that they are the light of the world, but he warns them to be careful about that. They are to preach openly and are not to keep to themselves what they have seen and heard. We are the successors of the apostles, we are the modern day heralds of the gospel and we too have a duty to make that message known to all whom we meet.
St Paul reminds the Corinthians in the second reading that he was no great orator but that what he preached came from his own faith in God.

Sixth Sunday in Ordinary Time
Ecclesiasticus 15:15-20; Psalm 118; 1 Corinthians 2:6-10; Matthew 5:17-37
The first reading this week comes from the Book of Ecclesiasticus and tells us that God knows all that we do and that he has never told anyone to do that which is wrong. We are also reminded that it is within our power to keep the commandments. The gospel passage from St Matthew sees Jesus commenting on the Law as the Jews had it and telling them that they have gone astray in their observance of it. We can only gain eternal life if we take on board the true message and wisdom of Christ and live that out in our daily lives.
The second reading from the first letter to the Corinthians tells us that there is wisdom or knowledge available to us in order for us to gain eternal life. This is not earthly wisdom but a wisdom which was worked out before the ages began and is a simple but powerful one.

Seventh Sunday in Ordinary Time

Leviticus 19:1-2, 17-18; Psalm 102; 1 Corinthians 3:16-23; Matthew 5:38-48

Today's first reading from the Book of Leviticus (one of the books of the Torah) and the gospel speak of love and how we should love one another. The first reading from the Book of Leviticus is brief but contains the key points or commands for living life as God wants us to live. In the gospel, Jesus tells us that the old way of 'an eye for an eye' has no place in the kingdom and will not lead to peace. He tells us that we must love even our enemies if we are to be his disciples and so bring lasting peace to the world.

The second reading tells us that we are temples of the Holy Spirit and we must do all that we can to protect and strengthen that temple. If we look after the temple within us and live according to the will of the Spirit, we will truly love our fellow men and women and so help make the kingdom of God a visible reality here on earth for all to see.

Eighth Sunday in Ordinary Time

Isaiah 49:14-15; Psalm 61; 1 Corinthians 4:1-5; Matthew 6:24-34

Today's readings again speak of God's love for us and how he is always watching over us. The first reading from Isaiah tells us that the Lord never forgets us, but is like a mother who always cherishes her children. The gospel echoes this and in it Christ is telling his disciples not to worry about tomorrow and where our next meal will come from, for God will always look after those who believe in him and call on him for help.

The second reading reminds us that while God is always there to help us in times of need, he is also there as our judge and it is to him that we must answer for our lack of belief and our wrong doings.

Ninth Sunday in Ordinary Time

Deuteronomy 11:18, 26-28, 32; Psalm 30; Romans 3:21-25, 28; Matthew 7:21-27

Our readings today speak of the covenant made with God as his chosen people. In the first reading from the Book of Deuteronomy we see Moses encouraging the people to keep God's words in their heart and in their mind. If they remain faithful to the covenant then they will be blessed, but if they stray from the covenant then they will be cursed. In our gospel reading from St Matthew, we see Christ telling the people that those who pay lip-service are not going to enter the kingdom. Those who will enter are those who listen to his word and put that word into action because this is true faith in practice.

Our second reading today and for the next fifteen weeks comes from St Paul's letters to the Christians in Rome and was written when Paul himself was in Corinth. Today he tells us that it is by faith that we are justified because simply keeping the law does not make us righteous – the heart might not be in the right place and so our actions are false.

Tenth Sunday in Ordinary Time
Hosea 6:3-6; Psalm 49; Romans 4:18-25; Matthew 9:9-13
Our readings today – like last week – speak of the covenant with God. In the first reading from the Prophet Hosea we are warned that our love for God and his word should not be blown away easily, as the dew quickly evaporates, but must be of stronger stuff. In the gospel, Christ is seen eating with those whom society considered sinners but he tells the people that it is those in need of conversion who are the ones who are called by him. We also have the call of the tax collector, Matthew, to be one of the Lord's followers and inner circle.

In the second reading from the letter to the Romans we are given the example of Abraham whose hope was also a source of strength which helped to bolster his faith. Both Abraham and Matthew are placed before us as examples of how we should trust in God – Abraham trusted even though the promise made seemed impossible; and Matthew completely changed his life when he received the call from Jesus. Everyone is in need of conversion and, like Abraham and St.Matthew, we must acknowledge that need in ourselves and take the message to heart.

Eleventh Sunday in Ordinary Time
Exodus 19:2-6; Psalm 99; Romans 5:6-11; Matthew 9:36-10:8
The theme of our readings today is very much one of calling. We are called to live as sons and daughters of God and to keep his

commandments and the covenant in constant faith and truth. Not only that, we are also called to go out ourselves and to proclaim the Good News and so make the kingdom visible. While all may not be able or called to do so as ordained ministers and religious, all are called to do so by the example of how they live their lives and in their dealings and relations with others. In our gospel text for today from St Matthew, we have the naming of the Twelve Apostles and the instruction to them to go out and spread the Good News. At the end of the text we are reminded that what we have received, we have received without charge and so we must pass that on without charge.

The second reading from the letter to the Romans reminds us that as Christ died to make us righteous in the eyes of God that he will not fail to save us should we go astray. We must remain faithful to him and live the kind of life he wants us to live. There will be times when we will go astray but we must always make the effort to secure our place in the kingdom.

Twelfth Sunday in Ordinary Time
Jeremiah 20:10-13; Psalm 68; Romans 5:12-15; Matthew 10:26-33

In our first reading we see the Prophet Jeremiah speaking of all those who are looking to bring him down. Yet in the second half of the reading he says that God is on his side and therefore he has nothing to fear. Our psalm could easily have been the words spoken to God by Jeremiah as he asked for help. In the gospel passage from St Matthew, Christ tells the Twelve that the soul is far more important than the body and it is the soul which they must be concerned with for the body is but a passing thing, the soul an eternal thing. The Lord is always at our side and therefore we must always be on our guard against anything that would lead us away from him. We must listen carefully and believe in his opening words: 'Do not be afraid.' We must let go of all that holds us back and become the people he wants us to be.

In the passage from the letter to the Romans, St Paul tells us that sin has always been in the world – even before the Law was set out. What is more significant than the presence of sin in the world is the fact that we have been redeemed by Christ's gift of his own life.

Thirteenth Sunday in Ordinary Time

2 Kings 4:8-11, 14-16; Psalm 88; Romans 6:3-4, 8-11; Matthew 10:37-42

In our first reading from the second Book of the Kings, we see the Prophet Elisha rewarding a Shunammite woman for her kindness to him by telling her that she will bear a son within a year. She and her husband had made him welcome whenever he passed and had even built a small room for him. Being childless was a great stigma at the time and so he lifts that stigma as thanks for her kindness and hospitality to him. Christ echoes this in the gospel passage in that he tells us that we must always show kindness and hospitality to others. In this way we are living out the gospel precepts and will be rewarded. There is also a reminder that in welcoming others we are welcoming Christ himself who is to be found in the hearts of others. We must be worthy of the life Christ won for us and be prepared to defend it and nourish it. Otherwise, in our case, Christ's sacrifice will have been for nothing.

St Paul tells us in the second reading that we have already died with Christ in baptism and now live a new life with him. As Christ was raised from the dead so too will we be raised for living a life worthy of that great gift.

Fourteenth Sunday in Ordinary Time

Zechariah 9:9-10; Psalm 144; Romans 8:9, 11-13; Matthew 11:25-30

The first reading from the Prophet Zechariah tells us that the Lord will come in victory but he will also come very humbly and riding on a donkey. This reminds us of the Lord's triumphant entry into Jerusalem on Passion Sunday – the fulfilment of this prophecy. In the gospel, Jesus says that his way of life can be discerned by little children, so simple is his way. His way is one of humility and gentleness and if we live as he did then we too will inherit everlasting life. There is also a reminder that little children trust their parents and that this is the way in which we should approach the gospel and faith in God. If we act too much like adults and try to scientifically explain things then we run the risk of missing the message itself. We need to trust God and his Son in a child-like way.

In the second reading St Paul tells us that we already have the Spirit of Christ living in us and that, as a result, there is no reason why we should not live the life Christ wants of us. Our spiritual selves are far more important that the unspiritual side and we must allow the spiritual side to dominate our lives. If we were to do this then we would very quickly transform our world.

Fifteenth Sunday in Ordinary Time
Isaiah 55:10-11; Psalm 64; Romans 8:18-23; Matthew 13:1-23
Today's first reading and the gospel are linked by seeds. In the first reading Isaiah tells us that both rain and snow water the earth and cause the seeds to grow and provide us with food. In the gospel, Christ speaks of a sower sowing his seed and of the different places where the seed fell and grew. We are the seed and Christ the water which nourishes us and causes us to grow. The reading today should prompt us to look honestly at our own lives and see which seed we happen to be – fruitful or fruitless.
St Paul, in the second reading, tells us that no matter what happens to us there is a glory awaiting us which is beyond compare. In order to attain the glory which has been promised us we must nurture the seed within us and listen to the word of God and put it into practice every day. Only then will we become a successful harvest and help others to grow also.

Sixteenth Sunday in Ordinary Time
Wisdom 12:13, 16-19; Psalm 85; Romans 8:26-27; Matthew 13:24-43
Our readings today speak to us of the mercy of God and of his judgement. God knows all things and he knows the secret thoughts of our hearts and of our prayers, though we are not always able to express these. He is merciful to the repentant and his Spirit is always with us to help and guide us. The Word of God has been given to us but we must be wary of those who seek to stifle that presence and that life. What God seeks is honesty, integrity and faith. The first reading from the Book of Wisdom speaks of the sovereignty of God and of his power but also of his great lenience for his people. The gospel sets three parables before us today – that of the darnel sowed among good seed, of the mustard seed and the parable of the yeast. Upon hearing the gospel we should ask ourselves whether we are the good seed or the weeds and whether or not we help in the growth of the kingdom.

The second reading, from the letter to the Romans, reminds us that the Spirit comes to help us in our weakness. If we allow the Spirit to work in us then we will be able to live the gospel precepts but also to give true glory and praise to God. This is the Spirit, the Advocate, which Christ promised us before the Ascension.

Seventeenth Sunday in Ordinary Time
1 Kings 3:5, 7-12; Psalm 118; Romans 8:28-30; Matthew 13:44-52
Our first reading today comes from the first Book of the Kings and shows us Solomon who has just succeeded his father, David, as King of Israel. The Lord comes to Solomon and tells him to ask for whatever he wants but Solomon asks for just one thing – 'a heart to understand how to discern between good and evil'. And this, the Lord grants him. In the gospel, Jesus likens the kingdom of heaven to fine pearls for which a person will give up everything else to attain them. The message is that the way to the kingdom is through wisdom and not through riches. We are also told in the second half of the passage that the Lord will separate the good from the bad at the end of time.
In the second reading, St Paul tells us that the Wisdom of God is the Word of God and by taking it to our hearts and living according to its values then we will share the Lord's glory.

Eighteenth Sunday in Ordinary Time
Isaiah 55:1-3; Psalm 144; Romans 8:35, 37-39; Matthew 14:13-21
Today's readings speak of being fed by the Lord. In the first reading from the prophet Isaiah, the Lord tells us to come and eat even if we have no money. If we do so then our soul will live. In the gospel, we see Jesus feeding the multitude with five loaves and two fish, which reminds us of the feeding of the Israelites in the desert with manna from heaven. The true bread is Christ himself which he gave us on Holy Thursday and it is the only nourishment we need in order to reach the kingdom, but only if we believe in it.
St Paul tells us in the second reading that nothing can come between us and the love of God and that the trials which come our way serve to strengthen our faith and the presence of God within each of us. In truth, the only things which can separate us from

God are the barriers we ourselves create or by our own rejection of the love of God.

Nineteenth Sunday in Ordinary Time
1 Kings 19:9, 11-13; Psalm 84; Romans 9:1-5; Matthew 14:22-33
The power of God is a common thread in our readings today. In the first reading we see that God was to be found not in the mighty forces of nature but in the gentle breeze. The holy Prophet Elijah had gone to Horeb and took shelter in a cave and only came out when he heard the gentle breeze for he recognised this as being the presence of God. In the gospel we see Christ having power over the physical forces of nature and walking on water. Christ is always with us whether it be in the gentle breeze or in mighty power. While God is the Creator of all that there is, he does not always make his presence known in a great show of power but is to be seen and felt even in the quietest and most still moments in life.

In the second reading, we see St Paul lamenting the fact that the Israelites have prayed for centuries for the Messiah and yet they refuse to accept Jesus as the Messiah despite his miracles and his teaching. We are called on to believe in Christ and his presence even though we cannot see him. We are asked to take to heart his words in today's gospel – 'Do not be afraid.'

Twentieth Sunday in Ordinary Time
Isaiah 56:1, 6-7; Psalm 66; Romans 11:13-15, 29-32; Matthew 15:21-28
In our readings for today we see that the word of God is meant not just for those who are baptised but for all peoples who live the gospel values. The one important criterion is belief in God. The first reading from Isaiah clearly tells us that those who live by God's word and are faithful to him will be joyful in his house of prayer as the Lord gathers to his holy mountain all those who live by his precepts. In the gospel we see Jesus encountering a Canaanite woman who asked him to heal her daughter. Despite her ethnicity she professes faith in Christ and her daughter is healed. We must all believe in God and his word and live lives worthy of the gospel values if we are to be saved.

The second reading from the letter to the Romans tells us that God is always merciful and that this mercy is always available to those who seek it. The mercy of God will always be there for us even if – for a time – we reject God and fail to live as he wants us to live.

Twenty-first Sunday in Ordinary Time
Isaiah 22:19-23; Psalm 137; Romans 11:33-36; Matthew 16:13-20
Our first reading from the Prophet Isaiah sees the Lord removing the key of the House of David from Shebna and giving it to Eliakim because the former had been a poor keeper of the key and servant of God. Eliakim is given full authority and whatever he closes will remain closed and whatever he opens will remain open. A similar scene is found in the gospel text from St Matthew in that, following his great profession of faith, St Peter is given the keys of the kingdom by Christ. The Lord tells Peter and his successors that whatever he binds on earth will be considered bound in heaven and whatever he should loose on earth will be considered loosed in heaven. Peter is also made the rock on which the Church is to be built.

In the second reading from St Paul to the Romans, Paul tells us that everything that exists comes from God, everything is by God and everything is for God. Our passage concludes with Paul telling us that it is to God that we should give glory for ever.

Twenty-second Sunday in Ordinary Time
Jeremiah 20:7-9; Psalm 62; Romans 12:1-2; Matthew 16:21-27
The Prophet Jeremiah in our first reading today is weary of proclaiming God's word because all he gets for doing so is insult and derision. This is not because the words he speaks are foolish but because the people are stubborn and are too fond of doing their own thing without giving any thought to God, from whom all things come. In the gospel from St Matthew, Christ tells those closest to him that he is soon to die. St Peter tries to change their path but the Lord is not happy with this for the disciples have failed to understand what his mission is all about. He tells them that his true followers must be prepared to suffer for him and to live according to his teaching and not according to the mores of their contemporary society. Those who are faithful to him will be rewarded by him.

Almost as a support to Jeremiah, St Paul in the second reading to the Romans urges his readers to offer their very lives to God and to live as God wants them to live. He calls on them not to live as those around them do but to allow the power of God to transform them in to what he wants them to be.

Twenty-third Sunday in Ordinary Time
Ezekiel 33:7-9; Psalm 94; Romans 13:8-10; Matthew 18:15-20
In the first reading from the Old Testament Prophet Ezekiel we are warned that if we do not try to turn the wicked from their ways then we will be held responsible for their punishment. This is a further reminder of our duty to spread the gospel. In the gospel for today, Christ echoes the words of Ezekiel that we must try to win people back to the right road to eternal life. He also reminds us that where we gather in his name, he will be there amongst us. The readings remind us today that we are a people who live in community and must therefore look after those in community with us. To help us in this we are also told in today's gospel passage by Christ that he will be with us even if there are only two or three gathered in his name.

In the second reading from Romans, St Paul tells us that love is the root of everything. If we act out of love then we will always be able to keep the commandments.

Twenty-fourth Sunday in Ordinary Time
Ecclesiasticus 27:30-28:7; Psalm 102; Romans 14:7-9; Matthew 18:21-35
Both the first reading and the gospel today speak of forgiveness. We are called on in both readings to remember the Covenants with God who forgave humankind again and again despite their sinful ways. The first reading from Ecclesiasticus opens by telling us that 'resentment and anger ... are foul things' and that these have no place in our lives. In our gospel passage we have the parable of the wicked servant who – despite being pardoned by the king of his debt – refused to pardon a fellow servant who was in debt to him. There is a reminder for us that if we are to expect forgiveness from God and from others then we ourselves must forgive those who we perceive to have wronged us and we should never harbour resentment.

In the second reading St Paul tells us that we belong to God whether we are alive or dead. If we belong to the Lord then we should forgive much.

Twenty-fifth Sunday in Ordinary Time
Isaiah 55:6-9; Psalm 144; Philippians 1:20-24, 27; Matthew 20:1-16
Our readings from Isaiah and from St Matthew's Gospel speak to us of the generosity of God which is beyond our understanding. Isaiah reminds us to seek the Lord and not abandon his ways like the wicked do. The gospel sees Jesus teaching about the mercy of God through a parable in which all people are treated very generously. All people are considered equal in God's eyes and there is a welcome and a place for each person in heaven if they live according to the gospel.

Our second reading now comes from St Paul's letter to the Philippians and in today's passage we read that Christ will be glorified in us and that Christ is our life. Paul is quite candid about the fact that he wants to die and live with Christ in heaven but at the same time he knows that Christ is with him and that he has a task to complete for Christ before he dies – the spread of the gospel. Christ can only be glorified in us if we live out the gospel in the sight of others with Christ as the guiding principle of our lives.

Twenty-sixth Sunday in Ordinary Time
Ezekiel 18:25-28; Psalm 24; Philippians 2:1-11; Matthew 21:28-32
The first reading from the Prophet Ezekiel tells us that we are the ones who are unjust when we go astray and not God. God punishes us for our sinfulness but he is just in doing so. We are also reminded that those who change their ways and repent of their transgressions are welcomed back by God. The psalm asks the Lord to be merciful and to teach us his ways. In the gospel, Jesus is admonishing some of the chief priests and elders for not listening to God's messengers. He tells them that those whom they consider to be sinners are actually getting in to heaven ahead of them because they are, in their own quiet way, believing in God. He points out to them that John the Baptist came and lived and preached in a way which they hold as exemplary and yet they refused to listen to him. We too are called on to believe in God and not fool ourselves with our own ideas.

St Paul tells us in the second reading that we must be the same as Christ who gave up everything and became like us in order to save us. We must give up our earthly ways and become like Christ if we are to enter the kingdom of heaven.

Twenty-seventh Sunday in Ordinary Time

Isaiah 5:1-7; Psalm 79; Philippians 4:6-9; Matthew 21:33-43

Through the Prophet Isaiah in the first reading the Lord speaks of a vineyard which he planted and which has yielded bad fruit. The Lord is now going to let the vineyard be destroyed and over-run. The good vines that were planted were the Lord's Chosen People but the bad fruit is their lack of belief and their sinfulness. In the gospel we have another parable concerning a vineyard. In this, the tenants try to take over ownership of the vineyard by killing the owner's son. We are reminded that while we may live in the Lord's vineyard here on earth we still owe our homage to God. We may try at playing gods but it will get us nowhere if we ignore the one true God from whom all things come.

In the second reading to the Philippians, St Paul tells us to pray to God if there is anything we need and that, at the very least, the peace of God will be granted to us.

Twenty-eighth Sunday in Ordinary Time

Isaiah 25:6-10; Psalm 22; Philippians 4:12-14, 19-20; Matthew 22:1-14

In the first reading from the Prophet Isaiah we are told that those who hope in the Lord will be raised up and will receive salvation. In this all their shame and troubles will be taken from them and happiness will be theirs. Our gospel text contains the parable of the king who held a banquet for his son's wedding but whose guests did not turn up. The banquet is the kingdom of heaven and the guests are men and women of every age and time. Those who do not heed the call of God and who ignore him will be left out in the dark when their time on earth comes to an end. It is a reminder that the message of God and places in the kingdom are offered to all but only those who are worthy will be allowed entry to the kingdom when the time comes.

In the second reading, St Paul tells his readers that he can master anything that may come his way because he has the Lord to give him strength. We are challenged today to live lives worthy of the invitation which the Father extends to us, knowing that he is with us to strengthen us just as he did St Paul.

Twenty-ninth Sunday in Ordinary Time
Isaiah 45:1, 4-6; Psalm 95; 1 Thessalonians 1:1-5; Matthew 22:15-21
In the first reading the Lord, speaking through the Prophet Isaiah, tells us that apart from him all is nothing. In the gospel, the Pharisees are trying to catch Jesus out but he turns the tables on them. They did not like paying taxes to Caesar and ask Jesus whether or not the taxes should be paid. If he says 'yes' then he will be seen as no friend to Israel and not a true Jew; if he answers 'no' then he could be denounced to the Romans as a trouble maker. He tells them that as Caesar's head is on the coins then Caesar has a right to claim them back. He uses this to say that all we have comes from God and therefore he is deserving of our praise, our thanks and our faith.
For the final weeks of this year our second reading comes from St Paul's letter to the Christians of Thessalonica. Today's reading is from the opening section of his first letter to the Thessalonians in which he reminds them of their faith, their love and their hope. Paul is giving them a little boost to keep them strong in faith. The same applies to us today.

Thirtieth Sunday in Ordinary Time
Exodus 22:20-26; Psalm 17; 1 Thessalonians 1:5-10; Matthew 22:34-40
In our first reading from the Book of Exodus the Lord is telling the people how they should behave towards the poor and the stranger. If they are not honest and upright with the poor and less fortunate then the Lord will be angry for he hears the cry of the poor and will answer their cries for justice. In the gospel, the Pharisees are still trying to trick Jesus and yet again they fail. He answers their question regarding the greatest commandment and goes on to tell them that they must love their neighbour as themselves – something they were not happy to do for they saw themselves as being greater than the majority of their neighbours. These readings challenge us to look at ourselves and to see how we treat our neighbours and particularly the poor.
St Paul continues to encourage the Thessalonians to remain

faithful to God in our second reading by telling them of how the reputation of their faith has spread to other places and so is an example for others.

Alternative Gospel for Mission Sunday – Thirtieth Sunday, Year A:
Matthew 9:1-8
In the gospel, we see the people follow Jesus and bring him a paralytic. He tells the man that his sins are forgiven and the scribes attack him. But the encounter reminds us that the love of God, the forgiveness and the healing of God are always available to us. It is the Mission of the Church to bring this healing, forgiveness and love to all people through knowledge of Jesus Christ.

Thirty-first Sunday in Ordinary Time
Malachi 1:14-2:2, 8-10; Psalm 130; 1 Thessalonians 2:7-9, 13; Matthew 23:1-12
In the first reading from the Prophet Malachi, the Lord is admonishing the priests for having strayed from the right path and for having taken the people with them. He will now deal with them harshly unless they amend their ways. In the gospel passage we are reminded to be a humble people and servants of the Lord and of each other. The scribes and Pharisees said and instructed the people in the right things but they themselves did the wrong things and so Christ encouraged his followers to be a humble people always doing what is right.
In the second reading, St Paul is encouraging the Thessalonians in their faith by reminding them that what they believe in is God's message and not some human thinking. This message of God is a living power among the Thessalonians. He also reminds them of the example he himself was when he lived among them – he worked quietly and was a burden on nobody.

Thirty-second Sunday in Ordinary Time
Wisdom 6:12-16; Psalm 62; 1 Thessalonians 4:13-18; Matthew 25:1-13
Our first reading from the Book of Wisdom speaks about wisdom and how it is to be found by those who seek her. We know that Christ is the Wisdom of God and those who seek him will

find him. As the first reading speaks of seeking wisdom so the psalm speaks of seeking God. The gospel reminds us that we do not know when the Lord will call us from this life and so we must always be ready, not like the foolish bridesmaids in the parable who forget to bring extra oil for their lamps and who were left out of the banquet.

In the second reading, St Paul tells us that those who have died in Christ have gone to God and therefore we should not grieve for them. This promise is also made to us but only if we die in Christ.

Thirty-third Sunday in Ordinary Time

Proverbs 31:10-13, 19-20, 30-31; Psalm 127; 1 Thessalonians 5:1-6; Matthew 25:14-30

The first reading from the Book of Proverbs speaks about the perfect wife and what a treasure is to be found in her. This comes from the closing section of the book and the woman, or wife, can be seen as Wisdom in everyday practical living. The gospel parable tells of a man who entrusted his property to others and went away. When he came back some of his servants had improved on what he had given them while another just hid it away. It is not enough for us to simply say that we believe in God – we must put that faith into practice and live it out in our lives so that we may give glory to God and help others to come to know him. In this way we will have taken what he gave us and improved on it and helped build up his kingdom.

In the second reading from the first letter to the Thessalonians, St Paul reminds us to be always ready for the Lord's coming because we do not know when it will happen. But when it does happen, we must not be found wanting.

Our Lord Jesus Christ, Universal King: Year A

Ezekiel 34:11-12, 15-17; Psalm 22; 1 Corinthians 15:20-26, 28; Matthew 25:31-46

Today is the last Sunday in the Church's year and is celebrated as the Solemnity of Christ the King. The image we have in our readings is of the king as a shepherd. In the first reading from the Prophet Ezekiel, the Lord says that he will be in the midst of his sheep so that he can keep all of them in view and look after them. The second reading from St Paul's first letter to the Corinthians speaks about the resurrection of the dead in which Christ is the first to be raised, and then all those who belong to Christ. In the gospel, Christ tells us that all peoples will be assembled before the throne of glory and they will be sorted out according to their deeds. Those who have believed in God and lived this faith out in their lives will be welcomed into the kingdom. Those who have not been faithful will not enter the kingdom. Christ is the supreme king and no matter who our civil leaders may be, we have a greater king in heaven who must be loved, obeyed and honoured.

SUNDAYS: YEAR B

In Year B our gospel is mainly taken from St Mark who was an interpreter for St Peter and so his writings come from the teaching and memory of Peter. It was the first of the gospels to be written and is dated to 64-67AD. It was written for the Christians in Rome who were undergoing persecution. There is a very strong emphasis on the kingdom of God and everything else is seen in relation to this. Those who wish to understand the kingdom need to look at the work and person of Jesus Christ as portrayed by Mark. The response to all of this – for Mark – is discipleship which means sharing in the mission of Christ. For Weeks 17-21 the gospel comes from the sixth chapter of St John's gospel which contains the 'Bread of Life Discourse.' The Old Testament texts are chosen in respect of the texts from these gospels.

The second reading texts for this year come from those attributed to St Paul and also from St James:

Week 1: The Lord's Baptism.

Weeks 2-14: 1 Corinthians was written about the year 54AD by Paul. It was probably written following reports Paul had received from some of his friends who had passed through or come from Corinth. 2 Corinthians was written about 55AD, again by Paul. This was in response to a serious deterioration within the community in Corinth and has much harsher tones.

Weeks 15-21: The Letter to the Ephesians was written between 80 and 100AD and is regarded as being Pseudo-Paul, in other words it wasn't written by Paul but is written in a style and with an understanding in line with Paul (Paul died about the year 67AD). The purpose of this letter was to instruct a number of Christian churches about the primacy of Christ and of his Church over everything.

Weeks 22-26: The Letter of St James was written about the year 70AD and is made up of a series of brief sections. The letter encourages people to have a practical and living faith rather than one which is simply theoretical.

Weeks 27-34: The Letter to the Hebrews was written between 80 and 90AD and is accepted that it was not written by Paul though it is attributed to him. It teaches that the old Covenants are now replaced by the one everlasting sacrifice of Jesus Christ. It also exhorts the reader to remain steadfast with the Christian faith.

First Sunday in Ordinary Time – the Baptism of the Lord
Isaiah 55:1-11; Psalm: Isaiah 12:2-6; 1John 5:1-9; Mark 1:7-11

In our first reading from the Prophet Isaiah we see the people being called by God to return to him and to abandon their wicked ways. The symbol of water is very evident in this reading as it is in all of the readings today. Our gospel passage recounts Christ's baptism by John as told by St Mark. In it, the Father witnesses to his own Son and says that he is the Chosen One, in fulfilment of the text from Isaiah.

In the second reading from St John's first letter we are told that we should love those with whom we come into contact because if we do not love them then we cannot possibly love God whom we cannot see.

Second Sunday in Ordinary Time
1 Samuel 3:3-10, 19; Psalm 39; 1 Corinthians 6:13-15, 17-20; John 1:35-42

Our readings for this Sunday focus on answering the call of God to be his followers and his disciples. In the first reading from the first Book of Samuel we see Samuel being called. Initially he thinks that it is Eli who is calling him but in time Eli realises that it is God who is doing the calling and tells the boy to answer with the words: 'Speak, Lord, your servant is listening.' In the gospel text from St John we read about how St Andrew became the Lord's first disciple and how he brought his brother, Peter, to the Lord with the words: 'We have found the Messiah.' We are encouraged to look at our own lives and to give our whole life to following Christ.

For today and the next twelve weeks our second reading comes from the letters of St Paul to the Christians in Corinth. In today's passage Paul reminds us that our bodies make up part of Christ's mystical body and so we should dedicate ourselves to the building up of the kingdom.

Third Sunday in Ordinary Time
Jonah 3:1-5, 10; Psalm 24; 1 Corinthians 7:29-31; Mark 1:14-20

Our readings today call on us to repent and to change our ways. They remind us that the pleasures of this earthly life are constantly changing and that only the Word of God can bring us everlasting happiness. In the first reading we see the Prophet Jonah being sent to Nineveh to preach the Word of God there. The people realise their folly and change their ways returning to the Lord once more. In the gospel from St Mark we see Jesus begin his public ministry with the words 'The kingdom of God is close at hand. Repent, and believe the good news.' He then goes on to call his first disciples. By virtue of our baptism we are each called to serve the Lord as did the people of Nineveh and the first disciples. We are challenged to say the words of today's psalm with conviction: 'Lord, make me know your ways ... make me walk in your truth.'

St Paul tells us in the second reading that the world as we know it is passing away. While the world is now a great age and does not appear to be coming to an end any time soon, the life of each of us on this planet is extremely short and rather insignificant. Therefore we should dedicate ourselves to the Lord so that we will inherit eternal life.

Fourth Sunday in Ordinary Time

Deuteronomy 18:15-20; Psalm 94; 1 Corinthians 7:32-35; Mark 1:21-28

In our first reading today from the Book of Deuteronomy, Moses tells the people that after he has gone the Lord will give them a great prophet who will teach them his ways. The people had grown tired of listening to God and wanted to listen to one of their own so the Lord agrees to appoint one of their own as his prophet. In the gospel we read how Jesus taught the people and that he commanded the unclean spirits with authority which they obeyed. In this we can see Jesus as the great prophet whom Moses spoke about. The Lord is our great teacher and the scriptures contain his teaching if only we had the courage to become familiar with the scriptures and to live out the teachings in our lives.

St Paul tells us that it is easier for the unmarried to devote themselves to the Lord because they do not have to worry about pleasing their spouse or looking after the family. In this, Paul is not being negative about marriage but he is reminding us that no matter what our status in life we must devote some time every day to the Lord.

Fifth Sunday in Ordinary Time

Job 7:1-4, 6-7; Psalm 146; 1 Corinthians 9:16-19, 22-23; Mark 1:29-39
The readings today speak of the healing and freedom brought to us by Christ and his gospel. In the first reading Job likens man's life to being little more than a slave who awaits his wages and has nothing else to look forward to. In the gospel we read about Jesus curing people and preaching the Good News to them. The crowds follow him wherever he goes because his words bring healing and freedom to them. We do not have Christ with us in the same way as the people in the gospel had, but we do have him present in our tabernacles and present in the words of sacred scripture. We are challenged today to listen to the words of Christ and to put our trust in them, knowing that they will bring us healing and comfort and free us from all that would enslave us in this life.

In the second reading St Paul tells us that he preaches the gospel in order to set others free, even though he doesn't get paid for it and has, in a certain sense, become the slave of all.

Sixth Sunday in Ordinary Time

Leviticus 13:1-2, 44-46; Psalm 31; 1 Corinthians 10:31-11:1; Mark 1:40-45
In our first reading today from the Book of Leviticus – one of the books containing the Law of Moses – we see Moses instructing that those suffering from leprosy must live as outcasts and that the priests must declare them as outcasts. While they were to live apart to prevent the spread of diseases, it was never decreed that they be treated shamefully. In our gospel for today we see Jesus – the eternal high priest – curing a man of his leprosy and bringing him back into society while Christ himself lives as an outcast. The reading is a reminder that the gospel and the love of God are inclusive and that everyone has a place in the kingdom.

In the second reading St Paul tells us that we should model ourselves on Christ and never do any harm to anyone no matter what they believe. As Christ brought outcasts back into society so we too should have genuine concern for those who are outcasts in our own society.

Seventh Sunday in Ordinary Time
Isaiah 43:18-19, 21-22, 24-25; Psalm 40; 2 Corinthians 1:18-22; Mark 2:1-12

In our first reading today from the Prophet Isaiah we see the Lord being annoyed with his people because they have troubled him with wrong doing despite all he had done. So he is now going to blot out everything and not remember their sins. In the gospel passage we see Jesus returning to Capernaum and word of his return spreads out across the countryside. Many people come to hear him and to be cured by him even to the point of peeling back the roof where he is and lowering a man down to him on a stretcher. Because of the faith of his friends, the man's sins are forgiven. This brings Jesus into conflict with the scribes because they believed that only God could forgive sins but they failed to see that Jesus was God despite the miracles or the cure of the paralytic which had just taken place before their eyes. In response to this, Jesus also healed the man of his paralysis.

St Paul in the second reading tells us that Jesus' teachings never wavered but were always constant and consistent. We are challenged today to be constant before God and to live the life of faith to which we are called.

Eighth Sunday in Ordinary Time
Hosea 2:16-17, 21-22; Psalm 102; 2 Corinthians 3:1-6; Mark 2:18-22

In our first reading from Hosea and the gospel text from St Mark we have the image of a bridegroom. Christ is the bridegroom who is married to his Church and who is forever attentive to the needs of the Church and its people and who is always faithful to it. The gospel tells us that we should always act as if the bridegroom were with us, and indeed he always is for Christ is present throughout all of creation which came into being through him. Therefore we should act as the first reading says: 'with integrity and justice, with tenderness and love'.

In the second reading from his second letter to the Corinthians, St Paul is praising the Corinthians for their faith and Christian living. He likens them to a letter of recommendation and says that they are a letter of recommendation both for the Good News and for himself.

Ninth Sunday in Ordinary Time

Deuteronomy 5:12-15; Psalm 80; 2 Corinthians 4:6-11; Mark 2:23-3:6
In our first reading from the Book of Deuteronomy, we see the Lord instructing the people to keep the Sabbath day as the day sacred to the Lord, as a remembrance of all that the Lord has done for them. Our gospel text seems to be at variance with this because Jesus and his disciples are doing things which were forbidden by the Laws. However, Jesus tells us that he is Lord of the Sabbath and greater than it and proves it by the miracle he worked. We are reminded to keep the Sabbath holy but not necessarily with the absolute rigidity that the Pharisees of the time were seeking.

In the second reading St Paul tells us that in each of us the person of Christ can be seen, and with Jesus in each of us there is no need to despair as long we allow him to work in us.

Tenth Sunday in Ordinary Time

Genesis 3:9-15; Psalm 129; 2 Corinthians 4:13-5:1; Mark 3:20-35
In our first reading today from the Book of Genesis we read of how the serpent successfully tempted Adam and Eve and caused them to break God's law. God visits the garden and discovers their wrong-doings. In the gospel we see the scribes looking upon Jesus as Satan and attributing his powers to the Prince of Darkness. We also see Christ's mother, Mary, referred to in the text. As sin entered the world through Adam and Eve so through Jesus (the new Adam) and with the help of Mary (the new Eve) sin is wiped away. Those who believe in God and carry out his will are the ones who will be regarded as the mother, brother and sister of Christ.

In the second reading St Paul assures us that he who raised Jesus from the dead will raise us from the dead and give us eternal life but only if we believe in him and live a life worthy of that faith.

Eleventh Sunday in Ordinary Time

Ezekiel 17:22-24; Psalm 91; 2 Corinthians 5:6-10; Mark 4:26-34
In our first reading from the Prophet Ezekiel we see the Lord likening his presence and his kingdom to a noble cedar tree. The birds and other creatures who come to shelter by it represent the people of God. In the gospel, Jesus uses similar imagery to show

that the kingdom grows quietly but constantly and provides shelter and support to all who come to it.

In the second reading, St Paul regards our current, physical life as being an exile from the Lord – only when we leave this life can we become one with him. Whether we are in this life or the next, our goal is to do his will and only by doing his will in this life can we attain union with him in the next.

Twelfth Sunday in Ordinary Time

Job 3:1, 8-11; Psalm 106; 2 Corinthians 5:14-17; Mark 4:35-41

In the first reading from the Book of Job the Lord reminds Job that it is the Lord who has power over the elements. Job has suffered tremendous loss and suffering and has begun to question how things happen. In the gospel we see Christ exercise this power by calming the storm when the disciples grew afraid. This also serves to remind us that amid the turmoil and difficulties of everyday life the Lord is always with us to smooth things over and to give us the strength to endure them.

St Paul reminds us in the passage from his second letter to the Corinthians that those who believe in Christ are a new creation and that Christ is always with them.

Thirteenth Sunday in Ordinary Time

Wisdom 1:13-15, 2:23-24; Psalm 29; 2 Corinthians 8:7, 9, 13-15; Mark 5:21-43

In our first reading today from the Book of Wisdom we are told that God takes no pleasure in death. The author tells us that God created us to live but that it was the devil's jealousy which brought death into the world. In our gospel reading from St Mark we see Jesus raise a little girl who had died. In so doing he shows that he has power over life and death and can give life back whenever he wishes. While on the way to the little girl a woman in the crowd touches the hem of Christ's cloak and is instantly cured because she believed in Christ. We are called on today to have faith in Christ and to share with others knowing that a great reward awaits us – that of eternal life with Christ.

St Paul reminds us in the second reading that we should share what we have with those who are in need but he tells us that we don't have to suffer hardship in order to satisfy their need. We give what we can without going short ourselves.

Fourteenth Sunday in Ordinary Time
Ezekiel 2:2-5; Psalm 122; 2 Corinthians 12:7-10; Mark 6:1-6

We read in the text from Ezekiel how the Lord spoke to the prophet and sent him to preach his word. Whether the people believe or not the prophet will still speak to them. In the gospel passage from St Mark we see Jesus being rejected in his own home town because the people thought they knew him. As a result of their rejection of him he is unable to do very much for them because his ministry and mission depend on people both listening and believing. Christ will not force any of us to do his will and if we don't want to do his will then we simply ignore him as did the people in his home town. Christ is no longer physically present with us as a preacher, but his Church is and she preaches his message and brings forgiveness whether people wish to listen or not. As members of that Church each of us was commissioned at baptism to preach that message.

St Paul tells us in the second reading that no matter what people say or think he will continue to preach the word of God to them. He may be weak in the eyes of the world but he knows that at such times he is strongest in his mission and that Christ is with him.

Fifteenth Sunday in Ordinary Time
Amos 7:12-15; Psalm 84; Ephesians 1:3-14; Mark 6:7-13

In our first reading we see Amos being dismissed by Amaziah because Amaziah does not like the message which is being preached by Amos. Amos tells him that it is not his own message but God's message and that he preaches at God's command. In our gospel we see Jesus sending out the Twelve in pairs to preach and to cure. They do so and are successful because they do so in his name and with his authority. No matter what people may think, the message of God cannot be silenced simply because they may not like what it says or who it is who is preaching. We are the successors to the Twelve and we are the Church and so we too should proclaim the kingdom of God to the people of our own time whether they like it or not, knowing that a great reward lies in store for those who do listen and believe.

For our second reading for the next few weeks we turn to St Paul's letter to the Christians at Ephesus. In today's passage we are told that we were chosen by God before the world was created to be his own people. In choosing us he wants us to live in love and to be spotless in his sight. We do this by believing in him and living according to his precepts.

Sixteenth Sunday in Ordinary Time
Jeremiah 23:1-6; Psalm 22; Ephesians 2:13-18; Mark 6:30-34

In our first reading we see the Lord condemning those shepherds who have not cared for their flocks but have allowed them to be scattered and destroyed. The Lord says that he will raise up true shepherds who will properly pasture his sheep. In the gospel passage from St Mark – which is the conclusion to the passage begun last week – we see the Twelve returning to Jesus after they had been preaching in his name and they return rejoicing. They go off to be alone and to rest but the people follow them because they want to hear more about Christ and his message. He takes pity on them and teaches them himself. Little has changed between Christ's time and ours – the world badly needs those who will preach Christ's message of salvation. No matter who we are or what we do in life, as baptised Christians we were all commissioned to go out and to preach the Good News of the kingdom both in word and in the example of our lives. There are still many in our world who have not heard about Christ or who have forgotten about him or not really come to know him. Each of us has a duty to bring our fellow men and women to the truth and the knowledge of God.

In the second reading St Paul tells us that Christ is the link which joins so many people together in peace. All who believe in him, regardless of their skin colour or their nationality, have a place in the kingdom and so all are brothers and sisters in the eyes of God.

Seventeenth Sunday in Ordinary Time

2 Kings 4:42-44; Psalm 144; Ephesians 4:1-6; John 6:1-5

Our first reading and our gospel are strongly linked today because they both contain a similar miracle – the feeding of many people with small quantities of bread and fish. In the first reading from the second Book of the Kings we see the Prophet Elisha feeding a hundred men with twenty barley loaves which they ate and still had some to spare though they were all satisfied. Our gospel for the coming few weeks comes from the sixth chapter of St John's gospel which is often referred to as 'The Bread of Life Discourse.' Alone among the gospels, St John's does not contain the Institution Narrative from the Last Supper and this sixth chapter is seen as a development of the theology of the Eucharist for John and his community. In today's passage we see Jesus teaching more than five thousand people who he then feeds with five barley loaves and two small fish. Again the people eat all they want and are satisfied and still have some left over. We know that Christ feeds us with even greater bread than the people received from Elisha or Christ because we receive Christ's own body and blood which bring us eternal life rather than the fleeting satisfaction the people received from the barley loaves.

In our second reading, St Paul tells us that there is only one baptism and that we all belong to the one Lord. Therefore, as members of the Body of Christ, we must live in charity and peace but above all we must believe in Christ if we are to receive the eternal life which he promised.

Eighteenth Sunday in Ordinary Time

Exodus 16:2-4; Psalm 77; Ephesians 4:17, 20-24; John 6:24-35

In our first reading from the Book of Exodus, the Jewish people are travelling through the wilderness away from Egypt and they complain that they have nothing to eat. So the Lord provides them with manna – bread from heaven – to satisfy them. In the gospel passage from St John we see Jesus telling the people that he is the bread of life. The bread which the people had every day did not last and so they sought for something better. What Christ gives is eternal and comes from God. That bread is given to us at every celebration of the Mass and it will bring us eternal life.

In the second reading St Paul tells us that we must undergo a spiritual revolution and put aside our material desires. In so doing we will draw closer to Christ and to the eternal life he has promised to each of us.

Nineteenth Sunday in Ordinary Time
1 Kings 19:4-8; Psalm 33; Ephesians 4:30-5:2; John 6:41-51

We see a very dejected and hopeless Elijah in the first reading from the first Book of the Kings for he is being hounded by the people. He goes into the wilderness to escape but the angel of the Lord comes to him with food and drink which strengthens Elijah so that he can make the long journey to Mount Horeb. In the gospel we see Jesus again teaching the people that he is the bread of life which has come down from heaven and which can bring them eternal life. He is also very clear that it is his flesh which will give life to the world.

In the second reading St Paul exhorts us to live in the Spirit of God and to believe in Christ. We are to live in peace and harmony with one another. If we believe in Christ then this will be easy to do and we will inherit the kingdom which Jesus promised us in the gospel.

Twentieth Sunday in Ordinary Time
Proverbs 9:1-6; Psalm 33; Ephesians 5:15-20; John 6:51-58

In the text from the book of Proverbs we see Wisdom preparing a banquet for the people and telling them that if they eat her bread and wine then they will live and walk in the ways of perception. Jesus is often seen as the personification of Wisdom and in our gospel text he tells us that he is the true bread which has come down from heaven. The people are not happy to hear this but he tells them that those who eat his bread – that is his own body – will live for ever and he will live in them and they in him. St Paul calls on us in the second reading to be filled with the Holy Spirit. He warns us against drugging ourselves with the ways of this world but tells us that we should redeem this present age by the way in which we live. In recognising the will of God and living according to that will we can inherit eternal life.

Twenty-first Sunday in Ordinary Time

Joshua 24:1-2, 15-18; Psalm 33; Ephesians 5:21-32; John 6:60-69

In our first reading we see Joshua calling the people together at Shechem and asking them whom they wish to serve – the true God or the gods of the local peoples. They opt for the true God who led them from Egypt and say that they will not desert him. In the gospel we come to the end of the sixth chapter of St John's gospel and with it the end of the Bread of Life Discourse. Jesus has told the people that he is the bread of life, that only those who eat of his flesh can have eternal life, and that he is the Son of Man. Many of those who had listened to him are not happy at these words and so they leave him and refuse to listen to him again. On behalf of the disciples St Peter says that he will stay with Christ because he has the message of eternal life. We too must ask ourselves whether or not we believe in Christ's message and whether or not we follow the Lord as the people in the first reading swore to do. If we truly believe in the words Christ spoke then that should be evident in the way in which we treat others.

In the second reading from the letter to the Ephesians, St Paul calls on us to love and respect one another for we are all part of Christ's mystical body here on earth. Paul also reminds us that this has many implications for us and for how we should live.

Twenty-second Sunday in Ordinary Time

Deuteronomy 4:1-2, 6-8; Psalm 14; James 1:17-18, 21-22, 27; Mark 7:1-8, 14-15, 21-23

In the first reading from the Book of Deuteronomy, we see that Moses has given the people the Ten Commandments and he encourages them to be faithful to them. By the people being faithful to them, non-believers will come to see that there is indeed a God to be followed – a God who is close to his people. In the gospel we see Christ admonishing the authorities for over-emphasising the letter of the Law and not adhering at all to the spirit of the Law. Our readings today remind us that the commandments and the Law of God are there, not to make life difficult, but to give life, to improve the quality of life which we already have. Only by keeping the commandments of God as he intended them can we grow and inherit eternal life.

Our second reading for the next five weeks comes from the Letter of St James and in today's passage he is calling on the people to be faithful to the Lord and to follow the word of God without making any changes to that word for it is already perfect. The word contains instructions for living under the law of God and inheriting eternal life.

Twenty-third Sunday in Ordinary Time
Isaiah 35:4-7; Psalm 145; James 2:1-5; Mark 7:31-37

In our first reading we see God speaking through the Prophet Isaiah and telling the people that the one who is to free them is coming. Those who are blind will see, the deaf will hear, and the land will once again become fertile. In our gospel text from St Mark we see Jesus restoring hearing and speech just as the Lord promised through the Prophet Isaiah. Jesus is the fulfilment of God's word and he does bring us salvation and freedom – freedom from all that would keep us separate from God. The psalm, which is a song of praise, also reminds us that the Lord has done much for us – he protects us, he feeds us, he is faithful forever. And with that in mind we approach the Lord in a spirit of praise and thanksgiving.

In the Letter of St James we read that we should never judge people using different standards – we should always deal with people by using the same criteria for each person because everyone is equal in the eyes of God.

Twenty-fourth Sunday in Ordinary Time
Isaiah 50:5-9; Psalm 114; James 2:14-18; Mark 8:27-35

In the first reading we read a passage from Isaiah which we usually associate with Christ for he did offer his cheek to those who tore at his beard and he willingly accepted insult and injury for he knew that God was with him. In our gospel text from St Mark we see Jesus questioning the disciples as to who they think he is. St Peter makes his great profession of faith by saying that Jesus is the Christ, the Son of God. Jesus then goes on to tell them that he is to suffer and die, in fulfilment of the text we read from Isaiah, but the apostles do not fully understand what he is saying and so Peter tries to persuade him not to go to Jerusalem. Jesus rebukes him because he was, albeit through a lack of understanding, preventing Christ from carrying out his salvific mission. When we too prevent the kingdom of God from being realised on earth – even if it is simply because we do nothing – then we are no better than Satan who does not want the kingdom of God to become a reality.

In our second reading from St James the apostle reminds us that faith without good works is dead. It is not enough to say that we love God – we must let that faith be seen by the way in which we live our lives but without showing off or drawing attention to ourselves. In this way the faith of others and our own faith may be strengthened and renewed.

Twenty-fifth Sunday in Ordinary Time
Wisdom 2:12, 17-20; Psalm 53; James 3:16-4:3; Mark 9:30-37
In our first reading from the Book of Wisdom we see the people plotting the downfall of a virtuous child of God. Much of what is said brings to mind the Passion of Christ and the suffering he went through in silence for us. In the opening part of the gospel we see Jesus speaking about his forthcoming sufferings while we also see the disciples arguing on the road about who is the greatest. They had misinterpreted Christ's teachings about the kingdom and presumed that it would be a kingdom in which they would have honour and prestige. Ambition is a good thing but only if it is kept in check and if pursued for the right reason. In the second reading St James reminds us to be peacemakers and never to allow our ambition to go unchecked for it can lead us far from the love of God. Peacemakers live out every aspect of the gospel and this brings others to the faith.

Twenty-sixth Sunday in Ordinary Time
Numbers 11:25-29; Psalm 18; James 5:1-6; Mark 9:38-43, 45, 47-48
In the first reading from the Book of Numbers we see that some of the people want Moses to stop Medad and Eldad from prophesying because they were not at the Tent of Meeting when the Lord sent his spirit on the people. But Moses will not stop them because they have received the spirit of God, even if they did not go to the Tent. What is important is that they have received the spirit and prophesy on behalf of God. In the gospel, as in the first reading, the disciples want to stop those who are not of

their group from preaching but Christ will not stop them. God gives his Spirit as he sees fit and we must work with the Spirit wherever he reveals himself.

St James gives us a reminder in the second reading that wealth can corrupt and that it cannot be taken with us to the next life. If we lay too much store on our wealth then we can become greedy and so fail to live the life to which the Lord is calling us.

Twenty-seventh Sunday in Ordinary Time
Genesis 2:18-24; Psalm 127; Hebrews 2:9-11; Mark 10:2-16
The readings for today speak of the importance of the unity of the family of God. In our first reading from the Book of Genesis we have the creation of woman from the second account of Creation. Woman is created from the rib of man as his equal. In the gospel we have Christ's teaching on divorce which went against the norms of his time for Moses had allowed divorce into Jewish life. Christ overturned that practice and gave a greater sanctity and status to this great act of union between a man and a woman. Though this is not easy for everyone to live, it is something towards which the world must strive if is to remain faithful to the teaching of Christ.

For the remainder of this liturgical year our second reading comes from the Letter to the Hebrews which is written to an unknown group and is attributed to St Paul though it is accepted that he did not actually write it. In today's passage the author tells us that we are all of the same stock as Christ – we are all sons and daughters of God and Christ is our brother.

Twenty-eighth Sunday in Ordinary Time
Wisdom 7:7-11; Psalm 89; Hebrews 4:12-13; Mark 10:17-30
In our first reading today from the Book of Wisdom, the author is speaking about Wisdom as the greatest possession of all. He compares gold, silver and other precious objects to Wisdom and finds them to be insignificant. Christ has often been seen as the personification of Old Testament Wisdom and so in the first reading we can see that Christ is the greatest possession of all. In our gospel we have the theme of possessions. Christ tells the rich young man who comes to him that he must give up all he has if he is to inherit eternal life. We all need certain possessions

and material goods if we are to live a relatively comfortable life but we must never place them before the Lord because they too will prove to be a block to Christian living and to eternal life. Christ is the greatest possession of all and he must be the only possession that we strive for. The text also tells us that we must give to the poor because all of our possessions are a gift from God and should be shared with those who are less fortunate so that they too may realise the presence of God in their lives.

In our second reading from the letter to the Hebrews, the author tells us that the word of God is alive and active. Many people feel that religious belief and the scriptures are a collection of old, dry words but not for the author. Christ is the Word of God and is very much alive and active in the lives of those who believe in him.

Twenty-ninth Sunday in Ordinary Time
Isaiah 53:10-11; Psalm 32; Hebrews 4:14-16; Mark 10:35-45

Our first reading today comes from the 'Suffering Servant' section within the book of the Prophet Isaiah. In the passage we see that the servant of God will suffer for the people in order to justify them. We know that the servant is Christ and through his passion, death and resurrection he has justified all human beings. In the gospel we see Jesus reminding the apostles, and us also, that those who wish to do the will of God and enter into eternal life must be the servants of all people. We cannot dominate people but must help all people to achieve perfection and this is done with a great deal of humility on our part and with an example of true Christian living. Most of us will not be called to suffer for our faith as Christ did, but the suffering servant is the example which we must follow.

In the second reading from the letter to the Hebrews, the author tells us that we can confidently approach Christ with our weaknesses because Christ was human and knows our faults. Because of this, Christ will be merciful and gracious with us.

Alternative Gospel for Mission Sunday – Twenty-ninth Sunday, Year B:
Mark 10: 42-45
In the gospel for today we see Jesus reminding the apostles of the importance of service. Some had thought that being his followers would give them special places and privileges among the people but he is telling them that this is not the case. The Mission of the Church is to spread the Good News of the kingdom and this can only be done through humble service. If we too serve our fellow men and women following Christ's example then they will see the Body of Christ visible among them and we will have answered the Lord's call to us as baptised Christians.

Thirtieth Sunday in Ordinary Time
Jeremiah 31:7-9; Psalm 125; Hebrews 5:1-6; Mark 10:46-52
The book of the Prophet Jeremiah was written just before the Babylonian captivity and in it the prophet predicts the downfall of the Jewish people because of their iniquities. In our passage today we see the Lord telling the people that he will bring them back to their home. Despite all they have done he will heal and cure those who are sick and will comfort the people as he guides them. The psalm continues the theme of bondage in Babylon. In the gospel we see Jesus restoring sight to a blind man. As with all the miracles worked by Jesus the blind man had to ask for healing, which reminds us that nobody will be forced to accept the love of God. Jesus is also the fulfilment of the text from Jeremiah because he is the one who is leading us to our true homeland – which is the kingdom of God – and he comforts us as he does so.
The author of the letter to the Hebrews speaks today of the priesthood. He reminds us that nobody chooses to be a priest but is called to that service by God himself. Priests come from among the people – they are not born into a special class with superhuman powers – they are regular human beings with the same faults and failings as everybody else and because of this are able to intercede for us and to minister to us on God's behalf.

Thirty-first Sunday in Ordinary Time
Deuteronomy 6:2-6; Psalm 17; Hebrews 7:23-28; Mark 12:28-34
In our first reading today from the Book of Deuteronomy we see Moses encouraging the people to follow the Law of God and to keep his commandments. If they do this then they will live in the Lord's favour. The passage concludes with the *Shema Israel* – the great command to love God which is so central to Jewish faith. In the time of Christ the scribes were a very important group within Judaism because they were the ones who interpreted the Laws and sacred texts for the people. In today's gospel we see one of the scribes asking Jesus about the most important commandment to which Jesus replies with the *Shema Israel* which we read in the first reading. The scribe applauds the answer and then goes on to give an explanation of the text and is in turn applauded by Christ because he is so close to the kingdom. The *Shema Israel* is a text which we too should take to heart and ponder on, as it reminds us of the central role which God should play in our hearts and in our lives.

In the second reading from the letter to the Hebrews we are told that Christ's power to save is utterly certain. Christ is the ultimate high priest who retains his priesthood for ever and whose sacrifice for sin need never again be repeated. In the Temple it was the custom for each high priest to offer regular sacrifices to the Lord to atone for the sins of the people, but for us this was done by Christ and need never again be repeated. Our sins are wiped away and will continue to be wiped away if we turn to the Lord and ask for forgiveness with a genuine heart.

Thirty-second Sunday in Ordinary Time
1 Kings 17:10-16; Psalm 145; Hebrews 9:24-28; Mark 12:38-44
In the first reading from the first Book of the Kings we see the great Prophet Elijah arriving in the town of Sidon. There he meets a widow and asks her to make some bread for him. The widow replies that she and her son have nothing, but Elijah tells her not to worry for she will not die of starvation if she does as he asks. The widow trusts him and the words which the Lord addressed to her through Elijah and so she goes and makes some bread for him and, miraculously, there is more than enough for her son and for her to live on. The psalm is a psalm

of praise for all that the Lord does for us. In the gospel text from St Mark we see Jesus teaching the people. He sees a widow putting two small coins in the collection plate while several wealthy men put in a lot more. However, Christ praises the widow because unlike the men she had no surplus and so the money she contributed was money that she needed to live on while the men put in money which they would not miss. We are reminded in this text that being charitable with our surplus wealth is very easy while giving of what we need is something very different but is what we are called to do as Christians. Only in this way can we truly show to others the love of God present in our world. As Christ gave all that he had for our sakes so we are called on to give of what we need for his sake.

We are again reminded in our second reading today from the letter to the Hebrews that Christ has abolished all sacrifice for sin by his sacrifice of himself on the cross. Therefore we should live as a redeemed people who believe in their redemption and who want to enter eternal life.

Thirty-third Sunday in Ordinary Time
Daniel 12:1-13; Psalm 15; Hebrews 10:11-14, 18; Mark 13:24-32

The Book of the Prophet Daniel is the earliest statement of belief in the resurrection of the dead in the Old Testament. The author speaks of those who have been 'sleeping in the dust' coming back to life. Of those who come back to life some will go on to everlasting life while others to eternal shame. The psalm asks God to keep us faithful to him. In the gospel, Jesus tells us that the Son of Man will come in his glory and will gather to himself all those who have been faithful to him. The text reminds us that this will be at a time that we do not know and so we must always be prepared. Jesus also tells us that his words will never pass away but will always be there to remind the people of the faith. No matter what might happen in our world the message of Christ will never be silenced.

In the second reading, the author reminds us that through his suffering and death on the cross, Christ has perfected us. We no longer have to make offerings for sins, for Christ has made the one eternal offering which was himself. To enter heaven therefore, we need only to believe in Christ, to confess our sins and to live out our faith as we are called to do.

Our Lord Jesus Christ, Universal King

Daniel 7:13-14; Psalm 92; Apocalypse 1:5-8; John 18:33-37

The last Sunday of the Church's year is always celebrated as the solemnity of Our Lord Jesus Christ, Universal King. It is a reminder that everything comes from God through Jesus who is king of all. The first reading is taken from the vision of Daniel in the Old Testament in which Daniel sees the sovereignty and eternal kingdom bestowed upon the Son of Man. In the second reading from the Book of the Apocalypse we read that not only has the Son of Man been made universal king, but that he has also made us a line of kings to carry on his work and to serve God. In the gospel we read from St John's account of the Passion of Christ and, in the excerpt we have, we see Jesus standing before Pilate who asks him if he is a king. He tells Pilate that he is but not of the same sort of kingdom that Pilate would be familiar with. An important element in the account is that Christ tells Pilate that he was born in order to serve the truth and that all those who believe in the truth will listen to him.

SUNDAYS: YEAR C

In Year C our gospel is taken from St Luke which was written between 80 and 85AD. As it was written after the destruction of the Temple in Jerusalem (70AD) it would appear to have been written for a community questioning God's faithfulness to his promises. For Luke, Jesus is the unexpected fulfilment of the promises which are now extended to those outside the Chosen People. Luke shows us a Jesus who is rejected by the religious leaders of the day but not by the common people who make up their own mind about him. The Old Testament texts are chosen in respect of the texts from this gospel.

The second reading texts for this year come from those attributed to St Paul:

Week 1: The Lord's Baptism.

Weeks 2-8: 1 Corinthians was written about the year 54AD by Paul. It was probably written following reports Paul had received from some of his friends who had passed through or come from Corinth.

Weeks 9-14: The Letter to the Galatians was written by Paul about the year 54AD to defend himself against people who were telling the Galatians that Paul had 'softened' the gospel in order to gain converts. In the letter, Paul gives an outline of the gospel as he believed and taught it.

Weeks 15-18: The letter to the Colossians is Pseudo-Paul and was written between 70 and 80AD and was written to bolster the faith of the people and to correct errors in the faith which had crept in because of failure to keep to the teaching already received.

Weeks 19-22: The Letter to the Hebrews was written between 80 and 90AD and it is accepted that it was not written by Paul though it is attributed to him. It teaches that the old covenants are now replaced by the one everlasting sacrifice of Jesus Christ. It also exhorts the reader to remain steadfast with the Christian faith.

Week 23: The Letter to Philemon is a private letter written by Paul to a friend. In the letter, Paul is urging Philemon to accept back – without punishment – his slave who had run away. This slave, Onesimus, has been converted by Paul. While Paul doesn't appear to favour slavery or to support it, he doesn't explicitly try to stop it which is an indication of the social norms of the time.

Weeks 24-30: The two letters to Timothy are regarded as not being from Paul, having been written about the year 100AD. They both encourage

*the recipient to maintain the structures already found in the Church
and in society and also the maintenance of 'good order.' They also give
some guidelines for such things as the appointment of bishops.*
*Weeks 31-33: The second Letter to the Thessalonians was written some-
where between 51 and 100AD which leaves its authorship and, therefore, its understanding, open for question. The emphasis in this letter is
on the Lord's second coming which will be one of triumph.*

First Sunday in Ordinary Time – The Baptism of the Lord
Isaiah 40:1-5, 9-11; Psalm 103; Titus 2:11-14, 3:4-7; Luke 3:15-16, 21-22
Our first reading today from the Prophet Isaiah is a call to the
people to rise up and be consoled, for their liberation is now at
hand. The Lord has now come to them and he will gather them
together as a shepherd gathers his sheep. It is an appropriate
text for the celebration of the Lord's baptism because with his
baptism Jesus began his public ministry – at his baptism he was
revealed to the people and God signalled his approval of him.
At the Epiphany we celebrated the revelation of our salvation to
the Magi but now we celebrate his revelation to all the people
and the preaching of the Good News. Our gospel passage recounts Christ's baptism by John in the Jordan as told by St Luke.
In it, the Father witnesses to his own Son and says that he is the
Chosen One in fulfilment of the text from Isaiah.
The second reading from St Paul also tells us that Christ was
filled with the Holy Spirit, that he cured those who came to him,
and that he is the Lord of all people. He also tells us that God has
no favourites – each one who does the will of the Father will
receive the inheritance promised if they believe in Christ. At our
own baptism we became God's chosen ones in a special way
and by living out Paul's instructions we will help to bring
Christ's glory to the whole world.

Second Sunday in Ordinary Time
Isaiah 62:1-5; Psalm 95; 1 Corinthians 12:4-11; John 2:1-11
A common theme in our readings today is that of marriage. In
our first reading from the prophet Isaiah we see that the Lord
will marry his people. As a result they will never be abandoned
by him but he will always delight in them. In the gospel text
from St John we have the miracle at the wedding feast in Cana. It

was Our Lady who noticed the potential embarrassment which the family were about to suffer and she asked her Son to intervene. Despite the fact that Christ's hour had not yet come, he answered his mother's request and, as a result, we are told that the apostles believed in him – they finally had proof that he was somebody great.

In the second reading from the first letter to the Corinthians, St Paul tells us that we each have gifts and that these gifts have been given to us by the Holy Spirit. No matter what the gift is or who has been given it, the gift is always given 'for a good purpose'. We come before the Lord today knowing that he is always with us and that he will answer our prayers and particularly the intercession which his Mother makes on our behalf.

Third Sunday in Ordinary Time
Nehemiah 8:2-6, 8-10; Psalm 18; 1 Corinthians 12:12-30; Luke 1:1-4, 4:14-21

In our first reading today from the Prophet Nehemiah, we see Ezra reading the Law to the people. They had assembled for the purpose of the reading of the Law so that they might know it and through it know how to serve their God in fidelity. As the psalm tells us: 'The law of the Lord is perfect, it revives the soul.' In the gospel we read from the opening chapters to St Luke's gospel in which he sets out why it is that he is writing the gospel. We also read of Jesus preaching in his home synagogue in Nazareth and telling the people that he is the fulfilment of the text. He came to bring the Good News to all peoples and he gave that message and mission to us. We do this by living according to the Law of God and by living as members of Christ's mystical body here on earth.

In the second reading St Paul tells us that we are all parts of the one body which makes up the Body of Christ. For a body to function perfectly it needs all the parts to work together in harmony. So it is with the Body and family of Christ here on earth: if the Church is to grow and be the true presence of Christ on earth, then all of us must do our share for that body.

Fourth Sunday in Ordinary Time
Jeremiah 1:4-5, 17-19; Psalm 70; 1 Corinthians 12:31-13:13; Luke 4:21-30
In our first reading today we read of the call of Jeremiah to be the Lord's prophet. He calls him to speak his words to his people and tells him straight out that he will be rejected by the people but he is still to go and speak to them, for the Lord himself will be with him. In our gospel passage we see Jesus preaching and at first the people marvel at what they hear. But as he speaks about the prophets Elijah and Elisha they become angry and drive him out of the synagogue, intending to kill him, because they do not want to hear his words. The readings remind us that we are called to proclaim the kingdom of God just as Jeremiah was called in his turn and that we will be rejected just as Christ was rejected. Just as God was with Jeremiah so too will he be with us in our mission.

In our second reading from the first letter to the Corinthians we have St Paul's tremendous passage on love which is common at wedding ceremonies and becoming common at funeral liturgies. Unless we have love as the guiding principle of our lives, then our work for the kingdom will not bear fruit.

Fifth Sunday in Ordinary Time
Isaiah 6:1-8; Psalm 137; 1 Corinthians 15:1-11; Luke 5:1-11
In our readings last week we saw the Lord calling us to be his prophets. In today's first reading we see Isaiah answering the Lord's call and volunteering to be the Lord's messenger to the people. At the same time, however, Isaiah acknowledges that he is not fit for this task for he is a sinner. The Lord then takes away his sin. In the gospel we see Jesus by the lake of Gennesaret where he meets Simon Peter, as well as the brothers James and John. They have been out all night and have caught nothing but, at Jesus' command, they cast their nets again and net a huge haul of fish. Peter realises he stands before someone truly great and asks to be left alone for he is a sinner. Still Jesus calls him and they follow him. Last week we were called to be God's prophets; this week we are reminded of those who answered that call and what it is that we are asked to preach. It is now for us to decide whether or not we want to answer the call and live

up to the commitments which were made at our baptism and which we ourselves renewed last Easter. There is also a reminder that God knows our inmost being, he knows of what we are made and still he calls us.

In the second reading we see St Paul reminding the Corinthians, and ourselves, about the basis of the Christian faith. He recalls their basic beliefs about Jesus and the resurrection as he taught them and he reminds them of how unworthy he himself was for this important work.

Sixth Sunday in Ordinary Time

Jeremiah 17:5-8; Psalm 1; 1 Corinthians 15:12, 16-20; Luke 6:17, 20-26

In our first reading today from the book of the Prophet Jeremiah we are reminded that we must always place our trust in God. While in life we have to trust in our fellow men and women – and this is a good thing – ultimately, we must place our trust first and foremost in God because there is only so much our fellow men and women can do for us while God can give us eternal life. This theme is continued in the psalm. In the gospel, we have St Luke's account of the Beatitudes – Christ's great blueprint for living as recounted by Luke. In all that is done or suffered, it is God who grants the reward, not man. All of this comes to pass because Christ has been raised from the dead.

In the second reading from the first letter to the Christians at Corinth, we are reminded that Christ's resurrection doesn't simply have an impact in this life but in eternal life. So too, trusting in man can only be for this life while trusting in God and living according to the Beatitudes and the gospel precepts brings eternal life to all.

Seventh Sunday in Ordinary Time

1 Samuel 26:2, 7-9, 12-13, 22-23; Psalm 102; 1 Corinthians 15:45-49; Luke 6:27-38

In our first reading from the first Book of Samuel, we read of an incident in the life of King David some time before he became King of Israel. David had been the loyal servant of King Saul but Saul feared and detested David's popularity amongst the people. So Saul set off in pursuit of David intending to end his life. David and his men come upon Saul during the night and creep into the king's camp but do not harm the king – David refuses to harm the Lord's anointed even when it was in his power to end the king's life. Our psalm reminds us that 'The Lord is compassion and love' and that he forgives us when we stray from his love. The gospel passage from St Luke is a continuation of last week's text in which we had the Beatitudes. Today we are told that we are to be compassionate to our fellow men and women just as God has been compassionate with us. The Old Law was very much an eye for an eye and a tooth for a tooth but the New Law – which Jesus has established – is built on forgiveness and not revenge, on reconciliation and not retribution, on love and not war. The last line of the gospel also reminds us that as we deal with others so too will we be dealt with by others.

In the second reading St Paul tells us that there are two key men: the first is Adam and the second is Christ. The second is the one whom we must follow if we are to gain eternal life and we do this by modelling ourselves on him and living according to the precepts which he laid down for us in today's gospel.

Eighth Sunday in Ordinary Time

Ecclesiasticus 27:4-7; Psalm 91; 1 Corinthians 15:54-58; Luke 6:39-45
In the first reading from the Book of Ecclesiasticus we are told that we should not praise a man before he has spoken, for it is in his speech that we find his true feelings and beliefs. The psalm reminds us that it is good to give thanks to the Lord and that the just will flourish. Taking up the sentiments of the first reading, Christ tells us in the gospel that a man's words come from his heart: if his heart is filled with love of the Lord then his words will reflect this and he will speak of peace, but if his heart is filled with malice then his words will be against the kingdom. Jesus also warns us about being hypocrites and tells us that we should not point out faults in others when we have faults of our own.

In the second reading St Paul reminds us that as long as we strive for the kingdom, death will have no power over us. Death only has power through sin but if we avoid sin and live lives according to the gospel then we will gain eternal life and will join Christ in defeating death.

Ninth Sunday in Ordinary Time
1 Kings 8:41-43; Psalm 116; Galatians 1:1-2, 6-10; Luke 7:1-10
In our first reading from the first Book of the Kings we see
Solomon giving instruction to his people. He tells them that people will hear of the nation of Israel and will then come to them
seeking help. When they come seeking they are to be given
every possible help and kindness. We can understand that as
Christians we are the successors to the nation of Israel as the
Lord's Chosen and so people will come to us seeking the kingdom and we are to offer them every help to enter that kingdom.
The psalm reminds us to 'Go out to the whole world and proclaim the good news.' In the gospel from St Luke we see Jesus
receiving a request to heal the servant of a Roman centurion. He
sets off to the man's house but the man doesn't feel worthy
enough to have Jesus under his roof but has such faith in Christ
that all he needs is for Jesus to say the word and his servant will
be healed. (words which we will use ourselves just after the
'Lamb of God')This is the sort of faith to which we are called – a
faith which does not need Jesus to physically walk into a room
for us to be convinced of his power. The centurion didn't see
Jesus and yet he believed that his request would be answered.
We too are asked to have complete trust in God and his Son no
matter what.
For the next few weeks we read from St Paul's letter to the
Christian community at Galatia and today he reminds us that
there is only one version of the Good News and that we must always be faithful to it and not throw in our lot with others who
preach a more relaxed version which only seeks to win human
approval.

Tenth Sunday in Ordinary Time
1 Kings 17:17-24; Psalm 29; Galatians 1:11-19; Luke 7:11-17
We read in the first reading today from the first Book of the
Kings that the son of the woman who has been looking after the
Prophet Elijah has died. She is distraught and asks Elijah to
bring her son back to life. He prays to God and the boy is restored to his mother. The woman now believes in Elijah and all
that he says. It is also proof that the Lord does answer our
prayers when we call to him. In the gospel we have an almost

identical incident from the life of Christ. As he was moving through the town of Nain he came upon a funeral procession in which an elderly widow was taking her only son for burial. Jesus felt sorry for the woman and restored the young man to life. A key phrase in the gospel are the words used by the by-standers: 'God has visited his people.' In the person of Elijah and of his divine Son, God visited two women and comforted them. Each day he visits us to hear our prayers and to comfort us and so all we need to do is to ask and he will answer us.

In the second reading St Paul tells us that the message which he is passing on to us is not a human message but is the very word of God. This message was given to him by God himself and therefore it is to be accepted as the truth and not some human work of fiction.

Eleventh Sunday in Ordinary Time

2 Samuel 12:7-10, 13; Psalm 31; Galatians 2:16, 19-21; Luke 7:36-8:3

In our first reading from the second Book of Samuel we read of the condemnation of King David who has arranged for the death of one of his officers so that he could marry the dead man's wife who was already pregnant with the king's child. David was the Lord's anointed and despite all that the Lord had done for him he still turned from the Lord. However, at the end of the reading we hear that the Lord has forgiven David's sins and David will not die for what he has done. The psalm is a prayer to God asking him to forgive our sins. In the gospel we see Jesus in the home of one of the Pharisees. While at table a woman of ill-repute comes in and washes his feet with her tears and wipes them with her hair. Jesus acknowledges that she is a sinner but he tells her that her many sins are forgiven. This is in stark contrast to the Pharisee and the others who had never given her a chance but continued to condemn her. In the second reading we are told by St Paul that mere observance of the Law will not bring eternal life. In his time people put too much emphasis on the letter of the Law rather than on faith and Paul is reversing this. If we have faith then we can be saved but if we simply carry out the letter of the Law and have no faith then we will not be saved. Part of that life of faith is acknowledging our sins and asking the Lord's forgiveness while also forgiving others who we perceive to have hurt us.

Twelfth Sunday in Ordinary Time
Zechariah 12:10-11, 13:1; Psalm 62; Galatians 3:26-29; Luke 9:18-24
In the first reading from the Prophet Zechariah, the Lord tells us that he will 'pour out a spirit of kindness and prayer' on his people. The people will mourn for the one whom they have pierced because of their sins. In the gospel we see Jesus at prayer when he asks his disciples who people think he is. The answer he is really after is who the disciples themselves think he is. St Peter answers immediately and says that he is 'The Christ of God' – showing that Peter has already grasped who Jesus truly is. Jesus then tells them to say nothing of this because his time has not yet come. He goes on tell them that he will suffer – he is the pierced one spoken of in the first reading and the fountain for the people will be his own blood. Those who want to follow him into eternal life must give up their life in this world in order to save it for eternal life.
In the second reading St Paul reminds us that we are all sons and daughters of God without any distinction. Therefore we should act accordingly and strengthen our faith so that, like Peter, we too can say without hesitation – 'You are the Christ of God.'

Thirteenth Sunday in Ordinary Time
1 Kings 19:16, 19-21; Psalm 15; Galatians 5:1, 13-18; Luke 9:51-62
In our first reading from the first Book of the Kings we see Elijah appointing Elisha as his successor as God had instructed him. Elisha was ploughing the land when Elijah found him and – having initially asked to say goodbye to his people – he leaves his men and his fields and follows the great prophet. In the gospel passage from St Luke we see Jesus heading resolutely for Jerusalem and his impending Passion and death. Along the way he meets three men: one who promises to follow him but is dismissed by Christ, and two others who are unable to follow him just then. Because of their conditions they are sent home by Christ. This is a reminder to us that following Christ is a wholehearted and total commitment – one which can have no conditions on our part.
In the second reading we are told by St Paul that the Spirit brings us liberty and so we should act accordingly. With the Spirit in us we will not act in any self-indulgent way but will

give ourselves completely to the Lord. We should pray, therefore, that we may have this Spirit in full measure so that we may answer the Lord's call to follow him with our whole heart, trusting in him alone.

Fourteenth Sunday in Ordinary Time
Isaiah 66:10-14; Psalm 65; Galatians 6:14-18; Luke 10:1-12, 17-20
In our first reading from the Prophet Isaiah we read that the Lord will send peace upon his chosen one like a flowing river. In the gospel we see the Lord appointing seventy two disciples and sending them out to spread his message. The first word they are to speak to people is the word 'Peace,' and they are to stay with the people and bring the Lord's healing and comfort to them. But Jesus is aware that they will not all be received with open arms for there will be those who do not want his peace and so will reject his messengers. In this case the messenger is to move on to those who will accept the message. As successors of the seventy two we have a duty and a responsibility to spread peace throughout the world, each in his or her own way. When we are rejected for doing this we must remember and take courage in the fact that Christ too was rejected and yet he has been raised to eternal life and we too will be raised for being faithful to him.
As we come to the end of St Paul's letter to the Galatians he reminds his readers that they are to remain faithful to the message of Christ. If they do not then they will not live in peace. He also reminds them that external signs, such as circumcision, are irrelevant compared to what is to be found within the heart of each believer.

Fifteenth Sunday in Ordinary Time
Deuteronomy 30:10-14; Psalm 68; Colossians 1:15-20; Luke 10:25-37
In our first reading from the Book of Deuteronomy we see Moses speaking to the people about the Word of God. He tells them that the word is very close to them – so close in fact that they can observe it. The word is not hidden from them in heaven but is among them: it is in their mouths and in their hearts. In our gospel text for today we have the story of the Good Samaritan. This kind man is shown in stark contrast to those who passed the victim by and did nothing and shows us that

there must be no discrimination in our hearts with regard to our fellow men and women. The Word of God is among us and he walks this earth in the hearts of all whom we meet if we but open our eyes to that and seek him there.

For today and the next three Sundays our second reading comes from St Paul's letter to the church in Colossae. In today's passage he tells us that Christ has existed before all time and from him comes all of creation. Everything that exists, even those in authority, owes their being to him. If we acknowledge that fact then we will find the Word of God wherever we go and we will be able to show that Word to our fellow men and women as did the Good Samaritan.

Sixteenth Sunday in Ordinary Time
Genesis 18:1-10; Psalm 14; Colossians 1:24-28; Luke 10:38-42
In our Old Testament reading today we see Abraham at the Oak of Mamre when three men pass by. He recognises them as friends and invites them to break their journey for some refreshments with him, before hurrying off to prepare a lavish meal for them. They ask after Sarah and tell Abraham that when they pass again the following year, Sarah will have given birth. We know in fact, that Sarah was well on in years but that the promise made was fulfilled in the birth of Isaac. In the gospel we see Jesus visiting the home of his friends Mary, Martha and Lazarus, though Lazarus is not mentioned in this passage. Mary sits down to listen to the Lord while Martha fusses over the hospitality. When she points this out to Jesus he tells her to follow Mary's example because while Mary is not being impolite about looking after her guest, she has recognised the importance of spending time with her Lord and listening to him as he speaks directly to her.

We are told in the second reading from the letter to the Colossians that the message of God was a mystery which was hidden for centuries but which, in Christ, has been revealed for all to see. If we are to see and understand this message then we must make time for the Lord when he passes our way, to prepare a place of welcome for him as did Abraham and to listen attentively to him as did Mary.

Seventeenth Sunday in Ordinary Time
Genesis 18:20-32; Psalm 137; Colossians 2:12-14; Luke 11:1-13
In our first reading from the Book of Genesis we see the Lord speaking with Abraham about the cities of Sodom and Gomorrah and their sins. The Lord decides to wipe them off the face of the earth but Abraham asks the Lord to relent for not all the people are evil. He begins by asking the Lord to spare them if there are fifty just men in the town and finally persuades the Lord to spare the people if there are but ten just men found there. The Lord listens to the pleas of Abraham and relents each time. The psalm is a hymn of thanksgiving to the Lord for listening to the cries of his servant. In our gospel text we see Jesus teaching the disciples how to pray and he gives them the 'Our Father.' He goes on to tell them – through an example – that if anyone calls on God, their prayers will not go unanswered. All too often people forget that 'no' is also an answer, as is silence. In answering our prayers the Lord does not always give us what we want because what we want might not be what we need or for our good.

St Paul tells us in the second reading that all our sins have been wiped away because they have been nailed to the cross with Christ whose sacrifice sets us free. No matter what we do we always have the Lord on our side and he is ready to forgive our sins and to answer our prayers whenever we turn to him in faith and trust.

Eighteenth Sunday in Ordinary Time
Ecclesiastes 1:2, 2:21-23; Psalm 89; Colossians 3:1-5, 9-11; Luke 12:13-21
Our first reading from the Book of Ecclesiastes is a stark reminder to us that all that we work for in life will go to someone else when our time on this earth is over. No matter how much we amass in this life it will not go with us beyond the grave. The psalm reminds us of how short life is. This theme is also found in the gospel where we see Jesus teaching people about the futility of amassing worldly wealth. The only wealth that is of real use to us is in the Spirit. This is not to say that we shouldn't work in this life but rather that we should have our goal fixed firmly on eternal life rather than on our bank balance.

The second reading too tells us that our thoughts should be on heavenly things rather than on the things of this earth. Only then can we inherit the kingdom and really reach out to our fellow men and women and lead them towards our true homeland in heaven.

Nineteenth Sunday in Ordinary Time
Wisdom 18:6-9; Psalm 32; Hebrews 11:1-2, 8-19; Luke 12:32-48
In our first reading today from the book of Wisdom we see that the virtuous will have the Lord on their side. When they turn to the Lord in sincerity and seek his help and protection he will be there to guard them. In our gospel, Jesus tells us to always stand ready and uses different examples to re-enforce his point. He tells us that if our treasure is to be found in worldly possession then our heart will be there rather than focused on the things of heaven where it belongs. We are also told that we are responsible for the things and people that are placed in our care and in this he includes the Good News of the kingdom. As baptised Christians we each have a duty to spread the news of the kingdom throughout the world in whatever way we can. One important point which the Lord brings out is that we do not know when we will be called to give an account of our stewardship and so we must always be ready whether we are called tomorrow or next year.

We now turn to the Letter to the Hebrews for our second reading for the coming weeks and in today's passage we are reminded of the faith of Abraham who went where the Lord asked him to go though he did not know what he would find there. If we have faith and live a life of faith then we will have nothing to worry about for the Lord will always be with us and our sights will always be firmly fixed on the kingdom. In this way, when the Lord comes, he will find us ready and waiting to enter our eternal inheritance.

Twentieth Sunday in Ordinary Time
Jeremiah 38:4-6, 8-10; Psalm 39; Hebrews 12:1-4; Luke 12:49-53
In the first reading we read of the attempted murder of the Prophet Jeremiah by some of the king's men. This was because the prophet had spoken the word of God to the people and they did not like what he said and were afraid that he would

influence the king. The psalm could easily have been the words on the prophet's lips as he sank into the mud: 'Lord, come to my aid!' In our gospel text for today we have an unusual lesson from Jesus in which he tells us that he did not come to bring peace but division. This seems to fly in the face of all that we have ever heard about Christ and yet when we look at places like the former Yugoslavia, like Rwanda, like Northern Ireland we see just how much belief in Christ has divided our world as people try to impose their understanding of the Good News on their neighbours. Yet, this is not the division which Jesus is speaking of for in reality he is talking about the division between good and evil, between those who opt for life over death. Only by following his ways can we walk the path of righteousness which leads to eternal life.

The author of today's second reading from the letter to the Hebrews urges us to keep our sights fixed firmly on Jesus in order to gain eternal life. He says this because of the number of opposing and competing views that were trying to win the allegiance of the people. In all of this we have the Lord as our advocate and the Holy Spirit as our guide.

Twenty-first Sunday in Ordinary Time
Isaiah 66:18-21; Psalm 116; Hebrews 12:5-7, 11-13; Luke 13:22-30
In our first reading we see that the Lord is going to gather all of his Chosen People from wherever they have been scattered and return them to Jerusalem. They will come in chariots, on horse back, on stretchers, but they will come to Jerusalem. In the gospel, Jesus tells us that there will be a gathering of the nations in the kingdom of heaven. But he also warns us that not everyone will be saved because there will be those who will not believe in him or in his message until it is too late and these people will be left out in the cold while the faithful will enter paradise to take their places along with the prophets of old. It is a reminder to us that we must live up to our responsibilities as baptised Christians sooner rather than later and to take an active part in the spread of the gospel.

In our second reading from the letter to the Hebrews, the author tells us that some of us will be punished by the Lord but this should not be a cause of worry for – in punishing us – the Lord acknowledges us as his sons and daughters. His punishment, therefore, is intended to make better people of us. Of course we can avoid such action by living according to the gospel precepts, beginning today.

Twenty-second Sunday in Ordinary Time
Ecclesiasticus 3:17-20, 28-29; Psalm 67; Hebrews 12:18-19, 22-24; Luke 14:1, 7-14
Our Old Testament reading today warns us to be a humble people. Humility is far better than pride and the humble are loved more than a generous giver because many people will take what they want from a philanthropist without thinking too much about him, so long as they can get what they can. The psalm reminds us that the Lord is the one who protects the widow and orphan and those who are powerless. The theme of humility is taken up in the gospel passage from St Luke where Jesus is the guest of a Pharisee. He also tells the people that those who give parties for the poor and the destitute are the truly generous ones for they are giving to people who cannot give to them in return. By giving to those who can give to us we do nothing but fool ourselves into false humility. The Lord knows the inmost heart and he knows whether we are really humble or not.
In our final excerpt from the letter to the Hebrews, the author reminds the Hebrews that they have come to the true God and with him everyone is regarded as a first-born son and therefore a citizen of heaven. As citizens of heaven, then, we should act like we truly believe and so show the way for others, that they too may become citizens.

Twenty-third Sunday in Ordinary Time
Wisdom 9:13-18; Psalm 89; Philemon 9-10, 12-17; Luke 14:25-33
The first reading from the Old Testament reminds us that without the Wisdom of God it would be impossible for us to know what lies in the heavens. We know that the Wisdom of God is Christ and that he died for us so that we might enter the heavenly kingdom. To help us reach that goal he sent us the Holy Spirit to be our guide. In the gospel passage from St Luke, Jesus tells us that we must give up all we posses if we are to be his disciples. While we do need some possessions in order to live or for the

world to develop, we must not put our trust in these possessions alone but must treasure God above all else. If we do this then we will come to know the Wisdom of God and will inherit the kingdom of heaven which is worth more than any earthly possession we could ever wish for.

In our second reading from St Paul's brief letter to Philemon, we read that Paul is sending Onesimus back to Philemon. Onesimus is a slave who has run away from his master. In sending him back, Paul is complying with the law but he is also doing so in the hope that Onesimus will be treated as a free man as his master is a Christian. Onesimus is returning because even though he does not know for sure what lies in store, as a Christian he has already been freed from oppression through the power of Christ. This is the spirit which we too must have and must place our trust in God rather than in the things and people of this life. Only then will we inherit eternal life.

Twenty-fourth Sunday in Ordinary Time
Exodus 32:7-11, 13-14; Psalm 50; 1 Timothy 1:12-17; Luke 15:1-32

In our first reading from the Book of Exodus we see Moses on the mountain with the Lord to receive the Ten Commandments. While Moses was on the mountain the people had turned from God and created a golden calf which they worshipped. The Lord is enraged and resolves to punish them but Moses pleads for the people before the Lord and the Lord relents. The psalm is a prayer seeking God's forgiveness and his strength. In the gospel text for today we have a number of stories about finding something which has gone astray and rejoicing at its return. The first sees a man who has lost a sheep, the second a woman who has lost a drachma and the third the story of the Prodigal Son. The stories, of course, symbolise the love of the Father for each and every one of us, a Father who is ready and waiting to accept us back after we have strayed from the right path. Once we turn to him he will restore us to that path and help us along the way to salvation. The stories came about because many of the scribes and Pharisees complained about Jesus eating and associating with people they regarded as sinners. Jesus tells them that the virtuous are already on the path to eternal life and so he does not need to convince them any further. But those who are straying from the path need a gentle reminder and that was why he associated with those who the self-righteous saw as sinners. It is also a reminder that the Lord judges by standards different to our own. Today we are challenged to honestly look at our own lives and to seek the forgiveness of God in order to prepare ourselves for entry to eternal life.

In the second reading, St Paul emphasises this point and tells us that Christ came into the world to save sinners, of which Paul says that he himself is the greatest. Paul also gives thanks to God for this.

Twenty-fifth Sunday in Ordinary Time
Amos 8:4-7; Psalm 112; 1 Timothy 2:1-8; Luke 16:1-13

In our first reading, the Prophet Amos speaks to the people on behalf of God and warns them to be honest and upright in their dealings with people, especially with the poor and those who have no voice to protect them from the unscrupulous. Our gospel passage sees Jesus warning us about the dangers of money and wealth. He affirms that money is necessary but also says that those who are dishonest when it comes to money will also prove themselves dishonest when it comes to real treasure – that is the treasures of the kingdom of God. The passage finishes with Jesus reminding us that, in reality, we can only serve one master and so we have a choice to make – to serve God or to serve the material things of this world – one will lead to eternal life while the other will lead to death.

In the second reading St Paul calls on each of us to pray for our fellow men and women through 'petitions, intercessions and thanksgiving' so that all may come to the true knowledge of God and so inherit the kingdom.

Twenty-sixth Sunday in Ordinary Time
Amos 6:1, 4-7; Psalm 145; 1 Timothy 6:11-16; Luke 16:19-31

Through the Prophet Amos in the first reading we see the Lord warning the people that because of their faith in earthly things and their disloyalty to him they will suffer destruction – all that they have will be taken from them because of their fickleness. The psalm reminds us of the faithfulness of God and of all that he does for his people. In the gospel, Jesus gives us the story of the rich man and the poor man named Lazarus. The rich man failed to really take notice of the poor man or to reach out to him and help him. As a result the rich man went to Hades while the poor man went to heaven. Despite all the warnings and all the teachings from and about God the rich man failed to heed them and so suffers after his death for his misdeeds. The story is a reminder to us that we have all been given the Good News with its promise of eternal life but it is now up to us to actually take those lessons on board and secure our place in heaven.

In the second reading from his first letter to St Timothy, we see St Paul encouraging Timothy to be faithful to the teaching to which he has dedicated his life so that he may secure for himself eternal life.

Twenty-seventh Sunday in Ordinary Time

Habakkuk 1:2-3, 2:2-4; Psalm 94; 2 Timothy 1:6-8, 13-14; Luke 17:5-10
In our first reading from the Prophet Habakkuk we are told that the 'upright man will live by his faithfulness'. At times we all struggle and wonder if God is present, but the reading reminds us that God is always there even in the most difficult of moments. In our gospel text from St Luke we see Jesus exhorting the disciples to unwavering faith in response to their quest for greater faith. They had asked him to increase their faith but his reply puts the onus back on them to increase their own faith. Faith is a free gift from God to all of his sons and daughters but it is also a gift which we must work at if it is to achieve its potential in our lives.

In our second reading we see St Paul exhorting his readers to 'fan into a flame the gift that God gave' them, a gift which was not a quiet thing but a thing of great power and love. This can be done with the assistance of the Holy Spirit if we but open our hearts to his power within us.

Twenty-eighth Sunday in Ordinary Time

2 Kings 5:14-17; Psalm 97; 2 Timothy 2:8-13; Luke 17:11-19
In our first reading today from the second Book of the Kings we read of the cure of the leper Naaman. He had come to the Prophet Elisha who told him to bathe seven times in the Jordan.

Having been cured, he returned to Elisha and proclaimed that he now believed in the one true God and that he would offer holocaust to none other. In the gospel we have the story of the ten lepers who were cured of their disease by Christ in answer to their request. Sadly, only one of the ten gave thanks for the cure and he, we are told, was a foreigner – someone who did not share the same faith as the Jews with Jesus. The story reminds us of Naaman in the first reading who was not a Jew but who gave thanks to God for his own cure. The point of the two stories is that we must give thanks to God for what we have because everything that we have comes from his bounty. All too often we take what we have for granted and it is only when others from outside the faith give thanks that we realise how arrogant we have really been.

In the second reading from his second letter to St Timothy, St Paul reminds us that God is always faithful. Even when we go astray and walk away from him, God is always there to welcome us back and to lead us home to paradise.

Twenty-ninth Sunday in Ordinary Time

Exodus 17:8-13; Psalm 120; 2 Timothy 3:14-4:2; Luke 18:1-8

In our Old Testament reading we see the Israelites engaging the Amalekites with Joshua at their lead. Throughout the battle, Moses remains on the hilltop and while his arms were raised the Israelites prospered, but, when his arms dropped, the Israelites suffered. The psalm is a hymn which reminds us that the Lord is at our side as our help and our strength as he was to the Israelites during the battle against the Amalekites. In the gospel Jesus tells a parable about a widow who comes before a certain judge. She continually pesters the judge because she did not have the money to bribe him. The moral of the parable is that as long as we believe in God and call on his name then we will prevail in the same way that the Israelites prevailed as long as Moses was able to keep the staff of God held up in his arms.

In the second reading we are told by St Paul to spread the Good News of the kingdom and to insist on it whether it is welcome or not. We are also to correct any errors in the faith or the preaching and we are to call people to obedience to the Good News. In all this we are to 'do all with patience and with the intention of teaching.'

Thirtieth Sunday in Ordinary Time

Ecclesiasticus 35:12-14, 16-19; Psalm 32; 2 Timothy 4:6-8, 16-18; Luke 18:9-14

Our first reading from the Book of Ecclesiasticus tells us that the Lord takes no account of our standing in the eyes of the world but that he listens to rich and poor alike. It also tells us that the prayer of the humble 'pierces the clouds' and does not go unanswered. Our psalm is a hymn of praise for all that the Lord has done for the poor who call to him. In the gospel we have the parable of the tax collector and the Pharisee who went to the synagogue. The Pharisee exalted himself in the eyes of God while the tax collector acknowledged himself as a sinner and asked the Lord for forgiveness. We can exalt ourselves in the eyes of our fellow men and women but the eyes of God penetrate the heart and the mind and know our true feelings and dispositions. Only the humble please God.

In our second reading we see St Paul telling St Timothy that he had been abandoned by everyone when he had been arrested but that God alone stood by him and gave him strength. Because Paul has the Lord faithfully on his side he will inherit the crown of righteousness, a crown which will also be granted to us if we serve the Lord in humility of heart.

Alternative Gospel for Mission Sunday – Thirtieth Sunday, Year C:

Luke 24:46-48

In the gospel we see Jesus pointing out to the disciples that scripture foretells that the Christ should suffer and rise from the dead. He also tells them that repentance would be preached to the whole world beginning in Jerusalem. The city of Jerusalem is where Christ was to suffer, die and rise again and it was from here that the disciples began the great work of spreading the Gospel message. We are the successors to the disciples and so on this Mission Sunday we are reminded that we too must preach the Gospel message to all people.

Thirty-first Sunday in Ordinary Time

Wisdom 11:22-12:2; Psalm 144; 2 Thessalonians 1:11-2:2; Luke 19:1-10

In our first reading from the Book of Wisdom we are told that

God created everything and having created it he loves everything in creation. The author also tells us that if there was something that God did not like that it would not be in creation for he would not have created it – a reminder that whatever we regard as being good or bad was all created by God. In the gospel from St Luke, we have the story of the tax collector, Zacchaeus, who was converted upon meeting Jesus and promises to make amends for anything he has done in the past while living a new life in to the future. The story is a reminder that while we may judge people by our own standards, they are not the standards which God uses.

In our second reading St Paul is writing to the Thessalonians to encourage them in the faith. In our passage today he prays that the name of Christ will be glorified in them and in their faith which he hopes will grow daily. We too must work to strengthen our faith every day in order that the name of God may be glorified in us and we, in turn, be glorified in and by him.

Thirty-second Sunday in Ordinary Time
2 Maccabees 7:1-2, 9-14; Psalm 16; 2 Thessalonians 2:16-3:5; Luke 20:27-38

In the first reading from the second Book of the Maccabees we have a section from the powerful story of a mother and her seven sons who were arrested for refusing to bow down before the false gods of the king or to defy the Laws of God. One by one they were tortured and put to death – in front of their mother – beginning with the eldest of the sons and finishing, finally, with the mother herself. Each proclaimed their faith in God and received a martyr's death to the astonishment of their torturers. Our psalm for today could easily have been the words on the lips of the young men and their mother as they died for the faith: 'I shall be filled, when I awake, with the sight of your glory, O Lord.' In the gospel Jesus tells us quite clearly that there is life after death and that we all have a place in that life with God. He reminds the Sadducees that Moses too held this belief but that over the centuries this belief has been lost to them. Those who are faithful to the Law and to God – such as the woman and her seven sons in the first reading – will rise from the dead and dwell for ever with God.

In the second reading St Paul prays that we may be kept safe from evil and from those who would lead us astray as the king and his minions tried in the first reading. If we trust in God then he will be at our side to strengthen and to protect us until we join him in paradise.

Thirty-third Sunday in Ordinary Time
Malachi 3:19-20; Psalm 97; 2 Thessalonians 3:7-12; Luke 21:5-19
In our first reading from the Prophet Malachi, we read that the triumph of God is at hand and his glory is soon to be revealed. The psalm calls on us to praise and glorify God. In the gospel, Jesus tells us quite clearly that we will be rejected by the world for believing in him because his message is something which many people do not wish to hear or to acknowledge. However, in giving us the warning he also tells us that he will be with us throughout and that while we may even have to give our lives for the sake of the message, we will reign for ever with him if we are faithful to him. On that day we shall see his glory and right-eousness shine out with him as foretold in the first reading.
In the second reading St Paul exhorts us to keep on working for the kingdom. He goes so far as to say that those who are not working but interfering with the work should not be fed. It is a reminder of how serious the spread of the gospel is – it is not some private message to be kept to ourselves but something which we should want to spread to the ends of the earth.

Our Lord Jesus Christ, Universal King
2 Samuel 5:1-3; Psalm 121; Colossians 1:12-20; Luke 23:35-43
Our first reading for today's Solemnity of Our Lord Jesus Christ, Universal King, comes from the second Book of Samuel where we read about the representatives of the people coming to David at Hebron and making him king over all their people. One of the reasons for doing so is because he is their own flesh and blood. This also reminds us that Jesus was of the royal line of David. Our second reading from St Paul reminds us that Christ is the Lord of all and everything comes from him – be it authorities and sovereignties. Our gospel text may seem a little strange for today coming as it does from the crucifixion where the good thief repents of his crimes and asks to be remembered.

Christ confirms the fact that he has a kingdom and tells the good thief that he shall be with his Saviour in that kingdom. As the liturgical year draws to a close it is appropriate that as we look back over it we acknowledge all that we have received from the Lord's goodness. It is also a good time to look forward while affirming that Christ is the Lord of all – he is the Universal King.

WEEKDAYS OF ORDINARY TIME: YEAR I

Monday of the First Week in Ordinary Time
Hebrews 1:1-6; Psalm 96; Mark 1:14-20

Our first reading comes from the letter to the Hebrews which is attributed to St Paul though not written by him. The letter is also written for an unidentified group. Nevertheless, the message of the letter is not to be ignored because of its authorship. In today's text, the Hebrews are told how God spoke to the people in former times by means of the prophets who delivered his message for him. Now, however, he has spoken to the people through his own Son. The author emphasises the fact that Christ is the Son of God and *is* God, and this highlights the importance of the message we have received. The beginning of Ordinary Time begins with Jesus starting out on his public ministry and calling the people to repentance. In today's gospel passage we also see him calling four fishermen (Simon, Andrew, James and John) to follow him and they do so without hesitation. Our readings today call us to repentance and to follow Christ with our whole heart, acknowledging the importance of the message and the true identity of Christ.

Tuesday of the First Week in Ordinary Time
Hebrews 2:5-12; Psalm 8; Mark 1:21-28

Again the author of the letter to the Hebrews speaks at length about the true identity of Jesus. He is at pains to make sure that we do not see Jesus as just another prophet or holy man but the Son of God who was perfect in everything. In the closing lines he also tells us that the one who sanctified us – Christ – and we who are sanctified are of the same stock, that is to say we are all sons and daughters of God and heaven is our true home. In our gospel text we see Jesus casting out an unclean spirit. The spirit recognised Jesus as the Son of God and acknowledges this. The people are amazed by how he speaks and they too recognise the authority with which he acts. The readings call on us today to recognise the authority of Christ and of his gospel and to conform our lives to it, for only then can we receive eternal life.

Wednesday of the First Week in Ordinary Time
Hebrews 2:14-18; Psalm 104; Mark 1:29-39

Having told us that Christ is the true Son of God and is God himself, the author of the first reading now tells us that Christ is also human. It was not the angels who needed to be redeemed but men and women and so Christ was born of human flesh and became one like us. There are a number of important points in today's gospel. The first is that Jesus cured people of their illnesses no matter what their complaint was. This shows how tremendous his power was. Secondly, he went away from the crowd so that he himself could pray. Even though he too was God he still prayed to the Father, he still spoke to the Father whenever he could and in private. Thirdly, he did not keep the message and his healing powers for those who were his friends but wanted to travel as far as possible to spread the good news as far as possible. The challenge for us today is to realise that Jesus was human like one of us and being human he knows our weaknesses. When we acknowledge this then we can pray to him knowing that he will listen to us and answer us. We must also realise that we too have a duty to spread the good news wherever we may go.

Thursday of the First Week in Ordinary Time
Hebrews 3:7-14; Psalm 94; Mark 1:40-45

We are reminded today of how the people in the wilderness rebelled against Moses and against God and turned their backs on God. We are also reminded of how he made a new covenant with his people despite all they had done. The writer does not want us to turn from God but to make sure that we help each other to remain faithful and on the path to eternal life as co-heirs with Christ. Jesus cures a leper in today's gospel passage, not because he had to but because he wanted to. Despite Jesus' warning the leper goes and tells others about the cure and the people begin to flock to Jesus. The readings remind us today that God wants us to be with him and will help us when we call to him and are faithful to him. God is not going to force salvation on us but will only grant us the salvation promised to us if we want it and to show that we want it we must be faithful to his word and to him.

Friday of the First Week in Ordinary Time
Hebrews 4:1-5, 11; Psalm 77; Mark 2:1-12

The author of the letter to the Hebrews reminds his readers that the promise made by God is still good and there is no time limit on it. But the promise can only be attained by being faithful. The Israelites who rejected Christ were not faithful and therefore have rejected their own salvation. Jesus has his first confrontation with the authorities in today's gospel text. A paralytic is brought to him and when Jesus tells him his sins are forgiven the scribes begin to question this. They believed that only God could forgive sins and to prove to them that he was from God and had the authority to forgive, Jesus cures the paralytic who then gets up and walks out in front of them. We are called to believe in Christ and to be faithful to God and to the gospel. We are also reminded that, if we do sin, Christ will forgive us if we ask for forgiveness.

Saturday of the First Week in Ordinary Time
Hebrews 4:12-16; Psalm 18; Mark 2:13-17

The word of God is something powerful and something from which we cannot hide. No matter what we do or say – in public or in the privacy of our hearts – all is known to God. Therefore we must always be on our guard and remain faithful. If however we do fall, the author of the first reading reminds us that Christ will be there to help us because he knows our weaknesses having been human like us. He will always be there to help and to pick us up when we fall. We see Jesus calling the tax collector, Matthew. We also see him admonished by the Pharisees for eating with those they considered sinners. It is worth noting that those who considered themselves virtuous were the very ones who rejected Christ, while those who acknowledged their sinfulness were the ones who embraced him. We are called to follow Christ as readily as St Matthew did and to remain faithful to him always. We are also told not to be like the Pharisees who coldly judged people without mercy, but to live a life of mercy and love.

Monday of the Second Week in Ordinary Time
Hebrews 5:1-10; Psalm 110; Mark 2:18-22

In our first reading today, the author of the letter to the Hebrews continues to explain about the person of Christ. Today they are told that Christ is a priest like all other priests, except that he is perfect. As those who become priests are called by God, so too Christ was called by God rather than opting for it himself. In this way he was like all other priests who are human and so knew our weaknesses. He also prayed to God for strength and support especially as he approached his own death. Again today we see the Pharisees objecting to the practices of Christ. While the Pharisees fasted publicly Jesus' disciples did not fast at all. Christ tells them that this is because he is with them. When he is gone from them then they will fast. Christ, who was with us as one of us, knows our faults and our failings and is always ready to help us when we call to him. As he himself regularly prayed to the Father we too must follow that example and pray to the Father in good times as well as in times of need.

Tuesday of the Second Week in Ordinary Time
Hebrews 6:10-20; Psalm 111; Mark 2:23-28

All that we do is remembered by God and never forgotten. The letter to the Hebrews uses the example of Abraham to show us that all that God promises will be fulfilled. God has promised us everlasting life and that promise will be fulfilled in the same way that Abraham became the father of a great nation. The Pharisees are unhappy with Jesus and his followers in today's gospel text because they do not keep the Sabbath in the same way as the Pharisees do. The Pharisees and many others had an extremely strict ban on doing any sort of work on the Sabbath and picking corn was against the Law. Jesus tells them that the Sabbath was made for man and not the other way around. In other words, the Sabbath is a day for remembering the goodness of God and giving thanks to him and while it does mean not working on the Sabbath day it does not mean that all physical exertion is banned.

Wednesday of the Second Week in Ordinary Time
Hebrews 7:1-3, 15-17; Psalm 110; Mark 3:1-6
The King of Salem was also Melchizedek, the priest of God. We often hear the phrase: 'You are a priest for ever, a priest like Melchizedek of old.' The author of today's first reading tells us that Christ is the high priest of this order and that, like Melchizedek, he is a priest for ever. But Christ's priesthood is not because of any law regarding his lineage, but because of his power over death and his immortality. Today's gospel has the same theme as yesterday's text – the Sabbath rest. Today we see Jesus in the synagogue where he cures a man with a withered hand. The Pharisees are not happy because, as far as they were concerned, nothing could be done on the Sabbath day. But Christ heals the man because it is a good thing to do and the right thing to do.

Thursday of the Second Week in Ordinary Time
Hebrews 7:25-8:6; Psalm 40; Mark 3:7-12
The theme of Christ's priesthood continues in the reading from the Hebrews. The text lays down the ideal of what a high priest should be and then goes on to say that Christ does fulfil this ideal perfectly. Therefore we can be certain of Christ's help when we call to him. In the gospel Jesus is being pursued by the people because of the miracles and cures he has worked. The people are coming from near and far just to see and hear him. As he casts out unclean spirits, these spirits recognise him for who he really is – the Son of God – but he warns them to keep quiet so as not to aggravate the authorities further.

Friday of the Second Week in Ordinary Time
Hebrews 8:6-13; Psalm 85; Mark 3:13-19
God made many covenants with his people in Old Testament times but the people regularly broke them. He then made a promise that he would make a new covenant with the people which would be everlasting. Our text from the letter to the Hebrews today speaks of this to show us that Christ is the new and everlasting covenant. Today's text from St Mark's gospel sees Jesus choosing his twelve closest companions. These twelve were to preach, to cure the sick and to cast out devils in his name. For us as baptised Christians, they are examples of the

sort of way in which we too must live out our faith – bringing the healing presence of Christ wherever we go.

Saturday of the Second Week in Ordinary Time
Hebrews 9:2-3, 11-14; Psalm 47; Mark 3:20-21

The author of the letter to the Hebrews reminds his readers that the blood which the priests sprinkled on people only restored their outward holiness – the inner sanctity of the person was never restored in this way. With Christ, however, we have the means of restoring our inner holiness through his blood which he gave for us. A characteristic of St Mark's gospel is that he likes to point out the people who did not always believe in Christ and sometimes paints a negative picture of them. Today we see him do this of Jesus' own relatives. Jesus had become quite the talking point and focus of attention and some of this attention was turned on them, particularly the attention of the authorities. They come in search of Jesus to take him home, thinking that he was out of his mind. It is quite easy at times to dismiss the teachings of Jesus as the talk of an attention seeker. However, when we look closely at the teachings of Christ we see that while they call for a radical conversion in our lives they are not attention seeking or mad. They are quite simple and possible and perhaps we do not want to live by them because they are so simple.

Monday of the Third Week in Ordinary Time
Hebrews 9:15, 24-28; Psalm 97; Mark 3:22-30

In our first reading from the letter to the Hebrews we are told that Christ offered himself for our sins. In Christ's time the high priest made offerings in the sanctuary time after time to redeem the people, but Christ only had to do this once: he suffered only once for our sins. The next time Christ appears on earth it will be to bring the reward of salvation to the faithful and not to deal with sin, which has already been dealt with by Christ. In our gospel text we see that Jesus has been casting out unclean spirits. The scribes believed that this was because he himself was Beelzebul – the prince of devils. But he tells them that if this were so then Satan would come to an end for a divided kingdom could never last. Christ can cast out spirits because he is greater than they and his authority is everlasting.

Tuesday of the Third Week in Ordinary Time
Hebrews 10:1-10; Psalm 39; Mark 3:31-35

We again read from Hebrews and about the Law of the Torah, which the Jews obeyed, but which did not win them life for they had to make sin offerings regularly. However, the law of Christ's gospel will win us life because we have been reconciled with God. If we live by the will of Christ then there will be no need for sin offerings because we will not sin. Today's gospel text is quite short and yet very profound. Jesus' family come looking for him and those with him tell him this. In reply he tells them that those about him are his mother and brothers and sisters. Those who hear his message and follow it, obeying the commandment of love and avoiding sin, are the true family of Christ.

Wednesday of the Third Week in Ordinary Time
Hebrews 10:11-18; Psalm 110; Mark 4:1-20

Speaking of the priests of his day, the author of the letter to the Hebrews tells us in today's reading that the sin offerings they made were insufficient for taking sins away. Christ's offering of himself on the other hand, is perfect and does redeem us, making us perfect in the eyes of God. No more sin offerings are necessary because all sins have been forgiven. Today's gospel text contains the story of the sower whose seed fell in various places. Some of the seed died, more of it produced a great crop. The seed, of course, is the word of God being planted in our hearts – in some people it will take root while in others it will be ignored. We are being challenged in this text to look closely at our own lives and our own response to God and we are asked to make a better effort in order to produce a harvest worthy of the redemption Christ won for us.

Thursday of the Third Week in Ordinary Time
Hebrews 10:19-25; Psalm 116; Mark 4:21-25

We are told in the first reading that now that our sins have been wiped away we can enter into the sanctuary ourselves. We do so through the door which is Christ himself. However, in order to be fit to enter, we are reminded that we must be pure and with a clear conscience. Our sins may have been washed away but we must still be on our guard and keep our souls spotless. Jesus tells his listeners in the gospel that nobody lights a lamp and then hides it away: they light the lamp to give light to themselves and to others. The readings challenge us to realise that we too are like lamps – if we hide away our faith then the kingdom of God will not be seen. By letting others see that we are Christians we will be helping them to grow in faith and we will also be making ourselves more worthy to enter the sanctuary.

Friday of the Third Week in Ordinary Time
Hebrews 10:32-39; Psalm 95; Mark 4:26-34

The Hebrews are reminded in today's first reading that when they first accepted the good news they suffered for it, but they got through the suffering. They are told that having come through this suffering they must still remain faithful even when there is nothing to challenge the faith. They must remain faithful for ever. In the gospel we see that Jesus continues to use parables to teach the people. Today he tells them that the kingdom grows silently and without ceasing, just as seeds grow silently and constantly in the ground. From small beginnings, the kingdom will grow like the mustard seed which, being the smallest of all seeds, grows to be the biggest shrub of all. Both readings challenge us to keep watch over our soul and to strengthen our faith. If we live a life of faith then our own faith will grow and with it the kingdom of God and the faith of those around us.

Saturday of the Third Week in Ordinary Time
Hebrews 11:1-2, 8-19; Psalm: Luke 1:69-75; Mark 4:35-41

Today, the author of the first reading uses the example of Abraham and Sarah to teach us about faith. Abraham was told that he would be the father of a great nation even though Sarah was barren. Sarah too believed that she would give birth because God had said it. They also moved to a different country at God's command. They did so because they believed and because they believed they were rewarded and the promises made to them were fulfilled. In the gospel, we see Jesus and the disciples out on the lake when a storm blows up. The disciples, terrified, waken him and he calms the storm, showing that he has power over the forces of nature. Both of our readings today challenge us to live by faith. Because the disciples had weak faith they were terrified in the boat even in the presence of their Saviour. Abraham and Sarah on the other hand, lived by strong faith and received a great reward. We too will be rewarded for living by faith and for helping to strengthen the faith of others.

Monday of the Fourth Week in Ordinary Time
Hebrews 11:32-40; Psalm 31; Mark 5:1-20

In our first reading from the letter to the Hebrews, the author speaks of some of the greatest heroes of the Jewish people – men who fought battles and conquered their enemies. He also speaks of the prophets who stood for the truth and did not flinch in the face of torture. Some were great warriors while others were weak but they all lived by faith, and because they had faith they achieved great things. In the gospel, Jesus cures a demoniac by casting out the evil spirits that had possessed him. The spirits instead entered a herd of pigs and were killed. The people were amazed when they saw this but were also terrified and asked Jesus to leave their area. Both of our readings speak to us about faith. The first reading speaks of those who had faith and lived by it while the gospel speaks of those who had little faith and did not want what faith they had to grow. Perhaps it was because they realised the conversion they would have to undergo if they were to become people of faith. We know what faith can do and what reward lies in store for us. We are given a choice – to be people of faith and enter heaven, or to be people who turn their backs on God, refusing to grow.

Tuesday of the Fourth Week in Ordinary Time
Hebrews 12:1-4; Psalm 22; Mark 5:21-43

Our extract from the letter to the Hebrews tells us today that having received the faith we should keep on believing and strengthening our faith. If we keep Jesus in mind then we will be able to do this for he too lived a life of faith. The life he lived is an example for us to follow, even if that means going to our death for the faith. Today's gospel text recounts two miracles for us. The first was the cure of the haemorrhagic woman who believed that she would be cured if she could even touch the hem of Christ's cloak. The second is the restoring to life of Jairus' daughter, because he had faith enough to ask for Christ's help.

Again today, our readings challenge us to look closely at our faith and to do what we can to strengthen it and live lives based on faith.

Wednesday of the Fourth Week in Ordinary Time
Hebrews 12:4-7, 11-15; Psalm 103; Mark 6:1-6

We read in the letter to the Hebrews that the Lord reprimands his children when they go wrong but the punishment is not meant to destroy them but to purify and make them better in the future. We see in today's gospel how Jesus is ignored by his own neighbours because they thought they knew him. Because of their little faith he could work no miracles among them, showing that if we really want to be better people we must believe in him and in the good news. Our readings today call on us to be people of faith and to live by faith.

Thursday of the Fourth Week in Ordinary Time
Hebrews 12:18-19, 21-24; Psalm 28; Mark 6:7-13

According to the text of today's first reading from the letter to the Hebrews, faith is leading us to something which we have never before experienced or could explain – it is leading us to our true homeland which is Mount Zion, the city of the living God. We are drawing closer to God himself because of our purification by the blood of Christ. In our gospel text we see Jesus beginning to send out the disciples to teach in his name. If they are welcomed in a place they are to stay and teach but if they are rejected, they are to leave at once. We too are called to preach the word of God in our lives by what we do and say. In that way we will draw closer to God and to Mount Zion and will help to bring many others to him also.

Friday of the Fourth Week in Ordinary Time
Hebrews 13:1-8; Psalm 27; Mark 6:14-29

The author of the letter to the Hebrews encourages us today to proclaim the good news in our lives and to help others to draw closer to God. He also reminds us that Christ is unchanging – he is the same yesterday, today and for ever. Today's gospel recounts the beheading of John the Baptist because of a rash promise Herod had made to Herodias' daughter. Again we are called to live by faith and to proclaim the gospel in our lives. John the Baptist believed in God and gave his life for that belief.

Saturday of the Fourth Week in Ordinary Time
Hebrews 13:15-17, 20-21; Psalm 23; Mark 6:30-34

As we conclude the letter to the Hebrews we are exhorted one last time to live according to the gospel, obeying the leaders of the church who are there to guide us towards God. In the gospel, the disciples have returned from their preaching and curing and a huge crowd gathers. They go with Jesus to rest but the crowd follows them and Jesus begins to teach them. The readings call on us to live Christian lives but also to play our part in the spread of the gospel.

Monday of the Fifth Week in Ordinary Time
Genesis 1:1-19; Psalm 103; Mark 6:53-56

Today we begin reading from the Book of Genesis and in today's passage we read of the first four days of creation. The author is not presenting scientific truth but is writing the basic truth that God is the benign Lord of Creation who has a plan for us. The psalm takes up the theme of creation and praises God for all that he has made. In our gospel we read that Christ's fame had spread throughout the countryside and that the people brought to him their sick whom he cured. God created everything there is and he holds all of it in view and so he is aware of our difficulties and the things that afflict us. Being so aware he is ready to help and heal us if we believe and call on him from our hearts.

Tuesday of the Fifth Week in Ordinary Time
Genesis 1:20-2:4; Psalm 8; Mark 7:1-13

Today we read of the conclusion of the seven days of creation and in the text we see that humans were the last to be created but they are also the jewel in the crown of God's creation. Being last created we were also entrusted with the stewardship of the earth, to look after it on God's behalf. The book is an important reminder about the role of God in creation and of the role of humans to rule over that creation in the way in which God intends. The psalm praises God for his magnificent creation. In our gospel text from St Mark we see Jesus at odds with the Pharisees who are being overly concerned with the Law. He admonishes them for clinging to human traditions while not being concerned with the law of God. We are challenged today to listen to the word of God and to carry out its precepts in our lives rather than being interested in what we ourselves want to do or in creating traditions to suit ourselves.

Wednesday of the Fifth Week in Ordinary Time
Genesis 2:4-9, 15-17; Psalm 103; Mark 7:14-23
Today we read of the second account of the creation of man from the Book of Genesis and in it we see that the Lord provided man with every good thing in the garden but forbade him to eat of one tree only – all else was his to taste. Our gospel passage for today is a continuation of yesterday's in which Jesus was questioned by the Pharisees because his disciples did not purify themselves before eating. His answer to them is that what goes in to a person does not make them unclean – all food is clean. It is what is inside their hearts and minds which makes them unclean and prone to do the wrong thing. This was difficult for the Jews of the time to hear and we know from elsewhere in the New Testament that St Peter himself had to receive a vision before he too preached the same thing. We are all aware of our shortcomings and the image of Adam in the garden reminds us of what we can be and what we must strive for.

Thursday of the Fifth Week in Ordinary Time
Genesis 2:18-25; Psalm 127; Mark 7:24-30
Today we read of the creation of woman from the second creation account and we see that woman was created as a helpmate for man, who was his equal and whose qualities complemented his. It was also the author's way of emphasising that marriage is between one man and one woman in happiness. In our gospel we see a Syrophoenician woman coming to Jesus because her daughter was possessed. Because she was a pagan Jesus told her that the believers had to be helped first but she reminded him that there was plenty of room for everyone at his table. Because of her faith in Christ's powers her daughter was cured, which also reminds us that there are plenty of people who may not belong to our church but who still have faith and are welcome in the kingdom. We are to keep in mind that we were created to live together in harmony, helping each other to fulfil our potential no matter what our creed or colour.

Friday of the Fifth Week in Ordinary Time
Genesis 3:1-8; Psalm 31; Mark 7:31-37

In our first reading we read of the temptation of Adam and Eve by the serpent and how it was successful in getting them to disobey God. This is where the Church's teaching on original sin comes from. The psalm is a reminder for us to acknowledge our sinfulness before God and to seek forgiveness. In our gospel we read of the cure of a deaf man with a speech impediment after Jesus calls him away from the embarrassing glare of the onlookers. The Lord uses the word 'Ephphatha' which is part of the ceremony of baptism for infants. The Lord is always close to us and wants to be closer still but we must want that too and we show that by living according to his precepts and avoiding sin.

Saturday of the Fifth Week in Ordinary Time
Genesis 3:9-24; Psalm 89; Mark 8:1-10

The first reading tells us of the expulsion of man and woman from the Garden of Eden because they disobeyed God's command and lost his divine friendship. In the gospel we see Jesus feed the multitude with a few small fish and some loaves. This is in contrast to the first reading where Adam and Eve were forced to till the ground and fend for themselves. God wants us to be with him but we can only be with him if we live life according to the gospel values. The gospel is also a reminder that we must always help those who are in need from whatever we may have, no matter how little.

Monday of the Sixth Week in Ordinary Time
Genesis 4:1-5, 25; Psalm 49; Mark 8:11-13

In today's reading from the Book of Genesis we see Adam and Eve now exiled from the Garden of Eden. They start a family and Eve gives birth to Cain and Abel – the former tilled the land while the latter became a shepherd. We are told that Abel prospered more than Cain and that this ultimately led to Cain slaying his younger brother. God punishes Cain for his sin but promises to punish even more those who might take Cain's life. At the end of the reading, Eve gives birth to her third son – Seth. In the gospel, Jesus is again in conflict with the Pharisees because they, after all that they had seen, still demanded a sign from Christ if they were to believe. If we are waiting for a sign before we believe then we will never have faith. We are reminded to always keep watch over ourselves and never allow envy or resentment to rule our actions, because God sees all.

Tuesday of the Sixth Week in Ordinary Time
Genesis 6:5-8; 7:1-5, 10; Psalm 28; Mark 8:14-21
The first reading from the Book of Genesis tells us of God's disappointment with man and woman who had drifted further and further from him and so he resolves to wipe them from the earth by means of a great flood. Only Noah and his family would be left to repopulate the earth. In the gospel Jesus warns his disciples not to be taken in by the sweet words of Herod and the Pharisees who no longer faithfully worship God but order the people for their own ends. The two readings remind us that our faith must be pure and must be based on God's word. If we live according to his word then we will know what the right way to act is and if we believe we will act accordingly.

Wednesday of the Sixth Week in Ordinary Time
Genesis 8:6-13, 20-22; Psalm 115; Mark 8:22-26
In the first reading we read of the end of the Flood and of Noah's sacrifice of thanksgiving to God. The psalm continues the theme of thanksgiving. In the gospel we see Jesus cure a blind man who gradually begins to see and this reminds us that faith grows over time and in time we accept the Lord more and more. We are reminded to give thanks to God for all that we have received in life no matter how trivial it may seem but also remembering to thank him for the gift of life itself. Faith grows over time but we must work at it all the time.

Thursday of the Sixth Week in Ordinary Time
Genesis 9:1-13; Psalm 101; Mark 8:27-33
God makes a covenant with Noah in our first reading from Genesis and uses the words he used in forging the original covenant with Adam and Eve. He sets the rainbow in the sky as a reminder of that covenant, though few people make that connection anymore. In the gospel from St Mark, Christ tells the disciples that he is to suffer grievously which upsets Peter who

tries to prevent the Lord from going to Jerusalem. He is admonished for this by Christ even though – moments before – he made his great profession of faith with the words 'You are the Christ.' Christ is the eternal covenant which surpasses all covenants. We are called on to have faith in him as did St Peter and to say with him every day: 'You are the Christ.'

Friday of the Sixth Week in Ordinary Time
Genesis 11:1-9; Psalm 32; Mark 8:34-9:1
In our final reading from the Book of Genesis we see how the people have strayed from the covenant and in their pride are trying to be as powerful as God by building a tower which would reach up to heaven. In their arrogance, God destroys the tower and confuses the people by giving them different languages so that they could no longer understand each other. Jesus warns us in the gospel of the futility of trying to win this world when in fact we should be striving to secure our place in heaven. Only those who follow Jesus truthfully and with a sure heart will enter the kingdom and their true inheritance.

Saturday of the Sixth Week in Ordinary Time
Hebrews 11:1-7; Psalm 144; Mark 9:2-13
Today we turn to the letter to the Hebrews and in today's passage we are told by the author of the importance of faith and that it is only by faith that we can become one with the Father. We cannot please God in anything we do unless we have faith. In the gospel we read St Mark's account of the Transfiguration of the Lord. The Transfiguration showed Christ in his glorified state but it also showed us what we can be if we live Christian lives and enter heaven. His appearance with Moses and Elijah is also significant as they stood for the Law and the Prophets – important pillars of the Jewish faith. The readings call on us to be people of faith and to believe in God without hesitation.

Monday of the Seventh Week in Ordinary Time
Ecclesiasticus 1:1-10; Psalm 92; Mark 9:14-29
Today we turn to the Old Testament Book of Ecclesiasticus, or the writings of Ben Sirach, who lived in the second century before Christ and whose Greek text was translated about the year 132BC. Sirach was a respected teacher of wisdom who had a school in Jerusalem and who also taught knowledge of the

scriptures. In our first reading today we are told that all wisdom is from the Lord, it is he who created her. No matter what mortal man may do he will never comprehend all wisdom because only one person is truly wise – the Lord. In our gospel today we see Jesus casting out a spirit because his disciples have not faith strong enough to do so. He rebukes them, not because their faith is small but because they haven't worked hard enough to understand what he has taught them and to truly trust in him. He also tells us that a key thing for us is prayer because this helps to strengthen our faith.

Tuesday of the Seventh Week in Ordinary Time
Ecclesiasticus 2:1-11; Psalm 36; Mark 9:30-37
Our first reading tells us that if we aspire to serve the Lord, then we must be ready for an ordeal because those who serve the Lord are not always welcome in society – either in Old Testament times or in our own day. To serve the Lord, as we are called to do, means a radical change in our lives and this confronts others who should also change their lives. Ben Sirach, the author of this book, also tells us to trust in God for he will help us. In our gospel passage we see Jesus telling the disciples of his impending death and resurrection though they fail to understand what he is saying. He goes on to tell them that those who wish to serve him must make themselves the servants of others in order to show their true faith and action, and must welcome others in Christ's name.

Wednesday of the Seventh Week in Ordinary Time
Ecclesiasticus 4:11-19; Psalm 118; Mark 9:38-40
Those who love wisdom and seek it earnestly will be protected by wisdom and led along the right path, a path which will bring them many blessings. The first reading from Ecclesiasticus also tells us that those who abandon wisdom – that is, the Lord – will be abandoned to their fate but those who remain steadfast will receive a great reward. Jesus tells us in the gospel that those who are not against God and his servants are for them for the disciples tried to stop a healer who was not one of their own company. What is important is that the person, that all of us, seek the face of the living God and make his message known throughout the world through prayer and action.

Thursday of the Seventh Week in Ordinary Time
Ecclesiasticus 5:1-8; Psalm 1; Mark 9:41-50

We are reminded in the first reading to remain steadfast and on the right path towards God. The author also tells us that we should not presume that our sins are forgiven and therefore make the mistake of adding more sins to our slate. We should always strive to do what is right and to remain close to the Lord making sure that our slate is clean at all times. He also condemns the false sense of power and security which comes from an abundance of wealth. The gospel continues this theme and we are told to always do what is right by Christ and always to welcome our fellow Christians. Even this little act of welcome will bring us closer to attaining our place in heaven. But if we prove to be an obstacle to others and block their path to heaven then we will lose our place in the kingdom and – it is Christ who says it – we will find ourselves cast in to hell.

Friday of the Seventh Week in Ordinary Time
Ecclesiasticus 6:5-17; Psalm 118; Mark 10:1-12

In the first reading from the writings of Ben Sirach we find an instruction about finding a faithful friend. The faithful friend is one who stands by us no matter what and is called a 'rare treasure.' We all know one person who can fill that role perfectly and that is Christ because if we trust in him and pray to him daily then he will walk with us wherever we walk and he will comfort us in our sorrows and show us the way when we are troubled. In the gospel we have Jesus' teaching on marriage in which he clearly forbids divorce and any remarriage which follows it and tells the people that it was because of their stubbornness that Moses allowed divorce in the first place but that it was not in keeping with God's will.

Saturday of the Seventh Week in Ordinary Time
Ecclesiasticus 17:1-15; Psalm 102; Mark 10:13-16

The first reading today tells us that men and women are made in the image of God. To these creatures he gave knowledge and understanding and placed them over all other creatures and established a covenant with them. But he warned them not to fall into wrong-doing because all that they do is seen by him. The psalm takes up some of the ideas of the first reading and repeats them saying that 'the love of the Lord is everlasting upon those who hold him in fear' or awe. Jesus tells us in the gospel that we must welcome the kingdom of God into our hearts and lives as little children welcome something that has been given to them. Only if we are open to the Lord like little children will we attain the promise made to us at creation and repeated by Christ. A childlike friendship with God is one which is humble, obedient and trusting.

Monday of the Eighth Week in Ordinary Time
Ecclesiasticus 17:24-29; Psalm 31; Mark 10:17-27
Our first reading today comes from the Book of Ecclesiasticus which was written by Ben Sirach who encourages his students to turn away from sin and wrong-doing and to return to the Lord for he is merciful and takes back those who seek him. Our psalm takes up this theme and speaks about the happiness of the man who has had his offence forgiven by the Lord. In our gospel, Jesus reminds us that we must make him the first person in our lives at all times. Material wealth may make our life comfortable but it does not bring the happiness which Christ offers to those who believe in him. We still need material things to live but we must never hold a greater affection for them in our hearts than we hold for Christ. True happiness lies in dedicating ourselves to the service of God and of others for the sake of the kingdom.

Tuesday of the Eighth Week in Ordinary Time
Ecclesiasticus 35:1-12; Psalm 49; Mark 10:28-31
Today our first reading calls on us to 'honour the Lord with generosity' and to keep his laws. What we have has come from the Lord and therefore we should share it with others so that they too may feel the love of God through us. The author – Ben Sirach – also tells us that those who give will be rewarded, but that our generosity must not be for any show of piety but must be genuine. In the gospel passage we are reminded that the reward promised to us is nothing short of eternal life. If we place Christ before all else then he will reward us but he also reminds us that fully living the Christian way of life will bring persecutions from those who are against the kingdom of God and against his believers.

Wednesday of the Eighth Week in Ordinary Time
Ecclesiasticus 36:1, 4-5, 10-17; Psalm 78; Mark 10:32-45

Ben Sirach, in the first reading, today calls on God to let the nations see that there is no God but our God – the true God. He asks the Lord to witness to those he created in the beginning and bless those who wait for their reward. He is writing at a time when Palestine had just come under Greek rule in the second century before Christ, and is asking for freedom for the Chosen People. The psalm asks that the Lord not hold the sins of our forefathers against us but that we be judged on our own merits. In the gospel, Jesus tells the disciples of his impending death and they are greatly disturbed. He also reminds them that as he came to serve the Father and not to be served, so too we should serve the Father in our daily life and also serve our fellow men and women in helping them to come to the Father and so enter eternal life. He is reminding them that authority is really about service rather than about power. Christ's life is the prime example by which we should live.

Thursday of the Eighth Week in Ordinary Time
Ecclesiasticus 42:15-25; Psalm 32; Mark 10:46-52

Our first reading today comes from the final section of Ben Sirach's book of wisdom and so is a hymn of praise for all the works of God. We are told that the glory of the Lord is to be found in creation which is all around us. Everything that the Lord has made is perfect for 'he has made nothing defective.' And whatever has been made compliments something else. In this way Ben Sirach was hoping to keep the Jews from being distracted by the new Greek culture which had just taken over control of Palestine. The psalm praises God for all that he has done. In the gospel we read of the restoration of Bartimaeus' sight by Jesus. Bartimaeus was healed because he asked to be healed and because he had faith in Christ. If we too ask for something and are people of faith then our prayer will most certainly be heard and answered.

Friday of the Eighth Week in Ordinary Time
Ecclesiasticus 44:1, 9-13; Psalm 149; Mark 11:11-26

In our first reading today we are told to praise illustrious men.

But the men we are to praise are not those who were wealthy or powerful but those who did good deeds, who kept the covenants and who passed these on to their children – these are the ones who are truly illustrious and worthy of praise. Ben Sirach, in writing about these men, is trying to show his readers and listeners that those who live God-fearing lives have already achieved wisdom and therefore do not need the philosophies and culture of foreigners. In the gospel we are reminded of the importance of the house of God as a house of prayer and how it should be kept sacred, through Jesus' cleansing of the Temple. We are also reminded of the importance of faith and of forgiveness – not just the forgiveness we receive from God but the forgiveness which others receive from us. If we come before the Lord to seek forgiveness then we must be willing to forgive those who have wronged us.

Saturday of the Eighth Week in Ordinary Time
Ecclesiasticus 51:12-20; Psalm 18; Mark 11:27-33
In the first reading, from our final passage from Ecclesiasticus, the author speaks of seeking wisdom and of following wisdom's instruction. As Christians we know that the wisdom of God is his Son, Jesus Christ, and that if we seek him we will find him and, having found him, he will guide us, through the Holy Spirit, in all things. In the gospel we see Jesus being confronted by the chief priests and the scribes because they are not happy with the way he teaches and what he teaches. They ask where his authority comes from but when they fail to answer his question he does not answer theirs. We know that his authority is from God because he is the Son of God who was sent to redeem us.

Monday of the Ninth Week in Ordinary Time
Tobit 1:3, 2:1-8; Psalm 111; Mark 12:1-12
Today we turn to the Book of Tobit which was possibly written by Jews in Egypt between the fourth and fifth centuries before Christ. In today's text we read of Tobit who was sitting down to a feast but, before he touched the food, he sent his son out to bring in someone who was in need to share in the meal. The son came back to say that one of their people had been killed and thrown in the market place. Tobit got up immediately and re-

covered the body and gave it a dignified burial. He shows concern for someone he did not know simply because he was one of his nation. It is also important because Tobit and the Jewish people were in exile in Assyria and many were struggling to keep faithful to their traditions and their Jewish roots. In our gospel text from St Mark, we have the parable of the vineyard in which the owner's son is murdered and thrown out. The earth, of course, is the vineyard and the workers represented the Jewish authorities of his day against whom Christ told this parable. The Jewish authorities wanted to arrest Christ there and then but couldn't for fear of the people. The earth still belongs to God and we look after it as his stewards but we must do so in a way which is in keeping with the will of God. We must have a concern for others and for all of creation just as Tobit did in our first reading.

Tuesday of the Ninth Week in Ordinary Time
Tobit 2:9-14; Psalm 111; Mark 12:13-17
In our reading today from the book of Tobit we see that Tobit looses his sight through a simple accident. The treatments only make his condition worse and yet he says nothing against God who could have prevented this from happening, even when his own wife says that there is no point in remaining faithful to God. As the psalm says, 'With a firm heart he trusts in the Lord.' In our gospel passage we see the chief priests and scribes at odds with Jesus and trying to catch him out. They ask him whether or not they should pay taxes to Caesar and he tells them that as it is Caesar's head on the coin, they should pay. He tells him to 'give to Caesar what belongs to Caesar – and to God what belongs to God.' We owe everything to God and we should thank and praise him for all that he has given us. He is the Lord of creation and is to be given true praise and acknowledgment at all times, even when things are not going our way.

Wednesday of the Ninth Week in Ordinary Time
Tobit 3:1-11, 16-17; Psalm 24; Mark 12:18-27
In our reading today from Tobit we see that Tobit is downhearted at the lot that has fallen to him and so he begins a prayer of lamentation to God. At the same time there is a woman named

Sarah who has been married seven times but all of her husbands have died before they came together. She too begins a prayer of lamentation to God and like Tobit, she too prays for death as a deliverance from her problems. Their prayers are answered and the Archangel Raphael is sent to them. This is an example of how we should trust in God and pray to him with confidence. In our gospel text we see Jesus being questioned by the Sadducees and he tells them that God is not a God of the dead but of the living. In other words, when we physically die in this life part of us lives on forever. The Sadducees denied this because they had not fully grasped the teachings in the scriptures and did not believe in resurrection. Their story of a woman with seven husbands reminds us of Sarah in the first reading. We have Christ's word for life after death and also the promise of eternal life to those who trust in him and believe in the promise he has made to us.

Thursday of the Ninth Week in Ordinary Time
Tobit 6:10-11, 7:1, 9-14, 8:4-9; Psalm 127; Mark 12:28-34
In our first reading today we see the marriage of Sarah to Tobias after Tobias has been sent to Persia to collect a sum of money for his father, Tobit. Sarah's father warns Tobias of the fate of those who marry his daughter yet Tobias goes ahead with the marriage regardless. The passage ends with the newly-weds in fervent prayer before God. We again see the scribes questioning Jesus in the gospel but this time his answer silences them. He tells the scribes, and us, that we must love the Lord our God with our whole being and we must also love our neighbour. These are the two greatest commandments and on these two all others hang: if we can live by these two then we will have no trouble in keeping the Law of the Lord and living righteously before him as his sons and daughters.

Friday of the Ninth Week in Ordinary Time
Tobit 11:5-17; Psalm 145; Mark 12:35-37
We read today of the answering of Tobit's prayer in the first reading and again, like Sarah's prayer yesterday, the answer is not what he asked for but is far better than he wished. Tobias is central to the story again today and again he goes and gives praise to God as soon as his father's sight is restored. This happens because

he follows the instructions of his travelling companion who happens to be the Archangel Raphael in disguise. The psalm is a hymn of praise which could have been the words used by Tobias. In the gospel we see Jesus upsetting the scribes by questioning their beliefs. He asks them how the Christ could possibly be the son of David when David himself refers to the Christ as his Lord. Again they fail to understand his teaching mainly because it would mean a conversion on their part and they did not wish to change their cosy lifestyle. He also tries to get them to understand that the Messiah will not be a political saviour. We must question ourselves from time to time to make sure that we are living according to the real word of God and not to what we would like him to be saying. The example for us today is Tobias who carried out God's will but was never slow to praise and thank him for his favours.

Saturday of the Ninth Week in Ordinary Time
Tobit 12:1, 5-15, 20; Psalm: Tobit 13; Mark 12:38-44
In our first reading the Archangel Raphael reveals himself and tells Tobit and Tobias that he was sent to test their faith and they have been found righteous. Before he leaves them he reminds them – and us – always to praise and thank God. He also tells them that while it is right to keep certain things secret it is always right to proclaim the works of God to all people. The psalm comes from Tobit's beautiful song of thanksgiving after Raphael has left them. In our gospel we have the story of the widow who put in very little to the offerings when compared to the money given by others and yet hers was the greater offering because she gave from what she needed while the others gave from their surplus and so would never miss it. We too are challenged to give as much as possible from what we have and not just from what we have over and above what is needed to live. We are reminded today to praise God and to give charitably to others.

Monday of the Tenth Week in Ordinary Time
2 Corinthians 1:1-7; Psalm 33; Matthew 5:1-12
In the first reading St Paul writes to the people of Corinth to strengthen them in their faith. This letter was written by Paul

about the year 57AD while on his third missionary journey to the Gentiles. Today he tells about the compassion of God who comforts us and helps us along the way no matter what happens to us. Having received God's consolation we are to go out and console others so that they too may feel God's presence and consolation through us. In our gospel reading for the next sixteen weeks we read from St Matthew's gospel and we begin with the Beatitudes – the radical blueprint for living which Christ left us. Matthew likens Jesus to Moses who gave the people a law for living while on another hilltop. If we can live out the beatitudes in our lives then we will give true glory and praise to God while allowing the world to see that there is a better way than the way it offers and that the peace of God is the true path to happiness and eternity.

Tuesday of the Tenth Week in Ordinary Time
2 Corinthians 1:18-22; Psalm 118; Matthew 5:13-16
St Paul tells us in the first reading today from his second letter to the Corinthians that the answer to all our prayers and God's promises are found in Christ. God assures us of this and has sent us the Holy Spirit who is present in us always. In our gospel we are told by Christ himself that we are the light of the world. Our world is in need of the true light that will guide it out of conflict and the darkness of sin into the true radiance of the Father's glory. We are that light but if we don't let our light shine then the world will never be saved. We are called on today to say 'yes' to the Lord, as Paul tells us Christ did, and so bring the world to him.

Wednesday of the Tenth Week in Ordinary Time
2 Corinthians 3:4-11; Psalm 98; Matthew 5:17-19
In our first reading today St Paul is reminding his readers that he is an administrator of God's covenant by the power of God. This new covenant is not written down like the tablets of stone given to Moses. It is far greater and is written by the Holy Spirit and therefore is also everlasting. This is the greatest covenant and one which we must live up to. It is also a living covenant as Christ lives for ever. In the gospel, Christ tells us that he did not come to abolish the old Laws as some had thought. He came

rather to complete them and give them their full meaning and he reminds us that we have to keep those Laws if we are to be his servants. We cannot be choosey in what we believe but must believe whole-heartedly in the Lord and in his Laws and commandments.

Thursday of the Tenth Week in Ordinary Time
2 Corinthians 3:15-4:1, 3-6; Psalm 84; Matthew 5:20-26
In our first reading today from his second letter to the Corinthians, St Paul tells us to remove the veil from over our minds which prevents us from listening to, understanding and accepting the word of God for what it is – the true word of God and not some human invention. In the gospel Jesus reminds us to be reconciled with our brother – that is, all those with whom we live or meet. He tells us that we sin even by thinking negatively about others and so we should make reparation for that before approaching the altar of God. We must lay aside all anger and resentment and live by the Law of the Lord in harmony and peace with one another and with God.

Friday of the Tenth Week in Ordinary Time
2 Corinthians 4:7-15; Psalm 115; Matthew 5:27-32
St Paul reminds us that with God on our side nothing can ever trouble us. We may be persecuted from time to time but this will never trouble us because God will be at our side to free us. If we believe in God and are open to the workings of the Holy Spirit we will live as true Christians and so bring glory to God. In the gospel we continue reading from St Matthew's section on the Sermon on the Mount where Christ lays down the blueprint for true Christian living. Today he gives us his instruction in favour of marriage and the indissolubility of marriage – a passage which few want to acknowledge today because it prevents them living the free and easy life they wish to live, with whoever they wish to live it. But Christ's teaching is clear and unambiguous – divorce is not in keeping with God's will.

Saturday of the Tenth Week in Ordinary Time
2 Corinthians 5:14-21; Psalm 102; Matthew 5:33-37
In our first reading St Paul reminds us of the great necessity of

reconciliation – reconciliation with our neighbour and reconciliation with God. Paul is an ambassador of this great work and so are we who have heard this message and who have been reconciled with God ourselves. The psalm today takes up this theme of reconciliation. In the gospel, Christ tells us that we should not swear. This may seem odd but when we think of the commandment – 'Thou shalt not take the name of the Lord your God in vain' – and the fact that everything we swear by comes from God in the first place, then in a way he is reminding us not to belittle God's name by using it in vain and so break the commandment. Our word should be our bond and when we say that we will do something then we should do it. If we are living truly Christian lives then people will need nothing more from us than a simple 'yes' or 'no.'

Monday of the Eleventh Week in Ordinary Time
2 Corinthians 6:1-10; Psalm 97; Matthew 5:38-42
In our first reading today from his second letter to the Christians in Corinth, St Paul is urging us to prove that we are servants of God. God has already given us the grace to do this work and he urges us not to neglect that grace but to work with it and so give glory to God in all things whether we are being persecuted, working or resting. In all things we must let the glory of God shine through so that others may come to believe in him. Paul also tells us that we should never put this duty off until tomorrow because we might not have a tomorrow. In our gospel for today, Jesus says the same thing but he tells us not just to do as we are told by those who don't believe or who are testing us, but to do what they have asked and more besides. We must not offer resistance to anyone because through it all we have Jesus with us to strengthen and guide us and to bring us to victory for the glory of God.

Tuesday of the Eleventh Week in Ordinary Time
2 Corinthians 8:1-9; Psalm 145; Matthew 5:43-48
In a very gentle way in the first reading St Paul is reminding the community at Corinth of their duty to live the gospel and also to aid in the spread of the gospel. He is in Macedonia and building up the church there and he tells the Corinthians of all that is

happening there so that they will feel, perhaps, a little envious and will work all the harder themselves to keep the faith. He also reminds them that Jerusalem is the focus of the faith. In our gospel we are called on by Jesus to be perfect just as our Father is perfect. This is not an easy thing to do and in particular he tells us that we should love our enemies, which many people shy away from. But given God's law of love we are not asked to like our enemies which is very different from loving them. In loving them we pray for their salvation and for an increase in them of the grace which has been poured out into the whole world. Nothing can disarm our enemies more than our prayers for them.

Wednesday of the Eleventh Week in Ordinary Time
2 Corinthians 9:6-11; Psalm 111; Matthew 6:1-6, 16-18
In our first reading today St Paul urges us to be cheerful givers. If we give to others out of charity it will mean nothing if we do so simply to fulfil the commandment to look after one another. However, if it is done out of genuine concern for the receiver then we will receive many graces and favours ourselves and will move a step closer to full union with God. Paul speaks of this because he was organising a special collection for the community in Jerusalem – the birthplace of the faith. In our gospel reading today from St Matthew we see Jesus instructing us on how to give to others and on how to pray – we are to do both without any show or arrogance. God alone sees all that we do in secret and God is the one we must please. Putting on an act for our fellow man is mere folly if it is simply done to win his approval. This doesn't mean that we don't make a special effort and dress appropriately when coming to church but it does mean that our reason for attending church must be of far greater importance than how people see us.

Thursday of the Eleventh Week in Ordinary Time
2 Corinthians 11:1-11; Psalm 110; Matthew 6:7-15
At the time that St Paul was writing to the Corinthians they had begun to fall away from the true faith and disunity was creeping in among them. Paul's letter was an attempt to keep them in tune with the correct gospel as is seen clearly in today's passage. He is telling them that the message which he brought is the right

one and that there is only one good news – anyone who comes with differences from this are not to be followed. As proof of what he is saying he tells them that he taught them for no fee because he did so out of love – love for God and love for the Corinthians. In our gospel we see Jesus teaching his disciples the 'Our Father.' It is a prayer which encompasses all of life – past, present and future and one which we should pray with great reverence and care. At the end Jesus also reminds us that we must forgive others who have hurt us or sinned against us because if we do not forgive others, then we have no right to expect God to forgive us the sins we commit against him and our fellow men and women.

Friday of the Eleventh Week in Ordinary Time
2 Corinthians 11:18, 21-30; Psalm 33; Matthew 6:19-23
Many people boast about their successes in life and the great things that they have done, so St Paul in our first reading to the Corinthians today boasts about himself also. But Paul doesn't boast about the wonderful things he has done or about the amount of travelling he has done, or about the number of times he has been in prison and punished by the civil authorities. He boasts about the occasions when he was in dangerous situations and in all his boasting he comes across as being weak or naïve. And yet all of this was done at the Lord's command so that the good news might spread throughout the land and because Paul's greatest treasure was Christ. In the gospel Jesus tells us that where our treasure is, that is where our heart will be found. On the last day there is little point if our treasure is in a bank vault and our heart with it, or in the jewels in our trinket box, because they are not the keys to heaven. If we wish to enter heaven then heaven must be our treasure so that our heart will always be there – in life and in death.

Saturday of the Eleventh Week in Ordinary Time
2 Corinthians 12:1-10; Psalm 33; Matthew 6:24-34
We have that great line in our first reading today from St Paul – 'For it is when I am weak that I am strong.' It is not always easy to see what Paul is saying here but when people are doing very well in life they tend to forget about God and all that they have

received from his bounty. When people are at their lowest ebb it is then that they turn to God and are most open to his mercy and generosity. So in a way Paul is telling us that we are the best Christians when things are not going so well for us. While this is true it is a reminder to us that we must always give thanks to God for what we have received whether it be family, material wealth, good health, or even the things which we regard as 'bad' – only then can we be true Christians all the time. Christ takes up this idea in the gospel and tells us not to worry about tomorrow but to live for today and leave tomorrow in his care. Everything else in creation does not worry and still it all continues to work smoothly. So we too should not worry about anything but live Christian lives in keeping with the gospel and in so doing give glory and praise to God.

Monday of the Twelfth Week in Ordinary Time
Genesis 12:1-9; Psalm 32; Matthew 7:1-5
We return to the Book of Genesis which we will read from over the next three weeks. Today we begin at the twelfth chapter where we see Abram being called by the Lord and told to move with his family to a land that the Lord would point out. Even though he did not know where he was going, how long it would take or what sort of welcome he would find there, Abram went without question because he believed in the Lord and knew that the Lord would look after him no matter what lay ahead. Our psalm tells us that those who have been chosen by the Lord will be blessed. In our gospel today we are reminded by Jesus not to be hypocrites but to remember that as we judge others so too we will be judged by others. Quite often the things we see in others which we don't like are only seen because we ourselves do the very thing we are giving out about. Therefore we should not judge others but should leave the judging to God and strive to make our lives perfect for the day when he will judge us. If we respond to the Lord with the same trust as Abram did, then we will not go wrong.

Tuesday of the Twelfth Week in Ordinary Time
Genesis 13:2, 5-18; Psalm 14; Matthew 7:26, 12-14

In our first reading today from the Book of Genesis we see disputes breaking out between Abram's people and the people of his nephew Lot, because the land is not able to provide for their combined numbers. Rather than fight over things, the two sit down and decide on a strategy and both go to live in peace – Lot to the good lands of the south near the Dead Sea, while Abram to the poor lands of the north. It is Abram's unselfish consideration for his kinsman that is placed before us. In the gospel, Jesus reminds us to protect and defend what is holy and not to give it to unbelievers. We must always treat others as we would like them to treat us and to settle arguments as quickly and amicably as did Abram and Lot. We are also told that the road to eternal happiness is the narrowest of roads because so many people take the road to perdition or hell. We should do all we can to ensure that we are one of the ones on the narrow road when our life comes to an end, and we do this by placing the needs of others before our own needs.

Wednesday of the Twelfth Week in Ordinary Time
Genesis 15:1-12, 17-18; Psalm 104; Matthew 7:15-20

In today's first reading we see the Lord reward Abram for his faithfulness and his willingness to go into the unknown for his Lord and God. Despite the fact that Abram has no children the Lord promises that he would be the father or a great nation. Part of the covenants of old was a ceremony which sealed the covenant. In the case of Abram, he and God were to pass between the animals prepared for sacrifice as a reminder that this lay in store for whoever broke the covenant. The psalm speaks of this covenant and of the 'children of Abraham' showing that the covenant has been fulfilled. In the gospel, Jesus is warning us about false prophets who pretend to come from him. He is telling us that there is only one kingdom and one good news and it is the only door by which we may enter. Others may come with promises of immortality but we must listen to what they say because in their speech we will know whether they are true or false prophets. How we act shows clearly the sort of person we are at the heart of our being. Through everything we must remain faithful to Christ and to his gospel alone.

Thursday of the Twelfth Week in Ordinary Time
Genesis 16:1-12, 15-16; Psalm 105; Matthew 7:21-29

In our first reading from Genesis we see Sarai, who is well on in years, giving her servant-girl to Abram in the hopes that this is how the Lord will give Abram his descendents. Sarai failed to have faith in the promise of God and followed a custom of the day for barren women – that of giving their servant-girl to their husband so that the girl may provide a child in her place. Hagar, the slave-girl, does indeed give Abram a son but this is not the child that the Lord had promised. Hagar's child was called Ishmael and he did indeed have many descendents for it is from him that the Moslem faith traces its lineage. In our gospel we come to the end of the passage on the Sermon on the Mount and today we are reminded by Christ that speaking about him and calling out to him in our need is not enough if we are to be saved. We can only call ourselves Christian if what we say is reflected in what we do. If we say one thing and do another then we are hypocrites and are not worthy of the kingdom or eternal life. We must also give an example to others of true Christian living and therefore we must put our professed faith in to practice each and every day.

Friday of the Twelfth Week in Ordinary Time
Genesis 17:1, 9-10, 15-22; Psalm 127; Matthew 8:1-4

There are two aspects to today's first reading from the Book of Genesis. The first is that every covenant had some form of sign or seal – for Noah, for example, it was the rainbow following the flood. For Abram and his followers it was to be circumcision and which was replaced by baptism for us. The second aspect is the promise made to Abram that Sarai would bear him a child. Abram laughs quietly at this because of his great age and yet the Lord proves that he has authority even over creation by allowing Sarai to give birth at such an advanced age. Not alone does the Lord say this but he names the child who will be born to them a year from now. It is also part of the covenant that their names now change to Abraham and Sarah. In the gospel passage from St Matthew we see Jesus curing a leper not because he had to but because he wanted to and because the leper too wanted it. The Lord will not force us to do anything against our will but he is always ready and willing to help us in any situation if only we would ask.

Saturday of the Twelfth Week in Ordinary Time
Genesis 18:1-15; Psalm: see Luke 1; Matthew 8:5-17
Quite often when we read the books of the Old Testament we find that we are reading the same incident twice but from two different perspectives. This is a reminder to us that several of the works were written by more than one person or group. We see that today as we have the second telling of the conception of Isaac by Sarah but this time from Sarah's point of view. It is now Sarah who does not believe, and even though she is not beside the angel when she laughs he knows exactly what she is thinking because nothing is hidden from God just as nothing is impossible for him. In our gospel today we have a passage containing several cures by Jesus. The important aspect to each one is that those who are cured are cured because they have faith or because those who sought the cure on their behalf had faith. One of those cured is the servant of a Roman centurion who is cured because the centurion himself had faith. The second was the cure of St Peter's mother-in-law. If we have faith then we can stand before the Lord and make our requests knowing that he will answer.

Monday of the Thirteenth Week in Ordinary Time
Genesis 18:16-33; Psalm 102; Matthew 8:18-22
In our first reading we see that the Lord has heard about the sinfulness of the city of Gomorrah and has decided to wipe out the city. However, Abraham has heard of the Lord's plan and pleads with him not to punish the just man along with the sinner and he pleads with the Lord to spare the just. At the end of the reading the Lord relents and promises not to destroy the city if there are but ten just men living within it. The reading reminds us that the Lord is always watching over us and is displeased with our sinfulness but he is always ready to relent and to accept us back, as is repeated in the psalm. In the gospel we see Jesus telling those who come to him to follow him. He makes that same invitation to each of us today and we can do this by keeping the commandments and believing in Christ and in his

gospel. We must remember though, that witnessing to the gospel will not be easy but that Christ is on our side and so we should not despair.

Tuesday of the Thirteenth Week in Ordinary Time
Genesis 19:15-29; Psalm 25; Matthew 8:23-27

In our previous section from Genesis we read that the Lord wished to destroy Gomorrah because of the sinfulness of the people but promised Abraham that he would spare it if he found ten just men living there. Today we see that only Lot, his wife and his two daughters were found to be just and the cities of Sodom and Gomorrah were destroyed after the angels had saved Lot and his family. In our gospel we see Jesus out on the lake with the disciples when a storm blows up and the disciples panic. Jesus calms the storm showing them his power and authority even over nature itself. This is a reminder of just who Christ is – the Lord of Creation – and that we should always strive to live out the gospel values, unlike the people of Sodom and Gomorrah. While we might feel as though we are alone in this, like Lot and his family, when all is said and done it is the Lord whom we must serve and not our fellow mortals.

Wednesday of the Thirteenth Week in Ordinary Time
Genesis 21:5, 8-20; Psalm 33; Matthew 8:28-34

Today we read from the Book of Genesis of Abraham's rejoicing at the birth of his son Isaac. His wife, Sarah, grows jealous of his first son, Ishmael, who was born to Sarah's servant-girl, and so she tells Abraham to send the servant-girl and her son away. Abraham is saddened by this but he does as she wishes. At the end of the reading we see that Ishmael too will be a great nation because he was the son of Abraham. In the gospel, Jesus heals two demoniacs and casts out their demons who enter a herd of swine and are destroyed. The local people implore Jesus to leave the area not because they had lost the herd but because they had little faith and did not want to change their comfortable lives. Faith in Christ calls for a radical change in our lives and one which we must make, no matter how uncomfortable it may make us feel for that is the only way to enter heaven.

Thursday of the Thirteenth Week in Ordinary Time
Genesis 22:1-19; Psalm 114; Matthew 9:1-8
Today we read of the sacrifice by Abraham of his son Isaac. What is remarkable about the story is that Abraham was willing to sacrifice his son because he believed in and trusted God so much. This is the faith to which each one of us is called. While this may seem a difficult thing to do we should not fear or worry for the Spirit is with us to help and strengthen us. The image of Isaac carrying the wood on which he was to be sacrificed reminds us of Jesus carrying the wood of the cross on which he became a sacrifice which saves us all. In our gospel passage we see Jesus at odds with the scribes because he has forgiven a paralytic his sins and told him to walk again. He did so not to show off but because the people who came to him had faith in him. The people are delighted to see this and they are filled with awe. Christ forgives our sins too if we turn to him in faith and he will help us in all our trials.

Friday of the Thirteenth Week in Ordinary Time
Genesis 23:1-4, 19, 24:1-8, 62-67; Psalm 105; Matthew 9:9-13
Our first reading today recounts the finding of a wife for Isaac. Sarah has died and Abraham is anxious that Isaac marry a woman of his own tribe so as not to contaminate the line chosen by God through marriage to a local Canaanite. Abraham's senior servant therefore travels back to Mesopotamia and is guided by the Lord who leads him to Rebekah. Upon returning to the land of Canaan they are met by Isaac who weds Rebekah. We again read in the gospel of Jesus coming into conflict with the Pharisees, this time because he was eating with people they considered to be sinners. He reminds them that healthy people do not need a doctor and so he has come to call the sinners to repentance because the virtuous are already on the right path. It is a reminder to us that even those who consider themselves to be virtuous are sinners because they have judged others by their own standards and have not been merciful in their consideration of others. When it comes to faith we must not consider others to be inferior to us but must always realise that we can be better than we currently are.

Saturday of the Thirteenth Week in Ordinary Time
Genesis 27:1-5, 15-29; Psalm 134; Matthew 9:14-17

We read in the first reading that Isaac is now an old man and calls his eldest son, Esau, to him to give him the blessing which belonged to the first-born son according to tradition, even though Esau had surrendered his birthright to Jacob. Rebekah, however, overhears the conversation and sends Jacob in to get the blessing. Isaac is fooled by the disguise and blesses his second son rather than the firstborn. Despite Jacob's deception in obtaining his father's blessing, the Lord chooses Jacob and so we are reminded that God's ways do not always fit the pattern we expect. Jesus is questioned in the gospel by some of John the Baptist's disciples about fasting. Christ's disciples did not fast while the others did and Jesus tells them that this was because he was with them. He uses the example of a wedding banquet at which people do not fast as long as the bridegroom is present, for he is the reason for the rejoicing. When Christ is taken from them they will then fast, but not as long as he is alive.

Monday of the Fourteenth Week in Ordinary Time
Genesis 28:10-22; Psalm 90; Matthew 9:18-26

We read in our first reading today about 'Jacob's Ladder.' Jacob had been travelling to Haran to find a wife and to get away from the wrath of his older brother, Esau. As it was night he stopped to rest and slept on the ground. As he was sleeping the Lord appeared to him in his dreams and promised him that his descendents would be great – the same promise he made to Abraham, Jacob's grandfather. The ladder of angels which Jacob saw symbolises the communication between God and man. The stone which Jacob had used as a pillow he sets up as a monument to the Lord. In the gospel we see Jesus curing two people. A woman in the crowd touched his cloak and the bleeding disease she had suffered from left her. In the second he raises a girl to life after her father had asked him to come to the house to save her. The key in these two miracles is faith. The woman didn't ask to be cured but believed that even if she just touched his cloak that she would be healed. The little girl didn't ask to be restored to life but her father had faith in Jesus. We too are called on to have faith in Christ because, for people of faith, anything is possible.

Tuesday of the Fourteenth Week in Ordinary Time
Genesis 32:23-33; Psalm 16; Matthew 9:32-38

In our first reading we see Jacob returning to his own country fourteen years after he had left for Haran to find a wife. As they cross the river Jabbok the Lord comes and wrestles with Jacob who fights with great strength all night. During the encounter the Lord changes Jacob's name to 'Israel' which means 'one who struggles with God.' Later this title becomes the name of the Jewish nation. We read in St Matthew's gospel that some of the Pharisees believe that Jesus is able to cast out devils because he is the prince of devils. However, Jesus feels sorry for the people because they have no real teachers to guide them in the faith and to lead them towards God. So he tells his disciples to pray for more people to come forward to lead the flock. This is a reminder to us to pray for vocations – not just to the priesthood and religious life – but also that we ourselves will have the faith and the courage to lead others to God by our own example of living the gospel.

Wednesday of the Fourteenth Week in Ordinary Time
Genesis 41:55-57, 42:5-7, 17-24; Psalm 32; Matthew 10:1-17

In our reading from Genesis we now move ahead several years and see Joseph in Egypt as the pharaoh's main steward. Israel's sons had sold Joseph into slavery because they were tired of his perfect ways and the fact that their father appeared to love him more than all of them put together. So they sold Joseph as a boy to some traders and Joseph ends up in Egypt where he becomes one of the chief stewards to the Pharaoh. Years later his brothers come to Egypt to buy grain for there is a famine in their own country. They do not recognise Joseph but he recognises them and has them detained for some days. In our gospel reading we have the naming of the twelve apostles and these Jesus sends out to proclaim the good news. We are the successors to the Twelve and it is our duty to proclaim the good news in all that we do and say.

Thursday of the Fourteenth Week in Ordinary Time
Genesis 44:18-21, 23-29, 45:1-5; Psalm 104; Matthew 10:7-15
In our reading from the story of Joseph in the Book of Genesis we see Joseph finally revealing himself to his brothers. Despite the way they had treated him, he forgives them and welcomes them with open arms. In some ways the scene reminds us of Christ who, on the cross, forgave those who rejected him and treated him shamefully. In the gospel we see Jesus instructing the Twelve before he sends them out in his name. We received the faith for nothing and so should pass it on to others for nothing. We should also welcome those who come in Christ's name and listen to their teaching.

Friday of the Fourteenth Week in Ordinary Time
Genesis 46:1-7, 28-30; Psalm 36; Matthew 10:16-23
In the first reading from the Book of Genesis we read of the moment when Israel (Jacob) is reunited with his long-lost son Joseph. Israel also takes his whole family and settles in Egypt at Joseph's request where they enjoy peace. Before moving to Egypt, the Lord appears to Israel to tell him that he will be with him and make him a great nation in Egypt. Jesus continues instructing the Twelve in the gospel before sending them out in his name. He reminds them that it will not go as smoothly as they might think and that they will be harassed from time to time and have to suffer for him, but through it all the Holy Spirit will be with them to guide and strengthen them. The Holy Spirit is also with us and so we should take up the mantle of the Twelve and preach the kingdom of God to all whom we meet.

Saturday of the Fourteenth Week in Ordinary Time
Genesis 49:29-33, 50:15-26; Psalm 104; Matthew 10:24-38
We read of the death of Jacob, now Israel, in our reading from Genesis today and of his wish to be buried in his native Canaan – the Land of Promise – rather than Egypt. Jacob's sons now fear Joseph's wrath for what they did to him as a boy now that their father is dead, but Joseph forgives his brothers, reminding them that a great good has come of their evil intent. Joseph too dies and before he dies he instructs them that, when they leave the land of Egypt, they are to take his bones with them. We continue

reading in the gospel from the instruction Jesus gave to his apostles before they went out to preach on his behalf. He again reminds them that a difficult road lies ahead and he tells them not to fear what people may do to their bodies but to fear what the prince of darkness may do to their souls if they do not trust in Christ alone. That same warning is given to us. We quite often spend far more time worrying about our physical body than we do about our soul, even though the soul is far more important and is the immortal part of us.

Monday of the Fifteenth Week in Ordinary Time
Exodus 1:8-14, 22: Psalm 123; Matthew 10:34-11:1
Today we begin reading from the Book of Exodus which continues where we finished in the Book of Genesis last week. Almost 200 years have now passed in Egypt since the death of Joseph and his brothers and a new Pharaoh comes to power who knows nothing of the history of the Israelites in Egypt. He therefore has the Israelites enslaved and begins killing their sons out of fear that they may not be as loyal as he would like. Our gospel passage today from St Matthew seems at first a little odd because Jesus tells his disciples that he did not come to bring peace but the sword. We know from bitter experience that this is correct for there are many places in the world where long and bloody battles have been fought because of religion and because of different views within Christianity, even within our own country. But Christ tells us that we should welcome all people regardless of their religious beliefs because, if we welcome those who are holy and help those who come to us, then we will bring peace to our world and the gospel of Christ will spread throughout the world.

Tuesday of the Fifteenth Week in Ordinary Time
Exodus 2:1-15; Psalm 68; Matthew 11:20-24
To help stamp out the Jewish race the Pharaoh had decreed that all Jewish males were to be killed at birth but today we read in Exodus that Moses was not killed but was hidden by his mother. Eventually she placed him in a basket in the river because she could no longer conceal him. The child is found by the Pharaoh's daughter who takes him home and entrusts him to his own

mother. He lives in Pharaoh's house and flees when he kills an Egyptian for striking a Hebrew. From here on, Moses will be central as we read about the return to the promised land. In our gospel text we see Jesus admonishing those towns in which he had worked miracles because, despite all they had seen, they still refuse to change their ways and to live according to the Law of God. This is a reminder to us that we must be converted daily to the gospel and play our part in the building up of the kingdom of God. It is also a reminder that Jesus had been busy in other parts of the Holy Land but that not all of it is recorded in the gospels – again showing us that in fact we know only small though significant parts about his life on earth.

Wednesday of the Fifteenth Week in Ordinary Time
Exodus 3:1-6, 9-12; Psalm 102; Matthew 11:25-27
In our first reading from the Book of Exodus we read of the first encounter between God and Moses in the burning bush. The Lord has heard the cry of his Chosen People in Egypt and he appoints Moses to be his instrument in delivering them from their slavery. Moses is unsure about this but the Lord tells him that he will be with him. This promise to be with Moses is heard time and time again throughout the Old Testament and also in the promise of Jesus to his apostles, 'I will be with you always.' In the gospel, Jesus praises his Father for revealing the mysteries of the kingdom to mere children. All too often today people scrutinise their faith so much that they destroy it. The mysteries are called mysteries precisely because we do not have the capacity to understand them and yet that does not mean that they are false or to be ignored. A child accepts what he or she is told and believes in it and that is what we are asked to do. If we truly believe in Jesus and his word, no further proof should be necessary for the Lord will not deceive us as he only seeks our good.

Thursday of the Fifteenth Week in Ordinary Time
Exodus 3:13-20; Psalm 104; Matthew 11:28-30
In our text from Exodus we see Moses still questioning God about sending him to be the one to win freedom for the Israelites. A person's name has always been important for the Jews as it tells a lot about the person and so Moses asks God for

his name. The Lord replies, 'I Am who Am,' and for the first time reveals himself as Yahweh, the God of power. The sacred name tells us that, unlike the pagan gods, this is a God who lives and he now hears the cry of his people and is about to act. By contrast we see Jesus in the gospel calling the people to him and telling them that he is gentle and humble of heart. And yet both of these images are of the same God who is at once powerful and gentle, who hears his people when they cry to him and will come to their aid. It is a reminder for us that God can do all things for us, but at the same time he is not a God to be feared but one who genuinely cares for each of us.

Friday of the Fifteenth Week in Ordinary Time
Exodus 11:10-12:14; Psalm 115; Matthew 12:1-8
We now move ahead in our reading from Exodus to the instructions for the first Passover. The Pharaoh has still not agreed that the Hebrews may leave Egypt so the Lord is going to smite the firstborn of both man and beast in the land. The Hebrews are told how to prepare and how to avoid the death which is about to come, for only those who prepare properly will be saved. This meal became an annual remembrance of how God delivered his people from slavery in Egypt. From this meal comes our Eucharist which reminds us that, through Jesus, the world has been delivered from slavery to sin. In the gospel we see Jesus in conflict with the Pharisees for apparently breaking the Sabbath, though in fact it was the disciples who committed the crime and not Jesus. Christ was not against observing the Sabbath but he was against the Pharisaic over-development of Sabbath legislation. He reminds them of what happened in the past and tells them that man is greater than the Sabbath and not the other way around. He does not suggest that the Sabbath should not be observed but to keep a perspective on things and not kill off the day completely.

Saturday of the Fifteenth Week in Ordinary Time
Exodus 12:37-42; Psalm 135; Matthew 12:14-21
In the reading from the Book of Exodus we see the Chosen People finally leaving Egypt. The Lord has heard their cry and is now leading them to a better life through the desert and across

the Red Sea. The psalm is a hymn of praise to God for freeing his people. In the gospel we read of the Pharisees plotting against Jesus while he goes off quietly and cures those who come to him seeking his comfort. He tells them to say nothing about him because his time has not yet come and he has more to do. Today, in our own time, however, the Lord's time has come and we all have a duty to proclaim the risen Lord who sets his people free from all that keeps them captive, but only if they turn to him in faith and seek his help.

Monday of the Sixteenth Week in Ordinary Time
Exodus 14:5-18; Psalm: Exodus 15:1-6; Matthew 12:38-42
In our first reading from the Book of Exodus we see that the Passover has taken place and the Israelites are now marching out of Egypt. The Pharaoh, regretting his decision, changes his mind and goes after the Israelites who immediately question Moses for freeing them. Their old life of servitude was what they wanted in the face of danger because they still did not trust the Lord but Moses leads them on and the Egyptians follow. The psalm tells us what happens when the two groups reach the Red Sea. In our gospel text we again see Jesus at odds with the scribes and Pharisees who still do not believe him and, despite all the signs they had seen, ask for more extraordinary signs so that they might believe. Jesus rebukes them and reminds them of Jonah who was thought to be dead for three days and also Solomon whose wisdom is well known. He is greater than all of these because he is the absolute revelation of the Father. Many today do not believe because they have never seen Jesus and want a sign before they believe. Only when they open their eyes to the message of Christ will Christ become visible to them.

Tuesday of the Sixteenth Week in Ordinary Time
Exodus 14:21-15:1; Psalm: Exodus 15:8-10, 12, 17; Matthew 12:46-50
Today we read of the end of the Egyptians who were chasing the Israelites as the latter fled from Egypt. At the Lord's command the Red Sea was parted and both groups went on dry ground. When the Israelites were clear across, the Lord allowed the sea to return to its normal path and so the Egyptians were destroyed. The text is a reminder that the Lord did fulfil his

promises to his people even though they initially had little faith. The promise to Abraham, Isaac and Jacob is now being fulfilled for them as they head towards the promised homeland. The psalm is a hymn of triumph for the freedom of the Israelites. In the gospel from St Matthew we see Jesus speaking to the crowds when his mother and family arrive to see him. Rather than going out to them he uses the opportunity to show that we are all his family – we are all his brothers and sisters – but only if we do the will of God. It is a great honour and privilege for us to be counted as his brothers and sisters but if we do not do the will of God and believe in Christ, then we are not worthy of such a title.

Wednesday of the Sixteenth Week in Ordinary Time
Exodus 16:1-5, 9-15; Psalm 77; Matthew 13:1-9
In our first reading from Exodus we see the people again complaining about how good it was back in Egypt where they had all the food they could eat. The Lord hears their complaints and gives them food – meat in the evening and bread in the morning. The text is a reminder that we all have a little 'Egypt' in us – we all have a comfort zone which we do not want to relinquish even for the sake of eternal life. However, we must give it up and if we make the effort to do so then the Lord will be with us to help us achieve perfection. St Matthew presents us with the parable of the sower in our gospel and it is a story which we are all familiar with. The seed is, of course, the word of God and the ground represents each of us. The seed is useless if it finds no nourishment just as the word of God will be dead in us if we make no effort to practice the faith or to live out the gospel values. We are called to renew ourselves daily and to nourish the faith which was given to us at baptism.

Thursday of the Sixteenth Week in Ordinary Time
Exodus 19:1-2, 9-11, 16-20; Psalm: Daniel 3:52-56; Matthew 13:10-17
In the text from Exodus we see the Israelites reach the mountain of Sinai and there the Lord comes to meet them on the mountain. In several places in the scriptures God comes to meet his chosen ones on mountains and they are sacred occasions. In today's text we see the people preparing for three days before they meet the Lord. In the gospel, the disciples question Jesus'

tactic of teaching through parables. He tells them that those who
have faith will understand what he is saying but that those who
do not believe, or who do not wish to believe, will not understand. The message of Christ is a simple one but only for those
who wish to inherit eternal life by following Christ.

Friday of the Sixteenth Week in Ordinary Time
Exodus 20:1-17; Psalm 18; Matthew 13:18-23
In our first reading from the Book of Exodus we see Moses with
the Lord on Mount Sinai and there the Lord gives him the ten
commandments. These are the most basic instructions on which
our Christian moral code is founded. The psalm tells us that
these instructions are perfect and to be trusted. In our gospel
text for today, Jesus explains the parable of the sower to the disciples. He explains the different types of people in the world:
those who do not understand Christ; those who initially receive
the word but do nothing about it; those who receive it but who
worry about the things of this world; and those who receive the
word and live it out in their lives. The question for each of us
today is – which one am I? If we are honest about the answer,
what are we going to do to make the word grow even more in
and through us?

Saturday of the Sixteenth Week in Ordinary Time
Exodus 24:3-8; Psalm 49; Matthew 13:24-30
In today's text from Exodus we see Moses presenting the ten
commandments to the people and the people affirm that they
will 'observe all the commands that the Lord has decreed.' This
is a further covenant with the people through Moses for if the
people keep their word then they will inherit life. In our gospel
we have St Matthew's version of the parable of the weeds growing with the good seed. The farmer's servants are scandalised to
see the weeds but he tells them to do nothing but to have
patience and wait, for at harvest time – at the last judgement –
the good will be separated from the bad and the bad will be
thrown on the fire. This is a parable regarding the kingdom
which has a mixture on earth of saints and sinners who will be
sifted at the last judgement. Again we are challenged to ask ourselves on which side of the divide we lie and what are we going

to do to ensure that we are among those found worthy to enter the Father's kingdom.

Monday of the Seventeenth Week in Ordinary Time
Exodus 32:15-24, 30-34; Psalm 105; Matthew 13:31-35

In our last passage from the Book of Exodus we saw the people saying that they would obey the Lord's commands and now today we see them worshipping a calf of gold. Moses had been a long time on the mountain and they had complained to Aaron so he made a golden idol for them to keep them quiet. Moses smashes the tablets of the Law – showing that the covenant they made with the Lord has been broken. He then returns to the Lord to seek forgiveness. The Lord tells him that he, Moses, will not be held responsible for the actions of the people for they are the ones that strayed so quickly, but they will be punished when the time comes. In the gospel we see Jesus continuing to teach through parables. Both of today's parables refer to the kingdom which begins as a small movement (Christ and his Apostles) and which suddenly grows and is revealed in all its grandeur. We are the leaven in society and without us the kingdom will not grow or flourish and the world will not achieve justice and peace.

Tuesday of the Seventeenth Week in Ordinary Time
Exodus 33:7-11, 34:5-9, 28; Psalm 102; Matthew 13:36-43

In today's text from Exodus we see Moses meeting the Lord in the tent of meeting and on the mountain top where he asks the Lord to forgive the stupidity of the people and to take them again as his heritage. Moses spent forty days and nights on the mountain in the presence of God and received again the two tablets of the Law. The psalm reminds us that the Lord is compassion and love and that he forgives those who have sinned. In today's gospel we see Jesus explaining the parable of the weeds, or the darnel, to his disciples. The weeds are the followers of the prince of darkness while the good seeds are the followers of Christ. At the end of time the good will be separated from the bad and the good will enter heaven while the bad will be cast below where there will be weeping and grinding of teeth. This is yet another reminder for us to examine our lives and see where we are for we do not know when judgement day will come for each of us – maybe tomorrow, maybe next year.

Wednesday of the Seventeenth Week in Ordinary Time
Exodus 34:29-35; Psalm 98; Matthew 13:44-46

In the first reading from the Book of Exodus, Moses returns to the people with the tablets of the Law. His face is now radiant because he has been in the presence of God and this happens every time he meets with God. Jesus tells us in the gospel about a man who finds a field with a hidden treasure – he sells everything he has and buys the field. The kingdom of heaven is the most prized possession in existence and if we only realised this we would do all we could to make sure that we too attain it. We do so by believing in Christ, by daily converting to the gospel and by proclaiming the good news wherever we go.

Thursday of the Seventeenth Week in Ordinary Time
Exodus 40:16-21, 34-38; Psalm 83; Matthew 13:47-53

We read of the construction of the first tabernacle by Moses in the Book of Exodus. The tabernacle contained the Ark of the Covenant with the tablets of the Law and there the Lord dwelled. When the Lord left the tabernacle the Israelites moved on but when he was in the tabernacle they rested. In today's gospel passage we have another parable about the kingdom of God, this time using the analogy of fishermen. The parable reminds us that there are both saints and sinners here on earth but the final sifting should be left to God. Those who are worthy will enter heaven; those who are not worthy will not enter. Again we are challenged to look closely at our own lives and to do all we can to ensure that we are on the right path for entry into heaven, if that is truly what we seek.

Friday of the Seventeenth Week in Ordinary Time
Leviticus 23:1, 4-11, 15-16, 27, 34-37; Psalm 80; Matthew 13:54-58

In our reading from the Book of Leviticus the Lord instructs Moses about the solemn festivals which are to be held by the Jewish people each year – Pesach (the Passover) and Yom Kippur (the Day of Atonement). These are important reminders each year for the people of all that the Lord has done for them. In the gospel we see Jesus returning to his home town and teaching the people. His 'old neighbours' however, dismiss him because they did not want their comfortable little world to be changed.

As a result of their lack of faith he could work few miracles. Faith and healing are both gifts from God and if we refuse faith then we also refuse healing. We are all like the Nazarenes at times and need to remind ourselves that it is the kingdom we are talking about and that Jesus is the gate to that kingdom.

Saturday of the Seventeenth Week in Ordinary Time
Leviticus 25:1, 8-17; Psalm 66; Matthew 14:1-12
In the text from Leviticus we read of the establishment of the jubilee year. The Lord instructs the people that every fiftieth year is to be a special year for them and they are to return to their own clans that year to celebrate the sacred jubilee. Part of the jubilee was also the practice of leaving the land fallow for that year to allow its fertility to return. It is a reminder that God is the Lord of Creation and the owner of all that exists. In the gospel text we read of the martyrdom of John the Baptist at the hands of Herod the Tetrarch. John died because of the vanity of Herod who had made a rash promise to a beautiful girl and was afraid to go back on it even though he knew that what he was about to do was wrong. It is not always easy to do the right thing but when it comes to the kingdom of God, the right thing is the only thing to do for it will secure our place in heaven alongside John the Baptist and those who gave their lives for the sake of the kingdom.

Note: In the eighteenth week of Sunday Cycle A, read Tuesday's gospel on Monday and use the special gospel on Tuesday.

Monday of the Eighteenth Week in Ordinary Time
Numbers 11:4-15; Psalm 80; Matthew 14:13-21
In our first reading from the Book of Numbers we have the account of the people complaining that all they have to eat is manna which they have now grown tired of. The Lord is angry but Moses pleads with him out of fear. We can also sense Moses' frustration at the constant whining of the people who still prefer their life of servitude under the Egyptians to their life of freedom under God. In the gospel we see Jesus feeding the multitude from five loaves and two fish. The people came wishing to listen to him even as he mourned for John the Baptist and they

received more than they had expected. Those who turn to the Lord in faith and openness of heart will be fed and strengthened by him for their earthly journey.

For Year A: Use Tuesday's gospel

Tuesday of the Eighteenth Week in Ordinary Time

Numbers 12:1-13; Psalm 50; Matthew 14:22-36

In the first reading today from the Book of Numbers we see that Moses has married a Cushite woman which did not find favour with Miriam and Aaron, so they speak against Moses. Part of their anger also comes from jealousy at the fact that they did not have the same standing in God's eyes as their brother Moses. They too had acted on behalf of God but Moses was the one with all the glory. The Lord is angered by this and he summons the three of them to the tent of meeting where he reprimands Miriam and Aaron for speaking against his servant. As the Lord departs, Miriam is turned into a leper. Aaron asks the Lord for forgiveness but it is the prayer of Moses which sees Miriam cured – proving his closeness to God and his superiority. The psalm reminds us of Aaron and Miriam asking for forgiveness for speaking against Moses. In the gospel we see Jesus walking across the lake to the disciples who were fishing. Peter begins to walk across the water to him but he doubts what he is doing and flounders. The episode is a further reminder that Christ is the Lord of all Creation and has power even over nature itself. It also reminds us that with faith in Christ we can overcome anything and be successful in our endeavours.

For Year A: Matthew 15:1-2, 10-14

In our gospel text we see the scribes and Pharisees again questioning Jesus about the actions of his disciples, this time with regard to washing before eating. He tells them that what God has planted is good and that what a person eats does not make them bad. Rather, what is within the person makes them bad. Because the scribes and Pharisees have failed to grasp this they are like blind people. We too will be blind if we do not listen to the message of the gospel and live that out in our own lives.

Wednesday of the Eighteenth Week in Ordinary Time
Numbers 13:1-2, 25-14:1, 26-29, 34-35; Psalm 105; Matthew 15:21-28
In our first reading today from the Book of Numbers we see that
Moses has sent men into Canaan to check out the country. They
come back and give a favourable report as to its fertility but a
negative one as to the people they wish to displace. The people
again complain against God and doubt his ability to deliver the
land to them. Therefore he punishes them by allowing them to
wander for a generation in the desert so that most of their current number will never see the Promised Land. In the gospel
text from St Matthew we see Jesus initially refusing to help a
woman because she was of the wrong tribe. However, when she
proves her faith, he grants her request and cures her sick daughter. We are reminded that simply asking the Lord for something
is useless unless we have faith and demonstrate that faith by living Christian lives.

Thursday of the Eighteenth Week in Ordinary Time
Numbers 20:1-13; Psalm 94; Matthew 16:13-23
We see the people continue their complaints against God in the
reading from the Book of Numbers. Again the complaint is
about food so the Lord orders Moses to strike the rock so that
water would flow for the people. Moses does this but not quite
as the Lord commanded, so Moses is told that he will not lead
the people into the Promised Land. The psalm reminds us of the
complaining of the people. In the gospel for today we have St
Peter's great profession of faith: 'You are the Christ, the Son of
the living God.' Christ then goes on to predict his death in
Jerusalem and Peter pleads with him not to go there and, for this,
the Lord rebukes him for trying to prevent what must happen.
Despite his profession of faith Peter still did not fully understand what that profession really meant. Whenever we seek to
prevent the spread of the kingdom – knowingly or otherwise –
we are taking the place of Satan. God's ways are not our ways
and so we should always be open to the work of God in our
lives.

Friday of the Eighteenth Week in Ordinary Time
Deuteronomy 4:32-40; Psalm 76; Matthew 16:24-28
In the first reading from the Book of Deuteronomy, the last book of the Pentateuch, we see Moses rallying the people to return to God by reminding them of all that God had done for them both in Egypt and in the wilderness. The psalm takes up this theme. In the gospel we see Jesus teaching his disciples that those who directly seek happiness and pleasure will never find it but if they seek to do God's will then they will find true happiness. We each have a cross to bear and we must gladly take that up as Jesus took up his cross. We can only have life if we follow Jesus' example and remain faithful to God for true life is found, not on this earth, but in the kingdom to come.

Saturday of the Eighteenth Week in Ordinary Time
Deuteronomy 6:4-13; Psalm 17; Matthew 17:14-20
In our first reading today, Moses gives the people the *Shema Israel* (Listen, Israel) which Christ later identified as the greatest commandment. These are the words which orthodox Jewish men wear on their foreheads and on their arms when praying. It is recited by all Jews in their morning and night prayers. It is also in the scroll found at doorways where we would have a holy water font. In the gospel we see Jesus growing impatient with his disciples because they had been unable to cure a boy of his possession. Despite all they had seen and heard the disciples still have little faith and Jesus tells them that if their faith were stronger they could do anything. So too with us. If we have real faith in Christ and not just lip-service then we will overcome all adversities in life and gain eternal life.

Monday of the Nineteenth Week in Ordinary Time
Deuteronomy 10:12-22; Psalm 147; Matthew 17:22-27
In our first reading today we see Moses calling the people to-gether and reminding them of the importance of looking after the neediest people in their society – the poor, the orphaned, the widowed. He reminds them also of God's love for them and urges them not just to have faith but to let that faith be seen in how they live their lives. In our gospel text we see Jesus predicting his coming death at the hands of men but also his

resurrection. The disciples are saddened to hear of his coming death but the prospect of his resurrection has little impact on them for they still did not fully understand all his teaching. We are reminded today to be faithful to God and to give thanks to him for all that we have received from his bounty and to let others see that faith at work in our lives.

Tuesday of the Nineteenth Week in Ordinary Time
Deuteronomy 31:1-8; Psalm: Deuteronomy 32:3-4, 7-9; Matthew 18:1-5, 10, 12-14
We read in our text from Deuteronomy that Moses is appointing Joshua – his military commander – as leader of the Israelites as they now cross into the Promised Land. Moses himself is now quite old and the Lord has already told him that he will not enter the land with the people. In the gospel text Jesus tells us to be like little children for they are the most precious in the eyes of God and their angels are continually in the presence of the Father. Today, children are protected in our society but, in the time of Christ, they had little standing or protection. Their example of trust is what we must strive for and work towards every day.

Wednesday of the Nineteenth Week in Ordinary Time
Deuteronomy 34:1-12; Psalm 65; Matthew 18:15-20
Today we read of the death of Moses and how Joshua, son of Nun and military commander, led the people to the Promised Land. Before he dies, Moses ascends to the top of Mount Nebo close to the Dead Sea where he has a good view of the land the Chosen People are now about to enter. In preparing Joshua for this moment, we are told that Moses laid his hands on Joshua, a ritual which is still part of the Ordination Rite to this day. Our psalm is a hymn of praise for all the Lord has done. In the gospel, we see Jesus giving instructions for sorting out legal problems. It may seem odd that he would tell his followers to treat people like pagans and tax collectors if they did not listen but then we must remember that the tax collectors he had with him were those who demonstrated their faith in him and so were welcomed into his flock. In the last part of the passage he tells us that where two or three are gathered in his name that he is there among them. This is not simply confined to prayer and

the church but could be any gathering for prayer, business, etc, and which should begin with a prayer to the Lord for guidance.

Thursday of the Nineteenth Week in Ordinary Time
Joshua 3:7-11, 13-17; Psalm 113A; Matthew 18:21-19:1
In the reading from the Book of Joshua we see that the Ark of the Lord leads the people on dry ground across the Jordan River into the Promised Land. The Ark reminds us of the cloud which guided the people out of Egypt, and the crossing of the River Jordan reminds us of the crossing through the Red Sea. The journey which began so long ago has now reached its conclusion and fulfilment. The psalm summarises some of the events which have taken place since the Passover in Egypt. In the gospel, Jesus reminds us of the importance of forgiveness. We are forgiven by God for what we have done wrong when we go to confession but the sacrament is negated if we ourselves do not forgive those who have hurt us or sinned against us. Jesus uses a story to illustrate this for his listeners. It is not always easy to forgive others but it is something which we must be prepared to do because it would be hypocritical of us to expect forgiveness for what we have done while we withhold forgiveness from others.

Friday of the Nineteenth Week in Ordinary Time
Joshua 24:1-13; Psalm 135; Matthew 19:3-12
In our first reading today from the Book of Joshua, the Lord speaks through Joshua and reminds the people of all that he has done for them – how he freed them from slavery in Egypt, fought battles on their behalf and gave them a land that they never worked and towns that they never built. The psalm is a hymn of praise for all this. Our gospel text today is not an easy one for many people for it deals with marriage and in it Christ is quite clear that marriage is indissoluble regardless of the circumstances. The Jews were allowed to divorce and so Christ was very much out of step with the tradition within which he had grown up but he tells the people that they only have divorce because they were stubborn people. However, he tells us that divorce is not in keeping with the Divine plan and so is not acceptable.

Saturday of the Nineteenth Week in Ordinary Time
Joshua 24:14-29; Psalm 15; Matthew 19:13-15

Our reading from the Book of Joshua sees Joshua asking the people which god they wish to serve – the true God or the gods of the land they have just entered. They wish to serve the true God and Joshua reminds them that if they go astray they will be cast off by the God they have sworn to serve. Joshua renews the covenant that was made on Mount Sinai and then divides the land among the tribes of Israel. Again today we see Jesus welcoming children and reminding his listeners to be like children in their faith. Too often we try to rationalise things or explain them scientifically and so miss the mysterious and the divine at work in our world. But a child trusts their parents implicitly and this is what we too must do. Only by trusting God completely can we inherit eternal life.

Monday of the Twentieth Week in Ordinary Time
Judges 2:11-19; Psalm 105; Matthew 19:16-22

In our first reading today from the Book of Judges we see that the people have quickly deserted the way of the Lord and do all that is against his will and so he allowed them to be taken and subjected by their enemies. He appointed judges for them but as soon as each judge died they behaved worse than ever before because even though the leadership was strong, they themselves were weak. This sequence of events took place over a period of about 150 years from the time the Chosen People arrived in the Promised Land to the time of the first king. This also corresponds to the time when the Hebrews moved from being nomads to being settled farmers. In the gospel we have the story of the rich young man who comes to Jesus seeking eternal life. He has kept the commandments but Jesus tells him that he must give up all that he has. To most people the young man deserves eternal life because he did no wrong but Jesus makes a distinction between being good and being perfect. It's easy enough to be good but it takes real conviction to be perfect.

Tuesday of the Twentieth Week in Ordinary Time
Judges 6:11-24; Psalm 84; Matthew 19:23-30

In our reading form the Book of Judges we see the Lord appointing Gideon as the one who will free his people from the oppression of the Midianites who were roving bands of nomads from the Arabian desert. We are reminded in this of Christ for scripture referred to his birthplace as the least of the tribes and this is how Gideon refers to himself. He seeks a sign that it is the Lord who is speaking and he receives one and so believes. In our gospel text the disciples are worried that they will not be able to enter the kingdom of heaven given what Jesus tells them. But he reassures them and us by telling us that while relying on our own abilities we cannot enter heaven, but with God on our side we can enter and receive our inheritance. We, like Gideon, have been given a mission but, unlike Gideon, we will not be given a specific individual sign but must trust in the Lord and live Christian lives. If we wait for a sign we will be waiting a long time and may miss the kingdom completely.

Wednesday of the Twentieth Week in Ordinary Time
Judges 9:6-15; Psalm 20; Matthew 20:1-16

In our first reading we see that the people have proclaimed Abimelech as their king despite the fact that the Lord was their king. In his story about trees, Jotham suggests that Abimelech will not be a good king and that in fact a king is not what the people need at all. In the gospel text from St Matthew, we see Jesus using a parable in which a landowner pays all of his servants the same wages though some had worked only an hour while others worked for the full day. The workers are, naturally, unhappy though he paid them according to the agreement he made with each one. The Lord has made an agreement with each one of us which is that if we keep his commandments and live according to the gospel then we will inherit eternal life. What is important is that we look after ourselves and not be worrying or be nosey about others and what they are doing or not doing as the case may be. The Lord deals with each person individually and while we worship collectively and live as members of one family, we must look after ourselves and make sure that we are truly living out the gospel values.

Thursday of the Twentieth Week in Ordinary Time
Judges 11:29-39; Psalm 39; Matthew 22:1-14

In our reading today from the Book of Judges we see Jephthah being successful over the Ammonites. But the victory comes at a high price because he must now sacrifice his daughter – his only child – in return for the victory and the vow he had made to God. We are reminded of Abraham who was willing to sacrifice his only son and of Christ, who gave himself to fulfil the Covenant Promise. In the gospel we have the parable of the marriage feast to which none of those who were initially invited bother to attend. The wedding banquet represents the kingdom and God is the king who issues the invites. He is under no obligation to issue the invites but he invites everyone and anyone just as he has invited all of us. An important part of accepting the invite is that we prepare ourselves properly for admittance to the banquet and that means converting our lives to the gospel. There is a note of urgency in the text which reminds us to convert today and not tomorrow, for tomorrow may never come for some of us.

Friday of the Twentieth Week in Ordinary Time
Ruth 1:1, 3-6, 14-16, 22; Psalm 145; Matthew 22:34-40

Our first reading today comes from the Book of Ruth and in it we see Naomi returning to her own people for she has heard that the Lord is with them and looking after them. She herself has suffered the loss of her husband and her two sons and now one of her daughters-in-law is returning to her own people. But the second daughter-in-law – Ruth, a Gentile – will not leave her but clings to her and takes Naomi's people as her people and Naomi's God as her God. In the gospel Jesus is questioned by the authorities as to what he saw as the greatest commandment. He quotes the *Shema Israel* ('Listen, Israel ...' – Deuteronomy) as the core of the faith. He also adds love of neighbour as the second commandment. Our Lord then says that everything hangs on these two commandments because if we fulfil the letter of the Law but without love of God or love of neighbour then our observance of the Law will be of little value to us. In all that we do we must work from a foundation of love.

Saturday of the Twentieth Week in Ordinary Time

Ruth 2:1-3, 8-11, 4:13-17; Psalm 127; Matthew 23:1-12

We see Ruth being rewarded in the first reading for her kindness to her mother-in-law, Naomi. In time she marries a man of her father-in-law's tribe, named Boaz, and she gave birth to a son whose grandson was King David. In our gospel text, Jesus tells the people to do what the scribes and Pharisees tell them to do for they have authority, but he also tells them not to do what the scribes and Pharisees actually do for they do it for show. Our faith and the expression of our faith must be genuine for if it is done for show then people will see through this very quickly and God quickest of all. Our lives must be humble and genuinely Christian if we are to inherit the kingdom.

Monday of the Twenty-first Week in Ordinary Time

1 Thessalonians 1:1-5, 8-10; Psalm 149; Matthew 23:13-22

Today we begin reading from St Paul's first letter to the Thessalonians which was written in Corinth between 50-51AD, possibly following reports received from St Timothy. In today's opening section we see Paul reminding them that God loves them. Many of Paul's letters were written to bring his readers back to the right path and to keep them faithful to God. In this letter he does this by reminding the people of all that they have received from God and of the great faith they had from the outset. The Christian community at Thessalonica was founded there by Paul about twenty years after the resurrection on what was an important point on the trade routes between east and west. The psalm is a hymn of praise for God. In the gospel we see Jesus rebuking the scribes and Pharisees because they have become too interested in technicalities and are, therefore, a block to the people drawing closer to God. This is a constant reminder to us that we can become too engrossed in details and so miss out on a wonderful and intimate relationship with God who does so much for us.

Tuesday of the Twenty-first Week in Ordinary Time

1 Thessalonians 2:1-8; Psalm 138; Matthew 23:23-26

In our first reading St Paul is reminding the Thessalonians of how he and his companions conducted themselves when they were in Thessalonica – they brought them the message with humility. When Paul first visited Thessalonica there were those who refused to accept his word and the faithful had to smuggle him out of the city. In the gospel passage for today, we again see Jesus scolding the scribes and Pharisees and calling them hypocrites because they have again been more concerned with the little details and have forgotten about the virtues of justice, mercy and good faith. They are more concerned with their external appearance while inside they are a poor example for the people. We must convert internally every day and in this way we will give an external example to others of true Christian living.

Wednesday of the Twenty-first Week in Ordinary Time
1 Thessalonians 2:9-13; Psalm 138; Matthew 23:27-32
St Paul tells the Thessalonians in the first reading of how he slaved for the people in order to bring them the good news. He reminds them that he was a tentmaker and was therefore able to live off his own independence and not be a burden to others while preaching the good news. This was possibly added to quieten those who tried to discredit Paul by saying that he preached solely for money. In our gospel text for today, Jesus continues to berate the scribes and Pharisees and he tells them that, while they appear to be good on the outside, on the inside they are full of hypocrisy for they are no better than those who killed the prophets. There is a contrast in our readings today between the single-minded Paul of the first reading, who wants people to be saved, and the Pharisees of the gospel who are looking after their own reputations and status rather than leading the people to God.

Thursday of the Twenty-first Week in Ordinary Time
1 Thessalonians 3:7-13; Psalm 89; Matthew 24:42-51
In our first reading we see St Paul praising the Thessalonians because he has heard from St Timothy of their great faith. He is currently in Corinth where things are not going so well for him and he tells them that he wishes he could see them again as this would be a boost to him. Having praised them he goes on to encourage them to a greater love than they already have, a love which would encompass the whole human race. In the gospel

we see Jesus exhorting the people to be always ready because nobody knows when this life will end. We cannot be Christians whenever it suits us but must always live out our Christianity so that whenever the Lord does call he will find us ready and pure.

Friday of the Twenty-first Week in Ordinary Time
1 Thessalonians 4:1-8; Psalm 96; Matthew 25:1-13
We see St Paul in our first reading explicitly calling the people of Thessalonica to holiness and to avoid anything which would lead them into sin and away from God. Sexual immorality was widespread in Paul's day and he was aware that the Thessalonians were living in a society in which this was very common. He reminds them that each person can become a temple for the Holy Spirit and therefore every human being must be treated with great respect. In our gospel text today we have the same theme as yesterday – that of being ready. Today Jesus uses the parable of the foolish bridesmaids who were caught out when the bridegroom arrived at an unexpected hour. Those who are prepared and have lived good lives will enter the kingdom with the Lord, but those who have not, will not necessarily enter because they may not have time to repent and return to the right path. It is quite easy for us to assume that we have years left in us yet, but, for some, it could all end today.

Saturday of the Twenty-first Week in Ordinary Time
1 Thessalonians 4:9-11; Psalm 97; Matthew 25:14-30
St Paul continues to encourage the people to love one another and today he tells them that it was from God that they learned to love, and that with the help of God and their willingness they will learn to love even more than they do at present. He also reminds them that he taught them to live in such a way that others would see Christianity in action and so come to believe. We have the parable of the talents in our gospel text for today and it is a reminder to us that we all have talents but that we won't fully realise those gifts unless we actually try. Some have huge and obvious talents but everyone has small talents too and these are just as important as the big obvious ones that some people seem to have. In any case we must work to the best of our ability for the sake of the kingdom.

Monday of the Twenty-second Week in Ordinary Time
1 Thessalonians 4:13-18; Psalm 95; Luke 4:16-30
In our first reading today St Paul is encouraging the Thessalonians to remain faithful to God and he tells them that those who are faithful will be taken up to heaven to be with Christ. Some in Thessalonica had been worrying about their dead relatives and were beginning to despair like some of the pagans. Paul reminds them of how non-believers mourn when people die but that as believers there is no need to mourn: full union with Christ is what we seek and that with this thought we should console each other and remain in hope. For the remainder of this liturgical year we read from St Luke's gospel and in today's text we see Jesus returning to his home town of Nazareth for the first time. He reads from the prophet Isaiah and then instructs the people, telling them that he is the fulfilment of the text he had just read. They were enraged because they thought they knew him from his childhood, and so they took him to one of the high ridges on which Nazareth is built and tried to kill him, but he slipped away. The text is a reminder that the message of God is not dependent on the messenger for its validity and that Christ is present in each person no matter how well we think we might know them. We must always be open to seeing and hearing the word of God in others.

Tuesday of the Twenty-second Week in Ordinary Time
1 Thessalonians 5:1-6, 9-11; Psalm 26; Luke 4:31-37
St Paul in the first reading for today is encouraging his readers to remain faithful to God and to the good news which they received from Christ. He refers to 'the day of the Lord' which is a phrase found in the Old Testament and which was used by the prophets to indicate that a new phase of human existence was about to begin as God cleansed the world. He says this because the new phase had just begun with the resurrection of Christ and so the people were to change their way of life in keeping with Christ's sacrifice for them. They are also to encourage one another to remain faithful so as to receive the reward which God has for all who believe in him. The psalm echoes Paul's sentiments. In the gospel passage from St Luke we see Jesus in Capernaum where he heals a possessed man whose demons

recognise him as the 'Holy One of God.' The people are impressed by Jesus not simply because of his teaching but also because of the authority with which he teaches.

Wednesday of the Twenty-second Week in Ordinary Time
Colossians 1:1-8; Psalm 51; Luke 4:38-44
Today we begin reading from St Paul's letter to the Colossians which he wrote while under house arrest in Rome (61-63AD) following news of a crisis in Colossae. The purpose of this letter was to bolster the faith of the community but also to correct errors and heretical tendencies which had been introduced into the community's faith. Paul begins by giving thanks for the people and their faith and telling them about how the good news is spreading throughout the world. In our gospel text we see Jesus healing people and casting out devils. He then tries to go to a quiet place while the people try to stop him because they want to keep him to themselves but he tells them that his message is for all people and so he has to go and sow the seeds in other towns and places. The message is for all people and we have a duty to help in the spread of that message wherever we may find ourselves.

Thursday of the Twenty-second Week in Ordinary Time
Colossians 1:9-14; Psalm 97; Luke 5:1-11
St Paul continues to praise the people of the small town of Colossae today for their faith and in this way to encourage them to grow ever deeper in the faith. He reminds them that, through Christ, God has taken them out of darkness and forgiven them their sins. In today's gospel text we see Jesus calling Simon Peter and his companions to be his followers. They do so after they make a huge catch of fish on the lake, though they had caught nothing in the same place only a few hours before. What is key in this text is the complete and total response of Peter and his companions to Jesus' call – 'they left everything and followed him.' This is in sharp contrast to the people in Nazareth, whom we read about on Monday, who wanted to kill Jesus after they had listened to him. A question for us today is whether or not our response is as total as that of Simon Peter, and, if not, why not?

Friday of the Twenty-second Week in Ordinary Time
Colossians 1:15-20; Psalm 99; Luke 5:33-39

In our first reading today we have a hymn in which the author reminds us of the central role of Christ in creation as its Lord. It is through Christ that all things are created and he is the perfection towards which creation is to move and to which we are being called. St Paul speaks elsewhere of Christ as being the Head of the Church (his Body) and this reaches its high point in this text. The Pharisees in the gospel are questioning Jesus as to why his disciples do not fast like so many others. In his reply he tells them that as long as he is with them they will not fast. He also goes on to speak about new and old wine. The implication is that the new wine stands for the good news and the old stands for the Mosaic Law. He doesn't do away with the old because God's will is also to be found in the old but the old is completed by the new. Jesus is showing how the Jewish people of his day preferred the old wine of tradition to the new wine he was offering them.

Saturday of the Twenty-second Week in Ordinary Time
Colossians 1:21-23; Psalm 53; Luke 6:1-5

In the first reading St Paul reminds the Colossians of what they used to be and what they are now through the death of Christ. He wants them to continue on the path which brings them to greater union with God rather than the path which will take them further from God's love – he wants them to go forwards rather than backwards. Again in today's gospel we see the Pharisees quizzing Jesus about the actions of his disciples who are breaking the Sabbath by picking corn. In reply Jesus tells them that in fact he is Lord of the Sabbath – he is not there to decide over Sabbath disputes but is the Lord of the Sabbath. In this way he is also telling them that as the Sabbath is subordinate to him then so too is the Law which they follow and use against the disciples. It is a reminder to us that Christ is Lord of all and it is to him that we owe our homage.

Monday of the Twenty-third Week in Ordinary Time
Colossians 1:24-2:3; Psalm 61; Luke 6:6-11

As we read St Paul's letter to the Colossians we see Paul telling them that he is happy to suffer for them because he believes so completely in the message he brings them and in Christ who is their salvation. So precious is the gift which he is handing on that he is happy to bear any hardship for their sake even though he has never seen them. This is part of Paul's writing style to encourage the people to remain faithful to the message. In the gospel text we again see Jesus in trouble with the Pharisees on a Sabbath day. He questions them and asks them if it is lawful to do good on the Sabbath because they would allow nothing to be done. What Christ does on the Sabbath is good for he healed a man with a withered hand. We are again reminded not to create too many laws and to make them our god, but to serve God alone in purity and sincerity of heart.

Tuesday of the Twenty-third Week in Ordinary Time
Colossians 2:6-15; Psalm 144; Luke 6:12-19

St Paul reminds the Colossians of what it is that Christ has done for them and for us – he has forgiven all our sins, he has shared his divinity with us and he has freed us from all that would keep us from God's love. These are Paul's reasons for us to continue growing in the faith. The psalm is one of praise for God. In the gospel we see Jesus choosing his twelve most intimate followers and then going on to cure those who come to him. What is key in the text is that before he made his decision, Jesus 'spent the whole night in prayer.' This is a reminder to us that we too should pray to the Lord for guidance no matter what decision we have to make in life and no matter how trivial it may seem. With the Lord on our side to help us we should ask for that help so that we will be able to see our decision through to a successful end.

Wednesday of the Twenty-third Week in Ordinary Time
Colossians 3:1-11; Psalm 144; Luke 6:20-26

St Paul tells the people in his letter to the Colossians that through baptism and accepting Christ as their Saviour they rid themselves of all that was impure and made themselves spotless. He now encourages them to remain spotless and faithful to that new life which they received in Christ and he gives them a few examples of the sort of things – every day things – which must not be allowed to creep back in to their lives. Our psalm is a continuation of yesterday's hymn of praise. In the gospel we read Luke's account of the Beatitudes. We have heard these beautiful phrases many times throughout our lives and several times a year but do we really pay any attention to them? Do we see them as lovely phrases or do we see them as a radical blueprint for living and one which we should try to practice in our own lives? Only when we see them as the latter and actively live by them can our world change for the better and so acknowledge that there is a God who is close to his people.

Thursday of the Twenty-third Week in Ordinary Time
Colossians 3:12-17; Psalm 150; Luke 6:27-38
In our closing section from the letter to the Colossians, St Paul exhorts us to put on love as the garment which covers all others and keeps all the garments of good living pure and spotless. In so doing we will put others before our needs and will please the Lord in all things. Paul also speaks about how important gratitude is as part of our daily lives. A similar theme is found in the gospel where we continue reading from the Sermon on the Mount. Today Jesus is teaching the people to be compassionate just as God is compassionate and he uses very concrete and familiar examples to teach the people. The one we should always look to and try to imitate is God, because he is perfect and shows us the way to eternal life.

Friday of the Twenty-third Week in Ordinary Time
1 Timothy 1:1-2, 12-14; Psalm 15; Luke 6:39-42
We now turn to St Paul's first letter to St Timothy, written in 65AD, which opens with an invocation of God's grace. Paul goes on to tell Timothy that he, Paul, was found to be worthy by God to be his messenger and this is a reminder that anyone can become God's messenger at any time if they are willing to convert and become a true believer. Paul was one of the greatest persecutors of the early church and yet he has been found worthy to

become its greatest messenger to the Gentiles. Paul received a personal and unambiguous call on the road to Damascus but we are called every day by virtue of our baptism, though not always as clearly as the call Paul received. In the gospel, Jesus is telling his disciples of the necessity to have the eyes of faith opened by his teaching so that they may lead themselves and others along the path that leads to life. Only when they have come to an understanding of the faith can they effectively teach it to others and build up the faith of the community.

Saturday of the Twenty-third Week in Ordinary Time
1 Timothy 1:15-17; Psalm 112; Luke 6:43-49
In writing to St Timothy, St Paul reminds him that Christ came to save sinners. As an example and proof of that, Paul says that he himself was the greatest of sinners and now he is counted as an apostle – appointed by God himself. Anyone who believes and is daily converted to the gospel can become a disciple. In the gospel, Jesus too reminds us of the necessity of daily conversion and really living out the gospel message in our lives. Simply acknowledging Jesus will do nothing for us but if we acknowledge him and live out the gospel every day then we will be on the right path to eternal life as he has promised us. This will also give a very good and encouraging example to others of real Christian living and so help the building up of the kingdom.

Monday of the Twenty-fourth Week in Ordinary Time
1 Timothy 2:1-8; Psalm 27; Luke 7:1-10
In our first reading from his first letter to St Timothy, we see St Paul exhorting Timothy and his companions to pray because this is what pleases God and it will also help others to come to salvation which is what God wants. There is also a reminder in the letter that God's offer of salvation knows no limits. The psalm reminds us that God listens to us when we call to him in prayer. In our gospel passage from St Luke, we see a centurion coming to Jesus to plead for the life of his servant. The man's request is answered because of his faith even though he is not of the House of Israel. This is the faith to which we are called – a faith which trusts Jesus completely in all things. It also shows us that God does answer our prayers, particularly when those prayers are for others.

Tuesday of the Twenty-fourth Week in Ordinary Time
1 Timothy 3:1-13; Psalm 100; Luke 7:11-17

Our first reading today from the first letter to Timothy gives us guidelines for the sort of people who should be admitted to service in the church as presidents of communities (bishops) and as deacons. It gives us an image of the early hierarchy of the Church with a married clergy and women working closely with deacons. St Paul also comments on how other people too should live. It is a good reminder to us that what we do is done in public and that we are answerable to the community as well as to God and we should always give a Christian example in living. In our gospel we see Jesus comforting the widow of Nain and restoring her only son to life. This is a further sign for the people of the greatness of Christ but also shows his compassion for those who suffer. The widow had lost the only person she had left in this world who would look after her and take care of her and so Christ answered her need by restoring her son to her. Luke is the only evangelist who records this miracle but it fits with his image of Jesus who always feels deeply the distress of his people. The Lord always comforts us in our sorrows and supports us in our pain, and while not always as obvious as in today's gospel he is always there to help us and to give us strength.

Wednesday of the Twenty-fourth Week in Ordinary Time
1 Timothy 3:14-16; Psalm 110; Luke 7:31-35

St Paul in his first letter to St Timothy reminds his co-worker that the mysteries of our religion are very deep. He offers no explanation because none could do justice to God but he does give a very brief summary of the mystery. The letter also shows Paul's concern for Timothy himself who is now looking after the church in Ephesus where Paul himself had spent time. In the gospel we see Jesus teaching the people. He puts it to them that when John the Baptist appeared and didn't act as they would expect, they called him a mad man. Yet when Christ himself appeared among them doing what they expected John to do, they likewise would not accept him but called him a drunkard. Christ is pointing out that the people do not decide what the messenger should be like. The messenger is appointed by God and acts on his behalf proclaiming the message as God has instructed. It is for the people to recognise the messenger and to listen to and accept the message if they are to attain eternal life. We must never see God and his message in our terms.

Thursday of the Twenty-fourth Week in Ordinary Time
1 Timothy 4:12-16; Psalm 110; Luke 7:36-50
Again today St Paul reminds St Timothy, and those who read the letter, that what we do and say must be done properly and with care because it is done in public. As Christians we speak and act on God's behalf as his disciples and so others must see that in the way we live our lives. Timothy is the 'bishop' of Ephesus and so must lead the flock by example and show to those who criticise him that he is right and a dedicated servant of the Good News. In the gospel we see Jesus at table with some Pharisees when a woman of ill-repute comes into the room. She anoints Christ's feet with her tears and wipes them with her hair. The polite guests are indignant that he should put up with this but he points out that she has done this because she loves him as her Saviour while the host failed to show him as much love or respect. Here again Christ is looking at the inner person and judging in a way which we usually overlook. We are reminded to be Christ-like in our actions and in our dealings with others no matter who they are, for Christ is dwelling in each one of us.

Friday of the Twenty-fourth Week in Ordinary Time
1 Timothy 6:2-12; Psalm 48; Luke 8:1-3
St Paul calls upon St Timothy to be saintly in all that he does and to seek only the profit of spirituality and not material possessions. The latter we cannot take with us and so we should and must concentrate on the spiritual. Paul was also aware that Timothy was going to encounter those who would seek to make financial gain out of preaching and he did not want Timothy to fall in to the same trap but to stick to the sound principles for a happy life as given by Christ. The psalm reminds us that we cannot buy life from God or avoid the grave. In the brief gospel text for today we are given the names of some of the women who accompanied Jesus on his travels and looked after his needs. These were loyal to Christ even to following him to Calvary and assisting with his burial.

Saturday of the Twenty-fourth Week in Ordinary Time
1 Timothy 6:13-16; Psalm 99; Luke 8:4-15
St Paul continues his exhortation to Timothy today and reminds him that Christ is the source of all life and so he must remain steadfast as a servant of Christ. As Christ bore witness before Pontius Pilate so too Timothy must bear witness until the end of his life. In our gospel passage we have the familiar parable of the Sower going out to sow seed. The different places where the seed fell represent humankind's response to Christ. The important phrase for us is 'Listen, anyone who has ears to hear!' If we truly listen to the word of God then we will grow in faith for we will realise the great promise that awaits those who listen, hear and take to heart the word of God.

Monday of the Twenty-fifth Week in Ordinary Time
Ezra 1:1-6; Psalm 125; Luke 8:16-18
For the next three weeks we return to the Old Testament for our first reading, beginning today with the book of Ezra which was probably written in the third century before Christ but concerning the return from Exile in 515-513BC. In our section today we see God moving the heart of King Cyrus to allow the Jews to rebuild the Temple in Jerusalem, which had been destroyed by the Babylonians and who were later defeated by the Persians who now rule the land. In the gospel text we have the parable of the lamp in which Jesus reminds us that nothing is secret. We live and work in communities and so what we do will ultimately be known to the community but, more importantly, everything is known to God. Our faith too is something which is not strictly private for the Christian community is a public one and we are called to proclaim our faith in public, though not so as to gain any adulation from others but so that others may see our example and, through us, come to know the living God.

Tuesday of the Twenty-fifth Week in Ordinary Time
Ezra 6:7-8, 12, 14-20; Psalm 121; Luke 8:19-21
In the text from Ezra we read of the Israelites completing the Temple to God at the command of King Darius (it was begun under the rule of Cyrus). This was completed about the year 515BC on what was the site of Solomon's magnificent temple.

When the Temple was completed they restored the priesthood to it as Moses had prescribed in the Torah. The psalm speaks of rejoicing during the pilgrimage to the Temple in Jerusalem. In the gospel, Jesus tells us that those who listen to his word and carry out his wishes will be regarded as his mother and sisters and brothers. It is a challenge to us to ask ourselves if we are worthy of those titles and, if not, what are we willing to do to be seen as the close family of Jesus.

Wednesday of the Twenty-fifth Week in Ordinary Time
Ezra 9:5-9; Psalm: Tobit 13:2, 4, 6, 8; Luke 9:1-6

Today, Ezra the priest praises the Lord for he has given the people a refuge even after they had sinned against him which resulted in their slavery to the Persians. They were in slavery because they did not keep the covenants and had strayed from the Law of God. Yet God is still faithful to them and has moved the heart of the king to allow them to rebuild the Temple and now they have a place in which to worship and to continue their faith. The psalm reminds us that while God punishes us for our transgressions he is still merciful. In the gospel we see Jesus sending out the Twelve on their first solo mission to preach in his name. They are to preach and to heal and to prepare the people for the Good News. We too were commissioned at our baptism and have been sent out every day since to preach and to heal, but how many of us have actually done that for even a few minutes a day? If we were all to be faithful to our promises then this world would be a better place.

Thursday of the Twenty-fifth Week in Ordinary Time
Haggai 1:1-8; Psalm 149; Luke 9:7-9

Our reading today goes back a few years in the history of the Israelites to about the year 520BC. Work on the reconstruction of the Temple has slowed down at this point and the Lord sends the prophet Haggai to remind the people that while they live in very fine dwellings, the Temple of the Lord is still lying in ruins. The Lord instructs them to consider how life has gone for them and to then go and prepare the materials for the new building. In the gospel today we see that Herod has become aware of the presence of Christ in his jurisdiction. He has also heard the people speaking about Jesus and it shows us that despite his many signs and miracles and his preaching, the people still do not see Jesus as the Messiah. They still think he is John the Baptist or one of the ancient prophets come back to life. We too must ask ourselves who Christ is for us. Is he simply a saintly man, someone who preached about love and moral living or is he really our Lord and Saviour?

Friday of the Twenty-fifth Week in Ordinary Time
Haggai 1:15-2:9; Psalm 42; Luke 9:18-22
The Lord speaks through the prophet Haggai in the first reading and tells the people that he will bless the Temple which they are about to build him and it will be greater than the Temple of old. The people had become disheartened as they built this new structure because it had none of the splendour and magnificence of the building which had been commissioned by Solomon. The psalm reminds us to always hope in the Lord no matter what. In the gospel text for today we see St Peter make his great profession of faith when Jesus asked the disciples who they say he is. In their reply they also tell him what the people think and it echoes the text we had yesterday in which Herod reminds others that he had John the Baptist beheaded. Jesus is the Christ of God and that is the faith that we are called to repeat with Peter each day. But do we truly believe that or are we still blind like the people of the time? For if we truly believed, then our lives and this world would be so much better.

Saturday of the Twenty-fifth Week in Ordinary Time
Zechariah 2:5-9, 14-15; Psalm: Jeremiah 31:10-13; Luke 9:43-45
In the first reading today from the Prophet Zechariah (written between 520-517BC) we see the Lord telling the people that he will be the wall around Jerusalem which will protect the city and its people. At the same time he will be the glory which dwells in the midst of the people in the centre of the city. The people will not need to build a stone wall around the city for the Lord himself will be their protector when he returns to Zion. For the second time in the gospel this week we see Jesus telling the disciples that he will be handed over and will eventually die. They still do not understand what he is saying and they are too

afraid to ask. We have the benefit of their accounts of the life, death and resurrection of Christ and so we know that there was no need for them to be alarmed but to rejoice for salvation was in their midst. How much more they could have enjoyed the living presence of Christ had they known what we know? And yet we have this knowledge but do we really enjoy living in the presence of Christ, knowing that salvation has not only been promised to each one of us but has been guaranteed through the death and resurrection of Christ?

Monday of the Twenty-sixth Week in Ordinary Time
Zechariah 8:1-8; Psalm 101; Luke 9:46-50
In the first reading today from Zechariah we see that the Lord has now decided that the time of exile for the Jewish people is to come to an end and he is going to bring them home to Jerusalem. There are a number of prophecies about the future of the Jewish people contained in this book. The Lord tells the people that he will fill Jerusalem with both young and old which symbolise both prosperity and peace. The psalm speaks of the Lord rebuilding Jerusalem. In the gospel, we see the disciples arguing over who is the greatest. Jesus reminds them that all are to be servants – servants of God who holds everyone equal in his eyes.

Tuesday of the Twenty-sixth Week in Ordinary Time
Zechariah 8:20-23; Psalm 86; Luke 9:51-56
In the first reading we see that when the Lord has rebuilt Jerusalem the renown of the city as the dwelling place of God will spread far and wide. On that day people from other nations and creeds will seek the city to draw close to the Lord. This is about the year 520BC and is an encouragement to those who are rebuilding the Temple to continue in their work. In the gospel, Jesus now turns resolutely towards Jerusalem and his impending death. On the way some people and villages do not accept him and the disciples want to destroy them but Jesus stops them. This is a reminder that nobody will be forced to believe in Christ or in his way. It is for each man and woman to make up their own mind and to follow their own path in life. The first reading puts it before us that if we are truly living Christian

lives and giving a perfect example to our fellow men and women then they will come to us and ask us to lead them to the Lord. However, unless we give the example they will never see the path to salvation.

Wednesday of the Twenty-sixth Week in Ordinary Time
Nehemiah 2:1-8; Psalm 136; Luke 9:57-62
In our text from Nehemiah we have a further telling of the rebuilding of Jerusalem written about the third century before Christ on events that took place between 538 and 515BC. Nehemiah seeks to rebuild the ancient defences of the city and tells the king of his dream. The heart of the king is moved to grant Nehemiah his request and renew the city's walls. Again we see that the Lord moves the heart of the king to allow this to take place even though the king was not a Jew. In the gospel, we see people coming to Jesus to be his followers but each one has a condition to fulfil before he takes the path with Christ. We are reminded that we cannot place conditions on our following of Christ – we follow him wholeheartedly or we don't follow him at all. If we follow him then we will inherit eternal life.

Thursday of the Twenty-sixth Week in Ordinary Time
Nehemiah 8:1-12; Psalm 18; Luke 10:1-12
In our first reading today we read of the people gathered in the square to hear the word of the Lord read by Ezra and explained by the Levites. They are told that the day is sacred to the Lord and that they are to be happy and not sad. Ezra had spent time in exile with his fellow Jews and only returned to Jerusalem because he felt called to help the people rebuild their faith according to the Mosaic Law. Much of the faith of the people after this return from exile is shaped by Ezra. The psalm reminds us of the importance of the Law of God in our lives. In the gospel we see Jesus sending out seventy-two of his followers to preach in his name. We are their successors and therefore we have a duty to bring the gospel message to all people wherever or however we meet them.

Friday of the Twenty-sixth Week in Ordinary Time
Baruch 1:15-22; Psalm 78; Luke 10:13-16
In our first reading today we go back in time to about the year 587BC, close to the start of the Babylonian exile. It is a text that was sent by the exiles to those Jews who had been left behind in Palestine and was a public confession of their sins which caused their exile in the first place. The people are sinners while God is integrity. For their sinfulness and disloyalty the people acknowledge that they have suffered disasters. In the gospel from St Luke we see Jesus lamenting the fact that people and places have not accepted his message despite the miracles they have seen him work. Jesus was sent by God and those who reject him or his messengers ultimately reject God himself.

Saturday of the Twenty-sixth Week in Ordinary Time
Baruch 4:5-12, 27-29; Psalm 68; Luke 10:17-24
In the first reading the Prophet Baruch reminds the people that God, who punished them by bringing disaster on them, will redeem them and make them a nation again, but only if they themselves call on God. It is a reminder that the punishment by God is not a permanent thing but something which only lasts for a time and which can be ended if those who are being punished repent of their sins. In the gospel we see the seventy-two return to Jesus rejoicing that they have been successful in his name. He tells them to rejoice – not because they were able to cast out spirits – but because their names are written in heaven. Those who do the will of God have their names written in heaven and so they can rejoice. We too will have our names written in heaven if we live according to his commandments and let others see Christ present in their midst through our lives.

Monday of the Twenty-seventh Week in Ordinary Time
Jonah 1:1-2:1, 11; Psalm: Jonah 2:3-5, 8; Luke 10:25-37
Today we begin reading from the Book of Jonah and in the text we see the Lord calling on Jonah to be his messenger to the Ninevites. Jonah does not want this work and so tries to escape from the Lord by taking a ship to Tarshish. While on the voyage the ship encounters a storm and the others on the ship throw Jonah overboard in order to save themselves. The story is

thought to represent the Jewish attitude to foreign nations from about 539 to 333BC when the Jews held that other nations, and particularly the pagans, could never be the recipients of God's mercy. In the gospel we see a lawyer trying to outsmart Jesus but instead he gets the parable of the Good Samaritan. The parable was told to point out that our neighbour is not simply the person who believes what we believe or who lives in the same district. Our neighbour is anyone we encounter. Not alone must we acknowledge them as our neighbour, we must treat them with the respect that a son or daughter of God deserves. Only then can we truly be their neighbour and be worthy of the kingdom of God.

Tuesday of the Twenty-seventh Week in Ordinary Time
Jonah 3:1-10; Psalm 129; Luke 10:38-42
In our first reading we see God again calling Jonah to be his messenger and this time Jonah answers positively. This reminds us that there is no getting away from God – we cannot hide from him especially when he has work for us to do on his behalf. Jonah goes and preaches to the Ninevites and they believe in his words and renounce their ways. It was a reminder to the Jews that all people are worthy of hearing the word of God and that those other nations could easily respond far more positively than the Jews themselves. If we go and proclaim God's word at his request then he will be with us and will bring success to our endeavours. At the same time, we should not place ourselves above others because of our beliefs. In the gospel we see Jesus visiting the home of his friends Martha and Mary. There Mary sits down and spends time with the Lord while Martha fusses over being a good hostess. When she speaks to Jesus about this he tells her to be more like her sister – to take time with the Lord. It is all too easy to become pre-occupied with other things and not to give the necessary quiet time with the Lord each day. It is Mary's example which we are called on to follow today.

Wednesday of the Twenty-seventh Week in Ordinary Time
Jonah 4:1-11; Psalm 85; Luke 11:1-4
In the first reading from the Book of Jonah we see Jonah very annoyed with God because the Lord has relented and allowed the Ninevites to live. He reminds Jonah that he has put much

effort in to creating the world and all it contains and so he has every right to be angry when part of that creation turns sour but also every right to be merciful when that misguided part decides to change its sinful ways. Jonah was aware that God was going to be merciful and, like the Jews of the fifth century before Christ, he didn't want God to show mercy to anyone but the Jewish people. In the gospel we see Jesus praying. His disciples, wishing to be like their master, ask him to teach them how to pray and so he gives them the 'Our Father.' This one prayer sums up all of life – past, present and future; it asks the Lord for forgiveness while asking for the strength to forgive others and it asks the Lord to protect us from all temptation.

Thursday of the Twenty-seventh Week in Ordinary Time
Malachi 3:13-20; Psalm 1; Luke 11:5-13
Today we turn to the Book of Malachi, written about the middle of the fifth century before Christ, for our first reading and in it we see the Lord comforting those who are not pleased that the sinful seem to prosper as much and sometimes better than those who are God-fearing. But the Lord consoles them by telling them that the day of judgement for the sinful is fast approaching and that when it arrives it is those who have been God-fearing who will have the sun of righteousness shining on them. Our gospel text today is a continuation of yesterday's passage in which Jesus taught the disciples to pray and today we are told that those who pray to God will have their prayers answered. He doesn't tell us that we will get what it is that we are asking for but he does tell us that our prayers will be answered, especially if we are consistent in our prayers.

Friday of the Twenty-seventh Week in Ordinary Time
Joel 1:13-15, 2:1-2; Psalm 9; Luke 11:15-26
In our first reading today from Joel, written sometime between 400 and 350BC, the author is calling on the people to repent for the day of the Lord is at hand. The prophets called the people to repentance and to the observance of the covenants and this is what Joel does in our first reading. The people are being punished by the Lord with a locust plague but if the people repent then they will be saved. In the psalm we are reminded that

while the Lord will judge his people he will do so in justice and fairness. In the gospel we see Jesus asserting before the people that he is not Beelzebul – the prince of devils. He can cast out devils because he has authority over them – not the authority of the prince of devils but the authority which comes from being the Lord of Creation. He also tells us that those who wish to enter the kingdom must always be on their guard so that they are not distracted from the right path to the kingdom.

Saturday of the Twenty-seventh Week in Ordinary Time
Joel 4:12-21; Psalm 96; Luke 11:27-28
In today's text from the prophet Joel we see the Lord telling the people that their sins are more easily harvested than a full and plentiful harvest. But he is soon going to deal with his people and on that day he will weed out the good from the bad. In addressing Jerusalem, Joel addresses the nation, for Jerusalem stood for and represented the country. Afterwards the just will flourish. In the gospel, a woman calls out to Jesus and comments on how fortunate his mother was to have borne such a son. He replies that those who listen to the word of God are even more fortunate than his mother. This was not to denigrate his mother but to show the great importance for all of us to listen to God's word and to live that out in our lives.

Monday of the Twenty-eighth Week in Ordinary Time
Romans 1:1-7; Psalm 97; Luke 11:29-32
We now return to the New Testament and over the next four weeks will take our first reading from St Paul's letter to the Romans which was written to the church in Rome (though it was not founded by Paul) between 57 and 58AD. In today's passage we have Paul's opening comments in which he tells the people that he was called by God to be a disciple and to preach about Jesus Christ. The opening, or salutation, of the letter contains many of the truths of the faith held by the early Church. In the gospel we see Jesus teaching the people and he reminds them of Jonah who was sent to the Ninevites to bring them back to the right path, which we read of last week. He tells them that there is something greater than Jonah in their midst and that their generation is in more need of conversion than were the

Ninevites. Unlike the Ninevites, however, their generation will not listen or repent and so will be lost. We each have a duty to preach the good news as Paul did and to bring the message of salvation to all people so that they may change their ways as did the people of Nineveh.

Tuesday of the Twenty-eighth Week in Ordinary Time
Romans 1:16-25; Psalm 18; Luke 11:37-41
In today's passage from the letter to the Romans, St Paul reminds us that the everlasting power and divinity of God are visible in his creation. Even if God did not speak to his people directly they could still know him through his creation. In the letter Paul also points out what sort of lives people lead when they don't have faith in God. In the gospel, we see Jesus admonishing the Pharisees because they are too concerned with external things and are not at all concerned with what is to be found in the heart of a person. He reminds them that God made the inside and the outside of everything and that therefore both inside and outside are clean. However, what is within a person is of far more importance than what is on the outside. The Lord also tells us that giving to charity is one way of cleansing the heart.

Wednesday of the Twenty-eighth Week in Ordinary Time
Romans 2:1-11; Psalm 61; Luke 11:42-46
St Paul tells us in the first reading that God will reward all those who have been good and who keep to his ways. Those who refuse to repent and continue in their sinful ways will always receive their reward but each person's reward depends on what it is they have done in life in terms of faith and helping their fellow men and women. The response to the psalm reminds us of this. We again see Jesus admonishing the Pharisees in the gospel and he does so today because they have failed to be just or to love God – they have been too interested in the minutiae of the Law. He reminds them that they too will die but that they will be quickly forgotten because of their example. He admonishes lawyers (theologians of the day) because they heaped burdens on the people instead of helping them.

Thursday of the Twenty-eighth Week in Ordinary Time
Romans 3:21-30; Psalm 129; Luke 11:47-54
In the first reading St Paul tells us that we are justified by faith and not by mere observance of a Law. Keeping the Laws of God are important but if they are not done from a faith-driven desire then they are worthless. Faith is all important if our actions are to be seen as Christian and Christ-like and so bring us to eternal life. Paul also tells us that we do not earn faith because of our good works and so should never use our good deeds as a way of showing off our faith. In our gospel passage for today we again see Jesus admonishing the Pharisees for their lack of honesty before the Lord. They build the tombs for the prophets who their own forefathers had killed and so their generation will now pay for the slaughter of the prophets. The Pharisees then begin a 'furious attack on him to try to catch him out.'

Friday of the Twenty-eighth Week in Ordinary Time
Romans 4:1-8; Psalm 31; Luke 12:1-7
Our passage today from the letter to the Romans continues yesterday's theme in which St Paul tells us that we are not justified by our works but by our faith. He takes as an example Abraham, our Father in Faith. Abraham did many good things and could have boasted about them but what justified him was the fact that he put his faith in God. This was partly to 'correct' a belief – then prevalent among the Jews – that saw Abraham justified because of his actions after God's call rather than because of his faith in God. In the gospel text we see Jesus teaching the people and his disciples and reminding them that everything that is said and done is known to the Father. He also tells the disciples that they need not fear those who can kill our mortal bodies but to fear those who can kill the spirit also which is far more serious as this is the immortal part of our being. Trust in God will prevent such a thing from happening.

Saturday of the Twenty-eighth Week in Ordinary Time
Romans 4:13, 16-18; Psalm 104; Luke 12:9-12
St Paul again uses the example of Abraham in our first reading today to point out that Abraham was justified because of his faith and so too are all those who are his sons and daughters in

the faith if they too believe in God. Again, Paul is 'correcting' a belief among the rabbis of the time that Abraham was justified because of the Law of Moses rather than because of his belief in God. They are justified not because they are his biological descendents but because of their faith in God as Abraham had faith. In the gospel, Jesus tells the disciples that those who openly opt for God will have Christ on their side before the throne of God but that those who openly opt against God will have no one on their side. Christ will support those who believe in him but those who do not believe will be on their own. Those who do opt for God will not just have Christ on their side in heaven but will also have the Holy Spirit with them to guide them in all that they do and say.

Monday of the Twenty-ninth Week in Ordinary Time
Romans 4:20-25; Psalm: Luke 1:69-75; Luke 12:13-21
Before St Paul became a Christian he was a Pharisee and the Pharisees believed that people were justified if they adhered to the letter of the Law and so they lived their lives in fidelity to the Law. Now a Christian, Paul realises that more than mere adherence to laws is necessary – we must also have faith. He reminds us of Abraham who had complete faith in God even though he had no idea where God was leading him and when the promise made by God seemed to be impossible in view of how old he and Sarah were. Our psalm today is the familiar text of the *Benedictus*. In the gospel we are reminded by Jesus not to lay store on earthly things for these will not last or bring happiness. We must always place God above all else and see material things as secondary, requiring only what we truly need rather than what we want. Jesus tells the story of a rich man who died without learning this lesson.

Tuesday of the Twenty-ninth Week in Ordinary Time
Romans 5:12, 15, 17-21; Psalm 39; Luke 12:35-38
In the first reading from his letter to the Romans, St Paul tells us that as sin entered the world through one man so also the world is redeemed through one man. The first man is Adam and the second is Christ. No matter how many sins people may commit the grace of God is ever more abundant and salvation awaits

every human being if they have the courage to accept it. In the gospel, Jesus reminds us to be always ready for we do not know when the master will return. He uses the analogy of the servants waiting for the master to return from his wedding banquet. No matter what time he returns he will want them to be waiting for him. However, he will expect more than to find them waiting but to also find his house in good order. We are the stewards of God's creation and so he will expect to find his house in good order when he comes to visit us.

Wednesday of the Twenty-ninth Week in Ordinary Time
Romans 6:12-18; Psalm 123; Luke 12:39-48
St Paul tells us today that we must not let the ability to sin reign in our lives. We all have the ability to sin and in today's world the great temptation is to follow ways which are not God's ways and to do whatever it is that we want to do. We must resist this and instead become enslaved to righteousness, which does not mean living a dull life. Again in our gospel passage for today we are reminded by the Lord to be always ready for the moment when he calls us to give an account of our lives, and not just of our lives but of our stewardship of his creation and as witnesses of his gospel. Those who have been faithful to the Covenant sealed in the Blood of Christ will be rewarded. The important point to note is that the Lord does not tell us when he will come to visit us. For most of us there are many years to come, yet, for many others, tomorrow could be the day they meet the Lord.

Thursday of the Twenty-ninth Week in Ordinary Time
Romans 6:19-23; Psalm 1; Luke 12:49-53
We continue reading from the letter to the Romans where we are told that we have been freed from the slavery of sin by Christ and that now we have the ability to live lives of righteousness. In so doing we will achieve eternal life with the Father. In talking about 'wages,' St Paul is referring to the wages a Roman soldier would have received and the 'gift' reminds the people of the gift the emperor gave out to people. Both remind us that our sins bring us closer to death or separation from God and that our sharing in eternal happiness is due entirely to the love of God. The psalm tells us of the happiness of the people who place

their trust in God and live by his ways. In the gospel we see Jesus telling the people that he has brought division with him. This may seem odd but when we look at it we realise that he is talking about division between those who believe in him and those who do not believe in him. The divisions which we see between those who do believe in Christ are at odds with his message. But in the world we see a very clear distinction between those who accept Christ and make every effort to live Christian lives faithful to the gospel and those who do not accept him and continue in their own ways. Unity can only be achieved when we show others that belief in Christ is the right way to live and that it is not a dull and boring way to live but a path of joyfulness and fulfilment.

Friday of the Twenty-ninth Week in Ordinary Time
Romans 7:18-25; Psalm 118; Luke 12:54-59
In today's passage from the letter to the Romans we see St Paul openly speaking of the struggle taking place within him – the struggle between living the gospel values and living the easier and more carefree life which so often leads to sin. He knows what the right thing to do is and yet he struggles. In this, any of us could replace Paul's name with our own. The gospel message is not always easy to live but with the help and the grace of God, who is always at our side, it is very possible. In the gospel passage today from St Luke, we see Jesus admonishing the people for not being able to read the signs of the times. They can make many other predictions regarding what they see and yet they cannot read the most obvious things before them, such as the presence of the Messiah. We have the Messiah in our midst always and yet we too fail to read the signs of the times and follow him in complete sincerity.

Saturday of the Twenty-ninth Week in Ordinary Time
Romans 8:1-11; Psalm 23; Luke 13:1-9
We are told in today's text from the letter to the Romans that we are saved because of the incarnation. In Christ's taking human form he destroyed the power of death over us and restored us to God. In taking human form he gave us the perfect example by which to live. The man who lives by the 'flesh' is the man who

lives by his own devices and who is, therefore, somewhat weak. The man who lives by the 'spirit' is the one who allows the Holy Spirit and the message of the gospel to rule in his life and guide all his actions. In the gospel, Jesus tells us that unless we repent and amend our lives in conformity to the gospel, we will perish. The traditional Jewish belief was that whatever evil befell people was a result of some sin they had committed. But Christ says that this is not so – God does not punish us in this life for whatever sins we commit. We can live life on this earth as we desire and will not be punished for it in this life. However, we will have to answer to God in the next life for whatever we do in this one.

Monday of the Thirtieth Week in Ordinary Time
Romans 8:12-17; Psalm 67; Luke 13:10-17

St Paul reminds us in today's extract from the letter to the Romans that we must live by the Spirit if we are to be saved. We must give up our unspiritual and sinful ways and turn to the Lord, otherwise we will be lost. In the society in which Paul lived, to be adopted into a family was to receive all the rights and privileges of that family. He extends this to remind us that we have been adopted as sons and daughters of God and that we, therefore, share the same rights and privileges of Christ, who is our brother. The psalm further reminds us that the Lord saves us. In the gospel we see Jesus healing a woman on the Sabbath which infuriates the officials in the synagogue causing one of them to speak out against Jesus. But Jesus' reply shows that there is nothing in the Law which forbids good deeds being carried out even on the Sabbath. The officials had failed to see that adherence to the Law alone could not save them – they missed out the teaching on faith. It also shows that while salvation is in their midst, some Pharisees have been too blinded by the Law to see that salvation.

Tuesday of the Thirtieth Week in Ordinary Time
Romans 8:18-25; Psalm 125; Luke 13:18-21

In the letter to the Romans St Paul acknowledges that we do suffer in this life but he goes on to say that those sufferings are nothing compared to the glory which is to be revealed at our resurrection. That glory is in the next life and we must be patient for it will not be revealed to us in this life, though it is there for each one of us. The psalm supports Paul's teaching: 'Those who are sowing in tears will sing when they reap.' In the gospel passage for today, we see Jesus talking about the kingdom of God and his message is that it is something which has the power to transform society. It may start with humble beginnings but it has the power to be a great transforming and growing force which can bring peace, beauty and shelter to our modern and often wayward world. However, it can only grow if each member of the Church plays their role in the building up of the kingdom, otherwise the kingdom will remain very small.

Wednesday of the Thirtieth Week in Ordinary Time
Romans 8:26-30; Psalm 12; Luke 13:22-30
In the first reading today from the letter to the Romans we are told that the Spirit of God is with us and helps us to communicate with God and to do his will. With such an advocate and guide always with us to help us become true images of Christ, how can we fail to live Christian lives? There is a sad reminder in the gospel for us today. We are told that there are two paths which we can follow in life – the path outlined by Christ or the path which allows us to do what we want to do. The sad reminder is that the majority of people opt for the latter which may make them happier in their own eyes in this life but which ultimately will not lead to eternal life. Jesus tells us that in fact fewer people follow his path and yet they are the ones who gain eternal life while the others are turned away. The challenge for us today is to look at our own lives and to consider honestly and openly whether we are on the narrow path of righteousness or the broad path which ultimately takes us further from God. It is our Lord himself who reminds us that there is an alternative to heaven and that some people are refused entry to heaven.

Thursday of the Thirtieth Week in Ordinary Time
Romans 8:31-39; Psalm 108; Luke 13:31-35
St Paul tells us in the first reading that the love of God is always there waiting for us and that nothing can block God's love for us. God always loves us but if we reject that love then that love cannot come to fruition in us. God is always with us to help and

to strengthen us in our weaknesses. The psalm calls on the love of God to save us. In our gospel passage Jesus speaks of his death. He says that he must go to Jerusalem for it would not be right for him to die outside Jerusalem, the holy city. This also fulfils the words written in scripture about him.

Friday of the Thirtieth Week in Ordinary Time
Romans 9:1-5; Psalm 147; Luke 14:1-6
In today's text from the letter to the Romans we see St Paul speaking honestly about the Jews – the people with whom he had shared his faith for so long. He doesn't speak negatively about them but speaks about them in a very Christian manner and also with a note of sadness. Over the next three chapters of his letter he tries to explain the place of the Chosen People in salvation history. He is sad because the Jews have rejected Christ: they heard the message of Christ as he heard it and yet they have rejected it and decided not to follow him. The Jews were always the Chosen People and in the life of Christ they were offered the Good News first but rejected it. We again see in the gospel that Jesus is being watched closely by the Pharisees on the Sabbath. Again he cures someone and again the Pharisees and some of the witnesses fail to hear his teaching that it is not against the Law to do good for another human being on the Sabbath. For them, any act which appeared to be work or servile was strictly forbidden on the Sabbath. We must ask ourselves whether we simply go through the motions of fulfilling the commandments or do we live our life because we believe in the word of God.

Saturday of the Thirtieth Week in Ordinary Time
Romans 11:1-2, 11-12, 25-29; Psalm 93; Luke 14:1, 7-11
In the closing section of today's text from his letter to the Romans, St Paul tells us that the love which God has lavished on each and every person will not be taken away from them. That love is given for all time but it is up to each individual to accept that love and they can do so whenever they wish. By way of example, he tells us that the Jews were the Chosen People and that, while they may have rejected Christ, they are still the Chosen People and can accept Jesus whenever they want and so really

feel the love of God present in our world. The psalm reminds us that the Lord does not abandon his people. In the gospel we see Jesus giving the Pharisees a lesson in humility. He tells them that they must be a humble people because if they try to exalt themselves they could end up being very embarrassed when their true standing is exposed. So too with us: in the eyes of God we are all equal and so we should live lives of humility if we are to truly please the Lord.

Monday of the Thirty-first Week in Ordinary Time
Romans 11:29-36; Psalm 68; Luke 14:12-14

Today we continue the theme which St Paul ended with in our first reading last Saturday – that the Lord does not take back his love from those to whom he has given it. In short, he has bestowed his love on all people and it is for each person to accept that love and to let it take root in their lives. Paul is reminding his Gentile readers how God was generous with them after the Jews had rejected his gift of salvation. In our gospel passage for today we again see Jesus dining with the Pharisees (which shows his close ties with them even if he and they did not always agree). At the meal he tells them that they should not invite people to their parties who will later invite them to other parties. They should invite those who cannot repay them for in doing this they are showing mercy and generosity and reaching out to others and, in this way, making them more fully a part of society. This is more in keeping with the Law of God than mere adherence to the letter of the Law.

Tuesday of the Thirty-first Week in Ordinary Time
Romans 12:5-16; Psalm 130; Luke 14:15-24

As we move into the closing sections of St Paul's letter to the Romans we see Paul giving some little gems of advice. Today he tells us that we are all part of Christ's mystical body but each with a particular role to play. He also tells us that our love for others and for God should be genuine and not a pretence, and that we should treat everyone with kindness. The psalm asks God to keep our souls in peace – if we live according to Paul's instructions then we will have peace in our souls. In the gospel we see Jesus as a guest at a meal but very quickly he becomes the host and begins to teach those gathered. He tells them that the Chosen People were the first to be told the Good News but as they have rejected it, the message is to be given to others who are just as worthy as the Chosen People. The use of force at the end should not be seen as against people's will, for in Middle Eastern custom it was polite for rich and poor alike to refuse hospitality until the host took them gently by the hand to show that the invite and the hospitality were genuinely offered. Those who reject Christ and his message will have no place in the kingdom.

Wednesday of the Thirty-first Week in Ordinary Time
Romans 13:8-10; Psalm 111; Luke 14:25-33
Love, St Paul tells us today, is the answer to all the commandments. If we live from the well-springs of love then we will have no problem in keeping the commandments and in drawing closer to God and to our neighbours. In the gospel we see Jesus speaking in parables and laying out clearly what discipleship means. We are each called to be disciples of Christ but that discipleship requires certain commitments on our behalf. Ultimately we must place Christ at the very centre of our lives and before all other things, including family. Becoming a disciple is not an easy thing and so we must weigh it up very carefully but, ultimately, if we do take up the call then the reward will be great indeed.

Thursday of the Thirty-first Week in Ordinary Time
Romans 14:7-12; Psalm 26; Luke 15:1-10
In the first reading today St Paul reminds us that we are all sons and daughters of God and that we must not judge others. When our time on this earth comes to an end we will each be judged by the Father. We have enough to do to make sure that we ourselves pass the great judgement without commenting on how others may fare at their judgement – we will only be judged on the state of our own souls. He also says that Christ is sovereign over the living and the dead – he is the supreme Lord of Creation. In our gospel we see the scribes and Pharisees complaining that Jesus was spending time with sinners. But he tells them that they are the very people that he needs to spend time with because those who are faithful to God and without sin are

already on the path to salvation, while those who are still sinning are the ones in need of conversion. The just need no further guidance but the sinner does. We should ask ourselves today which category we fall into and why, and, answering that, what are we going to do to make ourselves more worthy of the kingdom.

Friday of the Thirty-first Week in Ordinary Time
Romans 15:14-21; Psalm 97; Luke 16:1-8

As St Paul concludes his letter to the Romans he again reminds them that what he does he does for Christ and not for his own glory. Paul is but an instrument for Christ and goes where the message has not been preached so as to bring the good news of salvation to as many people as possible. Today's passage from St Luke's gospel is an odd one because on first reading it appears that Christ is suggesting that we should imitate the wrongly-accused steward who sought to get even with the master who was about to punish him. But if we read it at a different level we see that at the end of the passage the master praises the steward and does not punish him even though the steward's actions to protect himself meant that his master lost some of his due. The parable therefore is one about loving one's enemies because the master praised rather than punished the servant. We too are called on to love our enemies though this is not always an easy thing to do but it is what is required of those who wish to be true disciples of Christ. There is also a reminder that we will often do whatever we can to 'save our neck' in this life but will do little to save our salvation for the next life until it is too late.

Saturday of the Thirty-first Week in Ordinary Time
Romans 16:3-9, 16, 22-27; Psalm 144; Luke 16:9-15

Today we conclude our reading of the letter to the Romans and we see St Paul ending in typical fashion – by greeting the people and giving glory to God. We also hear the names of some of those people who looked after Paul in Rome and made their homes available for the work of spreading the gospel. The psalm too gives glory and praise to God. In the gospel we see Jesus telling his listeners to use money and possessions to gain friends. In this he means that we make friends with the poor and destitute by sharing our wealth with them. In this way we fulfil the gospel imperative to share with others and so prove that we can be trusted with the riches of the kingdom for the possessions we have come from God and therefore we must share with our fellow brothers and sisters.

Monday of the Thirty-second Week in Ordinary Time
Wisdom 1:1-7; Psalm 138; Luke 17:1-6

For the final few weeks of the Church's year we return to the Old Testament and this week we read from the Book of Wisdom which was written about the year 50BC in the Egyptian city of Alexandria and attributed to King Solomon. In the opening section we are told that Wisdom is a friend to man but will not make itself known to those who try to test it or seek to outsmart it. Neither will it be found by those who devote their lives to sin. Wisdom is the Spirit of God who moves throughout the world. In the gospel, Jesus tells us that we must forgive those who have done wrong to us if they come back and seek forgiveness. No matter how often someone may wrong us if they come seeking forgiveness then we must forgive them. In the same way we too should seek forgiveness of those whom we have hurt, and that includes God. We cannot go to God to seek forgiveness if we do not forgive others and we cannot expect others to forgive us if we do not seek their forgiveness and acknowledge that what we ourselves have done is wrong.

Tuesday of the Thirty-second Week in Ordinary Time
Wisdom 2:23-3:9; Psalm 33; Luke 17:7-10

Our reading today from the book of Wisdom is a very familiar one which is quite often heard at funerals. It tells us that we were made imperishable but that death came through the devil. It goes on to tell us that 'the souls of the virtuous are in the hands of God' – a very consoling image and one which clearly shows the author's belief in eternal life with God. Those who join God in the next life will sit with him in the kingdom and will not just praise and worship him but will judge the peoples of this world with God – they will fully share in his glory. In the gospel, Jesus reminds the disciples that they are servants and in carrying out his will they are not to look for praise or to have people wait on their every wish for they are doing no more than their duty. We too have a duty like the first apostles and that is to spread the good news of the kingdom wherever we may go and to do so without looking for reward or favour.

Wednesday of the Thirty-second Week in Ordinary Time
Wisdom 6:1-11; Psalm 81; Luke 17:11-19
In the first reading today the author reminds rulers of nations that they hold office from God in whose name they must govern the people. Those who abuse their office and act unjustly and unlawfully will be punished by the Lord. But those who have been merciful will be rewarded by God. In our gospel text, we have the story of Jesus' encounter with the ten lepers. He cures all ten but only one comes back to thank Jesus, and he the foreigner among them. This is a reminder that we have all received something from God's bounty and we must all give thanks to him. Sadly, it happens all too often that those who have grown up in the faith have taken such generosity for granted and so fail to thank God, unlike those who have come to knowledge of God later in life than most and who fully appreciate what it is that they have received. Let us spend some time today giving thanks to God for what we have received.

Thursday of the Thirty-second Week in Ordinary Time
Wisdom 7:22-8:1; Psalm 118; Luke 17:20-25
In the opening part of today's first reading we read of some of the qualities of Wisdom. This passage gave rise to many others in the New Testament and also gave rise to Wisdom being identified as the Son of God because of the qualities described here. In the second part we read that Wisdom moves through all things and through all generations, leading people to the knowledge of God. The psalm tells us that the word of God stands unchanging and for ever. In the gospel passage, Jesus tells the Pharisees that the coming of the kingdom will not be something that can be seen, in fact it has already arrived. The kingdom of God is already among us and we should waste no time looking for signs but should live as members of that kingdom. We are reminded not to be as blind as the Pharisees who failed to see in his teaching and preaching the presence of the kingdom among them.

Friday of the Thirty-second Week in Ordinary Time
Wisdom 13:1-9; Psalm 18; Luke 17:26-37
The author of the book of Wisdom questions how men of learning and science can understand so many things and yet fail to understand or come to know God. God is in all the things that they study and understand and yet they fail to see him. The author of Wisdom, while saying that the pagans are misguided for their worship of nature, does say that unlike the Jews of their day, the pagans do actually worship God in his creation though without realising it. The psalm also tells us that the heavens proclaim the glory of God. In the gospel, Jesus tells us that the glory of the Son of Man will be revealed suddenly. He reminds us of Noah and Lot who heeded the Lord's word and were saved, while those who did not, perished. We do not know when the Lord will call each one of us to give an account of our stewardship so we must always be ready for that day.

Saturday of the Thirty-second Week in Ordinary Time
Wisdom 18:14-16, 19:6-9; Psalm 104; Luke 18:1-8
In the first reading today we are reminded of the flight of the Israelites from Egypt and how they passed through the Red Sea in safety. This was done because the Lord was faithful to his people. It also reminds the people how nature can be controlled by God to bring good things for those who fear him but punishment on those who do not carry out his will. The psalm continues this theme and calls on us to remember all that the Lord has done for his people. In the gospel we are told by Christ that those who call to the Lord and who seek justice will be helped by the Lord even if that help appears to be slow in coming. No matter what happens we must never lose trust in the Lord but must continue to make our prayers known to the Lord in trusting confidence.

Monday of the Thirty-third Week in Ordinary Time
1 Maccabees 1:10-15, 41-43, 54-57, 62-64; Psalm 118; Luke 18:35-43
This week we read from the Old Testament books of the Maccabees which deal with the revolt led by Judas Maccabeus in 167BC against the Seleucids. While a historical work, it shows God's salvific plan at work in the Maccabean revolt against the

pagans. In our opening passage today we see the background to Judas' revolt. Many of the people had taken up the pagan ways and rejected God, preferring instead to do as the king dictated. But a few did remain faithful and even gave their lives for that faith. The psalm takes up the theme of the downfall of those who reject the law of God. In the gospel text from St Luke we see Jesus restoring sight to a blind man. He did this not because he had to but because the blind man asked for it and because Jesus wanted to help him. The third important 'ingredient' in the story is that the blind man had faith. God wants to help us but he can only do so if we have faith and if we ask.

Tuesday of the Thirty-third Week in Ordinary Time
2 Maccabees 6:18-31; Psalm 3; Luke 19:1-10
In today's passage from the second Book of the Maccabees we read of the courage and the martyrdom of Eleazar. He was an elderly Jew when the king ordered profane sacrifices to be made but Eleazar, believing in the one true God, refused to even give the semblance of giving in and betraying his God. He preferred to be an example to young and old to the death and so he died for what he believed knowing that God would look after him. The psalm could easily have been the prayer on Eleazar's lips as he was being martyred. In the gospel we read of Jesus' encounter with Zacchaeus, the tax collector. The people are indignant that he should visit with such a sinner but during the course of the evening Zacchaeus converts and makes amends for what he has done wrong. It is a reminder to us that we should never judge others because we do not know what they are like deep down and also that the Word of God is available to all people and that it has the power to work miracles in everyone.

Wednesday of the Thirty-third Week in Ordinary Time
2 Maccabees 7:1, 20-31; Psalm 16; Luke 19:11-28
Today we read of the slaughter of seven sons before the eyes of their mother. They had been arrested for not carrying out the pagan king's profanities but for standing by their faith. The mother is implored to save the lives of her sons but she too stands by the faith and so they die the death of martyrs. She is the last to die having watched each of her sons – from the eldest

to the youngest – put to death before her eyes. The psalm is a prayer of the faithful before God. In today's gospel passage we have the parable of the man who went abroad to become king and left his possessions with his servants. In this parable Jesus is talking of himself and when he returns he will ask each person for an account of their stewardship. Those who have been faithful will be greatly rewarded. Those who have refused his kingship will be punished. It is a reminder that being a true Christian will involve a certain amount of risk-taking in this life – but there will be no reward without risk-taking.

Thursday of the Thirty-third Week in Ordinary Time
1 Maccabees 2:15-29; Psalm 49; Luke 19:41-44
In our reading today from the first Book of the Maccabees we read of a revolt against the pagan king Antiochus and his acolytes. Mattathias protects the integrity of the altar erected for lawful sacrifice offered to God by slaying the one who was attempting to commit a pagan act. He then goes on to slay the king's commissioners and to rally the people. With the help of his five sons and some of his neighbours, his act of defiance lasted about three years in the small town of Modein, about 24 kilometres northwest of Jerusalem. In our gospel text we see Jesus arriving at Jerusalem and he pauses before going in to the city. He pauses to weep at the stubbornness and the blindness of the people who have heard his teachings and seen his miracles and yet fail to see that he is their Messiah. Despite their rejection of him, Jesus still loves the people as he loves each one of us, whether we wish to acknowledge that love or not.

Friday of the Thirty-third Week in Ordinary Time
1 Maccabees 4:36-37, 52-59; Psalm: 1Chronicles 29:10-12; Luke 19:45-48
In our first reading today we see that Judas Maccabeus (whose surname is the Hebrew word for hammer) and his followers have been successful in their revolt and have liberated the people about the year 165-164BC. The first thing they set about doing is cleansing and re-dedicating the Temple in their joy at being free to worship the true God. This rededication is recalled in the Jewish celebration of Hanukkah (Festival of Lights)

which coincides with Christmas. The psalm is a hymn of praise for God. In our gospel we see that Jesus has entered Jerusalem and now takes possession of the Temple. As Judas Maccabeus and his followers cleansed the Temple, so Christ drives out from the Temple all those who were defiling it. Christ is now moving closer to his crucifixion as the officials become worried about his preaching and seek an opportunity to be rid of him.

Saturday of the Thirty-third Week in Ordinary Time
1 Maccabees 6:1-13; Psalm 9; Luke 20:27-40
Today's first reading sees the pagan king Antiochus returning to his home having found out about the fall of his forces in Jerusalem. He takes to his bed and soon is at death's door where he realises that he is dying as a result of his greed. In the gospel, Jesus is quizzed by the Sadducees about life after death. He tells them that God is a God of the living, that there is life after we have died and that our earthly marriages are of no consequence there. Some of those who were listening only accepted the Torah as being authoritative and quote Moses against Jesus, and so he quotes Abraham and others to show that he is right in what he says. What is important is that we live in such a way that we will be worthy of heaven.

Monday of the Last Week in Ordinary Time
Daniel 1:1-6, 8-20; Psalm: Daniel 3:52-56; Luke 21:1-4
For the last week of the church's year we read from the Book of Daniel written in 165-168BC but including events as far back as the rule of King Nebuchadnezzar in 605-562BC. The king enforced his own religion and had four young Israelites brought to his palace to be educated. These were placed in the care of Ashpenaz who educated them but helped them to avoid some of the pagan practices of the king. These four – Daniel, Hananiah, Mishael and Azariah – became friends of the king because of their wisdom which had been given them by God. The book was written to strengthen the faith of the people who were being suppressed by the Syrians. The psalm is a hymn of praise for God. In the gospel we see a poor widow putting all she had into the collection plate in the synagogue. Jesus praises her because from what she needed to survive she gave all she could to help others.

It is easy for us all to put something in the plate when it comes from the surplus that we have and doesn't really make a difference to our daily lives. True charity is when we gave from what we need to live each day and this is what we are called to do as followers of Christ.

Tuesday of the Last Week in Ordinary Time
Daniel 2:31-45; Psalm: Daniel 3:57-61; Luke 21:5-11

In our reading today from the Book of Daniel we read that King Nebuchadnezzar has had a vision and is unable to interpret it. Daniel is brought to him and tells him what he has seen and interprets the vision. Daniel predicts that the king's successors will not be as successful as he for they will turn from God and so their kingdom and his line will fall. It is a reminder for the people of the second century before Christ, who are under the rule of the Syrians, that the Syrian kingdom too will fall as its king does not worship the one true God. Our psalm is again one of thanksgiving taken from the third chapter of the Book of Daniel. In the gospel, Jesus predicts the demise of the Temple which was so central to the Jewish faith and nation. He also warns his audience not to listen to those who will come pretending to be him for there is only one Messiah and he has given us the message of salvation, showing us the way to reach that salvation.

Wednesday of the Last Week in Ordinary Time
Daniel 5:1-6, 13-14, 16-17, 23-28; Psalm: Daniel 3:62-67; Luke 21:12-19

In our passage from the Book of Daniel for today we see that King Nebuchadnezzar has been succeeded by his descendent, Belshazzar, who profanes the sacred vessels brought from the Temple in Jerusalem by Nebuchadnezzar. During the banquet a hand writes on the wall and the only one who can interpret it is Daniel. He predicts that Belshazzar's kingdom is to come to an end and will be split between two of his rivals. It is a further reminder to the persecuted Jews of the second century BC that the reigning King of Syria will fall because he does not worship the true God. Our psalm continues to be taken from the Book of Daniel. In today's gospel passage we see Jesus warning his disciples that difficult times lie ahead for them because they are his followers and that some will die as a result. He tells them not to prepare their defence but to trust in him for he will be their protection and their defence.

Thursday of the Last Week in Ordinary Time
Daniel 6:12-28; Psalm: Daniel 3:68-74; Luke 21:20-28
In our first reading we see Daniel being thrown in to the lions' den because he was praying to God and not to the king, though this greatly distressed the king for he was fond of Daniel. But Daniel was unhurt because he trusted in God and the king issued a decree that all his people were to tremble before the God whom Daniel worshipped. It is a reminder to the people of the second century before Christ who were persecuted by the Syrians always to remain faithful to God who will be their defender when the day comes. Christ again foretells the destruction of Jerusalem in our gospel for today. He also makes reference to the end times when the Son of God will appear in all his glory to bring to himself the righteous.

Friday of the Last Week in Ordinary Time
Daniel 7:2-14; Psalm: Daniel 3:75-81; Luke 21:29-33
In our reading from the Book of Daniel we read of a vision which Daniel had in which he sees the coming of the Son of God. On this Son is conferred the sovereignty of the earth and this sovereignty will be eternal. There are four visions in this section of the book and which are explained in tomorrow's passage. One of the visions speaks of 'one like a son of man, coming on the clouds of heaven.' This is an image which Our Lord used of himself in his teaching. In our gospel text Jesus speaks to the disciples about how people are able to read the signs of the seasons. In the same way these signs will indicate that the kingdom is at hand and that, while people may die, the words of Christ will never pass away.

Saturday of the Last Week in Ordinary Time
Daniel 7:15-27; Psalm: Daniel 3:82-87; Luke 21:34-36
Again today we read from Daniel's vision and at the end we are told that the sovereignty conferred on the Son of God will also pass to the saints of God and so we too become a line of kings to continue the kingdom. In our final gospel passage for this liturgical year we are reminded by Christ to always be on our guard against anything that would lead us away from God. We do not know when the end will come – today, tomorrow or next year – and so we must always be ready to answer the call of God and to stand before him with confidence.

WEEKDAYS OF ORDINARY TIME:YEAR II

Monday of the First Week in Ordinary Time
1 Samuel 1:1-8; Psalm 115; Mark 1:14-20

At the start of this year we begin reading from the Prophet Samuel and from St Mark's gospel. Samuel was a prophet but also one of the last military leaders who were referred to as judges in the eleventh century before Christ. In the text from Samuel we see Samuel's father, Elkanah, and his two wives – one who has had children and the other, Hannah, who is barren. They have gone to Shiloh to worship God at the Ark and the first wife taunts Hannah because of her barrenness. In St Mark's gospel we see that Christ now begins his mission – the time has come. Having begun proclaiming he begins to choose men to help him in his work. We too are asked to help in that work in fulfilment of our baptismal promises and each according to their abilities and talents.

Tuesday of the First Week in Ordinary Time
1 Samuel 1:9-20; Psalm: 1 Samuel 2:1, 2-8; Mark 1:21-28

In our first reading today from the first Book of Samuel, we read of Hannah going to the shrine of the Ark of the Covenant at Shiloh and asking the Lord to remove her stigma and grant her a child. The text shows us the great devotion Hannah had for the Lord and of the enormous pain which her barrenness caused her. The priest Eli initially thinks she has had too much to drink but quickly realises her situation. The Lord hears Hannah's prayer and grants her a son whom she names Samuel. The psalm is a hymn of praise which we could imagine Hannah singing. In the gospel, Jesus and his disciples are travelling and preaching. Jesus is also casting out unclean spirits. What strikes the people about him is the fact that he speaks with such authority – authority that even the unclean spirits obey. As a result, his reputation quickly spreads.

Wednesday of the First Week in Ordinary Time
1 Samuel 3:1-10, 19-20; Psalm 39; Mark 1:29-39

We read today of the call of Samuel and of his 'yes' to the Lord. His 'yes' meant that he became an important prophet and military leader for the people. The psalm takes up this theme of answering the Lord's call. The gospel recounts some more of the miracles worked by Jesus. It also tells us that he was keen to move about the towns and to preach to as many people as possible. In the Old Testament, Samuel is called to act on God's behalf, while in the New Testament, God himself is present among us and trying to lead as many people as possible to the kingdom through his own words. We too must share the Good News with as many people as we can for we are the successors to Samuel and to Christ. The gospel also reminds us that, even though many people were coming to Jesus, he still had time for prayer with his Father.

Thursday of the First Week in Ordinary Time
1 Samuel 4:1-11; Psalm 43; Mark 1:40-45
The reading from Samuel recounts a battle from the history of Israel in which the Israelite army are facing up to the Philistines. Realising their weakness the Israelites bring the Ark from Shiloh and while this strengthens them it is not enough for them to overcome their adversaries. The Israelite army is heavily defeated and the Ark taken from them while the shrine at Shiloh is destroyed. Our gospel passage is a continuation of yesterday's text and again we see Jesus curing the sick, this time a man with leprosy. After he has cured him he warns the man to say nothing of who cured him but the man tells everyone. As a result Jesus has to move around quietly but crowds still come to him. Those who went seeking Christ after they heard of him believed in him even though they did not know who he was. The Israelites in the first reading are given a lesson that everything they have is dependent on God just as the leper's health is dependent on his mercy. When we are at our weakest, we learn the true power and mercy of God.

Friday of the First Week in Ordinary Time
1 Samuel 8:4-7, 10-22; Psalm 88; Mark 2:1-12
The theme of trusting in God alone is continued in our first reading from Samuel. In the passage, set about the year 1020BC, we see the people of Israel rejecting God and seeking a human king. Samuel tells them what a king would do to them but they still

want one and so God instructs Samuel to give them what they want. In our gospel passage Jesus cures a paralytic by forgiving him his sins which appalls the scribes who were listening to him. For them, only God has the power to forgive. But Christ tells them that the Son of Man has such authority. We too are asked to believe in God and his Son and their authority and to have faith in them at all times even when it may seem difficult.

Saturday of the First Week in Ordinary Time
1 Samuel 9:1-4, 17-19, 10:1; Psalm 20; Mark 2:13-17
Today's excerpt from the Book of Samuel sees the prophet appointing a king for the Israelites as they had requested. The one he anoints is Saul who was out looking for his father's she-donkeys which had strayed. The anointing symbolises that Saul is now set apart from other men and has been given authority by God – a symbolic ritual which exists to this day in the ordination of priests and bishops and some royal coronation ceremonies. Our passage from St Mark's gospel shows us Jesus sitting down to dinner with tax collectors and sinners – people whom polite and strict Jewish society rejected. The message and example for us in these readings is that God does not judge by our standards but accepts all people and even calls them to high office. The challenge for us is to likewise accept all people – regardless of race, language, colour or religion – as Jesus did.

Monday of the Second Week in Ordinary Time
1 Samuel 15:16-23; Psalm 49; Mark 2:18-22
We continue our readings from the first Book of Samuel and today we see that Saul – the people's king who succeeded in driving the Philistines from the central valley – has failed as God predicted that he would. Saul did not listen carefully to the word of God and displeased God in the battle against the Amalekites, so now God has rejected him as king. The psalm takes up God's displeasure with Saul and says that offerings are not enough – love of the law and word must also accompany sacrifices. In today's gospel we see that while others are fasting, Jesus' disciples are not fasting and this causes trouble with the Pharisees. When asked, Jesus tells them that wedding guests do not fast when the bridegroom is present. We too are called on to

love God's law and to live according to that law but not grudgingly. We too must realise that Christ is always with us in all things.

Tuesday of the Second Week in Ordinary Time
1 Samuel 16:1-13; Psalm 88; Mark 2:23-28

Having rejected Saul as king over his people, God now sends Samuel out to find another king. However, Saul remains as king for the time being as the people were unwilling to loose their first king. Samuel goes to Jesse and from among his sons anoints the boy, David, as king to replace Saul. In so doing, God again shows that he does not judge by the standards of humans but appoints those who appear to be unfit for high office. God's spirit rests on David who will rule when the right time comes. In the passage from the gospel we see Jesus again being questioned about the actions of his disciples, this time for picking corn on the Sabbath. In reply he says that 'The Sabbath was made for man, not man for the Sabbath.' The Risen Lord has made the Sabbath a holy day, one which unites all Christians. It is a day to celebrate the freedom won for us by Christ's sacrifice.

Wednesday of the Second Week in Ordinary Time
1 Samuel 17:32-33, 37, 40-51; Psalm 143; Mark 3:1-6

In our first reading from Samuel we see that Saul's army has been in battle for some time with the Philistines and have not been able to overcome them. The battle field is not far from Bethlehem and the time is about the eleventh century before Christ. David now arrives and we read the familiar story of how he alone – with very little weaponry – slew Goliath. He is able to do so because God's favour rests on him but also because he did it in the name of the Lord. The psalm is in praise of God who helped him in battle. The gospel reading continues yesterday's theme of the Sabbath day. Today we see Christ healing a man even though any form of work was prohibited. Even though he was doing good and healing an invalid, the Pharisees now seek to silence him permanently.

Thursday of the Second Week in Ordinary Time
1 Samuel 18:6-9, 19:1-7; Psalm 55; Mark 3:7-12
In our first reading we see that Saul has now become jealous of
David because the boy is now more popular than the king, and
so Saul seeks to destroy him. Saul's own son, Jonathan, however,
intercedes on behalf of David and brings reconciliation between
Saul and David. Our gospel tells of the popularity of Jesus
everywhere he goes and of his many cures. Whenever he casts
out demons he always stops them revealing who he is – his time
has not yet come to fully reveal that he is the Son of God, because the people are not ready for that. Like the unclean spirits,
we too know that Jesus is the Son of God but do we always acknowledge that as did the unclean spirits?

Friday of the Second Week in Ordinary Time
1 Samuel 24:3-21; Psalm 56; Mark 3:13-19
In our first reading today we read that Saul is again looking for
David because he has heard rumours that he meant to do the
king harm. However, David is in a position to kill Saul but does
not take it because Saul is God's anointed. Instead he turns the
occasion into another reconciliation between them. Now Saul
acknowledges that David will be king and that the sovereignty
will be secure under David. Today's gospel shows us Jesus appointing the Twelve who were to be his closest companions and
commissioning them to preach in his name and to cure others.
As these twelve were commissioned so too are we, as their descendents, and we too are called to proclaim the kingdom of
God in our lives by what we do and say in keeping with our
baptismal promises to be the Lord's disciples.

Saturday of the Second Week in Ordinary Time
2 Samuel 1:1-4, 11-12, 17, 19, 23-27; Psalm 79; Mark 3:20-21
We now begin reading from the second Book of Samuel and
today we read that Saul and Jonathan have been killed in battle.
David, who at one time was at the mercy of the king, mourns
greatly for the father and son and we see his pain in today's text.
David now becomes King of Israel and at the same time one of
the most important figures in Jewish history. Our gospel reading today is very short and a little unusual. In the passage a

large crowd has gathered around Jesus and his family receive word of this. So, convinced that he is mad, they set out to bring him home. However, we must remember that Mark has a habit of portraying those around Jesus in such a light because they didn't always support him or believe in his message. Even today, Christians are sometimes considered mad because of the message they preach in his name.

Monday of the Third Week in Ordinary Time
2 Samuel 5:1-7, 10; Psalm 88; Mark 3:22-30
On Saturday, we read of the death of King Saul and of David's grief. Today we see the tribes coming to David and asking him to take up the kingship and to lead the country. This he does and reclaims the city of Jerusalem as it stands on the border between the two halves of the kingdom and which stood as an impenetrable fortress. We are told that in all he did, the Lord was with David, a theme which is continued in the psalm. In the gospel passage, Jesus has been accused of being Beelzebul and that this is how he can cast out unclean spirits. In reply he tells the people that a kingdom which is divided cannot stand for very long. The kingdom of God is here with us but if Christians do not stand together in unity and peace, then that kingdom too will be in trouble in our time. We have a duty to help build up, in our own small way, the kingdom of God.

Tuesday of the Third Week in Ordinary Time
2 Samuel 6:12-15, 17-19; Psalm 23; Mark: 3:31-35
In our first reading we see that David has now established himself in Jerusalem – the Citadel of David – and to complete the victory has brought the Ark of the Covenant into the city. The Ark was received there with great praise and rejoicing. This also served to unite the northern and southern kingdoms as both held the Ark in great reverence and so Jerusalem became, not just the political capital, but the focal point of all worship. In our gospel text for today we are told that Jesus' mother and family have come to get him, which we read of last Saturday. When told this he asks his listeners who the members of his family are. In answer to his own question he tells us that those who do God's will are his mother, and brothers and sisters. We must ask

ourselves each day if we live our lives well enough to merit being called his brothers and sisters.

Wednesday of the Third Week in Ordinary Time
2 Samuel 7:4-17; Psalm 88; Mark 4:1-20
Having now regained Jerusalem in our first reading, and having brought the Ark of the Covenant to Jerusalem, David now wants to build a solid house for the Ark. Through the prophet Nathan, David is told that God's favour rests on him and he will have great fame. As David wants to build a house for the Ark so God intends to make a royal family of David's line which will last for ever. The psalm repeats this. The parable recounted in the gospel for today is the Parable of the Sower, a very familiar parable to us. The question we must ask ourselves today is this: 'Which of the seed in the parable do I belong to?'

Thursday of the Third Week in Ordinary Time
2 Samuel 7:18-19, 24-29; Psalm 131; Mark 4:21-25
In our reading today from the second Book of Samuel, Nathan has told David that his house is to be blessed for ever and David goes and sits before the Lord in prayer in a quiet room in which is kept the Ark of the Covenant. David makes a hymn of praise to God for the gifts which God has bestowed upon him. St Mark, in his gospel today, recounts some of the short sayings of Christ. One line from the passage says that what we give is what we will receive. If we show mercy and help to others then we in our turn will also receive mercy and help. In other words, if we do not reach out to others as Christians then we cannot expect anything when our time comes.

Friday of the Third Week in Ordinary Time
2 Samuel 11:1-10, 13-17; Psalm 50; Mark 4:26-34
Today we have the beginning of the downfall of David. Having been promised great blessings by the Lord, David now breaks one of the commandments and commits adultery and leaves the wife of one of his generals expecting his child. He brings home Uriah the general – the woman's husband – to make it look like the child was conceived by him, but when this fails he sends Uriah into battle and ensures that he dies there so that he may

have the woman for himself on a permanent basis. The psalm is a song of lament by those who have sinned. Two more parables are recounted in the gospel from St Mark today. They are reminders that all we have and do and are come from God. There is also a reminder that the kingdom of God is secretly growing in the world.

Saturday of the Third Week in Ordinary Time
2 Samuel 12:1-7, 10-17; Psalm 50; Mark 4:35-41

In our reading from the second Book of Samuel we see that David is confronted by Nathan for the sin he has committed. As a result of his sin the child he is about to father with Bathsheba is to be struck down and his kingdom is also to suffer. David repents of his sin following the telling of Nathan's story and, as a result, the sin is forgiven by God though the trouble which David will encounter with his sons will serve as a reminder of his actions. In the gospel text, Jesus shows his power over nature. He and his disciples are out on the lake and a storm blows up which he calms. The disciples are frightened because they do not yet realise exactly who he is. As his presence brought peace and tranquillity to those who were with him on the boat, so too it will bring us peace and harmony when we are in trouble and turn to him in prayer.

Monday of the Fourth Week in Ordinary Time
2 Samuel 15:13-14, 30, 16:5-13; Psalm 3; Mark 5:1-20

The setting for today's first reading is a time during the rule of King David when the people had grown disenchanted with his rule and were looking to rebel. The rebellion is led by his son Absalom who declares himself king in the city of David. We see David fleeing and, as he goes, he is cursed by a relative of his own predecessor – King Saul – because he has committed murder. In today's gospel, we see Jesus curing a man who was possessed by many spirits. The people come to see what has happened but they do not rejoice as so many others had done. Instead they ask Jesus to leave their area. Though he had shown his power to them they were afraid to believe – perhaps they realised that his message would require a change in their lifestyle.

Tuesday of the Fourth Week in Ordinary Time
2 Samuel 18:9-10, 14, 24-25, 30-19:3; Psalm 85; Mark 5:21-43
In our first reading today, we see that David has defeated his son Absalom in thick forests east of the Jordan. We now see that Absalom is fleeing for his life because his gamble of making himself king to answer the people's needs has not paid off. The young man falls into the hands of his father's troops who kill him while he could not defend himself. Upon hearing the news David goes into mourning for the loss of his son. The text from St Mark's gospel for today is a well known double miracle – the cure of the woman with a haemorrhage and the cure of Jairus' daughter. The central point is faith: the woman had faith and she needed only to touch the clothes Christ wore to be cured; Jairus' daughter died before Jesus could reach the house and when the messengers informed him of this, Jesus told them to have faith and she would live. The faith of the woman is the faith to which we are all called.

Wednesday of the Fourth Week in Ordinary Time
2 Samuel 24:2, 9-17; Psalm 31; Mark 6:1-6
In today's first reading, David decides to take a census of the people but having done so regrets it and asks the Lord for forgiveness. The Lord gives him three penances and he must choose one. The one he chooses results in death and hardship. In the end David asks the Lord to punish him and his family and none else, for the sin was his alone. We are not told why the Lord became angry at the census but it is possible that it showed that David was relying more on human resources in leading the Chosen People than reliance on God. The psalm takes up this theme of seeking forgiveness. Jesus, in the gospel, is rejected in his own hometown because the people 'knew' him. Because of their lack of faith they could not be healed or cured. We have each received graces from God but they are nothing if we do not accept them and have faith in God.

Thursday of the Fourth Week in Ordinary Time
1 Kings 2:1-4, 10-12; Psalm: 1 Chronicles 29:10-12; Mark 6:7-13
We now come to the end of David's life in our first reading and he is to be succeeded by his son, Solomon. Before he dies, he

implores Solomon to live according to the decrees of the Lord – something he himself had failed to do on a number of occasions. The psalm acknowledges that God is the ruler of all and that everything comes from him. In the gospel we see Jesus sending out his disciples to preach in his name. This they do and they cure many people of illnesses and unclean spirits. They were able to do so because they believed in what they were doing. We too are called to have faith in Christ, to live according to the decrees of the Lord and to bring his healing and love to all whom we meet.

Friday of the Fourth Week in Ordinary Time
Ecclesiasticus 47:2-11; Psalm 17; Mark 6:14-29
The reading from Ecclesiasticus today was written about eight centuries after the death of King David. It recalls his deeds and while we know that David offended God, the reading shows that his life was really oriented toward serving God and the Chosen People. It ends by saying that God took away David's sins and established his dynasty as he had promised. In the gospel we read of the death of John the Baptist because of a promise foolishly made. John had faith in what he preached and ultimately this faith brought about his death. John has now fulfilled the role which the great prophet Elijah was to fulfil – that of preparing the way for the Messiah.

Saturday of the Fourth Week in Ordinary Time
1 Kings 3:4-13; Psalm 118; Mark 6:30-34
Solomon has now been proclaimed king after his father, David. He goes to the holy site of Gibeon to sacrifice there and while there the Lord tells him that he can have anything he asks for. Solomon doesn't ask for victories or armies or lands or riches. He asks simply for wisdom. Pleased with this request, God also grants him more than he had asked for. In the gospel we see the disciples returning from their mission, which has been very successful, so much so that people from many villages have followed them to hear more and to be cured. The preaching of the disciples and the faith of the people has brought them to the Lord himself.

Monday of the Fifth Week in Ordinary Time

1 Kings 8:1-7, 9-13; Psalm 131; Mark 6:53-56

In the reading from the first Book of the Kings, Solomon, now king, completes the wish that David once had – to build a house of stone for the Ark of the Covenant, that is, the casket containing the two tablets of the Law. Solomon builds the great Temple in Jerusalem and has the Ark placed within it. Our gospel theme is a continuation of last week's theme on faith. Jesus is moving through the countryside and the people are flocking to see him. Many hope for a cure and many ask that they be allowed to touch even the hem of his garments, for they believe that even this will cure them.

Tuesday of the Fifth Week in Ordinary Time

1 Kings 8:22-23, 27-30; Psalm 83; Mark 7:1-13

Solomon now goes in to the Temple he has had built and prays to God. First, he praises God and then he asks for two things in particular for the people: that God will always hear them, and that he forgives them their transgressions. St Mark shows us Jesus at odds again with the Pharisees. This time they are not pleased that the disciples do not follow the rituals for washing prescribed by the Law. Christ points out that the rituals are nothing without the correct disposition of mind and heart. While the Pharisees may fulfil the letter of the Law in what they do, they do so without any great conviction. This is a reminder to us that going through the motions of our own religion is not enough – we must have faith in God and believe in what we are doing and why we do it.

Wednesday of the Fifth Week in Ordinary Time

1 Kings 10:1-10; Psalm 36; Mark 7:14-23

In our first reading we see that the Queen of Sheba has heard of Solomon and has come to test him for herself, only to find that he is as wise as the rumours proclaimed. She praises him and acknowledges that what he has has come from God. The psalm speaks of committing one's life to God as Solomon did. Continuing from yesterday's gospel text, Jesus now addresses the issue of clean and unclean foods as the Jewish Law understood them. Christ proclaims all food to be clean because nothing that goes into man is unclean. He makes a very clear declaration that whatever comes from man and is regarded as unclean is a result of the man's interior disposition. Evil, etc, comes from within ourselves, not from what we eat.

Thursday of the Fifth Week in Ordinary Time
1 Kings 11:4-13; Psalm 105; Mark 7:24-30
The first Book of the Kings today tells us that despite all he has received from God, in his old age Solomon is persuaded by his foreign wives to follow other gods and to whose glory he builds temples. In his displeasure at this, the Lord declares that Solomon's kingdom is to suffer. The psalm tells of the sins of the people. In the gospel text for today, Jesus cures a little girl who had an unclean spirit. He did so because her mother, a pagan, showed that she believed in him and his power. The woman's faith and her love for her daughter are the examples we are called to imitate today rather than the example of Solomon who, for all his wisdom, wandered far from the Lord.

Friday of the Fifth Week in Ordinary Time
1 Kings 11:29-32, 12:19; Psalm 80; Mark 7:31-37
We are told in the first reading today that because of the sins of Solomon and his following of false gods, the Lord has decided to split the kingdom into two – the southern kingdom of Judah and the northern kingdom of Israel. The psalm is a warning from God not to offend him and also reminds the people of what he had already done for them – a reminder of their ungratefulness. Again in our gospel text, Jesus is seen healing a deaf mute. However, he does so in private, away from the crowd, and tells the man to say nothing of it – his reputation is already preceding him. But the man speaks of it and the people praise Christ.

Saturday of the Fifth Week in Ordinary Time
1 Kings 12:26-32, 13:33-34; Psalm 105; Mark 8:1-10
In our first reading we see that Jeroboam I is now ruler of Israel while Rehoboam (son of Solomon) is ruler of Judah. Jeroboam fears that if the people continue to go to the Temple in Jerusalem to worship that they will revert to following Rehoboam and the northern kingdom will be lost. So he abandons God and creates

two calves as false gods and has the people worship them. In the text from St Mark we see one of the miracles of the loaves and fish. An interesting point in the text is that the people had been with Christ for three days. We are told that there were about four thousand people and they had sat and listened to him in the countryside without food for three days whereas many people today find it difficult to sit in a church for even one hour a week. The Lord is always with us in the Blessed Sacrament and so it is important that we make an effort to spend some time in his presence each week, even if it only means arriving earlier than usual for Mass or staying on for a while afterwards.

Monday of the Sixth Week in Ordinary Time
James 1:1-11; Psalm 118; Mark 8:11-13
In the first reading, St James – the leader of the community in Jerusalem – tells us that we will be tried in various ways but that we should welcome such trials because they are for our own good and will make us better people. He tells us that we should always rely on the help of God in such situations. The letter of St James is different from the letters of St Paul because James' letter is written as a guide for all Christians rather than just to Christians of a particular place. The psalm takes up this theme and says that 'It was good for me to be afflicted.' The text from St Mark's gospel sees Jesus being tested by the people who would not believe him unless he showed them a sign from heaven. The author notes Christ's exasperation or frustration in the sigh which comes from Christ before he leaves them. While it is good for us to be tested, it is not good for us to test God.

Tuesday of the Sixth Week in Ordinary Time
James 1:12-18; Psalm 93; Mark 8:14-21
Continuing our reading of the letter of St James, who died a martyr's death about the year 63AD, the apostle tells us today that while God tests us he does not tempt us for that would prove nothing. It also cannot happen because God is good and to tempt would be to lead people into sin and God would not do that either. The lure of sin comes from ourselves and not from God. In the gospel passage from St Mark, Jesus is warning the disciples to be careful with regard to the Pharisees and Herod

but they do not understand him. We too must be on the watch against those who would lead us along false paths – paths which would lead us away from God's Law and his love. So too, we must not lead others along false paths of our own making.

Wednesday of the Sixth Week in Ordinary Time
James 1:19-27; Psalm 14; Mark 8:22-26

St James gives us a warning today in the first reading that it is not good enough to simply listen to the word of God – we must also put it into practice in our everyday lives. If we say we believe in God but fail to act accordingly, then our faith is dead because, if we truly believed, we would live out that faith in a very real and clear manner. The psalm tells us how the one who listens to God's word should live. In the gospel text from St Mark, we see Jesus cure a blind man in the town of Bethsaida in Northern Israel. The man's sight returns gradually which suggests to us that the more our faith in Jesus grows the clearer we will be able to see.

Thursday of the Sixth Week in Ordinary Time
James 2:1-9; Psalm 33; Mark 8:27-33

In our first reading today we are being told by St James not to make distinctions between people for any reason but to treat all as equals before God. He talks about how we might treat the rich and poor in different ways because of their wealth or standing but that this is wrong because all are equal in the eyes of God. In the gospel passage from St Mark we see St Peter making his great act of faith before Jesus: 'You are the Christ.' To be true followers of Christ we too must make this same profession every day and live the gospel values, particularly as we have the benefit of an established religious community, expert witness testimony of the life of Christ, and have been learning about and communicating with God since our earliest days. In the text, Jesus also remonstrates with Peter for trying to hold him back from going to Jerusalem and to his death with the reminder that God's ways are not our ways. Jesus could have done as Peter wished but it was only through his death and resurrection that we are saved.

Friday of the Sixth Week in Ordinary Time
James 2:14-24, 26; Psalm 111; Mark 8:34-9:1

St James again tells us in the first reading today that it is not enough to say we have faith in God – we must show that faith by the kind of life we live. If we truly have faith then we will do everything in accordance with that faith. In other words, our life will be marked by good works but these works will not be done to prove to others that we have faith but they will be done out of a personal conviction that this is what the Lord wants us to do. Our faith strengthens our good works and our good works strengthen our faith and the faith of others. Jesus tells his followers in the gospel that they must not cling to the life they have, but must give it up in order to be his true disciples. We must give up our life and live the life Christ calls us to live if we too are to be his true followers.

Saturday of the Sixth Week in Ordinary Time
James 3:1-10: Psalm 11; Mark 9:2-13

In the first reading we are given a warning by St James to be very careful about what we say – the tongue is a dangerous instrument and needs be watched vigilantly. He talks about how loose talk can destroy a person and suggests that idle gossip and chat is the mark of a fool. Today's gospel account tells of the Transfiguration of the Lord on Mount Tabor. The passage has a number of meanings and one of these meanings is that the transfigured Christ is an image of what each of us can be and what we will be like when we join him in the next life. But we must be careful because our shining robes are easily discoloured if we stray from the right paths.

Monday of the Seventh Week in Ordinary Time
James 3:13-18; Psalm 18; Mark 9:14-29

This week we continue reading from the letter of St James which today presents a very practical view of religion. James tells us that if we truly believe then our belief will be seen in the good works that we do because we will have the wisdom to discern what is right according to our faith. In the gospel, some of the disciples have been trying to cure a possessed boy but are unable to because they have not prayed for it. The boy's father does believe and asks Jesus to help the little faith he himself has. We too need to have our faith strengthened daily and would do well to pray for that strengthening, while living out our faith in concrete ways.

Tuesday of the Seventh Week in Ordinary Time
James 4:1-10; Psalm 54; Mark 9:30-37
St James is warning us in the first reading to make God our sole object and master – not this world and its contents. He paints a picture of people who are looking for things from God but not for the right motives; he talks of people who are not happy with what they have or who quarrel or who are willing to commit other wrongs in order to get what they want. By making God our sole master then such evils will not be found in us. If we place anything before God we cannot be God's followers and friends. In the gospel, Christ tells his followers that they must become as simple as little children and not seek after high office. Such things do not worry the minds of children and they trust those who are older than them for all that they need. Only by following the 'little way' of a child can they truly be his followers.

Wednesday of the Seventh Week in Ordinary Time
James 4:13-17; Psalm 48; Mark 9:38-40
In today's excerpt from the letter of St James we are reminded that everything we do is subject to the will of God and that this should always be kept in mind when making promises about the future. We should be more concerned with attaining eternal life than with what we will do a year from now. In the gospel, Jesus tells John that those who work miracles in his name are not enemies. Even if one is not of the same church as us, that does not mean they are wrong if what is preached is in keeping with the teaching of Christ.

Thursday of the Seventh Week in Ordinary Time
James 5:1-6; Psalm 48; Mark 9:41-50
In today's first reading St James the Apostle is warning the wealthy to be mindful of the poor and the suffering for it is at the expense of the poor that many rich people have acquired their wealth. There is a reminder here that those with wealth

must use it to help alleviate the plight of the poor. All are equal in the eyes of God and God is very much aware of those who use their wealth to help others. The psalm continues this warning to the rich. Christ warns us in the gospel to be always pure of heart and intention and to remain faithful to his teaching. He tells us that if our actions cause another to sin then it would be better for us 'to be thrown into the sea with a large millstone tied around [our] neck.' Our actions have an impact on others and all that we do should direct others towards the kingdom of God and not away from it.

Friday of the Seventh Week in Ordinary Time
James 5:9-12; Psalm 102; Mark 10:1-12
Again today, St James is warning us about living lives faithful to the gospel and not swearing falsely about ourselves or others. He also reminds the people to remain faithful to God even in the midst of affliction and pain. Today's gospel passage sees Christ being asked about divorce. He tells us that divorce is wrong in the eyes of God and that is the ideal which we must always keep before us. However, we are not given licence to condemn those who have divorced or whose marriages have broken down. The marriage bond is sacred and may not be broken in the eyes of God.

Saturday of the Seventh Week in Ordinary Time
James 5:13-20; Psalm 140; Mark 10:13-16
St James in the first reading tells us of the importance of prayer both in good times and in bad. He also tells us of the importance of leading people back to the church when they have gone astray, and of the importance of confession and anointing the sick. In all things God is ready to listen and to help his people. In the gospel, Christ tells us that if we do not welcome God's kingdom we will have no hope of entering it. He again uses the trust of a child to show us the approach we should have towards God – one of complete trust and confidence in an ever-loving and benign Father.

Monday of the Eighth Week in Ordinary Time
1 Peter 1:3-9; Psalm 110; Mark 10:17-27

This week we turn to the first letter of St Peter and in our first reading for today Peter is preaching to the people about Christ and the kingdom. He is reminding the people that they believe in Christ even though they have never seen him and so their faith will bring them to everlasting happiness. The Jewish people regard the Promised Land as their 'inheritance' and so Peter uses this word deliberately to show that the new inheritance – the new Promised Land – is to be found in heaven rather than here on earth. This inheritance is something which cannot be taken from us except by God. In the gospel from St Mark, we see a young man go away sad because he did not see that faith is a far more precious treasure than the gold he possessed. We are called to be like the people in the first reading – who believed though they had not seen Christ, unlike the young man in the gospel.

Tuesday of the Eighth Week in Ordinary Time
1 Peter 1:10-16; Psalm 97; Mark 10:28-31

In our first reading again today St Peter is telling us how we must believe – with a completely free and open mind in imitation of the holiness of God himself. In that way we will truly come to know God and be united with him. He also encourages us to do all we can today to believe in God rather than putting it off until tomorrow. Today's gospel is a continuation of yesterday's passage, and in it we see the disciples worrying about how they will enter heaven. Christ reassures them and tells them that whoever gives up all they have for him will receive a great reward in this life and in the next – though they will suffer for it. We too will share in that promise if we put Christ and the gospel before everything else in our lives.

Wednesday of the Eighth Week in Ordinary Time
1 Peter 1:18-25; Psalm 147; Mark 10:32-45

Today, St Peter reminds us of what Christ did for us – a sacrifice we should never forget for it was paid in his precious blood. Peter also uses the image of a 'spotless lamb' which is seen so often in Christian art. In today's gospel, Christ tells his disciples of his impending death, when the ransom will be paid for us.

Christ also tells them that they are to be the servants of all, not masters. We too are called to serve others just as Christ served us and redeemed us. Service is far more important and life-saving than power.

Thursday of the Eighth Week in Ordinary Time
1 Peter 2:2-5, 9-12; Psalm 99; Mark 10:46-52
St Peter continues to tell us in the first reading how to believe and act as children of God. We must set ourselves close to Christ and always act honourably among those who denounce us. We must hunger everyday for the food that will feed us spiritually and so show to those around us what it means to follow Christ. In the gospel, Jesus cures a blind man on the road to Jericho because the man asked for the cure and because the man had faith and trust in Christ. This is the sort of faith we are called to have – complete and total, even when others are trying to keep us down.

Friday of the Eighth Week in Ordinary Time
1 Peter 4:7-13; Psalm 95; Mark 11:11-26
Our first reading continues with St Peter giving instruction on the faith. We must have total trust and faith in God and must remember that he will test us from time to time so that we are truly worthy to be with him in paradise. In our gospel passage for today there are a number of topics raised. In the Temple, we see our Lord driving out the money changers who had defiled his Father's house. There is a reminder here that we must give due care and respect to the house of God for it is here that he dwells most visibly in our world. Also in the passage we are told to 'have faith in God' and we will be able to move mountains. Finally, we are told that we must repent of our sins but if we approach the Father seeking forgiveness we must be prepared to forgive those who have wronged us. Only in forgiving others can we expect forgiveness for ourselves.

Saturday of the Eighth Week in Ordinary Time
Jude 17:20-25; Psalm 62; Mark 11:27-33
Today we read from the letter written by St Jude who tells us that our faith is to be our foundation and we are to build upon

that foundation. This is done by helping others who are weaker in faith than we are, while all the time praying for a stronger faith for ourselves. Jude is also warning us to be careful about the instruction we take from some who appear to be preaching the gospel but who are preaching a tainted version. The psalm gives us a good example of what our prayer could be. In the gospel, Jesus is questioned by the scribes and elders about his authority. He posses a question for them and when they refuse to answer this he does not answer theirs. His authority comes from God but they will not accept this.

Monday of the Ninth Week in Ordinary Time
2 Peter 1:2-7; Psalm 90; Mark 12:1-12
St Peter tells us in the first reading for today that all we need for living has been given to us by Christ. It is all to be found in his words recorded in the gospels. The author also sets out certain virtues which we should all have as Christians and which reinforce our own faith and the faith of others. In the gospel from St Mark, we have the parable of the vineyard in which Christ tells a story about his Father and his dealings with humankind. The two readings today call us to be faithful and totally committed to Christ and to say, with conviction, the response to today's psalm: 'My God, in you I trust.'

Tuesday of the Ninth Week in Ordinary Time
2 Peter 3:11-15, 17-18; Psalm 89; Mark 12:13-17
In our first reading, St Peter is telling us that we must be living lives worthy of God while waiting for his day to come. Even though we have been redeemed we must still live lives worthy of that redemption. The author also warns against listening to those false preachers who may preach in such a way so as to delay or prevent our entry into the kingdom. In the gospel, the scribes and elders are trying to catch Jesus out and ask him about paying tax to Caesar. He tells them that they should pay money to Caesar because his head is on the coin, but they must give to God what belongs to him – faith and praise – for everything we have is his and from his bounty.

Wednesday of the Ninth Week in Ordinary Time
2 Timothy 1:1-3, 6-12; Psalm 122; Mark 12:18-27

St Paul is writing to St Timothy in today's first reading to strengthen Timothy in the faith and to encourage him to build up the faith he has already received. He is also telling him that the Spirit he has received is not to be kept quiet, but is to speak out through him and proclaim Christ and his message. At the time he was writing the letter, Paul was in prison in Rome and was unable to proclaim the good news and so had to encourage others like Timothy to continue the work in his place. In the gospel text, Christ is telling his listeners that God is the God of the living and that those who have died – such as Abraham, Isaac and Jacob – are alive with God. This is the great promise which awaits us. We have a duty to tell the world of this promise so that more people may become worthy of it and receive the promise themselves.

Thursday of the Ninth Week in Ordinary Time
2 Timothy 2:8-15; Psalm 24; Mark 12:28-34

Again today, St Paul is encouraging St Timothy (his successor in Ephesus) in the faith and helping to strengthen him by explaining some of the mysteries about Christ and about our redemption. Though a prisoner in Rome, Paul is aware that he can still live out his vocation as a messenger of the gospel by encouraging others, like Timothy, by providing them with inspiration through his writings and by explaining key passages in the life of Christ and of the Christian. In the gospel, Christ gives us the great commandment to love one another, which is second only to the commandment to love God above all else. These are still the greatest commandments for us today and from them all other commandments and precepts for living flow.

Friday of the Ninth Week in Ordinary Time
2 Timothy 3:10-17; Psalm 118; Mark 12:35-37

St Paul continues to teach St Timothy about the faith in today's first reading. He tells him that all of scripture is inspired by God and, therefore, we can trust it and draw closer to Christ by reading it carefully. Paul also talks about the persecutions he faced while on his missionary work as an inspiration for those who

are being persecuted for the faith to continue on for the prize
which is unmatched by humans. Our gospel text today is a
rather difficult one. The scribes seem to have a very narrow definition of 'Messiah' and the cornerstone of that definition was
that the Messiah would be a son of David. In our text, Christ is
pointing out that this alone is not adequate and that the definition of Messiah is greater than they were used to. It is easy for us
to understand because we know that he is the Messiah, though
not the Messiah that the scribes wanted.

Saturday of the Ninth Week in Ordinary Time
2 Timothy 4:1-8; Psalm 70; Mark 12:38-44
In today's first reading and final passage from his second letter
to St Timothy, St Paul is encouraging Timothy to go out and
preach about Christ and to make that his life's work. He also
speaks about his impending death and says that he is happy to
die for the faith. In the gospel, Christ warns about being too
'showy' in our religious practice. Instead, we must give all that
we can but quietly and without attracting the wrong sort of attention. He uses the image of a poor widow giving all she has as
the image we should try to emulate.

Monday of the Tenth Week in Ordinary Time
1 Kings 17:1-6, Psalm 120; Matthew 5:1-12
We turn back to the Old Testament for our first readings for the
coming weeks, and in today's reading from the first Book of the
Kings we see Elijah answering God's call and doing God's will.
This takes place about the year 850BC when Ahab and his pagan
wife, Jezebel, ruled the country. The queen persecutes the Jews
and Elijah warns the king that there will be a drought unless he
relents. Elijah leaves his home and goes east for refuge. In the
gospel from St Matthew, we have the Beatitudes from the
Sermon on the Mount. These short phrases give us the perfect
blueprint for living and for serving God. Elijah, even though he
never heard Christ's sermon, lived out the Beatitudes in his life
and in his dealings with people. We are called to be like him and
to put our trust in God, serving him alone.

Tuesday of the Tenth Week in Ordinary Time

1 Kings 17:7-16, Psalm 4; Matthew 5:13-16

Today, in our first reading from the Kings, we see Elijah being sent by God to a Sidonian town. Again, Elijah puts his trust in God and does as he is commanded. There is a famine in both Palestine and Phoenicia (Jezebel's homeland) and yet the widow is provided with enough food by God for herself and the holy prophet she looks after. Our gospel text from St Matthew sees Jesus telling his disciples that they are the light of the world. It is their task to light the way for the people toward God and to guide them home. Elijah too, was the light of the world in his time for he spoke to the people about God and showed them how to live in the sight of God. As the successors of Elijah and the disciples, we are the light of the world and it is our duty to proclaim Christ wherever we may be and to bring people to know him.

Wednesday of the Tenth Week in Ordinary Time

1 Kings 18:20-39; Psalm 15; Matthew 5:17-19

We read in the first reading today of the slaughter of the prophets of Baal on Mount Carmel by Elijah and how he won back the people for the Lord, even though he was the only true prophet left alive in Israel. The event takes place about three years into the famine brought on the people by the actions of King Ahab and his pagan wife, Jezebel. The psalm for today could quite easily have been the prayer on Elijah's lips as he called on God for strength and guidance. Today's gospel tells us that the Law and the prophets are still to be obeyed because Christ did not come to abolish them but to complete them, for they contained some inaccuracies which had crept in over the years. It is not enough to observe the mere letter of the Law but also the broader interpretations of the Laws. We are called on to be like Elijah and to stand up for God in the midst of adversity and to obey the Law and the teachings in all things.

Thursday of the Tenth Week in Ordinary Time

1 Kings 18:41-46; Psalm 64; Matthew 5:20-26

In the first reading from the Kings, Elijah foretells an end to the drought which Ahab's land had endured. He could do this because God's favour rested on him and he served the Lord alone. The psalm speaks to us of God's care for his earth and he provides what is necessary to make the land fruitful. The gospel passage reminds us that we must hold no grievances against our fellow men and women but must be reconciled with them before approaching the altar of God. It is not for us to judge others and, for the sake of the kingdom, we must forgive others and in that way people will see that we are true witnesses for Christ. Again we see that the strict interpretation of the Law is not always right, as Jesus tells us that anger is also to be avoided just as murder is also to be avoided.

Friday of the Tenth Week in Ordinary Time
1 Kings 19:9, 11-16; Psalm 26; Matthew 5:27-32
In today's text from the first Book of Kings, Elijah stands on Mount Horeb (also known as Sinai) and is visited by God. God does not come with great power but in the gentleness of a light breeze. When asked why he has come there, Elijah says that he is filled with a jealous zeal for God and because all other servants of God have been killed. The meeting with God on Sinai reminds us of the meeting between God and Moses on the same mountain when Moses was given the ten commandments. Elijah is now instructed by God to return to Palestine for the Lord has work for him to do and from which he cannot shy away. In the gospel, Christ speaks about divorce and adultery. This is often used to portray the Church in a negative way as being oppressive and uncaring but in this passage Christ is setting an ideal for us to strive towards. He also reminds us that we must keep the oaths we swear. Living out the values of the gospel is not always going to be easy but the standards are always necessary to guide and strengthen the people. We are called to be like the Prophet Elijah because people like him are needed to stand up for God and his Word, especially in today's world.

Saturday of the Tenth Week in Ordinary Time
1 Kings 19:19-21; Psalm 15; Matthew 5:33-37
In our first reading from the first Book of the Kings we see Elijah travelling to central Palestine in search of Elisha who has been

marked out by God as Elijah's successor. When he sees him, Elijah places his cloak over Elisha who understands this as being the call of God to serve him. Without hesitation, Elisha bids farewell to his family and his former life and becomes the servant of the one true God. In today's gospel, Christ tells us that if we live truly Christian lives then there will be no need to swear oaths in order for others to believe us. If we are Christian then we will always live by the truth and others will recognise this in us. We are called upon to become servants of God just as Elisha became one and to always live in honesty and uprightness.

Monday of the Eleventh Week in Ordinary Time
1 Kings 21:1-16; Psalm 5; Matthew 5:38-42
Today's first reading sees Naboth – a just man – being stoned to death so that the king can have himself a vegetable garden. Naboth refused to hand over what had been handed down to him by his forefathers and even Ahab acknowledges this to be right. However, Queen Jezebel arranged for false accusations to be made against Naboth so that he could be tried as a traitor and the lands confiscated. In the gospel from St Matthew, Christ tells us to always turn the other cheek to the wicked. Naboth could be seen as a forerunner to Christ for both were wrongly accused and wrongly put to death. We are reminded of what lies can do and how they can destroy lives.

Tuesday of the Eleventh Week in Ordinary Time
1 Kings 21:17-29; Psalm 50; Matthew 5:43-48
Our reading today from the Kings is a continuation of yesterday's text, and in it we see Elijah confronting King Ahab. He accuses Ahab of killing Naboth and of doing what was wrong in the eyes of God. Having heard the predicted doom, Ahab repents. The psalm is one of pleading for mercy and would have been quite fitting if spoken by the king. Christ, in the gospel, tells us that we must love our enemies no matter what they have done to us. Only when we love them are we living truly Christian lives.

Wednesday of the Eleventh Week in Ordinary Time

2 Kings 2:1, 6-14; Psalm 30; Matthew 6:1-6, 16-18

Today's first reading sees Elijah being assumed into heaven – his work on earth now completed. In his place, Elisha takes over from his master as the foremost prophet in the land. In our gospel text, Christ is telling the disciples that they should not parade their religious practice in front of others or use it to show off. They should pray and fast quietly because God sees all that they do. Christ did not do away with prayer and fasting but changed how it should be done. We are called on to fast and to pray to our Father in heaven but without drawing attention to ourselves.

Thursday of the Eleventh Week in Ordinary Time

Ecclesiasticus (Sirach) 48:1-14; Psalm 96; Matthew 6:7-15

Today's reading from Ecclesiasticus is a hymn of praise for Elijah and Elisha and their service for the Lord. The author emphasises how the two prophets never tired of bringing the people back to God's way of living even when that work brought them great danger. The text from St Matthew's gospel sees Christ teaching his followers how to pray and in it he gives them the 'Our Father,' the Lord's Prayer. We are called on to pray to the Father and to serve him as did Elijah and Elisha. We are also asked to think carefully about the words of the Lord's Prayer and to try to fulfil each of its phrases.

Friday of the Eleventh Week in Ordinary Time

2 Kings 11:1-4, 9-18, 20; Psalm 131; Matthew 6:19-23

The reading from the second Book of Kings sees Queen Athaliah seizing power by slaying her grandsons. However, one male heir – Jehoash – is hidden by his aunt and survives the queen's massacre. Eventually the people revolt against her tyrannical rule and Jehoiada, the priest, has her removed from power and establishes a new covenant with God while destroying the temple of the Baals which Athaliah had built. In the gospel, we are told that we should not store up treasure for ourselves on earth for they are worthless. Rather, we are to store up treasure in heaven and this is done through upright living in the sight of God.

Saturday of the Eleventh Week in Ordinary Time
2 Chronicles 24:17-25; Psalm 88; Matthew 6:24-34

In our reading from the second Book of Chronicles, King Jehoiada is succeeded by Joash who quickly abandons the covenant with God and he and his people begin worshipping false gods. He has the prophet Zechariah – son of Jehoiada who saved the king's father – put to death in Jerusalem about 796BC. As a result, the land is taken over by the Aramaeans and the king dies at the hand of his own people. In the gospel, Christ tells us that we cannot serve two masters – we can only serve one. That master should be God. If we serve him faithfully then we will never have to worry about anything or even about tomorrow, for the Lord will look after us in all things. We are called to put our complete trust in God and never forget the Covenant he has made with us in the blood of his Son.

Monday of the Twelfth Week in Ordinary Time
2 Kings 17:5-8, 13-15, 18; Psalm 59; Matthew 7:1-5

We see in today's first reading that even though God had freed his people from the slavery in Egypt they soon fell away from the Covenant and so we see them again going into exile for their transgressions. The northern kingdom of Israel fell to the Assyrians about the year 721BC. Only the southern tribe of Judah remained faithful and free. Our gospel text tells us that we should never judge others but should look after ourselves. When we see faults in others we should realise that there are bigger faults to be found in ourselves. Today's readings give us a choice – be faithful to the Lord and his Word and thus live in peace and righteousness, or turn from him and suffer.

Tuesday of the Twelfth Week in Ordinary Time
2 Kings 19:9-11, 14-21, 31-36; Psalm 47; Matthew 7:6, 12-14

Despite being attacked by a more powerful nation in our reading from the second Book of Kings, Hezekiah prays to the Lord for deliverance for his people and, as a result of his trust in God, is delivered safely. The Assyrians – who had over-run the northern kingdom – were now attacking the southern kingdom and only one city remained free – Jerusalem. One could easily imagine today's psalm being sung following the defeat of

Sennacherib. In the gospel, Christ tells us to treat others as we would have them treat us. We are reminded to always remain faithful to the word of God and to always put our trust in him.

Wednesday of the Twelfth Week in Ordinary Time
2 Kings 22:8-13, 23:1-3; Psalm 118; Matthew 7:15-20

King Josiah is shown the Book of the Law in our first reading today which his people have just rediscovered in the Temple. He immediately orders that all it says is to be obeyed and makes a new covenant with God before the people. The psalm asks the Lord to teach us his statutes and that we may be careful to observe them. Christ warns us in the gospel today about listening to false prophets. In our day there are many false prophets with 'quick fix' solutions and easy ways to get into heaven. However, we must remember that there is only one way to enter heaven and that is through Christ – the Gate of the Sheepfold, the Way, the Truth and the Life.

Thursday of the Twelfth Week in Ordinary Time
2 Kings 24:8-17; Psalm 78; Matthew 7:21-29

The city of Jerusalem and the people go into exile in Babylon in our first reading from the second Book of Kings. This is about the year 597BC – 125 years after the northern kingdom had been over-run for the same reason, which was that the people and their king had turned from God and no longer trusted him. The magnificent Temple built by King Solomon is stripped of its glory. Our gospel tells us that we must build our house on solid ground if it is to remain standing and we are to be safe. The solid foundation is the word of God in which we must place all our faith and trust. If we walk away from it, we will be no better than King Jehoiachin and his people who fell to the Babylonians.

Friday of the Twelfth Week in Ordinary Time
2 Kings 25:1-12; Psalm 136; Matthew 8:1-4

Today we read of the total destruction of Jerusalem by the Babylonians. The once magnificent Temple of Solomon lies in ruins as do the city walls. The countryside becomes a barren wasteland – all because the people abandoned their God. The psalm is quite appropriate for this reading. Jesus cures a leper in our gospel text and what is important is that he did so because he wanted to. Christ always wants to help us but he will not force that help on any of us. He will give us his help only if we believe in him and ask for his help.

Saturday of the Twelfth Week in Ordinary Time
Lamentations 2:2, 10-14, 18-19; Psalm 73; Matthew 8:5-17
In today's first reading we read of the people's lament for all that has happened to them and the destruction of their nation because of their sinful ways. The text makes for sad reading as we hear what has happened to the people and the Promised Land. The psalm continues this theme. We again see Jesus curing the sick in today's gospel. The important key in today's reading is faith – the centurion had faith that Jesus could cure his servant even if Jesus never came near the house. That is the faith that we are asked to have in God and in his Son.

Monday of the Thirteenth Week in Ordinary Time
Amos 2:6-10, 13-16; Psalm 49; Matthew 8:18-22
Our first reading today comes from the Prophet Amos who served the Lord about the year 760BC. In our text, the Lord is recounting some of the many sins of his people. He reminds them of what he did for them and tells them how he will deal with them in a way that nobody in Israel will be able to escape. The psalm continues the accusations against the people. In the gospel, Jesus is calling the people to follow him, though some do not wish to come right away. The message in the readings for us today is that we are called to follow the Lord and to respond to that call immediately and not when we fell like it. Secondly, those who have been called are expected to live a life worthy of the Lord, one in keeping with the gospel values.

Tuesday of the Thirteenth Week in Ordinary Time
Amos 3:1-8, 4:11-12; Psalm 5; Matthew 8:23-27
Today's reading from the Prophet Amos continues yesterday's theme of reminding the people of how much they have sinned against God. They are also given warning that the Lord means to punish them for their sins. Today's psalm could easily have been the words on the lips of the Prophet Amos. In the text from

St Matthew's gospel, we see Jesus command the forces of nature and calm a storm. The readings remind us of the infinite power of God and that, in Jesus, he has made a covenant with us which we must honour.

Wednesday of the Thirteenth Week in Ordinary Time
Amos 5:14-15, 21-24; Psalm 49; Matthew 8:28-34
The Prophet Amos tells us in our first reading what it is that the Lord wants of us – justice and integrity. The prophet warns the people that the Lord is not deceived by their outward show of piety or their loud hymns of worship. Only when justice pre-vails will the Lord listen to his people. Our gospel sees Jesus dri-ving out demons from two demoniacs. The local people are afraid and ask Jesus to leave their area. The message of the Lord calls for a radical transformation in our lives if we are to be wor-thy of him. However, if we begin working towards integrity and justice then we will be well on the way towards that conversion which Christ asks of us.

Thursday of the Thirteenth Week in Ordinary Time
Amos 7:10-17; Psalm 18; Matthew 9:1-8
In today's first reading Amos is confronted by King Jeroboam and Amaziah, his royal priest. They do not like what Amos prophesies but in reply, Amos tells them that his words do not come from a group of prophets, like Amaziah, but directly from God. He then tells them how the kingdom will end. In the gospel, Jesus forgives a paralytic man his sins which outraged the scribes. He tells them that he has the power to forgive and heals the man to prove his authority. The people are amazed and pleased to see this. We are reminded that not everyone, such as Amaziah, speaks the truth but that the words of Jesus are truth and life.

Friday of the Thirteenth Week in Ordinary Time
Amos 8:4-6, 9-12; Psalm 118; Matthew 9:9-13
In the reading from the Prophet Amos the Lord tells his people that the punishment they will receive will be in the form of a famine. A spiritual famine is to fall upon them for their sins against the Lord in which they will not hear the word of the

Lord. In the gospel, Jesus is scorned by the Pharisees for eating with tax collectors and sinners but, in reply, he tells them that their sacrificial ways do not please him. What the Lord seeks is true mercy. Those who are virtuous are not called to conversion for their hearts are already set on God, but those who are still in need of conversion are the ones who are being called. If we in our day turn our backs on God then we live without his word, but if we seek God then his word will take root in our hearts and we will live the life he seeks.

Saturday of the Thirteenth Week in Ordinary Time
Amos 9:11-15; Psalm 84; Matthew 9:14-17
In the first reading from the Prophet Amos, the Lord tells his people that he will revive their fortunes and re-establish the kingdom of David. We know that this will happen in the person of Jesus, the Messiah. In the gospel, Jesus tells John the Baptist's disciples that his own disciples do not fast in his presence because they have the Lord of Life with them. When he is gone from them then they will fast and mourn. We have the Lord always with us and so we should rejoice and live by his precepts so that we may never be abandoned as were the people of old when they sinned against God.

Monday of the Fourteenth Week in Ordinary Time
Hosea 2:16-18, 21-22; Psalm 144; Matthew 9:18-26
In today's reading from the Prophet Hosea, who was writing about the year 755BC, the Lord is speaking of his relationship with his people. So strong is his love for his people that he speaks of marrying Israel for ever. Hosea was the first to use this marriage image when talking about God and his people but it is one which was to be used by later prophets and also St Paul. In the gospel, Jesus restores life to a little girl who has died. More importantly, he cures a woman whose faith was so strong that she believed that she would be cured even if she only touched his cloak. She was also courageous enough to own up when Jesus asked who had touched him – strict Jewish law would have decreed that she should not be in a crowd as that could result in those coming into contact with her being impure and unable to attend synagogue. We are called on to be like this

woman and to believe in God completely. He has chosen us out of all of creation to be his bride and therefore he will not abandon us.

Tuesday of the Fourteenth Week in Ordinary Time
Hosea 8:4-7, 11-13; Psalm 113; Matthew 9:32-38
In our first reading today we read that despite the fact that the Lord has chosen his people as his spouse the people turn from God and spurn him. He recounts their sins and how they abused his altars and created false idols for themselves. Now, God is about to punish them. In the gospel, Jesus is sorry to see many people coming to him for they have nobody to minister to them. We are called on to be labourers in this great harvest. We do not all have to become priests and religious but we are all called to live according to gospel values – in this way the kingdom of God will be strengthened daily and more people will become shepherds of the flock.

Wednesday of the Fourteenth Week in Ordinary Time
Hosea 10:1-3, 7-8, 12; Psalm 104; Matthew 10:1-7
Today we read in the text from the Prophet Hosea that Israel has turned from the Lord and worshipped false gods, and so the Lord is now going to punish the people. If the people had retained their integrity they would not be in such a situation. Hosea pleads with the people to change their ways and return to the Lord. In the gospel we see Jesus choosing his twelve closest companions and sending them out to preach in his name. Because Israel was the Lord's Chosen People through the ages, the apostles are told to go with the message to the house of Israel first and to leave the others aside for the moment. While the names of the Twelve appear in a few places in the New Testament no two lists are in the same order, though St Peter's name always appears first.

Thursday of the Fourteenth Week in Ordinary Time
Hosea 11:1-4, 8-9; Psalm 79; Matthew 10:7-15
The Lord recounts the sins of his people in today's first reading from Hosea. He also recalls some of what he did for the people and how he blessed them. While he is angry with his people he

will still keep his anger in check. He may punish this 'ungrateful son' but he will not destroy him. Today's gospel text continues on from yesterday's passage and in it we see Jesus instructing the Twelve before they go out in his name. We too need to be mindful of all that the Lord has done for us and we should give thanks for that each day, not just in our prayers, but by living lives worthy of the gospel which we can proclaim in the manner in which we live.

Friday of the Fourteenth Week in Ordinary Time
Hosea 14:2-10; Psalm 50; Matthew 10:16-23
In our first reading for today, the Lord speaks through the Prophet Hosea and tells his people what he wants of them. Those who listen and believe in the message will walk in right-eousness but those who reject it will stumble and fall. In our gospel passage Jesus continues to instruct the Twelve in today's text from St Matthew. In it he warns them of the hardships that will come but he strengthens them by telling them that they will have him with them and that the words they will speak will be from him – therefore they need have no cause for fear. We are called to live righteously before God and to remember that those who preach the true gospel in his name are doing so with the guidance of the Lord. As the people of the Old Testament were invited back to God despite their sins, so too we will be wel-comed if we ask the Lord for forgiveness.

Saturday of the Fourteenth Week in Ordinary Time
Isaiah 6:1-8; Psalm 92; Matthew 10:24-33
We now move to the book of the Prophet Isaiah and today's pas-sage recounts the call of Isaiah to be God's messenger. This took place about the year 742BC while the young Isaiah was visiting the Temple in Jerusalem. Though Isaiah felt unworthy of the task, the Lord was with him and so made him worthy. Isaiah re-sponded by accepting God's call and following the path of the prophets. Jesus' instruction to the Twelve continues in today's gospel reading and he tells them that no matter what happens they need have no fear. As Isaiah was called so too we are called to spread the gospel of Christ in our own way. If we truly be-lieve in God then we need have no fear of what others may say against us for living as Christians.

Monday of the Fifteenth Week in Ordinary Time
Isaiah 1:10-17; Psalm 49; Matthew 10:34-11:1

In today's passage from the Prophet Isaiah God tells his people that ritual sacrifice no longer pleases him. He wants the people to truly believe in what they are doing rather than just performing. He wants the people to be concerned with justice and peace. The psalm takes up this theme. In the gospel from St Matthew, we see Jesus telling his listeners that he has not come to bring peace but trouble. This is because his message calls for a conversion of heart and a new way of life which many will and, indeed, still do reject. Our readings challenge us to make this conversion and become true Christians in thought, word and deed.

Tuesday of the Fifteenth Week in Ordinary Time
Isaiah 7:1-9; Psalm 47; Matthew 11:20-24

In our first reading today from the Prophet Isaiah the Lord is telling his people to stand by him and they will be safe, but if they do not stand by him then they will not stand at all. This takes place about the year 733BC when the rulers of Israel (the northern kingdom) and Aram had forged alliances with foreign rulers. Isaiah tells King Ahaz of Jerusalem to place his trust in God and God will defend him. In the gospel, Christ exhorts his hearers to listen to him and to believe in him. Christ names a number of towns in which he had worked most of his miracles but where true faith had not materialised. He tells the people that these towns will be punished more severely than Sodom unless they listen and convert. We too are called to conversion of heart and a new way of life.

Wednesday of the Fifteenth Week in Ordinary Time
Isaiah 10:5-7, 13-16; Psalm 93; Matthew 11:25-27

The people are reminded by the Prophet Isaiah in today's first reading that kingdoms and powers rise and fall but that everything is subject to God's power. Isaiah foretells that the King of Assyria will be used by God as the stick to discipline the people of Judah for the sins they have committed. In the gospel, Jesus says that it is children who truly understand the message of the kingdom. By this he is saying that those with no preconceptions or theories can easily grasp the message he brings. To truly understand that message we need to have a clear mind and childlike trust.

Thursday of the Fifteenth Week in Ordinary Time
Isaiah 26:7-9, 12, 16-19; Psalm 101; Matthew 11:28-30
Our first reading today tells us that those who live righteously before the God who judges all will have a happy life. Those who do not live by the law of God will have a troubled life. Christ calls the people to himself in the gospel and tells them that if they believe in him he will support them. The yoke which each of us has to carry is an easy one because faith in Christ will make the burden lighter and easier to carry. True faith is what we must have and that faith is demonstrated in righteous living.

Friday of the Fifteenth Week in Ordinary Time
Isaiah 38:1-6, 21-22, 7-8; Psalm 38; Matthew 12:1-8
In our first reading we see that Hezekiah is now King of the southern kingdom of Judah. He is told by Isaiah that he is about to die so he prays to God and is cured because of his faith. In the gospel, Jesus admonishes the Pharisees for being too legalistic about the Sabbath day. His disciples had been out walking with him and had picked a few heads of corn as they passed through the corn fields. What the Lord wants is mercy and not legalism for only in mercy is true faith to be seen.

Saturday of the Fifteenth Week in Ordinary Time
Micah 2:1-5; Psalm 9; Matthew 12:14-21
Our first reading today comes from the Prophet Micah – a contemporary of Isaiah – through whom God warns that those who plot evil and mischief will themselves be plotted against by God. Micah speaks about how those who commit evil even lie awake at night thinking up even more ways to deprive the poor. In the gospel, Jesus is forced to move on from a particular district sooner than he intended because the Pharisees had decided to destroy him and were looking for a way to do it. As he goes he cures more people but tells them to say nothing about it – his time has not yet come. But our time has come and now is the time for us to live as true Christians and to proclaim the message of the Good News.

Monday of the Sixteenth Week in Ordinary Time
Micah 6:1-4, 6-8; Psalm 49; Matthew 12:38-42

Our first reading today comes from the Prophet Micah who lived in the eighth century before Christ. In it, we see God charging the people with the crime of abandonment – they have abandoned him. As witnesses he calls the mountains which have stood in silent watchfulness for centuries. At the end of the text we are told exactly what the Lord asks of us. In the gospel, Christ likens himself to Jonah who spent three days in the belly of the whale. Christ too was to spend three days in darkness before restoring the people to righteousness. If we wish to be worthy of God, then, we too, must 'act justly, love tenderly, and walk humbly with [our] God.'

Tuesday of the Sixteenth Week in Ordinary Time
Micah 7:14-15, 18-20; Psalm 84; Matthew 12:46-50

The Prophet Micah is calling on the Lord in the first reading to be merciful to his people and to pardon their sins and transgressions. The people wish to live under God's blessing as in the past and Micah's prayer to God is on their behalf. The psalm takes up this theme and asks the Lord to revive his people, to lead them in the right path. In the gospel, Jesus tells us that those who do the will of God are his brothers and sisters and mother. If we want to be called brothers and sisters of Christ then we too must denounce our sinful ways and do the will of the Father.

Wednesday of the Sixteenth Week in Ordinary Time
Jeremiah 1:1, 4-10; Psalm 70; Matthew 13:1-9

In our first reading today we read of the call of Jeremiah to be the prophet of God. Jeremiah is afraid – like Moses and so many other prophets – and does not want the job but the Lord strengthens him and the words that Jeremiah will proclaim are the words of God himself. This is about the year 626BC. The gospel text from St Matthew recounts the parable of the sower. The seed fell in various places and produced different effects. Today is a good time to ask ourselves whether we are the good and fertile soil of the parable or whether the Lord sees us as one of the lesser soils. As the Lord strengthened Jeremiah with his word, so too will he strengthen us if we allow him to do so.

Thursday of the Sixteenth Week in Ordinary Time
Jeremiah 2:1-3, 7-8, 12-13; Psalm 35; Matthew 13:10-17
In today's first reading the prophet Jeremiah is speaking on behalf of God and reminds the people of how good God has been
to them. Yet they have turned their backs on him and walked
away from him, preferring instead to put their trust in man-
made alliances with foreign groups. The psalm reminds us that
God alone is the fountain of life. In the gospel, Christ tells us that
he speaks in parables so that those who are open to him will understand. Those who are not open to him do not want to hear his
message because they know that it would force them to convert.
We are called today to conversion of heart and lifestyle. We are
called to acknowledge what we have received from God and to
be grateful for it and, in giving thanks, to be worthy of what we
have received.

Friday of the Sixteenth Week in Ordinary Time
Jeremiah 3:14-17; Psalm: Jeremiah 31:1-13; Matthew 13:18-23
The Lord calls his people back to him in the first reading from
the Prophet Jeremiah. He tells them that he will give them shepherds to guide them and that Zion will be their focal point as is a
throne in a throne room. Today's gospel text explains the parable of the sower. We are called on to be the rich soil in to which
the seed fell and produced a harvest. We are reminded today to
look into ourselves from time to time in order to rid ourselves of
anything which might reduce our faith and so separate us from
the love of God.

Saturday of the Sixteenth Week in Ordinary Time
Jeremiah 7:1-11; Psalm 83; Matthew 13:24-30
In our reading from Jeremiah today, the Lord is telling the people how they must behave towards God and towards others. If
they act according to his will, then he will stay with them. This is
about the year 609BC and Jeremiah is warning the people that
the fact that the Temple is in Jerusalem will not mean that
Jerusalem will stand against their enemies – God will only be on
their side to protect them if they are faithful to him. In the
gospel, Jesus uses another parable – that of the seed and the darnel which grow side by side – one useful, the other useless – but

the farmer leaves them both to grow until the harvest. In our world there are both good people and bad people and both grow and live side by side. The good should not worry that the bad grow and appear to prosper better than they, for the Lord will weed the good from the bad on the day of judgement. We must continue to live good lives converting ourselves more and more to the gospel.

Monday of the Seventeenth Week in Ordinary Time
Jeremiah 13:1-11; Psalm: Deuteronomy 32; Matthew 13:31-35
In our first reading today from the Prophet Jeremiah, we see that the Lord is dissatisfied with his people because they have not been faithful to him. He likens them to a rotting linen cloth which is good for nothing and which eventually decays to nothing. It is possible that Jeremiah is referring to the Babylonian captivity where the people would go into exile near the river Euphrates. The psalm, taken from Deuteronomy, continues this theme: 'You forget the God who fathered you.' Again in the gospel we see Jesus speaking to the people through parables because there are those who do not want to listen to his message and understand it. Those who do want to hear the word and believe will easily understand the meaning of the message and conform their lives to the truth, unlike the people in the first reading.

Tuesday of the Seventeenth Week in Ordinary Time
Jeremiah 14:17-22; Psalm 78; Matthew 13:36-43
In the reading from Jeremiah we read that the southern kingdom of Judah has been stricken with a drought because the people were unfaithful to the covenant. The people need food and call on God to be merciful to them and to end the drought. The people gather in Jerusalem for a penitential service in which they acknowledge that their sins have caused the drought. In the gospel, Christ tells us that on judgement day those who have not lived according to the will of God will be weeded out just as the darnel is weeded out and burned. Unlike the people in the first reading, we are called on to be faithful to God in good times as well as in bad.

Wednesday of the Seventeenth Week in Ordinary Time
Jeremiah 15:10, 16-21; Psalm 58; Matthew 13:44-46

The Prophet Jeremiah in our first reading realises that the message he preaches is a difficult one, one of dissention and one which has separated Jeremiah from his people and given him a sense of isolation. God, however, tells him to be faithful and he will strengthen him against those who do not wish to listen to him or his message. It is a reminder that, even in our day, following our Christian vocation is not always an easy one but that God is always with us to strengthen and guide us. Christ tells us in the gospel that the kingdom of heaven is a treasure beyond all price. We are called on to be like the Prophet Jeremiah, to preach the gospel of Christ no matter what the personal cost to us, knowing that there is nothing more valuable in this life than eternal life with God in the next.

Thursday of the Seventeenth Week in Ordinary Time
Jeremiah 18:1-6; Psalm 145; Matthew 13:47-53

We have the allegory of the potter in today's reading from Jeremiah. As the potter gently reshapes something which goes wrong and starts it afresh, so we are like clay in the hands of God who can restart creation whenever he wishes. Jeremiah realises that the sufferings the people are put through by God, are simply God's way of remoulding the people and coaxing them back to the covenant and their promises to him. Christ again tells us in the gospel that the good and the bad will be sifted on judgement day and only the good will be allowed in to the kingdom. We must allow the word of God to mould us each day in to a new people just as the potter moulds his clay.

Friday of the Seventeenth Week in Ordinary Time
Jeremiah 26:1-9; Psalm 68; Matthew 13:54-58

We see Jeremiah in the first reading preaching the word of God in the Temple. He tells the people that if they are not more faithful to God that God would destroy the Temple built by Solomon. This was blasphemous for the people, who nearly rioted, but Jeremiah reminds them that this happened before at Shiloh when the Lord allowed that most sacred of places to be destroyed by the enemies of Israel. In the gospel, we see Jesus being rejected by his own people because they think they know him just because he is from their district. In both readings the people had little faith and so the word of God could do no work in them. If we are not open to the word of God then it will not work in us either.

Saturday of the Seventeenth Week in Ordinary Time
Jeremiah 26:11-16, 24; Psalm 68; Matthew 14:1-12
The authorities wish to kill Jeremiah in the first reading because they did not like his message. He had predicted that God would destroy his own Temple in Jerusalem because of the sins of the nation. He tells the people that even if they kill him the message will be carried by others and it will never die because the message he brings are God's own words. In the gospel, we read of the beheading of John the Baptist for the sake of a foolish promise. The truth of the message and its constancy is put before us today and we are called on to believe it as the people did in the time of Jeremiah after they heard him speak.

Note that there are two sets of Gospel texts for Monday and Tuesday of this week depending on the Sunday Cycle:

Following Sunday Cycle A:
Monday of the Eighteenth Week in Ordinary Time
Jeremiah 28:1-17; Psalm 118; Matthew 14:22-36
We read in the first reading today how the prophet Hananiah gave a prophecy in the Temple which was false but which the people accepted and believed. Hananiah even takes on Jeremiah in front of the people but God assures Jeremiah that Jeremiah is the true prophet. For leading the people astray, Hananiah died. In the gospel, we see that Jesus has just heard of the death of his cousin, John, and goes away to be on his own. When he returns to the lakeside the disciples are having trouble fishing in their boats but he calls out to them and calls to Peter to walk across the water to him. St Peter starts out but soon his faith fails and he begins to sink. The text reminds us that we must trust the Lord at all times even when it is difficult to do so and our perceptions lead us astray.

Tuesday of the Eighteenth Week in Ordinary Time
Jeremiah 31:1-2, 12-15, 18-22; Psalm 101; Matthew 15:1-2, 10-14
We read in the first reading from the Prophet Jeremiah that despite the sins and transgressions of the people, which the Lord had punished them for, he is now going to restore the fortunes of Jerusalem and rebuild the city. This comes at the end of the Babylonian Captivity, about the year 539BC, and at a time when the people were disheartened at the restoration work which lay ahead of them. In the gospel, we see Jesus answering the questions of the scribes and Pharisees about ritual cleansing. He reminds them that what goes into a man is not what makes him unclean but what comes from within him. This was seen as an attack on the Laws concerning cleanliness from the Book of Deuteronomy and would not have gone down well with some of his listeners. However, the message is correct – what we have within us, and the choices we make along with the things we say and do, are the things which determine whether or not we are worthy enough to be in the Lord's presence.

Following Sunday Cycles B & C:
Monday of the Eighteenth Week in Ordinary Time
Jeremiah 28:1-17; Psalm 118; Matthew 14:13-21
We read in the first reading today how the prophet Hananiah gave a prophecy in the Temple which was false but which the people accepted and believed. Hananiah even takes on Jeremiah in front of the people but God assures Jeremiah that Jeremiah is the true prophet. For leading the people astray, Hananiah died. In the gospel, we read the account of the multiplication of five loaves and the two fish. This reminds us of the bread of life, the body of Christ, which brings us all to salvation. We must be always on our guard against false teachings which tell us what we want to hear and which ultimately lead us away from God. Only in the truth and in the Eucharist is our salvation assured.

Tuesday of the Eighteenth Week in Ordinary Time
Jeremiah 31:1-2, 12-15, 18-22; Psalm 101; Matthew 14:22-36
We read in the first reading from the Prophet Jeremiah that despite the sins and transgressions of the people, which the Lord had punished them for, he is now going to restore the fortunes

of Jerusalem and rebuild the city. This comes at the end of the Babylonian Captivity, about the year 539BC, and at a time when the people were disheartened at the restoration work which lay ahead of them. In the gospel, we see Jesus walking on water towards the disciples in the boat. St Peter tries to walk to him but his faith is not strong enough to make the journey. If we have complete faith in Christ we can overcome our fear and achieve great things for the kingdom. With our faith must also go conversion and repentance, as we are reminded in the first reading.

Wednesday of the Eighteenth Week in Ordinary Time
Jeremiah 31:1-7; Psalm:Jeremiah 31; Matthew 15:21-28
The Lord reminds us in our first reading that he has always loved his people with an everlasting love. And out of his love he is now going to restore the fortunes of his people. Again, this is following the end of the Babylonian Captivity and Jeremiah is painting a wonderful picture for the people of the new Jerusalem when all its people will come to it when the exiles are over. It is his way of encouraging the people to get on with the task of rebuilding the Temple and their dedication to the covenants with God. We read in the gospel of the cure of a young girl because of her mother's great faith and because she refused to take 'no' for an answer. Even though she was a Canaanite and not of the House of Israel, she had faith greater than some who had heard the Good News for themselves. With faith, we too can overcome the trials which afflict us throughout our life.

Thursday of the Eighteenth Week in Ordinary Time
Jeremiah 31:31-34; Psalm 50; Matthew 16:13-23
In the first reading from the Prophet Jeremiah, the Lord speaks of the new covenant he will make with his people and, in establishing this new covenant, he will wipe away their past sins. We know that this greatest of all covenants was fulfilled almost six centuries later in the life, death and resurrection of Christ. The psalm could easily be the prayer of one of the Lord's faithful who is waiting for the covenant to be established. St Peter's great profession of faith is our text in today's gospel. In it we

read of how Peter was made the first shepherd of the flock, a role which has been handed on through the papacy. Christ is now making his final preparations before he goes to Jerusalem where he will suffer and die for us and, in so doing, create the new and everlasting covenant spoken of by Jeremiah.

Friday of the Eighteenth Week in Ordinary Time
Nahum 2:1, 3, 3:1-3, 6-7; Psalm: Deuteronomy 32; Matthew 16:24-28
The first reading today comes from the Prophet Nahum in which we see the Lord restoring the fortunes of Israel and Judah but with a word of caution. Nahum was prophet at the time of the fall of Nineveh (in 612BC) which was the capital of the Assyrian Empire. The Assyrians had previously subdued the northern kingdoms of Israel but had failed to take Judah. In the gospel we are told that if we want to be a true follower of Christ then we must take up our cross – take up whatever it is that troubles us – and follow him. By offering up our sufferings to him he will strengthen us and we will be able to attain the promise of immortality which Christ has gained for us.

Saturday of the Eighteenth Week in Ordinary Time
Habakkuk 1:12-2:4; Psalm 9; Matthew 17:14-20
We are told in the first reading, this time from Habakkuk (written between 605 and 597BC), that if we live by faith then we will not flag like those who do not live at rights with God. We must not worry about how others live or how successful they appear to be but must look at how we ourselves live in the eyes of God. In our gospel text, the disciples have been unable to cure a boy and when they ask Jesus why this is he tells them that it is because of their lack of faith. While they believe in him they have doubts and uncertainties and this holds them back. Like the disciples, we too must have total trust and confidence in God, no matter what.

Monday of the Nineteenth Week in Ordinary Time
Ezekiel 1:2-5, 24-28; Psalm 148; Matthew 17:22-27
Today we begin reading from the Prophet Ezekiel and in today's text the prophet is describing what appears to be the glory of the Lord. The encounter takes place about the year 593BC during

the Babylonian captivity and sees God calling the Jewish priest, Ezekiel, to be his prophet. Ezekiel is to prepare the people for the destruction of Jerusalem and for its future glory. In our gospel passage we see Jesus again telling his followers that he will soon be put to death but that he will rise again to life. His listeners are saddened by this for they do not fully understand the meaning of his words.

Tuesday of the Nineteenth Week in Ordinary Time
Ezekiel 2:8-3:4; Psalm 118; Matthew 18:1-5, 10, 12-14
In our first reading we see that Ezekiel is being sent to the house of Israel by the Lord but before he goes, the Lord puts his words into Ezekiel's mouth. In consuming the scroll, Ezekiel is showing that he accepts the role of the prophet and that the words which he will preach from his heart will be the words of God himself. We are told by Christ in today's gospel that we must change and become as pure as little children if we are to enter the kingdom of heaven. Our trust in God must be as complete as that of a little child. As a child depends completely on their parents for everything, so too we must place our complete trust and confidence in God for all things come from him and he alone can save us.

Wednesday of the Nineteenth Week in Ordinary Time
Ezekiel 9:1-7, 10:18-22; Psalm 112; Matthew 18:15-20
In our reading today from the prophet Ezekiel we see the Lord sending out his messengers to weed out his faithful people from those who have departed from his Law. All of this comes to Ezekiel in a dream which goes on to show the glory of the Lord leaving the Temple in Jerusalem because of the sinfulness of the people. In the gospel, Jesus tells us that we must help keep our brothers and sisters on the right path, especially if they go astray from the word of God. Everything we do has an affect on others and so we must be very careful to live according to God's Law in public as well as in private. Our actions can build up or destroy the faith of those around us and we must never be found as a stumbling block to faith in God.

Thursday of the Nineteenth Week in Ordinary Time
Ezekiel 12:1-12; Psalm 77; Matthew 18:21-19:1

In today's first reading we see how Ezekiel is ordered by the Lord to leave the city because of its evil ways. But he is to do it in broad daylight so that the people will see what he does and may, in this way, be persuaded of their sinfulness and so return to God. These actions are to be a symbol of God's dissatisfaction with the House of Israel in the hopes that the people will heed what is happening and return to the right path. However, the people have grown stubborn and don't believe that God would destroy his own city. In the gospel from St Matthew, Christ tells us that there is to be no limit to the number of times we are to forgive others if they wrong us and seek forgiveness. As the Lord is merciful with us so we must be merciful with others.

Friday of the Nineteenth Week in Ordinary Time
Ezekiel 16:1-15, 60, 63; Psalm: Isaiah 12; Matthew 19:3-12

The Lord speaks to Jerusalem through the Prophet Ezekiel in the first reading and tells the city – which is a symbol of the Jewish nation – how he looked after it and nurtured it. But now the city has become infatuated with itself and is no longer faithful to the one who cared for it. Now is the time for the city and its inhabitants to remember the covenant and to be ashamed. Our gospel text is a particularly difficult one for it speaks of the Lord's displeasure with divorce as he tells his disciples that it is not in keeping with his Law or his vision for us. At the same time, he does not condemn those whose marriages have ended in this way.

Saturday of the Nineteenth Week in Ordinary Time
Ezekiel 18:1-10, 13, 30-32; Psalm 50; Matthew 19:13-15

The Lord tells us in the reading from Ezekiel that he will not punish whole groups of people for the misdeeds of a few but that he will punish the individual sinners for what they have done. Ezekiel is trying to get the people to accept responsibility for their own misdeeds rather than blaming those around them, or their ancestors, for their own sins and for the punishment which has befallen them. Again today we read in the gospel that we must become like little children in faith and trust if we are to enter the kingdom. At the time of Christ, children had no standing in society and so Christ's inclusion of them is important and shows the importance of a child-like trust and faith rather than one which uses reason and so reduces the faith.

Monday of the Twentieth Week in Ordinary Time
Ezekiel 24:15-24; Psalm: Deuteronomy 32; Matthew 19:16-22
In the first reading from the Prophet Ezekiel, the people have sinned and as a result the Lord is about to punish them. Ezekiel is told that his wife is soon to die which is a symbol of the destruction of the Temple in Jerusalem and of the grief which the people will have for their great loss. The psalm continues this theme. In the gospel we read the account of the rich young man who came to Jesus to be a follower. However he was unable to follow him because even though he had kept the commandments, he could not give up his wealth. It is one thing to have possessions but it is quite another to be too attached to them. To be true followers we must be able to give up all we have for the sake of the kingdom.

Tuesday of the Twentieth Week in Ordinary Time
Ezekiel 28:1-10; Psalm: Deuteronomy 32; Matthew 19:23-30
In our first reading we see God about to punish an imaginary prince in the port city of Tyre for the prince likened himself to a god and was not faithful to the true God. This comes from a section of the book of the Prophet Ezekiel in which warnings are given to the neighbouring kingdoms around Israel and Judah. The psalm, taken from Deuteronomy, could easily have been the words spoken by God in his anger. Today's gospel text follows on from yesterday's passage and in it Christ tells us that it is difficult to enter heaven if we place too much store on our possessions. First and foremost in our life must always be Christ and the kingdom. We need possessions to live comfortably in this life but we need Christ to live peacefully for all time.

Wednesday of the Twentieth Week in Ordinary Time
Ezekiel 34:1-11; Psalm 22; Matthew 20:1-16
We read in the first reading that the people have turned away from God and have been lured by other gods because their

shepherds – their religious and political leaders – have not looked after them properly. These shepherds are now to have their flocks taken from them and, ultimately, the Lord himself will be their shepherd. This latter part was fulfilled in the person of Jesus. In the gospel parable of the generous landowner, Christ reminds us that all are equal in the sight of God whether they be rich or poor, clergy or laity, young or old. All are judged equally in his eyes. No matter our station in life we have a duty to uphold God's word and to assist in its spread.

Thursday of the Twentieth Week in Ordinary Time
Ezekiel 36:23-28; Psalm 50; Matthew 22:1-14
In our first reading today from the Prophet Ezekiel the Lord tells his people that he will lead them to their own soil and bring them home from where they have been scattered. Once home he will give them a new spirit so that they will be able to keep his laws. This reminds us of the outpouring of the Holy Spirit on Pentecost Day. The psalm could have been the people's response to this: 'A pure heart create for me, O God …' Today's gospel parable speaks of the kingdom of heaven. The message of the kingdom was first proclaimed to the Jews who rejected it and so it was proclaimed to the Gentiles and hence to all people. We are all invited to the kingdom of heaven but unless we live a life worthy of that call we will not be allowed to enter. The Holy Spirit has been given to us to show us the way but we must receive him openly and without condition.

Friday of the Twentieth Week in Ordinary Time
Ezekiel 37:1-4; Psalm 106; Matthew 22:34-40
In our reading from the book of the Prophet Ezekiel we see that God is going to raise his faithful ones from the dead and give them new life. The bones symbolise the whole house of Israel which the Lord will bring back from Babylon to their own homeland in Palestine. In our gospel, the Pharisees are testing Jesus by asking him about the commandments. His answer is a reminder for us that we must place God above all else and love him with our whole being. Not alone this, we must also love our neighbour as we love ourselves. In giving us this commandment, Jesus put together two rules from the Old Testament and gave a greater standard to strive for and by which to live.

Saturday of the Twentieth Week in Ordinary Time
Ezekiel 43:1-7; Psalm 84; Matthew 23:1-12

In our reading from the Prophet Ezekiel we read of the Lord's glory returning to the Temple now that all things have been purified. When they have returned and restored the Temple, the basis of life for the people will be the presence of God in their midst. Christ warns us in the gospel about those who preach one thing while doing something completely different. While people may pay us respect for the positions we hold we must always remember that they are not lower than us – we are all equal. We must keep in mind that nobody is above us in the eyes of God for all are equal.

Monday of the Twenty-first Week in Ordinary Time
2 Thessalonians 1:1-5; Psalm 95; Matthew 23:13-22

This week we move from the Old Testament to the New Testament and today begin reading from St Paul's second letter to the Thessalonians – a community Paul had brought the Good News to about twenty years after the Ascension, between 50 and 51AD. We read in today's text how this young community was an example to other local churches because of their zeal for God. Paul also tells them that God judges them so that they may be found worthy to live with him in the kingdom of heaven. In our gospel text for today, Christ is rebuking the scribes and Pharisees for reducing the significance of the Temple and its altars and for giving greater importance to the materials from which they are made. The place where we gather for worship and the altar on which the sacrifice is offered is far more important than their material make-up.

Tuesday of the Twenty-first Week in Ordinary Time
2 Thessalonians 2:1-3, 14-17; Psalm 95; Matthew 23:23-26

Today, St Paul exhorts his readers in Thessalonica to remain faithful to Christ's message and not allow themselves to be led astray by false prophets or by those who proclaim that 'the end is nigh.' This was in answer to the idea that the Second Coming of Christ was about to happen very soon but Paul warns the people not to be deceived by false prophecies about this event but to remain faithful to the faith which he gave them. In our gospel, Jesus continues to rebuke the scribes and Pharisees. He tells them that they have been more concerned with the measure of things than with justice, mercy and good faith. He also tells them that what is in their hearts is of far more importance than their outward appearances. We too should be more concerned with our inner disposition than with how we dress and appear to others and we must make justice and mercy priorities in our whole life while building up our faith.

Wednesday of the Twenty-first Week in Ordinary Time
2 Thessalonians 3:6-10, 16-18; Psalm 127; Matthew 23:27-32
St Paul tells us in the first reading from his second letter to the Thessalonians that we must earn the bread we eat. This was because some in the community had believed that the Second Coming of Christ was imminent and had stopped working and begun to sponge off others. None of us should take advantage of the generosity of others but should earn what we get. Likewise, we should not presume that we will automatically get into heaven but should earn our place in the kingdom. Again today the scribes and Pharisees are admonished by Christ in the gospel for their hypocrisy. They give the outward appearance of holy men but inside are more interested in themselves than in the kingdom. There is no point in any of us giving an outward show of piety when we are dark and poisoned on the inside with self-conceit and pride.

Thursday of the Twenty-first Week in Ordinary Time
1 Corinthians 1:1-9; Psalm 144; Matthew 24:42-51
Today we turn to St Paul's first letter to the Corinthians which was written by Paul between 55 and 57AD, about five years after he had left the port town in southern Greece. In today's passage Paul tells us that we have been enriched with so many graces by God. If we put our faith and trust in Christ then he will keep us on the right path towards heaven. In the gospel, Jesus reminds us that we do not know the day or the hour when he will return, or indeed when we will be called to give an account of our life. Therefore, we must always be ready and must be living a Christian life at every moment by being faithful to Christ and to his gospel.

Friday of the Twenty-first Week in Ordinary Time
1 Corinthians 1:17-25; Psalm 32; Matthew 25:1-13
We are reminded by St Paul in his letter to the Christians in Corinth that for many people preaching about a crucified saviour is nonsense – the Jews could never accept a Messiah who suffers and the Greeks could never understand a God who dies. But for those of us who believe in the wisdom of God it is our salvation and our hope. We are reminded again in our gospel reading to be always ready for we do not know when the Lord will return or when he will call us to himself. Those who are ready and have lived a Christian life will enter the kingdom but those who have not been faithful will find themselves outside in the cold.

Saturday of the Twenty-first Week in Ordinary Time
1 Corinthians 1:26-31; Psalm 32; Matthew 25:14-30
There are those who consider Christians to be foolish because they believe in someone who was so weak that he was executed in a most demeaning way. But St Paul tells us in the first reading that God uses what appears to be weak to confound the mighty and to show his great power. It is only by placing our trust in the Wisdom of God that we will understand what it is the Lord wants of us and so enter heaven. In our gospel text we have the parable of the talents. We have all been given gifts and talents which we must use for the sake of the kingdom and the good of others. One such talent is our faith which was given to us at baptism. It is not simply enough to say that we believe in God but we must actively strengthen our faith and put it into practice in our daily lives through prayer and good works.

Monday of the Twenty-second Week in Ordinary Time
1 Corinthians 2:1-5; Psalm 118; Luke 4:16-30
St Paul tells the Christians at Corinth today that he did not use big arguments and philosophy to prove that God exists. Instead he preached a crucified saviour and allowed the Holy Spirit to work in him. For the remainder of this liturgical year we read from St Luke's gospel and today we see Jesus preaching in his home synagogue in Nazareth (Nazara). Here he is rejected by the people because they think they know who he is and because they do not like his message. No matter who preaches or how

they preach, the message of God is true and unchanging, but only with faith can the message have any impact in our lives.

Tuesday of the Twenty-second Week in Ordinary Time
1 Corinthians 2:10-16; Psalm 144; Luke 4:31-37
St Paul tells us that the message of Christ is for all people but unless we have faith and are disposed towards the Holy Spirit then the message will have no impact on us. The Holy Spirit will work in the Christian to reveal the mysteries of God and to bring understanding and acceptance of the message of the Good News. An important point in today's gospel passage concerns the authority of Christ. He has authority over all things including unclean spirits and the servants of Satan. Unlike many of those around him, the unclean spirits recognise his power and authority as the Son of God and so obey him. We too will be subject to his judgement on the last day and so we must make every effort to be found worthy through faith and right living.

Wednesday of the Twenty-second Week in Ordinary Time
1 Corinthians 3:1-9; Psalm 32; Luke 4:38-44
We read in the first reading from St Paul's first letter to the Corinthians that no matter who first brings the faith to us or who later nourishes that faith within us, that it is God who does the work. Those who bring the word to others and help them in their faith are fellow workers with God and we are all called to do this work. So there should be no factions aligning themselves with different preachers. In the gospel text, Jesus cures many people before going on to other towns which displeases the people for they wanted to keep him for themselves. However he tells them that his message is for all people. As Christians we have a duty to spread Christ's message to those whom we meet by what we do and say and not simply keep it to ourselves – this is one precious treasure which only grows through sharing.

Thursday of the Twenty-second Week in Ordinary Time
1 Corinthians 3:18-23; Psalm 23; Luke 5:1-11
St Paul tells us today that when it comes to Christ's message it is foolish to pretend to be wise or to understand it all. If we apply too much learning to the message, or if we scrutinise it too much,

we will miss the message completely. We need to approach it with an open mind and complete trust and confidence in God. In our gospel we read of the call of Simon Peter along with James and John. Simon, because he acknowledged himself to be a sinner, did not want the Lord with him. But Christ still called him because he knew Simon's potential just as he knows the potential of each one of us. Only when we truly acknowledge our weaknesses can we be true disciples for Christ.

Friday of the Twenty-second Week in Ordinary Time
1 Corinthians 4:1-5; Psalm 36; Luke 5:33-39
In today's first reading St Paul is addressing a group in Corinth who had been judging his work of spreading the Good News. Paul tells them that it is not for them to be his judge – that is God's role alone. He is happy that he has been God's faithful servant and is happy to be judged by God. In the gospel, the scribes and Pharisees rebuke Christ because his disciples did not fast. We fast in order to purify ourselves and bring ourselves closer to God. The disciples did not fast because they were in the presence of God.

Saturday of the Twenty-second Week in Ordinary Time
1 Corinthians 4:6-15; Psalm 144; Luke 6:1-5
St Paul tells the community in Corinth in the first reading that status in life and material possessions are of no importance when compared with Christ's message. He contrasts the selfish lives of some Christians in Corinth with the humiliating treatment of other Christians in Rome because of their belief in Christ. Paul's treatment as 'the scum of the earth' is something of joy for him because it comes from his steadfast faith in Christ. In the gospel, the scribes and Pharisees are again questioning Jesus because his followers do not strictly observe the Sabbath and so he tells them that he is Master of the Sabbath. He is reminding us not to be so caught up with the minute details of the Law that we miss the true reason for the Sabbath and so miss out on a lasting relationship with the Lord.

Monday of the Twenty-third Week in Ordinary Time
1 Corinthians 5:1-8; Psalm 5; Luke 6:6-11

In the first reading today St Paul sternly rebukes the Corinthians for allowing sexual impropriety into their midst and for allowing pride to spoil them. There is a reminder in this that sin is not just a private thing but has a social dimension – what we do has an affect on the lives of others. Paul sternly calls the Corinthians to conversion, to return to the right path. Again in our gospel today, we see the scribes and Pharisees trying to catch Jesus out on the Sabbath. However, he knows their thoughts and tells them that it is okay to do a good deed on the Sabbath. He then openly cures a man with a withered hand. We must keep all the commandments of God and not just our own interpretation of them. We should also never boast about being Christians but should boast about and proclaim the saving power of Christ.

Tuesday of the Twenty-third Week in Ordinary Time
1 Corinthians 6:1-11; Psalm 149; Luke 6:12-19

In calling the faithful to conversion today, St Paul tells the Corinthians that they should always show a unified front to non-believers. There is nothing more divisive and off-putting than public in-house fighting. Better still, the roots of division should be dealt with swiftly and public fighting avoided. Their baptism means that they must act in a different way to others – a way which will spread the gospel at every moment. In the gospel, Jesus appoints his twelve most senior followers. It is worth noting that among those was Judas – whom the Lord trusted as he did the others – even though Judas was to betray him. What is important for us is that before he made this important decision, Jesus spent the night in prayer. We too should pray for strength and guidance before making our own decisions, be they of great importance or everyday happenings.

Wednesday of the Twenty-third Week in Ordinary Time
1 Corinthians 7:25-31, Psalm 44; Luke 6:20-26

Today's reading from St Paul to the Corinthians is a little unusual but he was writing to a group beset with scandals at a time when it was thought that the return of Christ was imminent. In any case the important message for us today is one of chaste living. Whether we be married or celibate – we must be faithful to our status in life. Paul was writing at a time which saw many heresies being preached and the one he is referring to today is that marriage was a sin. Today we read St Luke's version of the Beatitudes, that radical blueprint for living which Christ taught his followers. To be true disciples we must strip away everything earthly from our lives and hunger for nothing but the word of God and the kingdom.

Thursday of the Twenty-third Week in Ordinary Time
1 Corinthians 8:1-7, 11-13; Psalm 138; Luke 6:27-38
At the time that St Paul was writing his letters to the various Christian communities he had established, there was the common practice of offering meat and other sacrifices to gods and idols. This meat was often sold in the market afterwards and some of the early Christians believed that in eating this meat they were as good as taking part in the sacrifice themselves. Paul reminds the Corinthians that there are no gods and idols – only the one true God – and so these sacrifices and scruples are meaningless. But he warns the people about taking advantage of those who are not as wise as they are in such matters because in doing so they are injuring the Body of Christ and so weaken rather than strengthen it. Our gospel is a continuation of the account of the Beatitudes in which Christ gives us some practical tips on how to live life properly as his followers. Above all he reminds us to be compassionate just as the Father is compassionate.

Friday of the Twenty-third Week in Ordinary Time
1 Corinthians 9:16-19, 22-27; Psalm 83; Luke 6:39-42
St Paul in our first reading talks of contestants in a competition who train for their event just so they can win a laurel wreath which withers. The wreath we are after is infinitely more valuable as it is the kingdom of heaven and so we must never become complacent but must always strive to attain that goal. In the gospel, Christ tells us that before we help others we must first take care of ourselves. We are called to spread the gospel but before we can do that we must acquaint ourselves with and believe in that gospel.

Saturday of the Twenty-third Week in Ordinary Time
1 Corinthians 10:14-22; Psalm 115; Luke 6:43-49

St Paul tells us today that because we share in the one body and blood of Christ we all form one body no matter how many of us there are. He also tells us that we either belong totally to Christ or to other idols – which today could be power, money, TV, etc – but we cannot belong to both and so must decide between the two. If we opt for Christ then the Eucharist will be the sacrificial meal which strengthens our bond with Christ and with one another. In the gospel, Jesus says something similar in that we cannot profess to be his followers and fail to fulfil his instructions. If we truly believe then we will act according to his will which is found in the gospels.

Monday of the Twenty-fourth Week in Ordinary Time
1 Corinthians 11:17-26, 33; Psalm 39; Luke 7:1-10

In our first reading for today St Paul is admonishing the Corinthians for the manner in which they celebrate the Eucharist. They had not been doing so in a fitting manner but, as they moved from house to house, the parties had become more lavish while the Eucharist was an almost 'by the way' happening. He reminds them of the true significance of the Eucharist. This passage is also the earliest record in the New Testament of the institution of the Eucharist on Holy Thursday night. Jesus meets a centurion in our gospel today whose faith is far stronger than many of those who follow him. He does not need Jesus to come to his house for his servant to be cured but only wants Jesus to will it or say it. This is the faith which we are all called to have – complete trust and belief in the Son of God no matter what.

Tuesday of the Twenty-fourth Week in Ordinary Time
1 Corinthians 12:12-14, 27-31; Psalm 99; Luke 7:11-17

In our first reading today St Paul uses the analogy of the body to speak about the Church. The body is made up of many diverse parts and yet they all work together to form a seamless and organic unit. So too with the Church – we all make up the Church which is the Body of Christ and of which Christ is the head. Though we are many people we still make up the one Body of

Christ, each with his or her own part to play. In our gospel we read of Jesus restoring a young man to life in the town of Nain for he had pity on the man's mother who was a widow. It also demonstrates Christ's power over death ahead of his own resurrection.

Wednesday of the Twenty-fourth Week in Ordinary Time
1 Corinthians 12:31-13:13; Psalm 32; Luke 7:31-35

Today's first reading is St Paul's beautiful passage on love from his first letter to the Corinthians. The greatest force we have is love and if we act and do everything from the principle of love then the kingdom of God will be ours. If we fail to act with love then nothing we do will matter at all. Paul writes about what love is not and then tells us what love is. In the gospel, Christ is rebuking the people because they do not listen to him because he does not act as they would have the Messiah act. John the Baptist did and they did not listen to him either. Christ has taught us to love one another following his example and that is the challenge for us today.

Thursday of the Twenty-fourth Week in Ordinary Time
1 Corinthians 15:1-11; Psalm 117; Luke 7:36-50

The message that St Paul preaches is the true message of Christ and he reminds the Corinthians of what it is he is preaching. He preaches about Christ crucified but also Christ risen from the dead. This latter part he backs up by talking about Christ appearing to himself but also to others following the resurrection – in some cases these accounts are found no where else in the Bible. In the gospel we read of Jesus forgiving a woman her many sins because of the way she treated him. The woman acknowledged her sins and bowed before Christ while the host who was giving the dinner failed to treat Jesus with such respect and reverence but continued to judge others according to his own standards and, in so doing, ignored his own sinful ways and his own need for conversion. We are called to repent of our sins, to forgive others and to love much.

Friday of the Twenty-fourth Week in Ordinary Time
1 Corinthians 15:12-20; Psalm 16; Luke 8:1-3

Today, St Paul reminds the Corinthians that Christ has in fact risen from the dead and that this is a pillar of the faith. It is also our salvation for if it did not take place then our faith would be in vain for there would be no hope and no salvation. In our gospel, Luke speaks of some of the women who followed Jesus on his travels and who had been cured by him. These women also witnessed to the events on Calvary, were present at his burial and saw the Risen Lord.

Saturday of the Twenty-fourth Week in Ordinary Time
1 Corinthians 15:35-37, 42-49; Psalm 55; Luke 8:4-15

We are reminded by St Paul in the first reading today that in order for us to rise with Christ we must first die to ourselves. In other words, those things which hold us to the ways of this world must die and we must be reborn as true Christians. Then we will rise with Christ and share his glory. Paul tells the Corinthians that just as a seed remains in the ground when the plant grows, so too our heavenly bodies will be unlike our earthly bodies which will remain here when we enter heaven. In our gospel we read the parable of the Sower, the Sower being Christ himself. We are challenged today to look honestly at ourselves and see which type of soil we are according to the parable. The challenge is for us to make ourselves the rich soil which will yield a rich harvest of faith and help others to reach the kingdom.

Monday of the Twenty-fifth Week in Ordinary Time
Proverbs 3:27-34; Psalm 14; Luke 8:16-18

Today we return to the Old Testament and to the Book of Proverbs in the section known as Wisdom Literature. The book is attributed to the wisdom of King Solomon and is aimed at the young and immature. We are warned in our passage for today that those who wilfully do what is wrong and who do not show kindness have no place with God. The psalm speaks of the sort of person who is pleasing to the Lord. In the gospel, Jesus tells us in the parable of the lamp that nothing is hidden from God – everything is seen by him. Therefore we must be careful to always act justly and righteously in all things.

Tuesday of the Twenty-fifth Week in Ordinary Time
Proverbs 21:1-6, 10-13; Psalm 118; Luke 8:19-21

We have a number of little proverbs in today's first reading from the Book of Proverbs which give pointers to the way we should think and act. The general theme is about the ways of evil men in comparison to those who are good-living. In the gospel we see Jesus being looked for by his family. He tells us that those who do his will are members of his family. If we are Christians then we should take every care not to let our family down, and in particular our brother, Christ, by doing or saying anything that is against his will.

Wednesday of the Twenty-fifth Week in Ordinary Time
Proverbs 30:5-9; Psalm 118; Luke 9:1-6

In the first reading from the Book of Proverbs we see the author remind us about the trustworthiness of God's promises. He then goes on to pray for sincerity and finally he asks to be protected against poverty but also against excessive wealth, for wealth can put a barrier between us and God. The psalm is a prayer to God to be guarded from evil ways. In the gospel we see Jesus sending out his Twelve Apostles to preach and to cure in his name. As Christians we too have an obligation to spread the Good News of the kingdom.

Thursday of the Twenty-fifth Week in Ordinary Time
Ecclesiastes 1:2-11; Psalm 89; Luke 9:7-9

Today we begin reading from the Book of Ecclesiastes written by an author named Qoheleth about the third century before Christ. He tells us that there is nothing new to be found in the world - everything there is has already existed but we do not have any memory of them. It is in the mind of God the Creator and the works of man are but mere vanity. In our gospel text, the works and teachings of Christ have come to the attention of Herod. He is unsettled because some people thought that Jesus was the Baptist – whom Herod had beheaded – come back to life. Herod had listened to John with curiosity but had not done as John had instructed. Now he is getting a second chance to do the right thing. We too get second chances though we do not always acknowledge or grasp them. However, we do not know when our time on this earth will end and so we need to listen to the word of God today and act upon it.

Friday of the Twenty-fifth Week in Ordinary Time
Ecclesiastes 3:1-11; Psalm 143; Luke 9:18-22
In our first reading today from the Book of Ecclesiastes, Qoheleth tells us that there is a time for everything. The reading reminds us that there is a rhythm in life and a cycle of change to all things. In our gospel, St Peter makes his great profession of faith when Christ asks his followers who they think he is. He also tells them that he is to suffer and to die. Today we are asked to look into our hearts and, for ourselves, answer the question, 'Who do you say I am?' We are also told that this event took place while Jesus and the Apostles were at prayer, again showing us how central prayer was in the life of Christ.

Saturday of the Twenty-fifth Week in Ordinary Time
Ecclesiastes 11:9-12, 8; Psalm 89; Luke 9:43-45
Today, Qoheleth – the author of the first reading – is reminding us of how foolish we can be, especially in our youth. It is in our young days that we should acknowledge the power of God and begin building up our faith so as to be able to bear the trials of the 'evil days' which come later in life. In our gospel text, Jesus again tells his disciples that he will be handed over to the power of men, though they do not understand what he is saying and are too afraid to ask. Yet he tells them to keep this always in mind and we are told elsewhere in the gospels that all these things fell into place for them following the resurrection.

Monday of the Twenty-sixth Week in Ordinary Time
Job 1:6-22; Psalm 16; Luke 9:46-50
This week we turn to the Book of Job which dates to about the beginning of the fifth century before Christ. In its opening section we see how Job was afflicted by Satan who wanted to prove a point to God. Job represents all those who serve the Lord faithfully and yet endure suffering in their lives. Despite his great misfortunes, Job still praises God and refuses to do or say anything wrong. In the gospel, the disciples have been arguing about who is the greatest but Christ tells them that the greatest

is actually the least. We are challenged today to be a humble people and to accept everything that comes our way – whether we see it as good or bad – with dignity and with praise for God.

Tuesday of the Twenty-sixth Week in Ordinary Time
Job 3:1-3, 11-17, 20-23; Psalm 87; Luke 9:51-56
In our first reading from the Old Testament Book of Job, we see Job cursing the day of his birth because of the misfortunes that have befallen him. However, he does not curse the Lord or sin because he believes that God does not punish without just cause and so would say nothing negative against God. In the gospel we read that Jesus resolutely headed for Jerusalem to suffer and to die for us. We are challenged to be Job-like and not to 'give out' to God when evil afflicts us but to see in it a way to show our love and trust for God and so be more worthy of the great sacrifice which Christ made for us.

Wednesday of the Twenty-sixth Week in Ordinary Time
Job 9:1-16; Psalm 87; Luke 9:57-62
In our first reading today Job tells his friends that God is always right for we do not know his mind. Therefore how can we be right and God be wrong? In his speech he outlines the greatness and the glory of the Lord. In the gospel we see a number of men coming to Jesus to follow him but each has a condition to be filled before they will set out with him. Our following of Christ must be unconditional if we are to be true disciples and so enter the kingdom of heaven.

Thursday of the Twenty-sixth Week in Ordinary Time
Job 19:21-27; Psalm 26; Luke 10:1-12
In our first reading Job is talking to his friends and still he does not condemn God for what has happened to him. Instead he knows that he will look on God. The psalm could easily be words spoken by Job – 'I am sure I shall see the Lord's good-ness.' In our gospel Jesus sends out seventy-two of his disciples to preach in his name and to heal the sick. We are again reminded that we are heralds of the gospel, each in his or her own way, and that we too must bring the healing presence of Christ to all whom we meet.

Friday of the Twenty-sixth Week in Ordinary Time
Job 38:1, 12-21, 40:3-5; Psalm 138; Luke 10:13-16

In our first reading for today, we come to the high point in the Book of Job. The Lord himself speaks with Job and questions Job about the world of nature because Job has told his friends that what has happened to him has its source in God and not in nature. At the end of the conversation Job declares that he has been frivolous and will not speak of this again. In the gospel, Christ tells his followers that those who reject their teaching of the good news reject not just those who proclaim it but also Christ and the Father. We know that those who reject the good news will not be allowed to enter the kingdom.

Saturday of the Twenty-sixth Week in Ordinary Time
Job 42:1-3, 5-6, 12-17; Psalm 118; Luke 10:17-24

In the first reading we see Job repenting for having questioned God's reasons for acting and for his own pride. Because he has been faithful, God rewards Job beyond his earlier fortunes. In the gospel, Christ's disciples come back rejoicing for they have had authority over the devil. They have been given power by Christ for the spreading of the kingdom. We too have a duty and a responsibility to pass on the message of the kingdom to those whom we meet by word and deed. Like Job, we will receive a great reward if we have been faithful to the gospel.

Monday of the Twenty-seventh Week in Ordinary Time
Galatians 1:6-12; Psalm 110; Luke 10:25-37

This week our first reading comes from the New Testament and today's passage comes from St Paul's letter to the Galatians written about 57-58AD. This was a predominantly Gentile Christian community in Northern Galatia in what is present-day Turkey. In today's passage Paul reminds us that there are those who preach different things and call it 'the good news'. We must be on our guard against them for there is only one gospel and we must accept it in its entirety. Believing in anything else can lead us from the truth and the love of God. In our gospel we have the story of the Good Samaritan which illustrates for us that everyone – including our enemies – is our neighbour and so we should reach out to them in their need no matter how inconvenient that might be. We have the example of Christ who cured people so long as they had faith in him.

Tuesday of the Twenty-seventh Week in Ordinary Time
Galatians 1:13-24; Psalm 138; Luke 10:38-42
In our reading from the letter to the Christian community in Galatia we are told how St Paul used to persecute the early Church. This all ended, however, when he answered the call of God to serve the gospel. Paul had been forced to defend himself because of Jewish teachers who had visited the area and told the people that Paul had no authority to teach. In the gospel, we see Jesus visit the home of his friends Martha, Mary and Lazarus. He is welcomed and Martha plays the host and fusses over food and other niceties while Mary sits at his feet. When Martha complains that Mary is doing nothing, the Lord tells her to relax and to take a leaf out of Mary's book because Mary is spending time with her Lord and listening to what he is saying. It is very easy for us to neglect quality time with the Lord in prayer and the reading of scripture but these are the things which make our relationship with him stronger.

Wednesday of the Twenty-seventh Week in Ordinary Time
Galatians 2:1-2, 7-14; Psalm 116; Luke 11:1-14
In our first reading St Paul continues to tell the Galatians of the work he has done in the name of the gospel, even to the point of disputing with St Peter – an acknowledgement of the foremost position of Peter among the Apostles. All this is to show them that he is trustworthy and that his message is the truth. In the gospel from St Luke, the disciples ask Jesus how they should pray and he teaches them the 'Our Father.' This one prayer covers every aspect of life and is a prayer we should use every day with sincerity and understanding.

Thursday of the Twenty-seventh Week in Ordinary Time
Galatians 3:1-5; Psalm: see Luke 1; Luke 11:5-13
St Paul is admonishing the Galatians in the first reading for they believe that they have received the Holy Spirit because they have kept the Law. Paul tells them that it has nothing to do with the Law but with their faith. In the gospel, Christ teaches us to

ask the Father for whatever we need. All our prayers are answered by God if only we would ask, though we might not always like the answer we receive. We are called on today to believe in God and to trust in him for if we simply keep the commandments but do not believe, it will count for very little.

Friday of the Twenty-seventh Week in Ordinary Time
Galatians 3:7-14; Psalm 110; Luke 11:15-26
In the first reading, St Paul tells the Christian community of Galatia that those who do have faith receive the same blessing as Abraham – 'our father in faith' – whether they be Jew, Gentile or pagan. Paul says that Christ came to free people from the Jewish Law and to give us the path of faith instead. Faith is what is important and it is a gift of God made available to all people. In our gospel, Jesus tells the people that he is not Beelzebul, the prince of devils. His power and authority over unclean spirits comes from God and not from the devil. In this way his kingdom is greater than that of his foes.

Saturday of the Twenty-seventh Week in Ordinary Time
Galatians 3:22-29; Psalm 104; Luke 11:27-28
St Paul tells us in the first reading that because of our faith in Christ we are all sons and daughters of God. In fact we are all either son or daughter because such distinctions do not exist in the sight of God. To Paul, the Law of Moses was no more than a 'guide' until such time as the people were mature enough to accept the path of faith. For Paul, that time has now arrived and the path has been given to the world through Jesus Christ. In the gospel we are told that those who are happiest are those who hear the word of God and keep it and live by it. We are challenged to hear the message of Christ in the scriptures and to live by that message every day of our lives and to participate in the spread of that message.

Monday of the Twenty-eighth Week in Ordinary Time
Galatians 4:22-24, 26-27, 31-5:1; Psalm 112; Luke 11:29-32
In our first reading from the letter to the Galatians we continue St Paul's explanation of how we have been freed from the Jewish Laws and given the path of faith by Christ. Paul talks

about Abraham's slave wife, Hagar and her child, Ishmael, who – for Paul's purposes – represent the Jewish people, and Abraham's free wife, Sarah and her child, Isaac, who represent Christians. Paul says that we have been born free in the waters of baptism because our slavery to sin has been broken by Christ. In the gospel the people are asking Jesus for a sign to prove that he is the Messiah. He doesn't give them a sign but reminds them of Jonah, telling them that they have something greater than Jonah in their midst.

Tuesday of the Twenty-eighth Week in Ordinary Time
Galatians 5:1-6; Psalm 118; Luke 11:37-41
Some of the Galatians believed they had to be circumcised and live under the Law in order to be saved. But St Paul tells them in the first reading that the Law cannot save them – faith is what they need in order to be saved and they should not worry about signs such as circumcision. Paul reminds them that true faith proves itself through charitable works and not through external signs on the body. In the gospel, Jesus admonishes a Pharisee for wanting to wash before meals when on the inside he was un-clean. The heart is what God looks at – not the outside. We too are called by both readings to look into ourselves and to make ourselves inwardly pure. One way of doing this is by giving alms to the poor.

Wednesday of the Twenty-eighth Week in Ordinary Time
Galatians 5:18-25; Psalm 1; Luke 11:42-46
In our last section from his letter to the Gentile Christians in Galatia, St Paul tells us that we should always live with the Holy Spirit guiding our lives. If we live by our own will then we only fall into sin. Paul tells us of the vices found in living by the flesh and the contrasting virtues found in living a life in the Spirit. Jesus, in the gospel, admonishes Pharisees and lawyers for putting obstacles before the people so that they cannot truly worship the Lord, especially when those things place the Pharisees themselves in elevated positions before the people.

Thursday of the Twenty-eighth Week in Ordinary Time
Ephesians 1:1-10; Psalm 97; Luke 11:47-54

We begin reading from St Paul's letter to the Christian community at the large seaport of Ephesus which he wrote while in
prison in Rome between 61 and 63AD. In today's passage Paul
tells us that God had a secret plan from the beginning of
Creation and that that plan has now been revealed. It is a plan
for all things to be united under Christ who shed his blood that
we might be saved. Again in the gospel from St Luke, Jesus is rebuking the officials for their hypocrisy because it prevents the
people from reaching closer union with God. That union was
destined from Creation and set in place by Christ.

Friday of the Twenty-eighth Week in Ordinary Time
Ephesians 1:11-14; Psalm 32; Luke 12:1-7

St Paul tells his readers in the letter to the Ephesians that they
have already been stamped with the seal of the Holy Spirit.
Therefore, the Holy Spirit is at work in them and brings them
freedom as sons and daughters of God. Paul reminds them that
the message was first preached to the Jewish people as the
'Chosen People' and then to all peoples and so they too have a
right to share in the salvation promised through Christ. Jesus
tells us in the gospel that what we do is known to God who
knows us intimately and cares for every fibre of our being.
Knowing this, and with the Holy Spirit working in us, we should
do everything to ensure that we live as God wants us to live.

Saturday of the Twenty-eighth Week in Ordinary Time
Ephesians 1:15-23; Psalm 8; Luke 12:8-12

In our first reading St Paul speaks to us today of the glories
which lie in wait for the faithful. All of this is in Christ who has
been made head of the Church, which is the Mystical Body of
Christ. In the gospel, Jesus tells us that if we reject him in the
presence of others then he will reject us in the presence of the
Father. To help us to stand faithful he has given us the Holy
Spirit to be our strength and protection. To deny Jesus is not
simply done in word but also by failing to act as Christians in
the sight of others. The rejection of Christ is also the rejection of
our hope.

Monday of the Twenty-ninth Week in Ordinary Time
Ephesians 2:1-10; Psalm 99; Luke 12:13-21

In the letter to the Christian community at Ephesus on the western shore of modern-day Turkey, St Paul reminds his readers that humans were sinners who were ruled by their physical desires. Despite still being sinners, God loved them greatly and sent his own Son to restore them to life. In the gospel, Christ reminds us of the folly of storing up material goods here on earth. They only serve to distract us from the true treasure which we should be seeking – that is a place in the kingdom. Considering the great love of God and the sacrifice he made for us we should always keep the kingdom as the sole goal of our lives.

Tuesday of the Twenty-ninth Week in Ordinary Time
Ephesians 2:12-22; Psalm 84; Luke 12:35-38

St Paul tells us in the first reading that before Christ there was only the Law and only Jews could worship God. Through Christ we all now have the means to salvation because we can all become Christians regardless of our birth. He goes on to speak about a household and how we are now all part of that household through the saving power of Christ. In the gospel we are told to be always ready because we do not know when the master will return to visit us. If we are living good Christian lives then we will be always ready and will not have to worry at the Lord's return or our call to heaven.

Wednesday of the Twenty-ninth Week in Ordinary Time
Ephesians 3:2-12; Psalm: Isaiah 12; Luke 12:39-48

We read in our first reading from the letter to the Ephesians how the grace of God is meant for all peoples – be they Jew, Gentile or pagan. With this grace we can confidently draw closer to God. We are reminded again in today's gospel that we do not know the hour when we will be called to give an account of our stewardship and of our lives. When the Lord does return he will want to know if we have done all that he has told us to do which includes being full participants in the spread of the Good News.

Thursday of the Twenty-ninth Week in Ordinary Time
Ephesians 3:14-21; Psalm 32; Luke 12:49-53

Today's first reading contains the prayer which St Paul prayed for the Ephesians – that their faith would grow strong through the power of the Holy Spirit. In the gospel we read an unusual passage in which Christ says that he came to bring division rather than peace. However, when we consider that he was talking about believer and unbeliever we can understand what he is saying. We are challenged to look into our hearts to see which category we fall into, knowing that faith calls for action in our lives rather than simply reciting words.

Friday of the Twenty-ninth Week in Ordinary Time
Ephesians 4:1-6; Psalm 23; Luke 12:54-59

St Paul reminds us in the letter to the Ephesians that we all form part of the Body of Christ and that we should do all we can to build up the unity of that body. He also tells us how that should be done – through charity, selflessness, gentleness and patience and by believing in God as the head of all. Jesus admonishes the people in the gospel for being able to read the weather but not being able to read the signs of the times and realise that he is the Messiah. We are challenged in our own day to read the signs of the times and to realise that we need Christ now more than ever before.

Saturday of the Twenty-ninth Week in Ordinary Time
Ephesians 4:7-16; Psalm 121; Luke 13:1-9

In our first reading for today, St Paul again uses the analogy of the body to say that we each have our own role to play in the Body of Christ. Each person's role is different but ultimately each is for the spreading of the gospel and the building up of the kingdom and we must do all we can to fulfil that role. In the gospel passage from St Luke, Jesus calls us to repentance in order to be saved. We should not put off our repentance until tomorrow but we should begin today for we do not know if we shall live to see tomorrow.

Monday of the Thirtieth Week in Ordinary Time
Ephesians 4:32-5:8; Psalm 1; Luke 13:10-17

Our first reading this week is again taken from St Paul's letter to the Christian community at Ephesus and in today's passage Paul encourages us to love others in imitation of the Father and the Son who both love much. Only in this way can we build up the kingdom of God and live righteously. The psalm speaks of how a good person lives. In the gospel, Christ heals a woman on the Sabbath which infuriates a synagogue official who tells the people to come to be healed on any day of the week except the Sabbath. The Lord answers and says that none of those present would hesitate to untie his donkey on the Sabbath in order to water the beast and therefore it is right to untie a fellow human from their bonds on the Sabbath. His words leave the officials confused while the people are happy to hear him.

Tuesday of the Thirtieth Week in Ordinary Time
Ephesians 5:21-33; Psalm 127; Luke 13:18-21

Our first reading from the letter to the Ephesians today does not appear to be very politically correct these days but St Paul's underlying message of respect is all the more important in today's overwhelming climate of individualism and self-centredness. Paul speaks of married life and says that a husband and wife should have the same relationship with each other as Christ has with his Church. Today's gospel sees Christ using two brief parables to show how the kingdom flourishes and grows. It can only grow if we allow it to do so and if we each help in its spread.

Wednesday of the Thirtieth Week in Ordinary Time
Ephesians 6:1-9; Psalm 144; Luke 13:22-30

Today's first reading is a continuation of yesterday's text from St Paul's letter to the Ephesians and sees great emphasis being placed on respect for one another. Today he speaks about the relationship between children and their parents and between slaves and their masters. Paul lived at a time when slavery was a way of life and his underlying principle is that all men and women should live in respect and love following the example of Christ. Jesus tells his listeners in today's gospel that everyone is invited to the kingdom where many will enter but not those who fail to do the will of God. Saying we believe in God is not enough unless we put that faith into practice.

Thursday of the Thirtieth Week in Ordinary Time
Ephesians 6:10-20; Psalm 143; Luke 13:31-35
St Paul tells us in our final section from his letter to the Christian community in the port city of Ephesus that it is the devil we must fear and not our fellow men and women. To combat the devil we must allow God to clothe us in spiritual armour and to pray constantly while spreading the gospel. In the gospel text some Pharisees come to warn Jesus to leave Jerusalem or he will die at the hands of Herod. However, he tells them that it is his destiny as a prophet to die in Jerusalem. He then weeps at the fact that Jerusalem has rejected both him and his message.

Friday of the Thirtieth Week in Ordinary Time
Philippians 1:1-11; Psalm 110; Luke 14:1-6
Today we begin reading from St Paul's letter to the Christians in the northern Greek town of Philippi. This was the first Christian community Paul had founded in Europe about the year 50AD, this letter being written about six years later when Paul was in prison. In our opening section, Paul tells the people that the work they have begun – that is, the spread of the gospel – will be completed by Christ when they are called home to heaven. Paul writes in glowing terms about the people and prays that their virtues may increase and that they may be blessed by the Lord. In the gospel, Jesus is again under scrutiny on the Sabbath as he goes to a meal in the home of a leading Pharisee. Before acting he asks if healing on the Sabbath is really against the Law given that those listening would unhesitatingly pull their ox from a well on the Sabbath if it fell in. His argument goes unanswered by those present.

Saturday of the Thirtieth Week in Ordinary Time
Philippians 1:18-26; Psalm 41; Luke 14:1, 7-11
In our first reading from his letter to the Philippians, St Paul says that he wants to die for the simple reason that he wants to go to heaven. However, he realises that he has an important mission to take care of before he dies and that is the spread of

the gospel. Paul also says that both life and death come under the influence of Christ and therefore he is happy to live but does not fear death. This mission is also our mission. Christ warns us in the gospel, in the story of the wedding feast, about being a humble people and about not seeking the highest honours. Humility will serve the kingdom, and ourselves, far better than pride and honours.

Monday of the Thirty-first Week in Ordinary Time
Philippians 2:1-4; Psalm 130; Luke 14:12-14
St Paul asks us in the first reading from his letter to the Philippians in northern Greece, to be a humble people and to always regard others as being better than we are. He also says that we should be of one mind thereby avoiding factions and divisions. In the Gospel, Jesus tells us that we should not do something for the sake of a reward or a returned favour in this life but that we should be charitable to those who cannot give anything back. Therefore our reward will be all the greater for it will be given in the next life.

Tuesday of the Thirty-first Week in Ordinary Time
Philippians 2:5-11; Psalm 21; Luke 14:15-24
In our first reading from the letter to the Christians at Philippi, we have one of the most beautiful passages in sacred scripture in which St Paul speaks about how much Christ gave up in order to become one like us. Given his great sacrifice how can we fail to make sacrifices which are as nothing in comparison to his? In the gospel, we have the parable of the man who gave a great banquet but whose original guests did not show up. He then gave his invite to others and they came. The message of Christ was first given to the Jews but they did not accept it so it was preached to the Gentiles and the pagans. Therefore all peoples have an invite to the eternal banquet of heaven.

Wednesday of the Thirty-first Week in Ordinary Time
Philippians 2:12-18; Psalm 26; Luke 14:25-33
St Paul exhorts us in the first reading from the letter to the Philippians to keep the faith and to continue working for the building up of the kingdom. Paul stresses how important it is

that the pagans in the town of Philippi should see a powerful example of Christian living demonstrated by the Christian community. Paul also speaks about the possibility of his dying for the faith which he embraces with joy. In the gospel, Christ calls us to give up our possessions in order to be true followers of his. While we do need certain things to live we do not need to be so attached to them that we cannot live without them or that they block Christ from our lives. Christ must be the one and only possession in life that we long and strive for.

Thursday of the Thirty-first Week in Ordinary Time
Philippians 3:3-8; Psalm 104; Luke 15:1-10
St Paul speaks about how perfect a Jew he himself was before his conversion. However, his former standing as a Jew is often a disadvantage because people are not always ready to accept that he is now a true Christian. If we want to be accepted as true Christians then we must convert today and not continue in our sinful ways. Christ tells us in the gospel that there is more rejoicing in heaven over the conversion of a sinner than for the right living of the virtuous. The virtuous are doing no more than is expected of them while the repentant sinner has come to accept the word of God and make it the guiding light in their life.

Friday of the Thirty-first Week in Ordinary Time
Philippians 3:17-4:1; Psalm 121; Luke 16:1-8
In today's first reading from the letter to the Philippians, St Paul calls on us to remain faithful because there is a glory awaiting us which only the faithful can attain. If we are unfaithful then we will be lost forever. Paul reminds us that our true homeland is in heaven where we will share in the glorified body of Christ. In the gospel we have the story of the steward who was to be sacked for his malpractices but who made a number of deals in order to secure his future. Our future is in heaven and so we should make that future secure by faith in God and living by the gospel.

Saturday of the Thirty-first Week in Ordinary Time
Philippians 4:10-19; Psalm 111; Luke 16:9-15
In our closing section today from his letter to the Christians at

Philippi, St Paul thanks the Philippians for their generosity to him and he tells them that their account in heaven is increasing because in helping him they are also helping in the spread of the gospel. He also tells them that he can overcome anything because he has the help of God on his side. In the gospel, Christ calls us to make God and heaven the only things that matter to us in life. Like the Philippians we are to help in the spread of the gospel in any way we can and that begins with the strengthening of our own faith in Christ and the resurrection.

Monday of the Thirty-second Week in Ordinary Time
Titus 1:1-9; Psalm 23; Luke 17:1-6
We begin this week with St Paul's letter to St Titus (in 65AD), a fellow missionary who he had left behind on the island of Crete to continue organising the Christian community there. In our opening passage Paul speaks of the sort of character a person should have if he wishes to be appointed as a sacred minister by Titus. In fact, as Christians, it is a standard by which we could all try to live. In the gospel, Christ tells us that we must forgive others who come to us seeking forgiveness and if they are sorry for the wrong they committed. It is a reminder that we cannot stand before God and ask him to forgive us if we have not forgiven others for the wrongs they may have committed against us.

Tuesday of the Thirty-second Week in Ordinary Time
Titus 2:1-8, 11-14; Psalm 36; Luke 17:7-10
St Paul speaks in the first reading from his letter to St Titus about how we should behave and act as Christians. We do this because of the glory which we are awaiting and which will be given us by Christ, though we do not know when. Paul also reminds Titus that the example of his own life in Crete will be very important for the growth of the faith there. The psalm continues Paul's theme. We are reminded by Christ in the gospel that we are servants of God and that really we should not expect praise for living as Christians because, in so living, we are simply doing our duty. Yet there are those who do it simply to earn the praise of others and the Lord knows this and will not accept it.

Wednesday of the Thirty-second Week in Ordinary Time
Titus 3:1-7; Psalm 22; Luke 17:11-19
St Paul continues to offer us a blueprint for living in the first reading from his letter to St Titus – his appointed leader of the Christian community in Crete. He also tells us that it was the compassion of God which saved us and nothing we ourselves had done when he sent his Son in to the world. We have the story of the ten lepers in our gospel passage for today. Only one man returned to thank Christ for the gift of health which Christ had given him and by this act of faith he was saved. How often do we stop to thank God for all that we have received? The greatest act of thanksgiving we could make would be to live righteously in keeping with the gospel.

Thursday of the Thirty-second Week in Ordinary Time
Philemon 7-20; Psalm 145; Luke 17:20-25
Our last section from St Paul this year comes from his letter to Philemon, a young well-to-do Christian who is a close friend of Paul, about Onesimus – Philemon's slave. He is asking Philemon to receive Onesimus back – not as a slave – but as a brother. Whatever our status or our role in life we are all brothers and sisters in the gospel and equal in the eyes of the Lord. In the gospel, Jesus tells the Pharisees that the kingdom is already with them though they have failed to see or realise it. He also tells his disciples that he is to suffer and be rejected. Still today, he suffers and is rejected when people reject his gospel and his Church.

Friday of the Thirty-second Week in Ordinary Time
2 John 4-9; Psalm 118; Luke 17:26-37
Today we turn from the letters of St Paul to the second letter of St John to an unknown Christian community. In the text, John reminds us of the great commandment to love one another. We are also told to be wary of those who teach a false gospel – all we need is to be found in the gospel we have already received. We are reminded by Christ in the gospel text from St Luke, that we know not when our time will come to an end and that we, like Noah and Lot, must heed the word of God today and be converted.

Saturday of the Thirty-second Week in Ordinary Time
3 John 5-8; Psalm 1; Luke 18:1-8

St John tells us in our reading from his third letter that we should support the servants of the gospel in any way we can for in supporting them we too help in the spread of the Good News. Of importance is our support of the missionary endeavour still taking place throughout the world. We are not all able to be missionaries but our help for them is our way of spreading the gospel of Christ. Through the parable of the unscrupulous judge and the poor widow we are told by Christ in the gospel that God will hear the prayers of his faithful ones and answer them even if he appears to take a long time in doing so. Therefore we are to persevere in our prayers and not loose heart.

Monday of the Thirty-third Week in Ordinary Time
Apocalypse 1:1-4, 2:1-5; Psalm 1; Luke 18:35-43

For the final two weeks of the Church's year we turn to the last book of the Bible – the Book of Apocalypse or Revelation – attributed to St John and put together between 70 and 95AD. The book is written in a style common at the time of Christ and the author addresses it to seven churches in what is today Turkey. In today's text the church in Ephesus is told that even though it worked hard for the faith it does not love as much as it did in the past. We are reminded that we cannot slip back to our old ways but must keep striving forward towards heaven. In our gospel text Jesus gives sight to a blind man because the man had faith and asked to be cured. This is a reminder that if we have faith then we can ask anything of God and he will answer us.

Tuesday of the Thirty-third Week in Ordinary Time
Apocalypse 3:1-6, 14-22; Psalm 14; Luke 19:1-10

In our first reading from the Book of the Apocalypse we see the Lord telling the churches of Sardis and Laodicea that he knows them well. He recounts their good points but also points out their flaws – for those in Sardis it is their lack of perfection which displeases the Lord, while he accuses the Laodiceans of being lukewarm in the faith. In the gospel, Jesus tells us that he came to save those who were lost but, like Zacchaeus, they will only be saved if they wish to be saved. Were the Lord to look closely at each of us, what flaws would he point out? More importantly, we must ask ourselves if we are willing to do what we can to eradicate those flaws and so enter the kingdom of heaven.

Wednesday of the Thirty-third Week in Ordinary Time
Apocalypse 4:1-11; Psalm 150; Luke 19:11-28

In our first reading from the Book of the Apocalypse, or Revelation, the author writes of the glory of God and of the praise given him by the host of heaven. The four principle creatures have been seen as the four Evangelists and indeed, the images found here are often used in art – the lion for Mark, the ox for Luke, the man for Matthew, and the eagle for John. This text was to give hope to those Christian communities who were being persecuted because of their faith. The gospel today gives us the parable of the man who was to be made king and who gave money to three servants. The first two servants made a profit with the money entrusted to them and they were rewarded for this while the third man did nothing and was punished. The money can be seen as our faith which we have a duty to build up and to strengthen while also helping the growth of the faith in the world. Lip-service to the Lord will count for nothing.

Thursday of the Thirty-third Week in Ordinary Time
Apocalypse 5:1-10; Psalm 149; Luke 19:41-44

We read in today's passage from the Book of the Apocalypse that Christ – the Lamb who was sacrificed – has, by his blood, redeemed us from death and opened the way to salvation for us. In our gospel text we see Jesus arriving at Jerusalem and he pauses before going in to the city. He pauses to weep at the stubbornness and the blindness of the people who have heard his teachings and seen his miracles and yet fail to see that he is their Messiah. Despite their rejection of him, Jesus still loves the people as he loves each one of us, whether we wish to acknowledge that love or not.

Friday of the Thirty-third Week in Ordinary Time
Apocalypse 10:8-11; Psalm 118; Luke 19:45-48

We continue to read of St John's vision of heaven in our first reading from the Book of the Apocalypse. In eating the scroll given him by the angel, John is indicating that he has fully understood the message he has received. (Similar to the Prophet Ezekiel centuries before) The sweet taste of the scroll signifies the glory of heaven which awaits us, while the bitter taste represents the trials that we must go through before entering into the glory promised us. In the gospel, Christ drives the money changers from the Temple and cleanses it. He then teaches the people every day in the Temple which infuriates the elders who wish to get rid of him. The people on the other hand, are so captivated by Christ's preaching that the authorities are unable to act against him for the time being.

Saturday of the Thirty-third Week in Ordinary Time
Apocalypse 11:4-12; Psalm 143; Luke 20:27-40
We continue our readings from the Book of the Apocalypse in which St John speaks about two men who witness for God – one who brings famine and the other who brings plagues - which could remind us of Elijah and Moses in the Old Testament. The two men are attacked by a beast who kills them. However, they are restored to life showing that God is more powerful than the powers of evil. This was a reminder for the people that, even though they may have to suffer for the faith, the power of God is greater and the promises he made to them will be fulfilled. In the gospel, Christ tells us that God is the God of the living for after this earthly life is over our soul goes to a place of never-ending life, as we have been reading from John's vision of that life in our first reading. Perhaps we could ask ourselves today if we are worthy of that never-ending life and, if not, to resolve to make ourselves more worthy.

Monday of the Last Week in Ordinary Time
Apocalypse 14:1-5; Psalm 23; Luke 21:1-4
Our first reading this week continues to come from St John's apocryphal dream and in today's passage we are told of the Just who have been allowed entry into heaven. The image speaks of the Lamb who stands in triumph at the end of the world surrounded by those who have been faithful despite their persecutions. This would have been a support to the early Christian communities who were being persecuted by the

Romans because of the faith. We have the story of the widow's mite in the gospel passage. For us to give away what is surplus is not really a sacrifice because we will not miss it. For us to give of what we need is real charity and a true sacrifice.

Tuesday of the Last Week in Ordinary Time
Apocalypse 14:14-19; Psalm 95; Luke 21:5-11

St John's vision today tells of the harvesting of the earth which will take place at the end of time. Christ is the one who will reap the harvest of those who have been faithful to him. In the second analogy we see an angel placing the grapes of the unfaithful in to the winepress of God's anger. In the gospel, Christ foretells the destruction of the Temple in Jerusalem and also warns his followers to be on their guard against those who claim to be messiahs and who preach of impending doom. The Temple was the most important place for the Jews and any talk of its destruction was seen as heretical and, therefore, the message of Christ would have been seen in a very poor light in certain quarters.

Wednesday of the Last Week in Ordinary Time
Apocalypse 15:1-4; Psalm 97; Luke 21:12-19

As we read from St John's vision in our first reading we should be encouraged to praise God by the vision of the Christians who have led victorious lives for the faith and the gospel. At the time that the book was written the early Christians were being persecuted by the Romans and so this book would have brought great consolation and encouragement for them. In our gospel passage for today, Jesus warns his disciples that they will suffer for him and that through it all he will be with them to strengthen them and to protect them. This protection will be ours also if we are willing to stand up for and witness to the Lord.

Thursday of the Last Week in Ordinary Time
Apocalypse 18:1-2, 21-23, 19:1-3, 9; Psalm 99; Luke 21:20-28

In our first reading we read St John's vision of how Babylon – representing the city of Rome and the greatest city of evil – has been destroyed by God for its wickedness. At the end of the passage the assembly of heaven sings a hymn of praise for the punishment of the city and for the fact that God 'judges fairly, he punishes justly'. Again in our gospel from St Luke, Jesus foretells the destruction of Jerusalem and the scattering of the people for their lack of faith and perseverance. He says that there will be many signs – terrifying and frightening signs – but that will be the time to stand confidently, for liberation will be near at hand.

Friday of the Last Week in Ordinary Time
Apocalypse 20:1-4, 11-21:2; Psalm 83; Luke 21:29-33
In our first reading from Apocalypse (Revelation) we are told that the dead are judged by God according to what they did in life in terms of their faith. In order to be saved their names had to be written in the book of life. We are told about the 1,000 year reign of Christ at the end of which the dragon (Satan) would be set free for a short time. Some Christian-based groups of our own time – such as the Jehovah's Witnesses – take this passage to be literally true and see the release of the dragon to be the great battle of Armageddon when sinful and unfaithful humans will be wiped out forever and only the righteous will live. Most Christian groups see the passage as an allegory to encourage the early Christians to remain faithful and to do all they can to ensure that their names will be found in the book of life. In the Gospel, Jesus tells us that even if the earth and heaven pass away his words will remain for ever. As sure as the trees bud and flower in summer, his words will come to pass.

Saturday of the Last Week in Ordinary Time
Apocalypse 22:1-7; Psalm 94; Luke 21:34-36
We conclude our liturgical year with part of the last chapter of St John's vision in which we are told that at the end of time the saints will live in never-ending light because the Lord will be shining on them. This will take place in the new Jerusalem, the heavenly city. In our final gospel text for this year, Christ reminds us to be always ready because we do not know when he will return and ask us to make an account of our lives. As this liturgical year ends, our readings cause us to reflect on the end times and the beginnings of eternal life with God. As we prepare to begin a new liturgical year, perhaps this is a good time to reflect upon our own lives and so make preparations for our own end and entry to eternal life.

SOLEMNITIES OF THE LORD IN ORDINARY TIME

The Most Holy Trinity: Year A
Exodus 34:4-6, 8-9; Psalm Daniel 3; 2 Corinthians 13:11-13; John 3:16-18
In the first reading from the Old Testament Book of Exodus we see Moses going back to the Lord with the two tablets to receive the Law from a tender and compassionate God. The God who gives the Law to his people is one who does so out of love for his people that – through observance of the Law – they may be drawn into his love and live in happiness. The second reading is quite Trinitarian in its closing words to the people of Corinth, a closing which we use at the start of the Eucharist, and which is a common feature of St Paul's letters. The gospel tells us that God sent his Son to redeem and to save the world. We are told that God did this because he wanted all people to 'have eternal life'. All who believe in Jesus and who live out that belief, will one day be joined with the Trinity in eternal life.

The Most Holy Trinity: Year B
Deuteronomy 4:32-34, 39-40; Psalm 32; Romans 8:14-17; Matthew 28:16-20
Today we keep the solemnity of the Most Holy Trinity when we acknowledge in a very special way that, while there is only one God, there are three persons in that one God – God the Father, God the Son and God the Holy Spirit. While we do not fully understand how this can be, it is a cornerstone of our faith. Many have tried to explain it such as St Patrick with the shamrock, but understanding is not necessary for faith. The readings are also 'trinitarian' in that the first reading from Deuteronomy sees Moses speaking about God the Father, while in the second reading St Paul speaks about the Holy Spirit, and in the gospel we have Jesus instructing his disciples. In his instruction Christ commissions all of us to spread the good news and for people to be baptised in the name of the Trinity – a very clear indication that God is one but with three persons.

The Most Holy Trinity: Year C

Proverbs 8:22-31; Psalm 8; Romans 5:1-5; John 16:12-15

It is our firm belief that God is a Trinity – the Father, the Son and the Holy Spirit – and even though we may not understand how this can be, today we celebrate that fact in the Solemnity of the Most Holy Trinity. Our readings for this solemnity reflect this Trinitarian aspect of God. In the first reading from the Old Testament Book of Proverbs we see Wisdom telling us that she had existed before anything was created and she was at the Creator's side through all of creation. Today, we understand Jesus to be the personification of Wisdom and so we believe that he was at the Father's side through all of creation. In the gospel reading from St John we see Jesus telling his disciples that he has many things to say to them, though not enough time, but that the Spirit will guide them after he has returned to the Father. The word 'trinity' may not have been used by Christ but in this short passage all three persons are mentioned by him and all are clearly equal. In our second reading from St Paul to the Romans, Paul too speaks of the Trinity because he tells us that through Christ we draw close to the Father with the persever-ance and hope given us by the Spirit. The Father wants us to be with him and his Son has shown us the way while the Spirit fort-ifies us for the journey. All that remains is for us to accept that guidance and follow the path marked out by Christ.

Body and Blood of Christ (Corpus Christi): Year A

Deuteronomy 8:2-3, 14-16; Psalm 147; 1 Corinthians 10:16-17; John 6:51-58

The first reading from the Book of Deuteronomy tells us that God humbled the people in the desert to see if they would be faithful to him or not. Throughout their wanderings he kept his people alive with manna – bread from heaven. The gospel pas-sage comes from St John's Bread of Life discourse. In the section we have today, Jesus tells us that he is unlike the bread – the manna – which the Jews received from God in the wilderness. The bread in the wilderness only satisfied them for a while whereas the food which Christ gives us is his own flesh and blood – food which will bring the believer to union with Christ and eternal life with the Father. In the second reading from his first letter to the Corinthians, St Paul tells us that while there may be many of us, through receiving the body of Christ we are all made one and become a single body, which has Christ as its head. Today's feast has the Last Supper on Holy Thursday night as its backdrop and origin but we celebrate it today in thanksgiving for the great gift we receive through the body and blood of Christ given for us.

Body and Blood of Christ (Corpus Christi): Year B
Exodus 24:3-8; Psalm 115; Hebrews 9:11-15; Mark 14:12-16, 22-26
In today's solemnity we celebrate in a very special way the real presence of the body and blood of Christ under the appearance of the bread and wine and which is reserved in the tabernacles in our churches and chapels. Christ made a new and everlasting covenant with us which brings eternal life to all who believe in him and this covenant was sealed in his blood. In our first reading from the Book of Exodus we see Moses sealing the covenant between the people and God with the blood of animals but, as we know, the people did not keep this covenant. In the second reading from the letter to the Hebrews the author speaks about the blood of Christ which not only brings eternal life but also purifies us. In the gospel from St Mark we have the institution of the Eucharist in which Christ gives his body and blood to his disciples. Christ is really, truly and substantially present in the bread and wine after the consecration and these remain forever his body and blood which we receive at Mass or return to adore in the Eucharistic presence in the tabernacle. There is no greater possession in the world than the body and blood of Christ but it is worthless to us if we do not believe and live the life to which it calls us.

Body and Blood of Christ (Corpus Christi): Year C
Genesis 14:18-20; Psalm 109; 1 Corinthians 11:23-26; Luke 9:11-17
Today we celebrate the great solemnity of *Corpus Christi* – the Body and Blood of Christ. Traditionally, this day was marked by processions with the Blessed Sacrament carried through towns and villages whose streets and neighbourhoods were cleaned up and decorated for the occasion. The solemnity marks one of the great mysteries of our faith and with it one of the

great gifts which God has given to his Church. We celebrate the fact that bread and wine become the very body and blood of Christ, and strengthen us and the Church along the path to salvation. In the first reading from the Book of Genesis we see Melchizedek offering bread and wine to God in thanksgiving for the victories achieved with God's help. This bread and wine is a foreshadow of the bread and wine offered by Christ at the Passover meal. The second reading from St Paul's first letter to the Corinthians reminds us of the first Eucharist in the upper room on Holy Thursday night. In the gospel we have St Luke's account of the miracle of the loaves and fish in which Christ fed a multitude that was hungry. Christ has told us that he is the bread of life and that those who partake of his body and blood will want for nothing because his body and blood will strengthen and guide us. It may be difficult to grasp how a small wafer or a drop of wine can be so important or undergo such a change, but faith is not dependent on proof and so we keep today's solemnity, asking the Lord to lead us toward our true homeland and to strengthen our faith in this most precious of sacraments.

Sacred Heart of Jesus
Celebrated on the Friday after the Body and Blood of Christ
The Solemnity of the Sacred Heart calls to mind images of the Sacred Heart in which the heart of Christ is emblazoned upon his chest for all to see. In the images Christ points to his heart which, on the one hand, invites us to draw closer to him and, on the other, reminds us that he has been rejected and his heart has been pierced because of that.

Year A
Deuteronomy 7:6-11; Psalm 102; 1 John 4:7-16; Matthew 11:25-30
In the first reading today from the Book of Deuteronomy we are told that God has chosen us out of his love for us despite all our faults. The psalm continues this theme of God's love for his people. The second reading from St John tells us that love comes from God and is a love which surpasses all others. In the gospel from St Matthew, Christ is calling us to himself and tells us to place in his care all our worries and troubles. In his great love for us he will ease our burdens. We too are called to love our fellow men and women, and Christ above all else.

Year B

Hosea 11:1, 3-4, 8-9; Psalm: Isaiah 12:2-6; Ephesians 3:8-12, 14-19; John 19:31-37

In the first reading from the prophet Hosea we see that the Lord recoils from doing harm to his people even though those people have turned against him. In the second reading from the letter to the Ephesians, St Paul reminds us that the love of Christ is beyond all knowledge but also means that we can 'approach God in complete confidence'. The gospel text from St John recounts the death of Jesus and how the soldier pierced his side with a lance. Christ died for us out of his great love for us that we might all be saved. The overwhelming message of this feast is that God loves us and is there to welcome us home with open arms if we have the faith and the courage to believe in him and the saving power of his Son.

Year C

Ezekiel 34:11-16; Psalm 22; Romans 5:5-11; Luke 15:3-7

For today the first reading and gospel present us with the image of the shepherd who looks after this sheep. Christ is not just any shepherd but one who loves his sheep, as we are reminded in the text from the letter to the Romans. Because of the love Christ has as a shepherd he is willing to do more for us than any mortal shepherd even to the point of laying down his life for us out of the great love he has for us. We know that Christ did this on the cross and that, in that action, he has redeemed us and brought us back into the sheepfold which is the kingdom of God. All we are asked to do is to have faith and to believe in the gospel.

FEASTDAYS AND MEMORIALS

1 January: Solemnity of Mary, Mother of God

Numbers 6:22-27; Psalm 66; Galatians 4:4-7; Luke 2:16-21

In our first reading today from the Book of Numbers we see God telling Moses how to bless the people in his name: 'May the Lord bless you and keep you ...' In our reading from Galatians we are reminded that Christ was born of a woman and therefore he was the same as we are. But in so doing, he has enabled each of us to become children of God just as he is the Son of God. In the gospel passage we see the Holy Family still in the stable or cave when the shepherds come, having been sent by the angels. The second part of the text recalls how he was named Jesus in accordance with the instruction of Gabriel at the annunciation. The woman referred to in Galatians is Mary and today we celebrate the fact that she is the mother of God which also declares Christ to be God. This does not place Mary in a position higher or more exalted than God, but simply acknowledges her as mother of his Divine Son.

January 25: Feast of the Conversion of St Paul, Apostle

Acts 22:3-16 or Acts 9:1-22; Psalm 116; Mark 16:15-18

St Paul had been the great persecutor of the early followers of Jesus and had put many of them to death. Today we celebrate his conversion and the readings show how he has changed and become one of the greatest preachers in the Church. In the first reading from the Acts of the Apostles, we hear Paul himself speak of his former life as a persecutor of Christianity and of his calling by Christ himself. The alternative reading from Acts gives a second telling of the event from a historical perspective. What is important in both accounts is that as Christ appeared to the Eleven in today's gospel and sent them out to spread the news of the kingdom, so too Paul has been commissioned by Christ for that same task. We are asked to convert daily to the gospel and to take its message to others, following the example of St Paul and in fulfilment of our own baptismal promises. Our gospel text is a post-resurrection encounter between Christ and the Eleven in which he commissions them to go out to the 'whole world; proclaim the good news.'

January 26: Memorial of Sts Timothy and Titus, Bishops
2 Timothy 1:1-8; Psalm 95; Luke 10:1-9

In our first reading today from St Paul's second letter to Timothy we see Paul describe Timothy as someone who was sincere in the faith. Paul is writing to him to encourage him to work to increase his faith, to 'fan into a flame the gift which God gave' him. That gift was something powerful with which to spread the faith. That gift has also been given to us and so the example of Timothy and Titus is placed before us as an encouragement to follow their example and the example of the apostles. Our gospel text from St Luke sees Christ sending out the seventy-two to preach in his name and to bring his healing power to others.

February 1: Feast of St Brigid, Virgin, Secondary Patron of Ireland
Romans 12:3-13; Psalm 148; Mark 3:31-35

St Paul reminds us in the letter to the Romans that each of us has been given a different grace or gift and that we should not boast about them. As the body must work as one, without one part being any better than another, so too the Christian community must work together as one for the good of the kingdom. The gospel text is quite appropriate for the feast we celebrate today for it tells us that those who do the will of God are truly the brothers and sisters of Christ. Brigid left us an example of this in her life in that she always did the will of God and placed Christ and others before her own needs.

February 2: The Feast of the Presentation of the Lord (Candlemas Day)
Malachi 3:1-4; Psalm 23; Hebrews 2:14-18; Luke 2:22-40

The reading from Malachi tells us that God will send his messenger to prepare the way and that, suddenly, the Lord himself will appear. This reminds us of John the Baptist's preaching. In the second reading from the letter to the Hebrews, the author tells us that Christ had to become human in order to fully represent us before God the Father. In our gospel passage from St Luke, we see Mary and Joseph going to the Temple with the infant Jesus to be purified. There, they meet Simeon and also Anna who both speak of the child as being salvation for all the nations. Simeon praises God and says that he can now rest in peace for he has seen the Saviour. Though he was the Son of God and himself God, Jesus was still brought up in the faith and with respect for the Law of Moses.

February 14: Feast of Saints Cyril & Methodius, Patrons of Europe
Acts 13:46-49; Psalm 116; Luke 10:1-9
These two men are responsible for bringing the good news to those who spoke the Slavonic language in the ninth century. Like Saints Paul and Barnabas in the first reading from the Acts of the Apostles, they proclaimed the message to those who had not heard the story of Christ and our salvation and in doing so they did as the seventy-two did in going out ahead of the Lord (St Luke). The response to the psalm sums up their mandate: 'Go out to the whole world, proclaim the good news.' Our gospel text from St Luke sees Jesus sending out the seventy-two in pairs to preach and heal in his name just as Cyril and Methodius did in their time. As they responded to the Lord's mandate so too we are challenged to follow their example and spread the Good News.

February 22: Feast of the Chair of St Peter, Apostle
1 Peter 5:1-4; Psalm 22; Matthew 16:13-19
In his first letter, St Peter tells us how he himself exercised his authority through a pastoral letter to those who were responsible for looking after the faithful. In the passage, Peter speaks of his being a witness to the sufferings of Christ – reminding his readers that he was present with the Lord and knew the human Christ. This letter also tells us how he implores all elders to be true shepherds to those entrusted to them by the Lord and to be perfect examples of living witnesses to the gospel. As Peter was the chief shepherd of the flock after Christ, the psalm for today reminds us that the Lord is the true Shepherd. The gospel passage from St Matthew shows Peter being appointed as leader of Christ's Church following his great proclamation of faith in Christ. While he was leader of the fledgling group he is also a powerful symbol of unity for the Church which continues right down to this day.

March 17: Solemnity of St Patrick, Patron Saint of Ireland

Jeremiah 1:4-9; Psalm 116; Acts 13:46-49; Luke 10:1-12, 17-20

All of our readings today are very appropriate for this celebration of St Patrick because they can all be seen as missionary readings, which is what Patrick was. In the first reading from the Prophet Jeremiah we see that Jeremiah was afraid to go and preach because he did not know what to say, but the Lord was with him and gave him the words and the eloquence to teach. In the second reading from the Acts of the Apostles we read of Saints Paul and Barnabas speaking boldly to the people about Christ and telling them that they had to go to the pagans for God's word is intended for all people. In the gospel text from St Luke we see Jesus sending out the seventy-two to preach his word and they come back rejoicing. Initially Patrick was a little hesitant about coming back to Ireland but God gave him the strength and the wisdom to do so and Patrick boldly proclaimed Christ in a pagan country and so he can now rejoice that his preaching has had such an impact. However, today's celebration also reminds us not to return to the pagan ways which Patrick took us from as our people appear to abandon his true legacy as the years pass by. Today's celebration is a call to return to that faith which Patrick devoted his life to and to return to the Lord.

March 19: Solemnity of St Joseph, Husband of the Blessed Virgin Mary

2 Samuel 7:4-5, 12-14, 16; Psalm 88; Romans 4:13, 16-18, 22; Matthew 1:16, 18-21, 24

In the first reading from the Prophet Samuel, we see God telling David that his throne will stand secure for ever through one of his line. The psalm repeats this promise. The passage from the letter to the Romans assures us that we are the spiritual children of Abraham and that we must have faith and belief like him. The gospel recounts the narrative of the vision Joseph had which told him to take Mary as his wife though she was already pregnant. In this way Jesus was born of the line of David and everything that God had promised to David and to Abraham was fulfilled. As Joseph trusted in the Lord, so we are called to that same trust and belief. The key element for us is that Joseph was a man of faith just as Mary was a woman of faith. Both had annunciations and both accepted what must have been quite troubling, but they did so without hesitation. In this way they ensured the prophesies and promises of the Old Testament while giving the child a strong faith-based family unit in which to grow up.

March 25: The Annunciation of the Lord
Isaiah 7:10-14, 8:10; Psalm 39; Hebrews 10:4-10; Luke 1:26-38

The readings for this solemnity all point towards one very important word: 'Yes.' They each speak of doing the will of God with open hearts. The gospel text recounts Gabriel's visit to Mary to tell her that she is to bear the Saviour of the world. Mary answers 'yes' to God and we too are called on to say 'yes' to him everyday of our lives and to trust in his goodness as completely as did Mary. Our gospel today also reminds us of Christ's 'yes' in the Garden of Gethsemane when he was faced with the prospect of dying for us. Yet in that 'yes' which caused his death he also secured our salvation. Now is the time for us to say 'yes' to him and to truly gain that salvation.

April 25: St Mark, the Evangelist
1 Peter 5:5-14; Psalm 88; Mark 16:15-20

In our first reading for this feast, St Peter gives instruction to the people on how they should live with one another. In the letter he makes mention of St Mark, who is one of his companions. The gospel account from Mark tells of Christ's commandment to his followers that they are to go out and spread his gospel everywhere. Mark himself did this through his travels with St Paul and later with St Peter and particularly through the written word of his gospel.

April 29: St Catherine of Siena, Doctor of the Church, Patroness of Europe
1 John 1:5-2:2; Psalm 102; Matthew 11:25-30

The first reading from the first letter of St John calls on us to live in the light, just as St Catherine of Siena did. If we live in the light we will not go wrong and we will live in truth before God and our fellow men and women. The gospel passage too can be applied to today's saint for she brought comfort to many who were poor through her gentleness and humility of heart. We too are called to look after others and to share our belongings, our time and our life with them.

May 3: Feast of Sts Philip & James, Apostles
1 Corinthians 15:1-8; Psalm 18; John 14:6-14
In our first reading for today, St Paul tells us of the resurrection of the Lord and of his first appearances to his followers, among them James. The gospel tells us that we must believe in Christ in order to have eternal life and that the message of Christ is the message of God. We are called on to believe just as Sts Philip and James did and to put that belief into practice in our lives.

May 14: Feast of St Matthias, Apostle
Acts 1:15-17, 20-26; Psalm 112; John 15:9-17
The reading from the Acts of the Apostles tells us of the election of Matthias as one of the Twelve to replace Judas Iscariot. We hear of St Peter's speech in which he says that Judas' fate had been foretold. He goes on to say that Matthias had been with them for a long time so that his testimony of the resurrection will be a first hand witness account. Of the two nominated, Matthias was the one elected. The gospel reading from St John reminds us that Christ has chosen us to be his own and to fulfil his work. If Christ has chosen us, who are we to say 'no'?

May 31: Feast of the Visitation of the Blessed Virgin Mary
Zephaniah 3:14:18 (or Romans 12:9-16); Psalm Isaiah 12:2-6; Luke 1:39-56
In the first reading from Zephaniah we are told to rejoice because the Lord, the king of Israel, is in our midst and has come to repeal our sentence. In the alternative reading from Romans, we are told to make the needs of our fellow men and women our special care. This is what Mary did when she went to visit her cousin Elizabeth in the final stages of Elizabeth's pregnancy. The gospel tells us of the encounter between the two women when Mary arrived at Elizabeth's house. It gives us the beautiful *Magnificat* – the hymn of Mary. We too are called to think of our fellow men and women in their need and to praise God for all

that we have been given in life, even if it is not what we expected. Mary is often seen as the Ark of the Covenant as she bore Christ within her for those nine months and Elizabeth rejoiced when she stood in the presence of that human ark, as did the child within her. Having received the Holy Spirit and also Christ at communion, we too are arks of God's word and so should act accordingly and bring his message and his peace wherever we go. A small point, but an important one, is that the child carried by Elizabeth (John the Baptist) leapt for joy in her womb when he heard Mary – he recognised who and what she was, and he also recognised the immense importance of the child she herself carried. Today also reminds us of the great part John would play in the spread of the gospel.

Saturday after the Second Sunday after Pentecost: The Immaculate Heart of Mary

Isaiah 61:9-11; Psalm: 1 Samuel 2:1, 4-8; Luke 2:41-51

The first reading speaks of rejoicing in God for what he has done for the speaker. It could so easily be the prayer of Mary in thanksgiving for the great honour which God has bestowed upon her in making her the mother of his Divine Son. The psalm continues this theme. The gospel text tells us how Mary stored up everything about her Son in her heart as a truly loving mother. No doubt Mary thought about these things from time to time – something which we too should do regarding Christ and his place in our lives.

June 9: Feast of St Columba (Colm Cille), Abbot & Secondary Patron of Ireland

Colossians 1:24-29; Psalm 15; Mark 10:17-30

In our first reading St Paul tells us that he became the servant of the Church to deliver God's message to the people. In the gospel we see the rich young man asking Jesus what he must do in order to inherit eternal life. Jesus tells him that he must give all he has to the poor and then follow Christ. These readings are very apt for the feast of St Colm Cille for he was of royal lineage but he gave up that privilege and gave his whole life to Christ, founding churches and monasteries wherever he went. As Colm Cille became a servant of the gospel of Christ we too are challenged today to continue his great missionary work in our own communities.

June 11: Memorial of St Barnabas, Apostle

Acts 11:21-26; 13:1-3; Psalm 97; Matthew 10:7-13

Our first reading from the Acts of the Apostles recounts some of the work done by St Barnabas in spreading the gospel of Christ in various communities. The gospel today sees Jesus sending out his apostles and telling them how they should act. We are called to be like Barnabas and to give our life to the service of God and the word.

June 24: Solemnity of the Birth of St John the Baptist

Isaiah 49:1-6; Psalm 138; Acts 13:22-26; Luke 1:57-66, 80

Our readings today speak to us about St John the Baptist and his life. John was the last of the prophets – those people who were called by God to remind the people of the covenants and to point out to them when they were straying from the Law of God. The first reading from the Prophet Isaiah reminds us of the messenger who would prepare the way for the Lord. In the second reading from the Acts of the Apostles we see St Paul speaking about John and his life's work. The gospel recounts for us the birth and how it was that John got his name. It also indicates the great destiny which lay before him as the cousin and herald of the Messiah. We also remember how some saw him as Elijah or one of the other great prophets come back to life.

June 29: Solemnity of Saints Peter & Paul, Apostles

Acts 12:1-11; Psalm 33; 2 Timothy 4:6-8, 17-18; Matthew 16:13-19

Our first reading from the Acts of the Apostles tells of the release of St Peter from prison before Herod could put him to death as he had St James. In the second reading, St Paul tells Timothy that he has been able to preach the good news because he had God at his side to give him power and to guide him. In the gospel, Jesus makes Peter the head of the Church and tells him that nothing will ever prevail against the Church. Our readings show us how we should live – by being faithful to God and not fearing what may come for God is always with us. They also remind us that even those who consider themselves to be 'ordinary' can become 'heroes' of the faith for these men were quite ordinary and quite unremarkable before they received the Holy Spirit – the same Spirit which we too have received. We are also reminded that they were old men when they were martyred because even in old age they witnessed for Christ. Regardless of our age or our standing in society we should always publicly acknowledge Christ as our Saviour.

July 3: Feast of St Thomas the Apostle
Ephesians 2:19-22; Psalm 116; John 20:24-29
The first reading from St Paul's letter to the Ephesians tells us that we are all part of God's household and that that household has the apostles and prophets for its foundations. In the gospel, we see St Thomas doubt the words of the others when they say that Jesus has risen and appeared to them. When Jesus appears to them again eight days later, Thomas is in the room and believes, once he can physically touch the Lord. In this way Thomas represents all peoples down through the centuries who have not personally seen the Risen Lord. Thomas' great declaration of faith – 'My Lord and my God' – should be all the proof we need.

July 11: Feast of St Benedict, Abbot & Patron of Europe
Proverbs 2:1-9; Psalm 33; Matthew 19:27-29
The first reading from Proverbs exhorts us to apply ourselves in seeking the truth for there is a great treasure to be found in the truth. When we discover it then we will 'understand what virtue is, justice and fair dealing.' In the gospel, Jesus assures Peter that those who have left everything for him will receive a great reward, that reward being eternal life. The readings are quite appropriate for the feast of St Benedict for they recount exactly the sort of life Benedict lived. We too are called to seek truth and to give up everything for the sake of Christ and the kingdom.

July 22: Memorial of St Mary Magdalene
Songs 3:1-4 (or 2 Corinthians 5:14-17); Psalm 62; John 20:1-2, 11-18
The first reading from the Song of Songs tells of a person seeking the one whom they love. Today we can understand it as Mary Magdalene seeking the Lord. In the gospel from St John we see Mary at the empty tomb and being greeted by Christ himself, now risen from the dead. For her faithfulness to him

she has been rewarded by being the first person to see the Lord after his resurrection and also by being the one to proclaim that news to the apostles.

July 23: Feast of St Bridget of Sweden, Patroness of Europe
Galatians 2:19-20; Psalm 33; John 15:1-8
The first reading from St Paul to the Galatians speaks very much of the life of St Bridget of Sweden. She gave what she had in the service of the poor and of Christ and the life she lived was not hers but Christ's. The gospel speaks of the vine whose branches bear much fruit if they remain pure and part of the vine tree. We are called to be like Bridget and to give of what we have in the service of the Lord and of his people. If we do so then we will produce much fruit for the kingdom.

July 25: Feast of St James the Apostle
2 Corinthians 4:7-15; Psalm 125; Matthew 20:20-28
In our passage from the second letter to the Corinthians St Paul tells us that, because he believes and proclaims the word of God, he will be raised to life with Christ. The death and the life of Christ are at work in him in a very powerful way. There is also a reminder that there will be trials in witnessing for the Lord. In the gospel we see Zebedee's wife coming to Jesus to ask that her sons sit at his right and left in heaven. Jesus can grant them places in heaven but only if they suffer for him through the spread of the gospel. We too are called to live lives worthy of the kingdom no matter what trials may come our way. We are to carry our cross every day for Christ and to proclaim the gospel by the example of how we live.

July 29: Memorial of St Martha
1 John 4:7-16; Psalm 33; John 11:19-27 or Luke 10:38-42
The first reading from St John's first letter speaks of love – love for God and love for others. Love was also a characteristic of Martha. We have two images of Martha presented to us in the gospels. The first is from St Luke in which we see Martha rushing about the house when our Lord arrives. She becomes annoyed because her sister, Mary, is sitting listening to Christ rather than looking after him. When she complains about this, Jesus tells her

to stop worrying and to sit in his presence and listen as her sister is doing. In the second image, this time from St John's gospel, we are presented with the arrival of Jesus at the tomb of his friend Lazarus. Martha greets him while Mary stays indoors. Martha says that if Christ had come sooner her brother would not have died but that whatever Christ asks of the Father will happen. When asked if she believed that Christ was the resurrection and the life, Martha answers that she does and that she believes him to be the Christ, the Son of God. This is the faith which we are all called to profess and to show in our lives through love of God and neighbour.

August 6: Feast of the Transfiguration of the Lord
Daniel 7:9-10, 13-14; Psalm 96; 2 Peter 1:16-19; Matthew 17:1-9 or Mark 9:2-10 or Luke 9:28-36

This feast recalls the day when Christ was on top of Mount Tabor with a few of his disciples and in their sight he was transfigured. The glory with which he stood before them is the glory which awaits us on the last day when we shall enter the kingdom of heaven and be counted among the elect. The first reading from the book of Daniel speaks of the glory of God, of his appearance and of his white robes. The second reading from St Peter (a witness to the transfiguration) also speaks of the glory of Christ.

Year A: The gospel text from St Matthew recounts the transfiguration of the Lord on the mountain in the presence of Peter, James and John. While the disciples look on Jesus is changed and his clothes appear as white as light while he speaks with Moses and Elijah. This suggests that Jesus is greater than both the Law and the Prophets. In the transfiguration we are given an insight into the glory which awaits us and so we are reminded to remain always faithful if we are to attain that glory.

Year B: The gospel text from St Mark recounts the transfiguration in the presence of three of Christ's closest companions and of how the appearance of Christ changed so much. We are given an insight today into the glory which awaits us and so we are reminded to remain always faithful if we are to attain that glory.

Year C: The gospel text from St Luke recounts the transfiguration of the Lord on the mountain in the presence of Peter, James and John. While the disciples look on Jesus is changed and his clothes appear as white as light while he speaks with Moses and Elijah. This suggests that Jesus is greater than both the Law and the Prophets. As with Christ's baptism in the Jordan, the Father's voice sounds from heaven to proclaim his satisfaction with his Son. We are given an insight today into the glory which awaits us and so we are reminded to remain always faithful if we are to attain that glory.

August 9: Feast of St Teresa Benedicta of the Cross (Edith Stein), Martyr & Patroness of Europe
Hosea 2:16-17, 21-22; Psalm 44; Matthew 25:1-13
In our first reading we see that the Lord will lure his faithful one and betroth himself to her forever. This is appropriate for this feast for we remember that Edith Stein was Jewish by birth and over time she sought to give herself to God through the Christian Church while not forgetting her Jewish heritage. In our gospel we have the parable of the ten bridesmaids who were waiting for the bridegroom's return. Some were foolish and were not ready for his return and so were left outside in the cold. Edith was ready when it came to her own death in the concentration camp and as that time loomed she also gave strength and solace to those around her. So today would be a good time to ask ourselves if we are ready for when the Lord calls us and have we done all that we could do to deepen our faith and to make God's presence visible in our world.

August 10: Feast of St Lawrence, Deacon & Martyr
2 Corinthians 9:6-10; Psalm 111; John 12:24-26
In our first reading today St Paul exhorts his readers to give alms to the poor and to look after them in any way possible, knowing that there will be abundant blessings from the Lord for this work of mercy. In our text from St John's gospel the Lord tells us that we must be like a grain of wheat because unless we die to the ways of this life and are born of the true and everlasting life, we will be lost for ever. Lawrence lost his life but he did so with a great heart because what he did was done for the Lord and so his name and his example lives on to this day. He is an example to us that the life to come is of far greater value than the

present life we live and that we should do all we can to secure our place alongside Lawrence in the kingdom.

August 15: Solemnity of the Assumption of Our Blessed Lady into Heaven

Apocalypse (Revelations) 11:19, 12:1-6, 10; Psalm 44; 1 Corinthians 15:20-26; Luke 1:39-56

The first reading from the Book of the Apocalypse refers to our Lady who, as Queen of Heaven, is robed in splendour and majesty. She gives birth to one of great importance who is taken directly to the throne of God, whose Son he is, while the Virgin flees to a special place – reminding us of her special place in heaven. In the second reading, St Paul tells us that Christ is the first-fruit – the first to rise from the dead. The gospel from St Luke contains the *Magnificat* – Mary's beautiful hymn which she said upon meeting her cousin Elizabeth shortly after the Annunciation. Today's solemnity commemorates our Lady's entry into glory, a glory which awaits us and which was prefigured on 6 August in the celebration of the Transfiguration of the Lord.

August 22: Memorial of the Queenship of Mary

Isaiah 9:1-6; Psalm 112; Luke 1:26-38

Our first reading today comes from the Prophet Isaiah and is commonly heard coming up to Christmas. In the text the prophet tells us about the Son who will be given to us and will bring us salvation through his self-sacrifice. The gospel text is St Luke's account of the Annunciation in which we hear how the Son spoken of in the first reading will be born. As always, the readings on memorials and feastdays of Our Lady remind us of her great service to the word and will of God.

August 24: Feast of St Bartholomew the Apostle

Apocalypse (Revelation) 21:9-14; Psalm 144; John 1:45-51

Our first reading from the book of the Revelations made to St John the Evangelist, speaks of the new Jerusalem which has twelve foundation stones. The new Jerusalem is a metaphor for the Church established by Christ and built on the foundation of the apostles themselves. The wall symbolises the people of God. In the gospel we see Nathanael (Nathaniel) being brought to

Jesus and we read of his declaration of faith because of what Jesus said to him. It is believed that this Nathanael is the St Bartholomew we honour today.

August 29: Memorial of the Beheading of St John the Baptist
Jeremiah 1:17-19; Psalm 70; Mark 6:17-29
The first reading sees the Lord telling Jeremiah not to be afraid but to stand up before the people and to preach as he has been commanded to by the Lord. The reading is also a good description of John the Baptist and his fearless belief in Christ who also stood before a king and gave him warning of how to act righteously before God. Both Jeremiah and John suffered violent deaths. The gospel passage recalls the martyrdom of John and how he died for the faith as a result of a promise vainly made to a lovely girl by Herod.

September 8: Memorial of the Birthday of the Blessed Virgin Mary
Micah 5:1-4 or Romans 8:28-30; Psalm 12; Matthew 1:1-6, 18-23
Our readings today may seem rather odd for the memorial of our Lady's birthday because they speak about the arrival of Christ. In the first reading from Micah we read that the saviour will arrive and then his people will live secure. In the gospel text from St Matthew we have the genealogy of Christ. But the readings do serve to remind us that if it wasn't for the generosity of Mary in answering God's call then Christ would not have been born and world history could have been very different. The memorial also serves to remind us that Mary was a human being just like us and that she had a birth just like us.

September 14: Feast of the Triumph of the Cross
Numbers 21:4-9; Psalm 77; Philippians 2:6-11; John 3:13-17
The first reading from the Book of Numbers recalls how the people in the wilderness had complained against God. For their ungratefulness, the Lord sent serpents among the people to punish them. Moses fashioned a bronze serpent to save those who were bitten by the serpents. The second reading from the letter to the Philippians is one of the most beautiful passages in scripture for it tells us of how Christ humbled himself to become one of us in

order to save us. Through his humility he was raised above all other creatures and won our salvation. In the gospel, Jesus tells us that he had to be raised high, just as Moses raised the serpent, so that all peoples may be saved and brought to eternal life. In the cross is our salvation and the salvation of all peoples and it is this redemption which we celebrate today.

September 15: Memorial of Our Lady of Sorrows
Hebrews 5:7-9; Psalm 30; John 19:25-27 or Luke 2:33-35
In our first reading from the letter to the Hebrews we read that Christ offered up prayer to God but still went to the cross to save the world. In the gospel from St John, we see Mary at the foot of the cross as her Son dies. In the alternative gospel from St Luke we see Mary and Joseph with the Christ-child in the Temple at his presentation. There they are met by Simeon who predicts that Mary would suffer as a result of being the mother of Christ. Today's memorial recalls Mary's suffering at seeing her Divine Son rejected and ultimately put to death. Through it all she never tried to prevent what was taking place because she trusted in God and in her Son. As she suffered she was comforted by God who comforts us in all our troubles.

September 21: Feast of St Matthew the Apostle and Evangelist
Ephesians 4:1-7; Psalm 18; Matthew 9:9-13
Our first reading today from the letter to the Ephesians speaks of the different gifts of God which have been given to the Ephesians, and how they should all be used for the building up of the Body of Christ. First among those are the apostles who gave their lives for the building of the kingdom – Matthew being today's example. The gospel passage tells the story of the call of Matthew from being a tax-collector to being a follower of Christ.

September 29: Feast of Sts Michael, Gabriel & Raphael, Archangels
Daniel 7:9-10, 13-14 (or Revelation 12:7-12); Psalm 137; John 1:47-51
The text from the Book of Daniel speaks of one of great age taking his seat upon his throne and receiving sovereignty, glory and kingship and with all peoples worshipping him. The alter-

native reading from the Book of Revelation tells of Michael the Archangel leading the hosts of angels into battle on behalf of the Lord against the dragon, known as the devil of Satan. They are victorious and the glory of the Lord is declared. In the gospel we see Jesus speaking with Nathanael when the latter came to him late at night. Nathanael says that Jesus is the Son of God and Jesus commends him for his faith. He goes on to tell him that he shall see great things in heaven including the angels who dwell in the Lord's presence and act as his messengers.

October 2: Memorial of the Guardian Angels
Exodus 23:20-23; Psalm 90; Matthew 18:1-5, 10
In our first reading we read of the Jews who have just left Egypt on their journey back to the Promised Land. As the journey is a long one the Lord is granting a guardian angel to them who will guide and protect them and speak God's word to them. For their part, the people must honour and respect the angel. In the gospel, Jesus tells us that we have guardian angels and that, particularly in the case of children, our guardian angels are in the presence of the Father in heaven and speak directly to him on our behalf.

October 7: Memorial of Our Lady of the Rosary
Acts 1:12-14; Psalm: Luke 1; Luke 1:26-38
The readings and the psalm today focus very much on Our Lady. In the first reading we see the apostles and a number of others gathered with Mary in the upper room between the Ascension and Pentecost. They are gathered together in prayer. The psalm is Mary's beautiful prayer, the *Magnificat*, in which she praises God. In the gospel, we see the archangel Gabriel greeting Mary at the Annunciation. She says 'yes' to God in complete trust and confidence. Today's memorial reminds us to be steadfast in prayer and always to trust in the Lord for he will be with us to strengthen and to guide us.

October 18: Feast of St Luke the Evangelist
2 Timothy 4:10-17; Psalm 144; Luke 10:1-9
In our first reading from his second letter to St Timothy, St Paul tells Timothy that he has nobody with him now except Luke.

The evangelist was a companion of Paul in the latter's second and third missionary journeys. Paul also tells of an occasion when he had to defend himself and only God was there to support him. In the gospel, the Lord sends out seventy-two disciples to preach and cure in his name. We are all reminded that we each have a role to play in the spread of the gospel. Tradition at one time thought Luke was a member of this seventy-two.

October 28: Feast of Sts Simon and Jude the Apostles
Ephesians 2:19-22; Psalm 18; Luke 6:12-19
Our first reading from the letter to the Ephesians speaks of the Church being founded on the apostles. St Paul speaks about the role the apostles played in the establishment of the Church and of how their lives can give a sure foundation to the faith of each of us. The gospel passage recounts the naming of the Twelve Apostles by Christ. What is significant about his choice is that they were ordinary people who believed in him and acknowledged their sinfulness and need of grace. More importantly, Jesus spent time in prayer before he made his choice. We too should pray before we make our own important decisions and try to live as the apostles did – completely faithful to the Lord.

November 1: Solemnity of All Saints
Apocalypse 7:2-4, 9-14; Psalm 23; 1 John 3:1-3; Matthew 5:1-12
In the reading from the Book of the Apocalypse the author speaks of the faithful who have died and are now radiant in the presence of God in heaven. They are radiant because their robes have been washed in the blood of the Lamb who is our redeemer. Before the final judgement all those who have been faithful will be given a seal on their forehead as the Jews sealed their doorposts on Passover night. In our second reading St John asks us to think of the love which God has lavished on us – a love which allows us to be called the sons and daughters of God and therefore grants us a place in heaven with God. For John, this means that anybody who thinks of this would automatically try to purify themselves and try to live up to this great gift and grace. In the gospel, we have Christ's tremendous blueprint for Christian living – the Beatitudes from the Sermon on the Mount – which has the power to transform our world but only if people

live out that teaching in their lives. These readings are apt for today's feast because the saints did live out the Beatitudes and did recognise and appreciate the great love which God lavished on them and so lived their lives in such a way that people could see the love of God in their midst. As a result, the saints – who were living, breathing human beings like each and every one of us – now enjoy the beatific vision in the eternal kingdom.

November 2: Solemn Commemoration of All the Faithful Departed

Isaiah 25:6-9; Psalm 26; Romans 5:5-11; Matthew 11:25-30 or Mark 15:33-39, 16:1-6

In our first reading from the Prophet Isaiah we read that the Lord of hosts will destroy death for ever. We know that Christ has triumphed over death and yet people still die. What is important for us to keep in mind is that while our earthly body may die our soul does not. It lives on and the banquet which Isaiah speaks about takes place in heaven. In the second reading St Paul tells us that we have been saved by Christ who died for us even while we were still sinning. This is the hope that we should have and if we live according to that hope then we will all be reunited in the kingdom where death has no power. In the gospel text from St Matthew we see Jesus praising the Father in heaven for revealing the mysteries to children rather than to the learned and the clever. The text concludes with Jesus calling to him all those who are overburdened. Matthew is reminding us that the way of Christ is a way of fulfilment at the end of which is eternal life and a time of rest which will never end. Only if we trust God like little children and act accordingly can we enter the kingdom of heaven. In the alternative gospel passage from St Mark we read of the death of Christ which is a moment of great despair for his mother and for the disciples. But in the second part there is a very obvious contrast because we now see the Risen Lord and so we are filled with great hope. Christ, who was human, has been raised from the dead and through his resurrection we too have the promise of resurrection and eternal life. Today in a very special way we pray for all who have died but we do so in hope – hope of the resurrection which has been promised to each one of us and to all who have died.

Any of the readings from amongst those from the Lectionary for the dead may be used today.

November 6: Feast of All the Saints of Ireland

Ecclesiastes 44:1-5; Psalm 14; Luke 6:17-23

The first reading from the Book of Ecclesiastes calls on us to praise illustrious men and then lists those who have held positions in society and who are remembered for their great and noble works. But in the last section it speaks of generous men and those who kept the covenants and handed them on to their children. Today we praise those Irish people who kept the faith which was handed on to them and for which they are now counted among the Communion of Saints, though their names have long since been forgotten. In the gospel, we have Luke's account of the Sermon on the Mount and the Beatitudes in which Christ is promising the kingdom to those who are poor in spirit. Those who live by the Beatitudes are those who will inherit the kingdom and be counted among the Communion of Saints.

November 9: Feast of the Dedication of the Lateran Basilica

Ezekiel 47:1-2, 8-9, 12; Psalm 45; 1 Corinthians 3:9-11, 16-17; John 2:13-22

In the first reading from Ezekiel we read how a stream flowed from the Temple and gave life in abundance wherever it flowed. If we look at the distance from the Temple as a timeline then we see that over time the river grows to become a great torrent with the Temple being Christ. What is in the river could be seen as the members of the Church and what is on the banks as those who come into contact with members of the Church. Whether the people be in the river or on the bank, all receive life from the river. In the second reading St Paul reminds us that we are all God's temple through the Spirit which has been given to us and therefore we must preserve this temple and strengthen it in the faith. The Temple is not just a stone building but it is each and every one of us who has God within them. In the gospel we see Jesus driving out of the Temple those who had dishonoured it. The church is the house of God and it is the source of life for us and that is what we celebrate today. It is our duty to build up the Church of God – the church within each of us and the church as the unity and gathering of all who believe in Christ.

November 21: Memorial of the Presentation of the Blessed Virgin Mary

Zechariah 2:14-17; Psalm: Luke 1:46-55; Matthew 12:46-50

As is so often the case on memorials of Our Lady, the readings focus very much on her Divine Son. Today's memorial is no different for the first reading sees the Lord telling us that he is coming to dwell in the midst of his people, and that he will make Jerusalem his very own. This reminds us of Christ who lived among the people and for whom Jerusalem was so important. In the gospel text we have the familiar story of Jesus being sought by his family. He tells the people that whoever does the will of God are his real family.

November 23: Feast of St Columban, Abbot

Isaiah 52:7-10; Psalm 95; Luke 9:57-62

Our reading from the Prophet Isaiah speaks of how all the ends of the earth shall see the salvation of our God and of how they will rejoice in that salvation. St Columban – as a monk and missionary – sought to bring that salvation to people by founding monasteries and teaching the people. The psalm commands us to 'proclaim the wonders of the Lord among all the peoples,' which is what Columban did. In the gospel passage from St Luke, we see some men telling Jesus that they will follow Jesus once they have taken care of certain things. However, Jesus tells them that they must follow him immediately. Columban did this even in the midst of difficulty. We are challenged today to be like Columban and to freely and readily go where the Lord leads and to spread his word in all we do and say.

November 30: Feast of St Andrew the Apostle

Romans 10:9-18; Psalm 18; Matthew 4:18-22

In the first reading from the letter to the Romans, St Paul speaks of the importance of spreading the Good News because if the Word is not spread then people will not hear of Christ and so will be unable to believe in him or to call upon him. In our gospel text for today's feast, we read of the call of St Andrew by Christ. Andrew responded generously to the Lord's call and without hesitation and he spread the gospel among the peoples even to the point of giving his life in martyrdom for Christ. His example of spreading the good news is set before us today and we are reminded that we have all been called by Christ to do the very same in our own day.

December 8: Solemnity of the Immaculate Conception of the Blessed Virgin Mary

Genesis 3:9-15, 20; Psalm 97:1-4; Ephesians 1:3-6, 11-12; Luke 1:26-38

Today's solemnity recalls the conception of Mary in the womb of her mother. It is fitting that she should be conceived free from the traditional mark of original sin as she would be the mother of Jesus Christ. Our first reading comes from the Book of Genesis and it reminds us of how sin entered the world through our first parents. Because of their sin, Adam and Eve were expelled from the Garden of Eden and a barrier was placed between humans and God. By contrast, Mary is often seen as the 'New Eve' for it is through her Son that we are restored to full unity with God. Our gospel text from St Luke recalls the Annunciation to Mary by the Angel Gabriel. In the scene Mary is greeted with the words, 'Rejoice, so highly favoured!' (Luke 1:28), which shows the special place Mary already had above the rest of the sons and daughters of God. Just as important, and indeed central, is Mary's 'yes' to the angel's message because it allows the poor decision of Adam and Eve to be reversed. The second reading from St Paul's letter to the Ephesians reminds us that God has chosen us in Christ to be his people and that Mary's immaculate conception was part of God's predestined plan for our salvation and glory. In order to achieve that salvation and glory we have to live the gospel values and say 'yes' to God everyday, just as Mary did. Falling as it does in Advent, this solemnity also reminds us of our preparations for the birth of Christ at Christmas and of the necessity to remove sin from our own lives.

December 26: Feast of St Stephen, the First Martyr

Acts 6:8-10, 7:54-59; Psalm 30; Matthew 10:17-22

Our first reading today from the Acts of the Apostles gives an account of Stephen's belief in the Son of God and of the 'great wonders and signs' he worked and which led to his arrest and trial before the supreme court of the Jews. It goes on to tell us of his martyrdom for holding such beliefs. The psalm could quite easily have been the last words of Stephen as he died: 'Into your hands I commend my spirit, it is you who will redeem me Lord.' In the gospel passage from St Matthew we see Jesus warning his followers that they will be handed over to others and betrayed for believing in him. But he tells them not to worry because they will have the Spirit of God with them and those who stand 'firm to the end will be saved'. Having just celebrated the birth of the Saviour, we are challenged to believe in him even to the point of dying for him as St Stephen did.

December 27: Feast of St John the Apostle & Evangelist
1 John 1:1-4; Psalm 96; John 20:2-8
In the first reading, St John is giving testimony that what he has said about Jesus is the truth. It is almost his affidavit that what he is saying is correct and not some made up story. He is writing this account because he wants to share his joyful friendship with God with others. In the gospel, we have the account of John and Peter going to the tomb having heard that Jesus was no longer there. John gets there first but waits for Peter – the first among equals – before he goes in. They see that Jesus has risen and they believe all that he has said and this is what John's testimony in the first reading points to. We too are challenged today to believe in God having been given assurances by John that Jesus is the Saviour.

December 28: Feast of the Holy Innocents, Martyrs
1 John 1:5-2:2; Psalm 123; Matthew 2:13-18
In our first reading, St John calls on us to live as children of the light always doing what is right and good. He also reminds us that – if we do go astray – the Lord will be our advocate and will return us to union with God. Our gospel passage today recounts the flight into Egypt of the Holy Family of Jesus, Mary and Joseph, and of the slaying of the Innocents by Herod in his attempt to kill the newborn king and so secure his own throne. The Holy Innocents gave their lives for Christ that he might live, reminding us of the presence and power of the forces of darkness in our world. We are called on to believe in God even to the point of dying for him.

LIVES OF THE SAINTS

January 1: Solemnity of Mary, Mother of God

Throughout the Church's liturgical calendar there are several solemnities, feast days and memorials of Our Lady. Today we celebrate Our Blessed Lady as the Mother of God which is not accepted by all Christians. For us, Jesus Christ is God the Son, the second person of the Most Holy Trinity. Therefore, as his mother, Mary is the Mother of God. However, this does not place Mary in a position superior to God or to her Divine Son but simply acknowledges her special connection with Jesus Christ. The Vatican II document, Lumen gentium, says: 'At the message of the angel, the Virgin Mary received the Word of God in her heart and in her body, and gave Life to the World. Hence she is acknowledged and honoured as being truly the Mother of God and Mother of the Redeemer' (Lumen gentium 52).

January 2: Memorial of Sts Basil the Great & Gregory Nazianzen, Bishops & Doctors of the Church

Basil was born in 329 in Cappadocia to a family which produced nine saints. During the course of his studies he met Gregory of Nazianzen and they became life-long friends. For a time after studies Basil was a teacher before becoming a monk and is regarded as the spiritual head of monks of the Eastern Church (as St Benedict is spiritual head of monks in the Western Church). In 370 he was made bishop of Caesarea and ac-quitted himself very well in his role as bishop. The Arian heresy (that Jesus is not co-equal with the Father but created by him) was strong at this time and Basil fought against this even to the point of taking on the Arianist emperor, Valens. His friend, Gregory, was born about the year 329 and likewise to a family of saints. After studies in law he followed Basil in the solitary life and was very shy compared to his friend. He was appointed bishop by Basil but never took up the office, instead acting as assistant-bishop to his father before being appointed to Constantinople in 380, though he resigned soon after. Basil died in January 379 and Gregory ten years later. Both are counted in the Western Church as being among the Four Greek Doctors of the Church while in the East they are two of the Three Holy Hierarchs – John Chrysostom being the third.

January 6: Solemnity of the Epiphany of the Lord

This solemnity recalls the visit of the Magi – the Three Wise Men – to the manger in Bethlehem where they found the Christ-Child. They had followed a star from the east and came to pay him homage – they discovered the Child by their own methods and not by the message of any angel. In the Eastern Churches this day is celebrated with more solemnity than Christmas Day for it is the day when the newborn Saviour was presented to his people. The peoples of the East were regarded as pagan peoples so the arrival of these three wise men – traditionally named Gaspar, Melchior and Balthasar – is significant for it shows that Christ is already winning the hearts and minds of people. The gold represents Christ's kingship, the frankincense his divinity, and the myrrh his burial.

January 15: Memorial of St Ita, Virgin

Ita (whose name means 'thirst for holiness') was born in the sixth century in the Deise near Drum, Co Waterford. She left home and went to Limerick in order to devote her life to God. She gathered a community of maidens around her and also ran a school for boys. Many miracles were said to have been worked by her. She died in 570.

January 17: Memorial of St Antony, Abbot

Antony was born to a wealthy family in Upper Egypt in 251 but lived a life of solitude and prayer in the desert. He is regarded as the Father of Christian Monasticism because he was the first hermit to form communities of hermits. He was much sought after by kings, bishops and crowds of people seeking advice. He died in his hermitage on Mount Kolzim near the Red Sea at the age of 105.

January 21: Memorial of St Agnes, Virgin & Martyr

Agnes was a girl of about 14 or 15 years of age when she was martyred and buried beside the Via Nomentana in Rome during the final years of the persecutions by the Emperor Diocletian (early fourth century). Near her grave a basilica was erected and a series of large catacombs excavated and which can still be visited today. Nothing definite is known about her martyrdom other than the fact that she died for believing in Christ. On this day lambs are blessed, whose wool is used to make the palliums for new metropolitan archbishops.

January 24: Memorial of St Francis de Sales, Bishop & Doctor of the Church

Francis was born in Savoy in 1567 to a noble family. Having studied law at Padua he gave up the legal profession and was ordained priest in 1593. He was made a bishop only six years later and was Archbishop of Geneva by 1602 – home of John Calvin (who broke from the Roman Catholic Church in 1530 and founded Calvinism). He founded the Visitation Nuns with St Jane Frances de Chantal and was noted for the great way he preached which brought many people back to the Catholic Church following the Reformation. He died at the age of 56 in 1622. He is the patron saint of journalists and other writers.

January 25: Feast of the Conversion of St Paul the Apostle

Paul (also known by his Jewish name Saul) was born in Tarsus in Cilicia in modern-day Turkey. He was educated and was a Pharisee which meant that he was well acquainted with both the Law and the Scriptures which is evident in his writings. As a faithful Jew he persecuted the early Christians until he was struck down on his way to Damascus to arrest some Christians. In this incident, the Risen Lord appeared to Paul and from then on Paul becomes the greatest champion of the faith and is known as the Apostle to the Gentiles. He met with St Peter and the other Apostles in Jerusalem on a number of occasions and undertook three great missionary journeys to spread the faith. These journeys took him through Palestine but also through Syria, Turkey, Crete, Greece and Malta. During some of these journeys he funded himself through his work as a tent maker. Eventually Paul ends up in Rome where, even under house arrest, he spreads the faith and writes some of the letters found in the New Testament to the churches he had founded on his travels and also to individuals to bolster their faith. These letters also contain Paul's understanding of who Jesus Christ is and the importance of the death and resurrection of Christ. He was beheaded during the persecutions in the reign of Emperor Nero.

January 26: Memorial of Sts Timothy & Titus, Bishops

Very little is known about these two saints who were companions and disciples of St Paul who is said to have written three letters to them and which are part of the canon of sacred scripture. Timothy was made bishop of Ephesus while still very young and is said to have been beaten and stoned to death in 97AD for fighting against heathen worship. Titus was made bishop of Crete though he still went on missions for Paul from time to time but always returned to Crete where he eventually died.

January 28: Memorial of St Thomas Aquinas, Priest & Doctor of the Church

Thomas was born in 1225 and was educated by the Benedictine monks of Monte Cassino before joining the Dominican Order. He spent his life teaching and writing in France and Italy and his two major works – the 'Summa Contra Gentiles' and the 'Summa Theologica' – are still studied today for the quality of their theology and philosophy. He died at the age of 49 while on his way to the second Oecumenical Council of Lyons in 1274. He is the patron saint of universities and schools.

January 31: Memorial of St John Bosco, Priest

Don Bosco was born in 1815 to a peasant family in Piedmont, Italy. After being ordained he established several boys' clubs and schools in Turin which very quickly flourished. He was also well known for his preaching and fund raising skills and he built several churches. In 1854 he founded what became the Salesian Congregation to educate and look after boys, and with St Mary Mazzarello he founded the Daughters of Our Lady Help of Christians in 1872 to educate and look after girls. He died in 1888.

February 1: Feast of St Brigid, Virgin & Secondary Patron of Ireland

Brigid was born near Dundalk about the middle of the fifth century. She became a nun and founded a monastery in Kildare (for both men and women) and became known for her love of justice, for her compassion for the poor, and for the many miracles she worked. She was the spiritual mother of Irish nuns for many centuries and is often referred to as 'Mary of the Gael' (Mary of the Irish). She died about the year 525.

February 2: Feast of the Presentation of the Lord (Candlemas Day)

On this day we call to mind the presentation of the child Jesus in the Temple by his parents in keeping with the Law of Moses. This event is recorded in today's the gospel. Today is also the formal end of the Christmas festival of light and the memorial of Christ's birth. Today, candles are blessed and carried in procession as a sign of our welcoming Christ the Light into our lives. It is also a special day in the Church's calendar when the Church prays for Consecrated Life – a life which is consecrated to God through prayer and service and which enriches and gladdens the Christian community. We also pray to God to help people to hear and answer his call and so consecrate themselves to the Lord.

February 3: Memorial of St Blaise, Bishop & Martyr (Optional)

Very little about Blaise is known with great certainty though it would appear that he had been a bishop in Armenia and was martyred about the year 316. Throats are blessed because it is told that he saved the life of a boy in whose throat a fishbone had lodged. The blessing of throats today is a reminder to us of the Lord's desire for us to be well and to remove suffering from our lives.

February 5: Memorial of St Agatha, Virgin & Martyr

The cult and veneration of Agatha goes back to earliest times though nothing is known of her life other than the fact that she was martyred in Sicily. She is among those named in the Roman Canon of the Mass (Eucharistic Prayer I).

February 6: Memorial of Sts Paul Miki & Companions, Martyrs

Paul was born in Japan between 1564 and 1566 and joined the Jesuits in 1580. Along with twenty-five other Christians – both religious and lay, Franciscans and Jesuits – he was tortured and martyred at Nagasaki in 1597.

February 10: Memorial of St Scholastica, Virgin

Scholastica was born in Umbria in the late fifth century and was the sister of St Benedict. She became a nun and eventually was prioress of her monastery near Monte Cassino which she ran under the direction and guidance of her brother. She died in 543 or 547.

February 11: Memorial of Our Lady of Lourdes (Optional)

In 1858, fourteen year old Bernadette Soubirous received a vision from Our Lady near the mountain village of Lourdes, in southern France. Initially, people refused to believe her but the apparitions continued. When Bernadette asked the Lady who she was she replied that she was the Immaculate Conception. In time the well and site of the apparition became a centre of prayer as people flocked to it to draw closer to Our Lady and in the hope of receiving a cure. Several miracles have taken place here. In recognition of this, Pope John Paul II named this particular day 'World Day of the Sick' in 1992. On this day, special liturgies may be celebrated which include the Sacrament of the Anointing of the Sick.

February 14: Feast of St Cyril, Monk & St Methodius, Bishop, Patrons of Europe

These two brothers were born about the year 825 in Salonika, were educated at Constantinople, and are regarded as the apostles of the southern Slavs to whom they preached the Gospel. In 863 they were sent as missionaries to Moravia. In 869 Cyril died in Rome but his brother was consecrated bishop and went back to Moravia and Pannonia (Hungary) with permission to use the Slavonic language in the liturgy. The Slavonic translation of the Bible is attributed to them. He was opposed by the German bishops and was for a time imprisoned. Methodius died in 885.

February 21: Memorial of St Peter Damian, Bishop & Doctor of the Church

Peter Damian was born in 1007 in Ravenna. Being unwanted as a child he was poorly treated but still managed to gain an education thanks to his brother who was archpriest of Ravenna. He became a monk in 1035 and was soon appointed abbot of Fonte

Avellana and later Cardinal-bishop of Ostia where he worked tirelessly for the Church and against clerical abuses such as simony and incontinence. He died in 1072 and was declared a Doctor of the Church in 1828.

February 22: The Feast of the Chair of St Peter

This feast has been observed in Rome since the fourth century. It celebrates the unity of the Church under the papacy and the readings recall Christ's choice of Peter as the rock on which he would build the Church.

February 23: Memorial of St Polycarp, Bishop & Martyr

Polycarp, Bishop of Smyrna, was a disciple of John the Evangelist and is regarded as one of the greatest of the Apostolic Fathers. He wrote a number of letters similar to St Paul and these were read publicly for many years. He was martyred at the request of the people by being burnt at the stake probably in 155.

March 1: Memorial of St David

David is the patron saint of Wales. He founded the monastery of Menevia (Mynyw) in the far west of South Wales and was bishop of those parts. His monks followed a very austere rule which brought David into conflict with other Christian leaders. David lived in the sixth century.

March 7: Memorial of Sts Perpetua & Felicity, Martyrs

Perpetua was a young married woman and Felicity was a slave when they were arrested in Carthage in 203 AD during the persecutions of Septimus Severus. Along with four men – Saturus, Saturninus, Revocatus and Secundulus – they were thrown to the beasts and thus martyred – those who did not die were killed by the sword. Their 'stories' are amongst the greatest writings of the martyrs and were written by two of the martyrs themselves. Perpetua and Felicity are named in the Roman Canon (Eucharistic Prayer I).

March 17: Solemnity of St Patrick, Patron of Ireland

Patrick was born between 385 and 389 in Roman Britain, probably Wales. About the year 403 he was taken as a slave to Ireland by pirates who used to raid the Welsh coast, and he remained there for six years before escaping back to Britain. However, he could hear the call of the Irish people to return to them so he studied and became a priest. He was consecrated bishop by St Germanus at Auxerre before returning to Ireland as a missionary and Bishop of Ireland in succession to St Palladius about 432AD. He travelled the country preaching the Gospel of Christ and baptising the people and established what was to become the primatial church of Ireland at Armagh in 444. He is said to have died at Saul in northeast Ireland about 461 and his remains are, according to tradition, buried at Downpatrick with St Brigid and St Columba (Colmcille).

March 19: Solemnity of St Joseph, Husband of the Blessed Virgin Mary, Protector of the Child Jesus

Little is known about Joseph except that he was of the line of David which was essential in order for Jesus to be legally of the house and line of David in fulfilment of the Scriptures. What is more important for us is the example which Joseph left us. He was a man of faith who played his role in God's salvific plan for us; he was obedient to the will of God; he had a love for the Law and its fulfilment; he showed piety and fortitude in times of trial; he had a chaste love for the Blessed Virgin Mary and he exercised his paternal authority with due care. He is therefore a true example of Christian living and is the Protector of the Church. Joseph is also the patron of carpenters and manual workers.

March 25: Solemnity of the Annunciation of the Lord

Today is celebrated as a solemnity as it recalls the day when the Angel Gabriel appeared to Mary and told her that God had chosen her to play an important role in the plan of salvation – that of bearing the Christ-child. Key for us is Mary's acceptance of this task even though the whole episode must have terrified her.

April 7: Memorial of St John Baptist de la Salle, Priest
John was born in Rheims in 1651 and was ordained priest in 1678. His life was devoted to education, especially education of the poor. He favoured group teaching rather than the teaching of individuals and founded the Brothers of the Christian Schools. However, his ideas met with opposition throughout his life. He died in 1719 and is the patron saint of school teachers.

April 11: Memorial of St Stanislaus, Bishop & Martyr
Stanislaus was born in Szczepanow in 1030 and became bishop of Cracow in 1072. It is said that he was martyred in 1079 by Prince Boleslaus II, who is said to have been a cruel and evil man and for which Stanislaus had excommunicated him.

April 25: Feast of St Mark, the Evangelist
There is not a huge amount known about St Mark. It was thought that he was the young man referred to in Mark 14:51-52 who fled at the arrest of Jesus, though there is no proof. He was a companion of St Paul on his first missionary journey as noted by Paul in his writings. Later he joined St Peter, on whose teachings his gospel is based and which was written for Christians who were being persecuted in Rome to show them that Christ too suffered but never gave up. According to tradition, he founded the Church in Alexandria and was probably its bishop when he was martyred about the year 74. The symbol for St Mark is the winged lion.

April 29: Feast of St Catherine of Siena, Doctor of the Church & Patroness of Europe
Born in Siena in 1347, Catherine became a Dominican Tertiary and lived a life of charitable works. She became involved in politics and was instrumental in getting Pope Gregory XI to leave Avignon for Rome. She died in 1380 leaving behind more than 400 letters and a great mystical work, 'Dialogue'. She was declared a Doctor of the Church in 1970, and Patroness of Europe in the Jubilee Year, 2000.

May 1: Memorial of St Joseph the Worker
This commemoration was established by Pope Pius XII in 1955. St Joseph is the patron of working people.

May 2: Memorial of St Athanasius, Bishop & Doctor of the Church

Athanasius was born in 295 or 297 in Alexandria. He attended the Council of Nicaea as a deacon in 325 and impressed the Council Fathers with his defence of the divinity of Christ. He became Bishop of Alexandria in 328 and served as bishop for forty turbulent years. He fought against the heresies of the time and particularly that of Arius (that Jesus is not co-equal with the Father but created by him) and, as a result, was exiled from his diocese on five occasions for a total of seventeen years. Yet he never ceased to defend Christ and his Church. He died in the year 373. He is one of the four great Greek Doctors of the Universal Church.

May 3: Feast of Sts Philip & James the Apostles

Very little is known about St Philip beyond the few mentions of him in the gospels. According to tradition, he preached the Gospel at Phrygia and died at Hierapolis, where he may have been martyred. Philip was originally a disciple of John the Baptist. The St James we celebrate today is the son of Alphaeus, also known as James the Less (that is, the Younger). He was the first Bishop of Jerusalem and the author of the epistle in the Bible which bears his name. He was martyred in 62AD either by stoning or by being thrown from the top of the Temple.

May 14: Feast of St Matthias the Apostle

Very little is known about St Matthias except that he is the one who was chosen by the Eleven to take the place of Judas Iscariot. He appears to have spent time working in Judaea before going east to Cappadocia. He is believed to have been martyred at Colchis and his relics later brought to Rome by St Helena.

May 26: Memorial of St Philip Neri, Priest

Philip was born in 1515 in Florence and spent most of his life in Rome. He became known as 'the second apostle of Rome' because of his untiring work for all those in the city whether they be Pope or servant boy. After his ordination (1551) he founded the Congregation of the Oratory and was particularly well known for his ministry in the confessional. He died in 1595.

May 31: Feast of the Visitation of the Blessed Virgin

This feast celebrates the visitation of Mary to her cousin, Elizabeth. She had been told at the Annunciation that Elizabeth was also to give birth and Mary goes to be with her.

June 1: Memorial of St Justin, Martyr

Born to pagan parents in Nablus, Palestine, Justin became a Christian when he was about 30 years old. He was a well known philosopher and was known as 'the Philosopher'. He wrote many works in defence of the faith and some of these – the 'Apologies' and the 'Dialogue with Trypho' – survive today. He also wrote our earliest account of baptism and of the Sunday Mass. He was martyred in Rome in 165, during the reign of Marcus Aurelius, by being beheaded along with five men and a woman.

June 3: Memorial of St Kevin, Abbot

Kevin (Coemgenus) was one of the great sixth-century Irish saints. He grew up in Kilnamanagh and later went to Glendalough to become a hermit and settled in Disert Caoimhghin, by the upper lake. In time, several other hermits joined him and soon the great monastic settlement of Glendalough grew up by the lakes and continued to spread after his death in 618.

June 4: Memorial of St Charles Lwanga & Companions, Martyrs

Charles Lwanga was in charge of the servant boys of King Mwanga of Buganda (Uganda). The king opposed both Christians and Muslims which led to an attempt by the British to remove him from power. During one persecution the king ordered his Christian servants to be executed. Some of the boys were quite young and only preparing for baptism at the time but, despite the pleas of their families to obey the orders of the king, they remained faithful to Christ. They were martyred by being burned to death at Namugongo in 1886 and canonized in 1964.

June 5: Memorial of St Boniface, Bishop & Martyr

Known as the 'Apostle of Germany,' Boniface was born in Devon, England, about the year 680 and christened Winifrid. He became a monk and left England in 716 to preach the Gospel in Germany. He was given the name Boniface by Pope Gregory II. He travelled throughout Germany and established monasteries and dioceses before carrying out an ecclesiastical reform in Gaul. He was consecrated bishop in 722 and was later Primate of Germany. In his seventies, he retired as bishop and travelled about the country again. He was martyred for the faith in Friesland in 754.

June 9: Feast of St Columba (Colum Cille), Abbot & Missionary, Secondary Patron of Ireland

Columba was born about the year 521 in Co Donegal of royal stock and having completed his studies spent 15 years founding churches and preaching in Ireland. In 561 – for reasons still not clear – he left Ireland for Scotland and arrived on the island of Iona with twelve companions. He preached the Gospel far and wide while returning to Ireland occasionally. His monastic rule had a great influence on Western monasticism. He died in 597.

June 11: Memorial of St Barnabas, Apostle

Little is known about Barnabas but, like St Paul, he is always counted as an apostle because he was divinely called to spread the Gospel with Paul. He is the one who was sent to Paul to 'bring him into Christianity' after Paul's vision on the road to Damascus, and is the one in Acts 4 who sold his land and gave the money to the common fund. He also attended the first council of the Church in Jerusalem with Paul. He is said to have been martyred in Cyprus.

June 13: Memorial of St Anthony of Padua, Priest & Doctor of the Church

Anthony was born in Lisbon, Portugal, in 1195. He first joined the Augustinian canons regular but later left to become a Friar Minor of St Francis and preached in Italy and France. He was known to his contemporaries as 'The Hammer of Heretics' for his dedicated preaching of the true faith. He has a reputation for retrieving lost objects of careless people. According to a story he received a vision of the Child Jesus and this is why statues of Anthony show him holding the Child Jesus. He died in 1231, was canonized a year later in 1232, and was declared a Doctor of the Church in 1947.

June 20: Memorial of the Irish Martyrs
Between 1579 and 1654, seventeen Irish people were put to death for the Catholic Faith during the persecutions in Ireland. Of the eleven clergy: nine belonged to religious Orders, four were bishops (three Religious), four were priests (one secular). Of the six lay people: one was a woman (Margaret Ball), three were sailors, and one – Francis Taylor – was Lord Mayor of Dublin. These seventeen were canonized in 1992.

June 21: Memorial of St Aloysius Gonzaga, Religious
The patron saint of Youth, Luigi Gonzaga was born in Castiglione in northern Italy in 1568. Born into high society he refused to allow corruption and worldliness take hold of his life, preferring instead to become a Jesuit. He joined the Society of Jesus in Rome in 1685 but after six years of tending to the sick he too became ill – probably with the plague – and died in 1591.

June 24: Solemnity of the Birth of John the Baptist
John was a cousin of Jesus and was just a few months older than him. In the gospel, John is the fore-runner to Christ and is known as 'the Baptist' because he was the one who began baptising with water for the forgiveness of sins. He suffered martyrdom by beheading because of a promise foolishly made by King Herod.

June 28: Memorial of St Irenaeus of Lyons, Bishop & Martyr
Irenaeus was born about the year 125 in Asia Minor and was a pupil of Justin Martyr and was influenced by St Polycarp. He came to Gaul as a missionary and was later made Bishop of Lyons. He is counted as one of the Fathers of the Church because of his writings and is celebrated in both the Eastern and Western Churches. He died sometime around the year 203, possibly by being martyred for the faith.

June 29: Solemnity of Sts Peter & Paul the Apostles
Today's feast celebrates the two founders of the Church in the city of Rome and has been observed in Rome since the fourth century. This date was traditionally considered the foundation day of the city of Rome by Romulus and Remus.

July 1:   Memorial of St Oliver Plunkett, Bishop & Martyr
Oliver was born in Meath in 1625 and ordained priest in Rome in 1654. Soon after he was made professor at the Propaganda Fide College and in 1669 was created Archbishop of Armagh and Primate of All Ireland. It was a difficult time for the Church in Ireland and even though he was on very good terms with the Protestant bishops, he was forced into hiding in 1673. Following his betrayal he was arrested and imprisoned in Dublin Castle. His trial in Dublin collapsed due to lack of evidence and he was sent to London where a grand jury said there was nothing to answer for. Following a third (fixed) trial he was sentenced to death. He was hung, drawn and quartered in 1681, the last Roman Catholic to be martyred at Tyburn, London. He was canonized in 1975.

July 3:   Feast of St Thomas the Apostle
Very little is known about Thomas other than what is found in the gospels. Also known as Didymus (The Twin) his questioning of Christ's teaching and his disbelief in the resurrection show that even the closest followers of Christ had doubts and that, even in doubting, the Lord is there to give strength and guidance. Tradition holds that he brought the faith to Southern India where he is said to have died. He is the patron saint of architects, builders and India.

July 11: Feast of St Benedict, Abbot & Patron of Europe
Benedict was born in central Italy in 480. He was sent to Rome to study but left the city for the life of a hermit in Subiaco, not far from Rome, about the year 500. So many gathered around him that he founded twelve communities of monks, but in time left them because of their lack of discipline. He moved to Monte Cassino and established the famous monastery there on the site of a pagan temple to Apollo. He wrote a Rule for the monks

which has become the foundation of spirituality and monastic life though it is not believed that he intended starting a religious order. He is the spiritual head of monks in the Western Church as St Basil is spiritual head of those in the Eastern Church. He died while at prayer in March 547 and was made Patron of Europe by Paul VI in 1964.

July 15: Memorial of St Bonaventure, Bishop & Doctor of the Church

Giovanni di Fidanza was born between 1218 and 1221 in Tuscany, Italy. He joined the Order of Friars Minor and rose through the ranks becoming the Order's seventh Minister General in 1257, devoting much time to the unity of the Order. He was approached with a view to making him Archbishop of York in northern England, but this he refused. Eventually he was made bishop of Albano, Rome, and a cardinal in 1273. One of the key mystical theologians and scholars of his time he attended the Council of Lyons in 1274 at which he died. One of his tasks at this council was the re-unification of the Latin and the Orthodox Churches which seemed to begin well but failed soon after his death. He was declared a Doctor of the Church in 1588.

July 22: Memorial of St Mary Magdalene

Mary of Magdala was one of the followers of Christ who is mentioned in all four gospels. She stood by the cross of Christ as he was dying and she was the first to see the risen Lord. Because she was the one who told the apostles that the Lord had risen, she is often referred to as 'the apostle to the Apostles.'

July 23: Feast of St Bridget of Sweden, Patroness of Europe

Bridget was born between 1302 and 1304 in Sweden and in 1316 was married to Ulf Gudmarsson and together they had eight children. She became the chief lady-in-waiting at the royal court of King Magnus II in 1335, possibly due to her father's post as a provincial governor. She was widowed in 1344 and from then on devoted her life to the poor and destitute. She travelled to Rome for the Jubilee Year in 1350 and spent the rest of her life there. She also established the Bridgettines though it never received official approval in her lifetime. She died in Rome in 1373 and her remains were returned to her native Sweden, to the Bridgettine monastery she had founded. Catherine – her fourth child – followed her mother and dedicated her life to the poor and to the strengthening of the Bridgettines. She too was widowed at a young age and she too was canonized.

July 25: Feast of St James the Apostle

Also known as James the Greater, he was the brother of St John the Apostle and Evangelist. Not much is known about him other than what is to be found in the gospels where he has a special place among the Twelve with Peter and John. In Spain it is believed that he preached the Gospel in the Iberian Peninsula and that his relics were buried at Santiago de Compostela, but this is not maintained outside of Spain. He was the first of the apostles to die having been martyred by Herod Agrippa between 42 and 44 AD.

July 26: Memorial of Sts Joachim & Anne, Parents of Our Lady

These are the names traditionally given to the parents of Our Lady, though nothing is known about them. Anne is the Patron Saint of Canada, women in labour, miners, cabinet-makers and home-makers.

July 29: Memorial of St Martha

Little is known about Martha other than what is recounted in the gospels. She was the sister of Lazarus and Mary, and a friend of the Lord. She is the sister who frets over the guests while her sister sits and listens to Jesus. She is also the one who addresses Jesus when he arrives following the death of her brother, Lazarus, and who makes her declaration of faith ('I believe you are the Christ, the Son of God, the one who was to come into this world').

July 31: Memorial of St Ignatius of Loyola, Priest

Born in 1491 in Loyola of noble stock, Ignatius became a soldier. Having been wounded in battle against the French, Ignatius began reading sacred texts while he was recovering from his injuries and then went on pilgrimage to the Holy Land. He became a priest and began founding the Society of Jesus (the

Jesuits) in 1534 and whose members are ready to serve the Church wherever needed. He died in 1556.

August 1: Memorial of St Alphonsus Liguori, Bishop & Doctor of the Church

Born near Naples in 1696, Alphonsus became a lawyer before becoming a priest, being ordained in 1726. He created the Redemptoristines in 1730 and founded the Redemptorists (Congregation of the Most Holy Redeemer – C.Ss.R) in 1732 to work among the country peasants. By the time of his death in 1787 however, the Redemptorists were in a terrible state though he was no longer at its helm to help heal the rifts. From 1762 to 1775 he was bishop of the small diocese of Sant'Agata dei Goti.

August 4: Memorial of St John Mary Vianney, Priest

Vianney, commonly known as the Curé d'Ars, was born in Dardilly, France in 1786. Due to his educational difficulties he was almost refused ordination but was ordained priest in 1815, being appointed curate in the town of Ars near Lyons in 1818, where he was to minister for the rest of his life. Nothing in life mattered to him except matters spiritual so that his clothes were falling apart, his food was insufficient and he hardly slept, but he still attracted thousands to his little church where many benefited from his hidden knowledge and his gifts of healing. It is said that over 1,000 people a week came to him in the twelve months before he died in 1859. He was canonized in 1925 and named patron saint of parish clergy four years later.

August 6: Feast of the Transfiguration of the Lord

This feast commemorates the day when Jesus, in the company of Peter, James and John, was transformed before their eyes on a mountain top. It reminds us of the various occasions in the Old Testament when people, such as Moses, met with God on mountains and spoke with him there. In the Transfiguration, God is heard to speak from heaven which re-enforces who Jesus Christ is for the Apostles who were with him.

August 8: Memorial of St Dominic, Priest

Born in Spain about the year 1170, Dominic first became an

Augustinian canon regular. Throughout this time the Albigensian heresy was prevalent across southern France due to a lack of proper teaching and preaching. As a result, Dominic founded the Friars Preachers (Order of Preachers – O.P.), more commonly known as the Dominicans, for the purpose of preaching the true faith and in particular to combat Albigensianism. He died in 1221.

August 9: Feast of St Teresa Benedicta of the Cross (Edith Stein), Martyr & Patroness of Europe

Edith Stein was born on October 12, 1891, the eleventh child of a Jewish family living in Breslau in what was then Germany (today Poland). She studied and became a lecturer of philosophy and knew many of the leading philosophers of her day including Edmund Husserl (for whom she was an assistant) and Martin Heidegger. She became a Catholic in 1922 having been moved by the life of St Teresa of Avila. Eleven years later she entered the Carmel at Cologne and took the name Teresa Benedicta of the Cross. During the Nazi persecution she moved to the Carmel in Echt, Holland, to ease things for the Carmel in Cologne but was arrested there and sent to Auschwitz. There she was gassed on August 9, 1942, offering up her holocaust for the people of Israel. Her writings are noted for their doctrinal richness and spirituality including 'The Hidden Life' and 'The Science of the Cross.' She was beatified by Pope John Paul II at Cologne on May 1, 1987, and canonized at Rome twelve years later. She was also named Co-Patroness of Europe.

August 10: Feast of St Laurence the Deacon, Martyr

Laurence was one of the seven deacons in Rome under Pope St Sixtus II. Three days after Sixtus was martyred in 258, Laurence was himself martyred by being roasted alive on a grid-iron. He is remembered in the Roman Canon of the Mass (Eucharistic Prayer I).

August 11: Memorial of St Clare, Virgin & Religious

Clare was born in Assisi 1193 and left home at the age of 18 to join St Francis of Assisi. Influenced by his ideas she established the first convent of Franciscan nuns, today known as the Poor

Clares, at San Damiano, and spent the rest of her life in that convent. She died in 1253 and was canonized two years later.

August 14: Memorial of St Maximilian Kolbe, Priest & Martyr

Maximilian was born near Lodz, in Poland in 1894 (then part of Russia). He became a Franciscan in 1910 and both his parents also entered religious orders. He also founded a community in Japan in 1930 and returned to Europe in 1936. With the Nazi invasion of Poland in 1939 he and his community gave shelter to Poles and Jews who were being rounded up by the Nazi regime. For this he was imprisoned in the Auschwitz Concentration Camp where he ministered to his fellow prisoners. In reprisal for an escape by some prisoners, the camp authorities took ten men to be starved to death, one of which came from Maximilian's bunker. Maximilian volunteered to take the man's place and so was deprived of food for two weeks. He was eventually put to death by lethal injection on August 14, 1941. He was canonized by his fellow countryman, Pope John Paul II, in 1982. Among those at the canonization was the man whose life he had saved by his heroic act in 1941.

August 15: Solemnity of the Assumption of Our Blessed Lady into Heaven

This solemnity celebrates the fact that at the end of Mary's life, her body was assumed into heaven rather than undergo decay in the earth. Though maintained by the faithful for centuries, it was only proclaimed a dogma of the faith by Pope Pius XII in 1950.

August 20: Memorial of St Bernard, Abbot & Doctor of the Church

Bernard was born near Dijon in France in 1090. In 1112 he joined the Cistercian monastery of Cîteaux along with thirty other young men. Soon after he established the monastery of Clairvaux and was its first abbot. He worked tirelessly for the unity of the Church and against heresies and was not afraid to dispute with princes or to give advice to popes. He took part in Oecumenical and other councils, travelled extensively to preach the faith and established 68 other Cistercian monasteries. He died in 1153 and was canonized twenty-one years later.

August 21: Memorial of Pope St Pius X

Giuseppe Sarto was born in 1835 and was ordained priest in 1858. He was made Bishop of Mantua in 1884 and eight years later was created Cardinal Patriarch of Venice. In 1903 he was elected Pope. During his pontificate he urged daily communion and facilitated the communion of children and the sick. He encouraged Bible reading and tackled Modernism. He died two weeks after the outbreak of World War I in 1914 and was canonized forty years later.

August 22: Memorial of the Queenship of Mary

This memorial celebrates the crowning of Mary as Queen of Heaven following the Solemnity of the Assumption seven days ago.

August 24: Feast of St Bartholomew the Apostle

Very little is known about Bartholomew apart from his being listed among the Twelve in the Synoptic gospels. Many scholars identify him as the Nathanael who came to visit Jesus under the cover of darkness in the first chapter of St John's gospel. Tradition holds that he preached the faith in India, though there is no evidence of this.

August 27: Memorial of St Monica

Born in North Africa to a Christian family in 332, Monica married a pagan, Patricius, who was converted due to her gentle ways. She then spent her energies in converting her eldest son – Augustine – to the faith. She followed him to Milan where she enlisted the help of St Ambrose, then Bishop of Milan, and in time Augustine was converted and became one of the greatest teachers in the Church. She died in Ostia in 387 while Augustine was taking her home to North Africa. Her last words, recorded in Augustine's 'Confessions' were – 'Lay this body wherever it may be. Let no care of it disturb you: this only I ask of you that you should remember me at the altar of the Lord wherever you may be' (Confessions Book 9, Chapter 11).

August 28: Memorial of St Augustine, Bishop & Doctor of the Church

Augustine was born in Thagaste in North Africa in 354, one of four children of St Monica. He studied law and spent several years of his life following the ways of Manichaeism and fathered a child with his mistress. He was converted through the prayers of his mother, St Monica, with the help of St Ambrose, Bishop of Milan, who baptised him in 387. He returned to Africa and was made Bishop of Hippo in 396 where he established communities of priests and nuns. His Rule for religious institutes is the basis for many Congregations and Institutes of Apostolic Life today. He became the greatest of the Latin Fathers of the Church and spent much of his energies fighting heresies. His two best known works are 'The Confessions' and 'De Civitate Dei' ('City of God') which are still influential today. He died in 430.

August 29: Memorial of the Beheading of St John the Baptist

As the name of this memorial suggests, today recalls the martyrdom of St John the Baptist, his last and greatest act of witness for Christ.

September 3: Memorial of St Gregory the Great, Pope & Doctor of the Church

Gregory was born about the year 540 to St Sylvia and her patrician husband who was a Roman senator. He first became a monk and was later appointed papal legate to Constantinople. He was elected pope in 590 – the first monk elected to this office. He was tireless in his defence of the primacy of Rome and in his encouragement of monasticism and the spread of Christianity. Much of his work still has an effect on the Church today in terms of the liturgy and the discipline of the clergy which he enforced. He is the fourth of the Doctors of the Western Church. He died in 604.

September 8: Memorial of the Birthday of the Blessed Virgin Mary

Though we do not know the year or the day when our Blessed Lady was born, we keep this memorial in her honour.

September 9: Memorial of St Ciaran of Clonmacnois, Abbot

Ciaran (Kieran) was born in Connacht and went to the monastic school at Clonard before spending some time on Inishmore with St Enda. Following a vision he left the western isles and travelled across Ireland to Clonmacnois where he founded one of the most famous monasteries in the country and where he was noted for his virtues and miracles. He died between 549 and 556.

September 13: Memorial St John Chrysostom, Bishop & Doctor of the Church

Born about the year 347-349 in Antioch, John was ordained in 386. His gifts of speech and eloquence gave rise to the name 'Chrysostom' – 'Golden Mouth'. He was made archbishop of Constantinople in 398 and was one of the greatest of the four Greek Doctors of the Church and one of the Three Holy Hierarchs along with Basil the Great and Gregory Nazianzen. He worked tirelessly for the spread of the faith and its defence against heresies. His courage brought him many enemies and he was banished from Constantinople by civil decree on a number of occasions, which the Western Church tried to resolve but in vain. He died in 407 during one such banishment.

September 14: Feast of the Triumph of the Cross

St Helena was, for a time, wife of Emperor Constantius and was the mother of Emperor Constantine I – the first emperor to become a Christian. With her son's approval she travelled to the Holy Land in search of the sacred places and relics associated with our Lord. Among the relics she discovered was the True Cross which she is said to have discovered on this day in 320 and in 335 had churches dedicated on Calvary and the True Cross venerated there. This annual feast is a chance for us – outside of the Easter Season – to reflect on the significance of the cross in our lives and of the redemption which Christ won for us by his death and resurrection.

September 15: Memorial of Our Lady of Sorrows.

Today's memorial recalls in a particular way the sorrows which Our Lady underwent as the mother of Christ.

September 16: Memorial of St Cornelius, Pope, & St Cyprian, Bishop, Martyrs

Cornelius was elected pope in 251 and was martyred two years later under the persecutions of Emperor Gallus. During the persecutions under the Roman emperors many Christians left the faith to save their lives eventually returning to the faith before they died or when the persecutions eased. Cornelius and Novatian clashed over this with Novatian saying they should not be re-admitted and Cornelius being more pastorally sensitive and forgiving. Part of this clash saw Novatian have himself elected as pope in opposition to Cornelius (Novatian was anti-pope from 251 to 258). Caecilius Cyprianus was born in North Africa at the start of the third century and became a lawyer before converting to Christianity and became a bishop in 249. He is remembered with Cornelius because he supported Cornelius in the struggle against Noviatian and was beheaded on the 14th of September, 258 on the instruction of Emperor Valerian. Both of these men are named in the Roman Canon of the Mass (Eucharistic Prayer I).

September 20: Memorial of St Andrew Kim Taegon, Priest & Martyr, St Paul Chong, Martyr & Companions

Andrew and his Companions are known as the Korean Martyrs for they were martyred in that country. Andrew was born in 1821 and ordained in 1845, just one year before he became the first Korean priest to be put to death for the faith. In all it is thought that up to 10,000 Koreans were martyred for the faith between 1791-1867, many of whom were lay-people. Pope John Paul II canonized a representative 103 martyrs in Seoul Cathedral on May 6, 1984.

September 21: Feast of St Matthew the Apostle

Very little is known about Matthew other than the fact that he was a tax-collector and wrote one of the Synoptic Gospels, which he wrote in Hebrew. Accounts of his martyrdom are unconfirmed.

September 23: Memorial of St Pius of Pietrelcina (Padre Pio), Priest

Francesco Forgione was born in southern Italy in 1887. He joined the Capuchin Friars and was ordained priest in 1910. He suffered from ill-health and was thought to have tuberculosis at one stage. While praying before a cross he received the visible stigmata on September 20, 1918. His fame spread far and wide after the end of the Second World War and crowds flocked to hear and see him. Many miracles have been attributed to him and he was a gifted confessor. He founded a hospital in 1956. He died on September 23, 1968, and was canonized in 2002.

September 27: Memorial of St Vincent de Paul, Priest

Vincent was born in France in 1581. He became a priest in 1600 and, on a visit to Paris, he met with Fr Bérulle and Mme de Gondi who changed his heart forever. He then became totally immersed in the plight of the poor and destitute. In 1625 he founded the Congregation of the Missions (the Vincentians) and, in 1633, the Daughters of Charity of St Vincent de Paul to carry on his work. He died in 1660 and is the patron saint of all charitable societies and in particular the society which bears his name.

September 29: Feast of Sts Michael, Gabriel & Raphael, the Archangels

Michael is traditionally regarded as the chief of the Archangels and a special protector against the attacks of Satan. Gabriel is the special messenger of the Lord who visited Mary at the Annunciation. Raphael is known as 'The Healer of the Lord' because he brought healing to people as found in the Book of Tobias and St John's gospel.

September 30: Memorial of St Jerome, Priest & Doctor of the Church

Eusebius Hieronymus Sophronius was born in Dalmatia between 340 and 347. He is regarded as the most learned Father of the Church in matters concerning the Bible. In 385 he retired to Bethlehem where he continued his great work of translating the Bible into Latin and also wrote several Biblical commentaries.

He could be quick to temper but also very quick to remorse. He referred to those who sought to amend the Bible as 'presumptuous blockheads'. In his Prologue to his commentaries on the Prophet Isaiah he wrote that 'Ignorance of the scriptures is ignorance of Christ.' For his services for Pope St Damasus he is depicted as a cardinal though he was never elevated to the College of Cardinals. He died in 420 in Bethlehem. Jerome is the patron of librarians.

October 1: Memorial of St Thérèse of Lisieux, Virgin & Doctor of the Church

Thérèse Martin was born in Alençon in France in 1873 and is popularly known as 'The Little Flower.' Whilst still young, and despite opposition, she entered the Discalced Carmel of Lisieux at the age of 15. By word and example she taught the novices virtues of humility. Following a difficult illness she died on September 30, 1897, and was canonized in 1925 with successive popes referring to her as 'the greatest saint of modern times.' She became famous for her 'Little Way' which is found in her remaining letters and her biography. She was declared a Doctor of the Church by Pope John Paul II in 1999. She is co-patroness of the Missions and secondary patron of France.

October 2: Memorial of the Guardian Angels

It is our belief that each of us has a guardian angel from birth who is there to help us in all things. It is also the belief that homes, cities and states also have guardian angels. A Votive Mass to the guardian angels has been in practise since the ninth century and, in 1670, Pope Clement X made October 2 an obligatory commemoration.

October 4: Memorial of St Francis of Assisi, Deacon

Francis was born in Assisi in 1181. After a pleasure-filled youth he left home and founded the Order of Friars Minor in 1209. Ten years later he went east to convert the Muslims but was unsuccessful either with the Crusaders or the Muslims. In 1224 he received the stigmata, the first recorded incident of the stigmata in history. With St Clare he established the Franciscan nuns in 1212. He died a deacon in 1226 and was canonized just two years later.

October 7: Memorial Our Lady of the Rosary

This memorial has been observed since 1571 when the Christians gained victory over the Turks through the intercession of Our Lady at the naval Battle of Lepanto.

October 15: Memorial of St Teresa of Avila, Virgin & Doctor of the Church

Teresa Sánchez de Cepeda y Ahumada was born in Avila in Spain in 1515. She entered the Carmelites and made great progress in the way of perfection and was granted mystical revelations. At this time religious life in Spain, and across Europe, was in need of reform and Teresa began this work with the monastery in which she was living. She also founded other monasteries under her strict reform and enlisted St John of the Cross to reform the male branch of the Order of Carmelites. After her death the reform she began eventually separated from the Carmelite Order to become the Order of Discalced Carmelites. She wrote a number of books which brought her to the attention of the Inquisition but which she persevered in writing and which show a profound insight into prayer. For Teresa, prayer was a conversation with a close friend and this can be seen in her many references to Christ. Her letters also show a tremendous humanity while gently bringing people back into line. Her best known works are 'The Way of Perfection' and 'The Interior Castle.' She died at Alba in 1582 and was canonized in 1622. Her writings have earned her the title of Doctor of the Church.

October 17: Memorial of St Ignatius of Antioch, Bishop & Martyr

Not very much is known about Ignatius except that in old age he was sent to Rome to be martyred with other Christians. On the long journey to Rome he wrote several letters to various Churches as did St Paul, and these letters are among the most important documents of the ancient Church. He died in 107 when he was thrown to the lions.

October 18: Feast of St Luke the Evangelist

Luke was from Antioch and was a physician when he met St Paul and joined him on his travels. He wrote the Acts of the Apostles and the gospel which bears his name but beyond that nothing is known of his life.

October 28: Feast of Sts Simon & Jude, the Apostles

Very little is actually known about these two apostles. Simon, known as 'the Zealous', is named in the list of the Twelve. Jude (Thaddeus) is believed to be the brother of James the Less and also the author of the epistle which bears his name. Tradition holds that Simon and Jude were martyred together in Persia but there is no proof for this.

November 1: Solemnity of All Saints

Today we celebrate not only the publicly canonised saints but also all those who have reached eternal life with the Lord, including our deceased relatives and friends who have died and are counted among the Communion of Saints.

November 2: Solemn Commemoration of All the Faithful Departed

Today we remember all the members of the Church who have died in Christ. While we remember them at their funerals and anniversaries we also remember them in a very special way on this day and pray for their eternal happiness. On this day, each priest has the privilege of celebrating three Masses.

November 3: Memorial of St Malachy, Bishop

Malachy O'More was born in 1095 at Armagh. He was known for his zeal and vigour and was Abbot of Bangor, Bishop of Connor and then Archbishop of Armagh and Primate of All Ireland. When the Irish Church was reorganised in 1139 he resigned and went on pilgrimage to Rome. On the way he stayed at Clairvaux where he became friends with St Bernard and arranged for the Cistercians to come to Ireland where they established their first monastery at Mellifont. On his second journey to Rome he again stayed at Clairvaux where he died in St Bernard's arms in 1148. He was the first Irish saint to be formally canonized.

November 4: Memorial of St Charles Borromeo, Bishop

Charles was born in 1538 to a privileged background – his mother was a Medici. Though he was ordained a priest in 1563 he had been made a cardinal three years earlier by his uncle, Pope Pius IV. He was responsible in part for reassembling the Council of Trent but his greatest achievement was in sorting out his own diocese and improving the liturgy there. He was also the first to begin what are known as 'Sunday Schools.' He was selfless during the plague and was one of the greatest churchmen of the Counter-Reformation. He died in 1584 and was canonized in 1610.

November 6: Feast of All the Saints of Ireland

On November 1st we celebrated the Feast of All Saints. Today we remember in a particular way all those Irish men and women who make up part of the Communion of Saints.

November 9: Feast of the Dedication of the Lateran Basilica

The Church commonly known as the Basilica of St John Lateran is actually dedicated to the Most Holy Saviour and St John the Baptist and St John the Evangelist and was first dedicated in 324AD. It derives its importance from the fact that it is the 'Most Holy Lateran Church, of all the churches in the city and the world, the mother and head' (Sacrosancta Lateranensis ecclesia omnium urbis et orbis ecclesiarum mater et caput – from an inscription on the front wall of the church). This basilica is also the Cathedral Church of the Bishop of Rome and Primate of Italy – the Pope (St Peter's in the Vatican is a basilica but not a Cathedral Church). In celebrating its dedication we celebrate the dedication of our own local churches also for they are all joined together.

November 10: Memorial of Pope St Leo the Great

Leo I was elected pope in 440 at a time when there were several heresies regarding the person of Jesus Christ prevalent in the Church. Nestorianism held that the two natures of Christ – the human and divine – were two completely separate persons while Monophysitism held that Jesus only had one nature as the human nature was replaced by his divine nature. Leo fought against these two maintaining that the human and divine natures of Christ are both present and inseparable. This he laid out in his 'Dogmatic Letter' to Flavian of Constantinople and which became a key discussion at the Council of Chalcedon in 451. Leo prevailed and his teaching is part of our faith to this day. At a time when civil order was breaking down in the Roman Empire he gave the Church an important role in civil and political society when he negotiated with Attila the Hun and Genseric the Vandal. He died in 461.

November 11: Memorial of St Martin of Tours, Bishop

Martin was born about the year 335 to a Roman officer and was himself drafted into the army. However, he believed that Christians should not take part in war and he refused to take part. He was a disciple of St Hilary of Poitiers and founded a community of hermit-monks which later became a Benedictine monastery. Reluctantly he was elected Bishop of Tours in 371, though he continued his monastic lifestyle as much as possible. He brought monasticism to Gaul and had a considerable influence on the Celtic churches. He died in 397.

November 12: Memorial of St Josaphat, Bishop & Martyr

Josaphat was born about the year 1580 in Vladimir in the Ukraine. He became a Byzantine Rite monk and later abbot of Vilna at a time when the Orthodox Dioceses in Kiev were united with the Holy See and to this union he devoted his life. In 1617 he was made Archbishop of Polotsk where he touched the lives of many people through his gentleness and wisdom. For his efforts to bring about union with Rome he was murdered by a mob in White Russia in 1623.

November 17: Memorial of St Elizabeth of Hungary, Religious

Princess Elizabeth, daughter of King Andreas II of Hungary and niece of St Hedwig, was born in Bratislava (in modern-day Slovakia) in 1207. At the age of fourteen she married Louis IV, Landgrave of Thuringia (Blessed Louis of Thuringia) and they had three children. Six years later, in 1227, her world was shattered when Louis died in a crusade. Eventually she gave up her finery and became a Third Order Franciscan and devoted her life to the poor – work which she had begun when Louis was alive and for which her in-laws were not happy but unable to do anything about while Louis lived. She died in 1231, aged 24.

November 21: Memorial of the Presentation of the Blessed Virgin Mary

Today's feast has been observed in the Church since the eighth century. We know that Mary said 'yes' to the message of the Annunciation but today's feast commemorates that Mary had a relationship with God before that – if not then the message of the Annunciation would not have been given to Mary. The feast of the Presentation of Mary recalls the Presentation of the Child Jesus in the Temple and suggests that Mary's life was, in some way, consecrated to God from her earliest years.

November 22: Memorial of St Cecilia, Virgin & Martyr

Very little is actually known about Cecilia. Tradition has it that she was married at a young age to Valerian, who later converted to Christianity, and was martyred with his brother, Tiburtius, both of them being later canonized. Cecilia was later martyred by beheading in her own home after the attempt to suffocate her failed. However, there is no proper record of this. It is thought that perhaps her following comes from the belief that she founded a church in Rome. She is the patron saint of musicians though for reasons unknown. She is named in the Roman Canon of the Mass (Eucharistic Prayer I).

November 23: Memorial of St Columban, Abbot

Columban was born in Leinster in the mid-sixth century and became a monk. He left Bangor for France and founded the famous monastery of Luxeuil in the Vosges. In 610 he was exiled from France by Queen Brunhilda and went to Italy where he founded the equally famous monastery of Bobbio. He defended and maintained Irish customs and his strict Rule was very influential on European monasticism during the sixth and seventh centuries. He died in Bobbio in 615.

November 24: Memorial of St Andrew Dung-Lac & Companions, Martyrs

Andrew Dung-Lac was a Vietnamese priest who worked to spread the Gospel in what was formerly known as Indo-China (Cambodia, Laos, Vietnam, Myanmar, Singapore and Thailand). Throughout the seventeenth, eighteenth and nineteenth centuries many Christians were martyred in Vietnam and the region for their faith – the first being Vincent Liem, O.P., who was beheaded in 1773. Today's memorial commemorates 96 native Vietnamese men and women, 11 Dominican missionaries from Spain, and 10 French missionaries. Andrew Dung-Lac was born in 1795 and was beheaded on December 21, 1839.

November 30: Feast of St Andrew the Apostle

Like so many of Christ's apostles very little is actually known about Andrew. He was the brother of St Peter, a disciple of John the Baptist, and was the first to be called by Christ. In St John's gospel he tells his brother of Jesus with the words – 'We have found the Messiah.' He is also mentioned in the gospels as the one who brought the Gentiles to Jesus and the one who pointed out the boy with the loaves and fishes. He is said to have preached the Gospel in Asia Minor and Greece and to have been martyred by crucifixion at Patras in Achaia. He is the patron saint of Scotland, Greece and Russia.

December 3: Memorial of St Francis Xavier, Priest

Francis Xavier was born in Navarre in 1506 and was one of the original seven companions of St Ignatius of Loyola, who founded the Jesuits. He was one of the greatest missionaries and concentrated his efforts on India and the Far East. He organised his newly-founded communities in such a way that they were well able to survive after he had moved to new territories. He died in 1552 on his way to China. He was named Patron Saint of the Foreign Missions and of all works for the spreading of Christianity by Pope St Pius X.

December 7: Memorial of St Ambrose, Bishop & Doctor of the Church

Ambrose was born sometime around the year 340 in Gaul. He was a lawyer and later became governor in what is today northern Italy. He had his offices in Milan where he was elected Bishop by popular acclaim of the laity and was consecrated on December 7, 374, even though he was still only preparing to be baptised. He worked untiringly for the Church and was not afraid of standing up to the Emperors in defence of the faith and of morals. He was a close friend of St Monica and baptised St Augustine. He died on Good Friday, 397.

December 8: Solemnity of the Immaculate Conception of the Blessed Virgin Mary

This solemnity celebrates the fact that Mary herself was conceived without original sin, a state which reflected the fact that she was to be the Mother of God. Though this belief was held for many centuries it was only formally proclaimed by the Church in 1854.

December 13: Memorial of St Lucy, Virgin & Martyr

Very little is known about Lucy though pious tradition says that she turned down the advances of a suitor who, in an act of rage, denounced her as a Christian and had her killed. She suffered martyrdom at Syracuse during the persecution under the Emperor Diocletian about the year 304. She is listed among the saints and martyrs in the Roman Canon of the Mass (Eucharistic Prayer I).

December 14: Memorial of St John of the Cross, Priest & Doctor of the Church

Juan de Yepes Alvarez was born in Fontiveros, Old Castile, Spain, in 1542 and became a Carmelite Friar in 1563. Having met St Teresa of Avila they became good friends and Teresa encouraged him to reform the male branch of the Carmelite Order as she was reforming the Carmelite nuns. This he did and founded a number of reformed monasteries. He was imprisoned by the Carmelites at Toledo for trying to reform them and later was badly treated by the houses of his own reform which he had established. It is as a mystic that John is known as a 'Doctor of the Church'. His best known writings and poems are 'The Ascent of Mount Carmel,' 'The Dark Night of the Soul,' and 'The Spiritual Canticle'. He died at Ubeda on December 14, 1591, and was canonized in 1726.

December 26: Feast of St Stephen, the First Martyr
Stephen was the first deacon and the first martyr for the Church. His martyrdom is recounted by St Luke in the Acts of the Apostles. He was stoned to death by the Sanhedrin at Jerusalem while Saul (the future St Paul, Apostle to the Gentiles) looked on approvingly.

December 27: Feast of St John the Apostle & Evangelist
The younger brother of St James the Greater, John was the only apostle that we know of who did not suffer martyrdom, but died at a good age in Ephesus maybe as late as 100 AD. He is attributed with authorship of the fourth gospel, of three epistles and of the Book of Revelation though it is doubtful that he is the author of the last of these. He is sometimes referred to as 'John the Divine' or 'John the Theologian.' Being 'the disciple whom Jesus loved' and the only apostle to be present at the foot of the cross, he was entrusted with the care of Our Lady by our Lord at the crucifixion.

December 28: Feast of the Holy Innocents
This feast recalls the slaying of the children under the age of two years by King Herod and which is recounted in St Matthew's gospel. They are venerated as martyrs not simply because they died for Christ but because they died instead of him.

Author's Note

Scripture Quotations are taken from:

The Lectionary. London: Harper Collins Publishers. 1981

For a much more detailed explanation of Biblical texts:

The New Jerome Biblical Commentary. Engelwood Cliffs, New Jersey: Prentice Hall. 1990.

For more information on the Saints:

Butler's Lives of the Saints (New Full Edition). Collegeville: Liturgical Press. 1995
The New Catholic Encyclopedia. Washington D.C.: Catholic University of America. 1967
A New Dictionary of the Saints. Tunbridge Wells: Burns & Oates. 1993.